The Day I Become a Butterfly

BY
SUMOMO YUMEKA

June

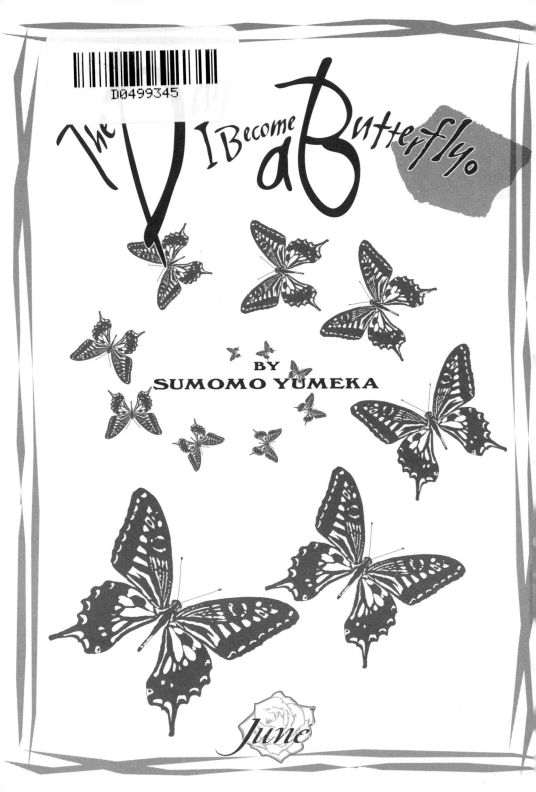

CONTENTS:

Translation	Sachiko Sato
Lettering	Replibooks
Editing	Bambi Eloriaga
Editor in Chief	Fred Lui
Publisher	Hikaru Sasahara

English Edition Published by
DIGITAL MANGA PUBLISHING
A division of DIGITAL MANGA, Inc.
1487 W 178th Street, Suite 300
Gardena, CA 90248

www.dmpbooks.com

First Edition: March 2007
ISBN-10: 1-56970-869-X
ISBN-13: 978-1-56970-869-9

1 3 5 7 9 10 8 6 4 2

Printed in China

THE DAY I DECIDED TO GO ON
LIVING MY LIFE WITH YOU IS THE
DAY I BECAME A BUTTERFLY.

THE DAY I BECOME A BUTTERFLY

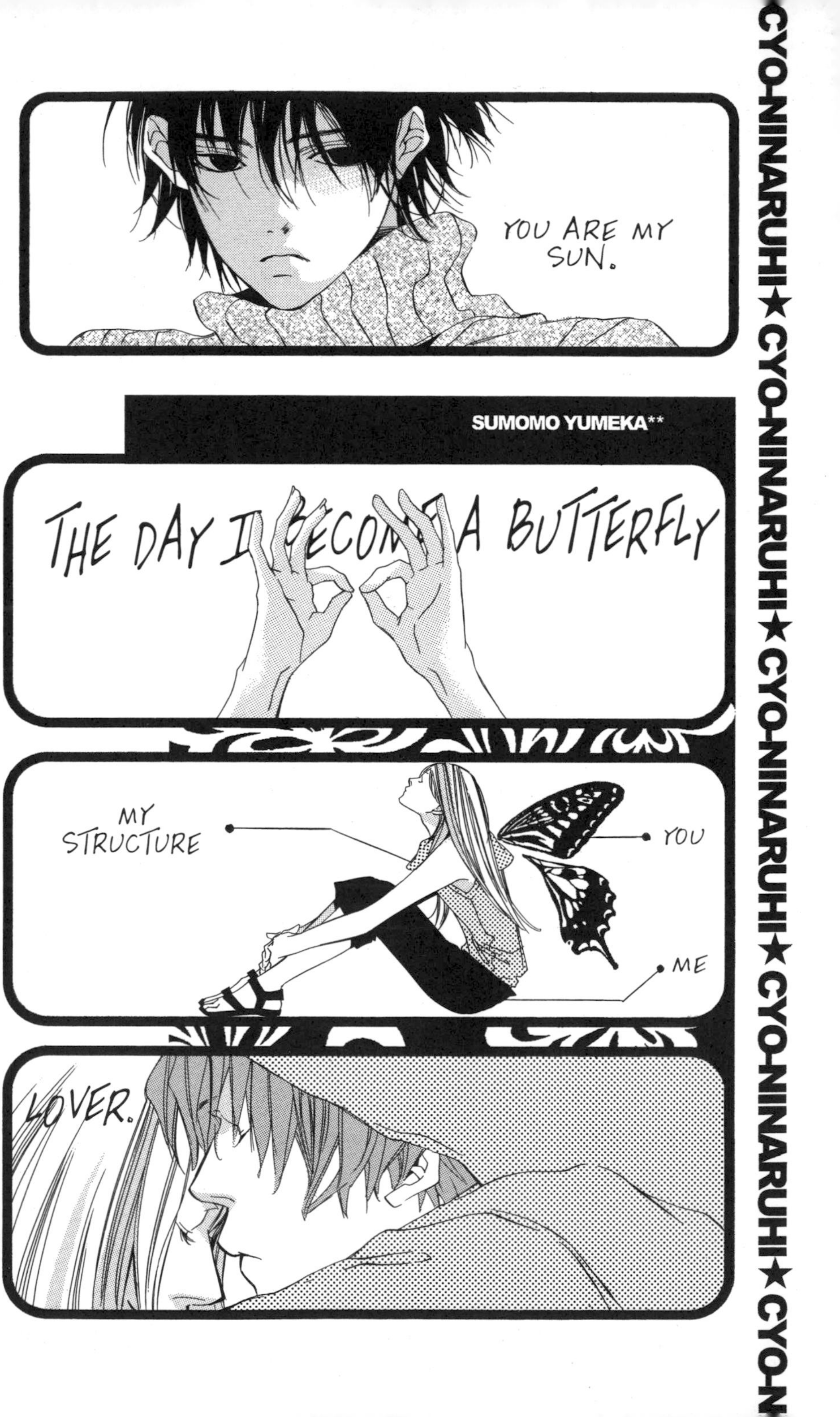
YOU ARE MY SUN.
SUMOMO YUMEKA**
THE DAY I
ECOM
A BUTTERFLY
MY STRUCTURE
YOU
ME
LOVER.
CYO-NINARUHI★CYO-NINARUHI★CYO-NINARUHI★CYO-NINARUHI★CYO-N

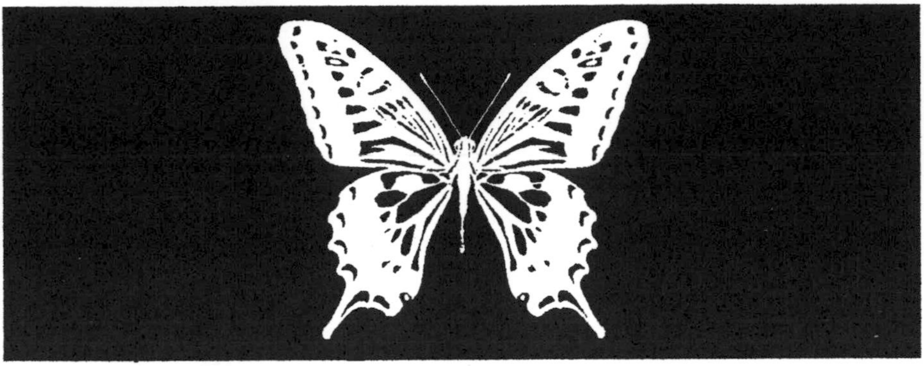

THE DAY I BECOME A BUTTERFLY

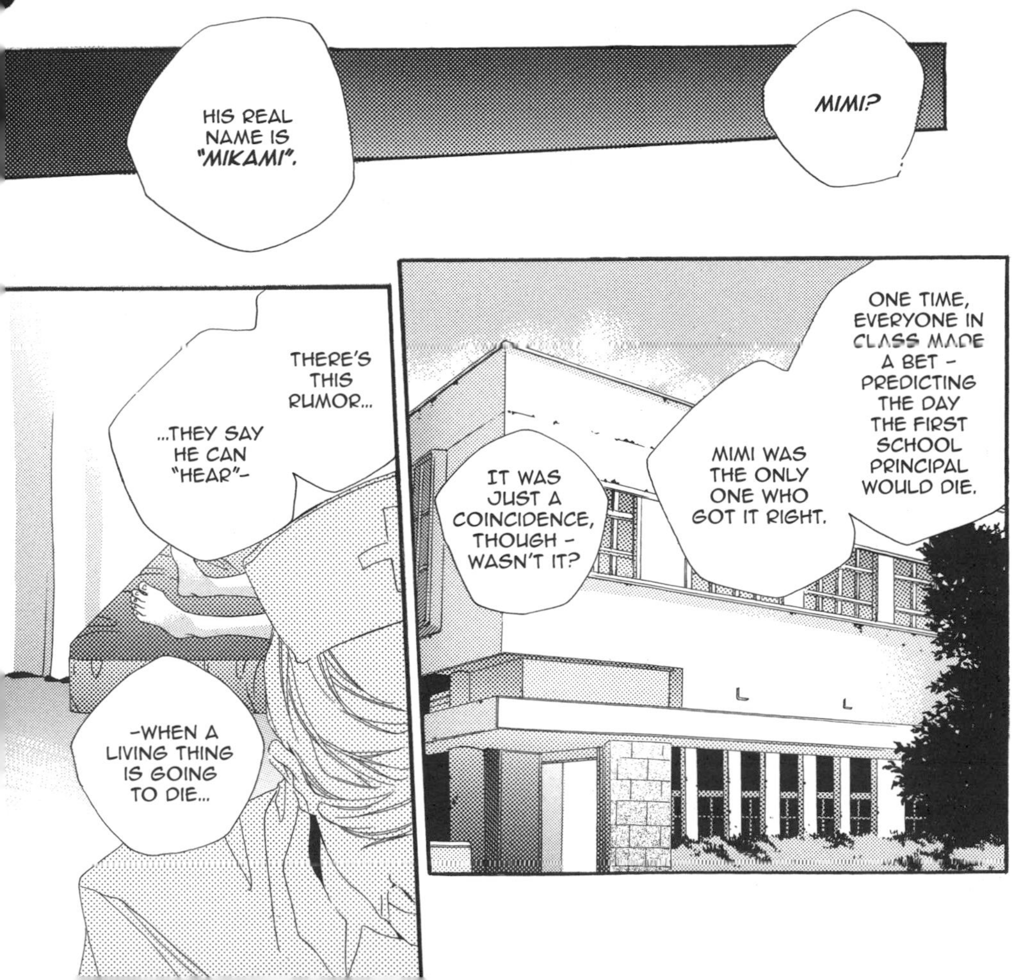
MIMI?
HIS REAL NAME IS "MIKAMI".
ONE TIME, EVERYONE IN CLASS MADE A BET - PREDICTING THE DAY THE FIRST SCHOOL PRINCIPAL WOULD DIE.
MIMI WAS THE ONLY ONE WHO GOT IT RIGHT.
IT WAS JUST A COINCIDENCE, THOUGH - WASN'T IT?
THERE'S THIS RUMOR...
...THEY SAY HE CAN "HEAR"-
-WHEN A LIVING THING IS GOING TO DIE...

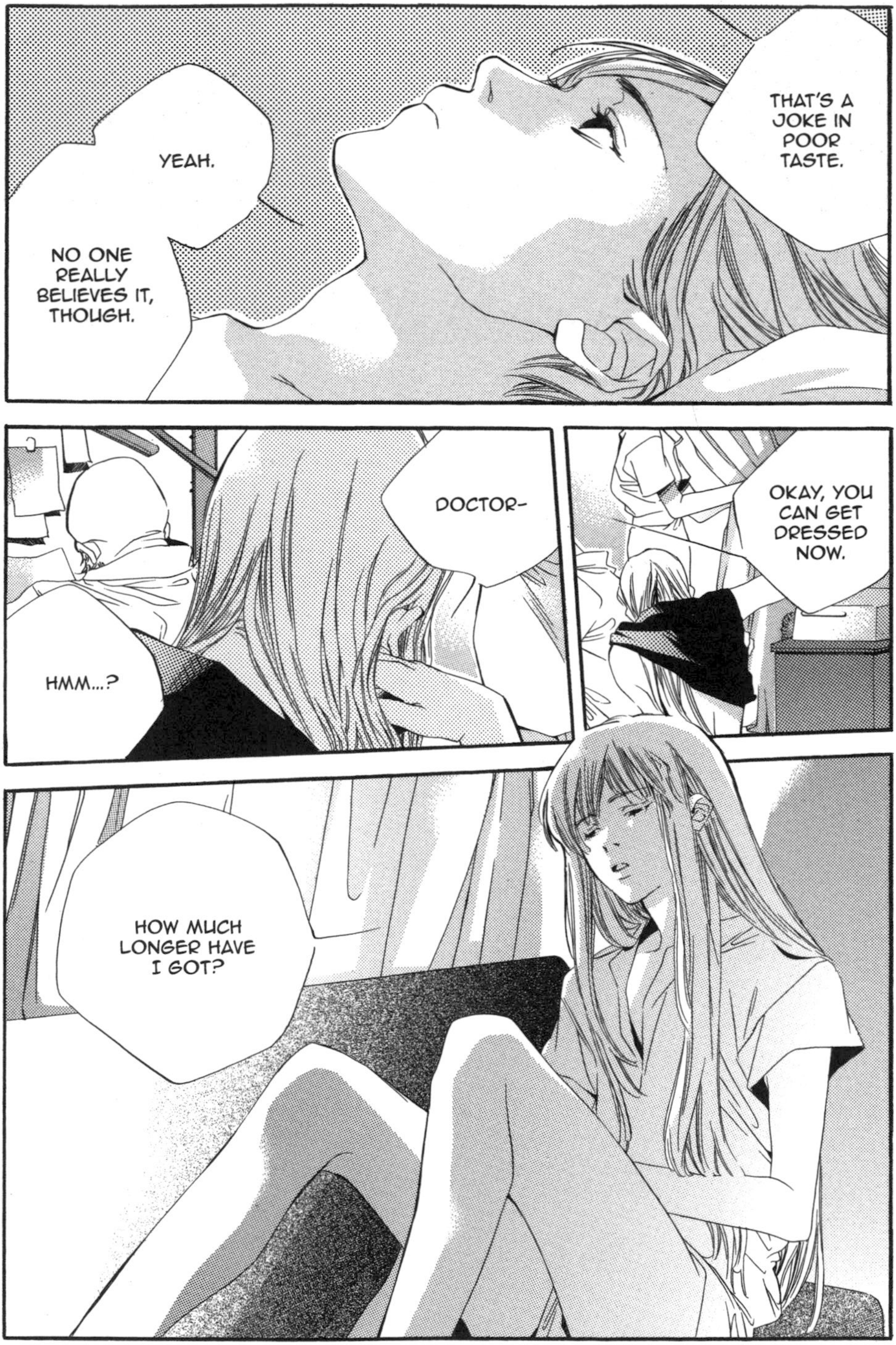
THAT'S A JOKE IN POOR TASTE.
YEAH.
NO ONE REALLY BELIEVES IT, THOUGH.
OKAY, YOU CAN GET DRESSED NOW.
DOCTOR-
HMM...?
HOW MUCH LONGER HAVE I GOT?

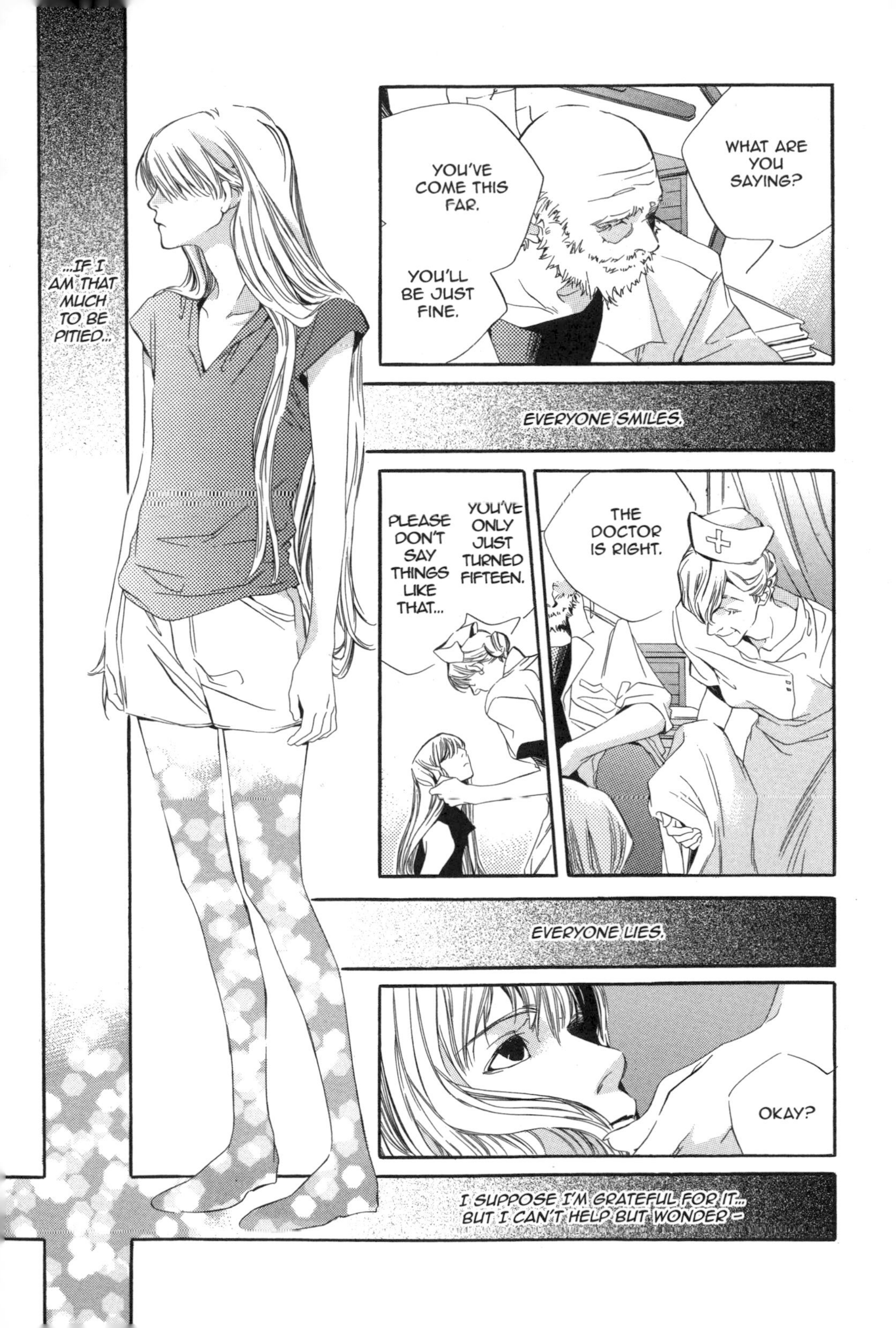
WHAT ARE YOU SAYING?
YOU'VE COME THIS FAR.
YOU'LL BE JUST FINE.
EVERYONE SMILES.
THE DOCTOR IS RIGHT.
YOU'VE ONLY JUST TURNED FIFTEEN.
PLEASE DON'T SAY THINGS LIKE THAT...
EVERYONE LIES.
OKAY?
I SUPPOSE I'M GRATEFUL FOR IT... BUT I CAN'T HELP BUT WONDER –
...IF I AM THAT MUCH TO BE PITIED...

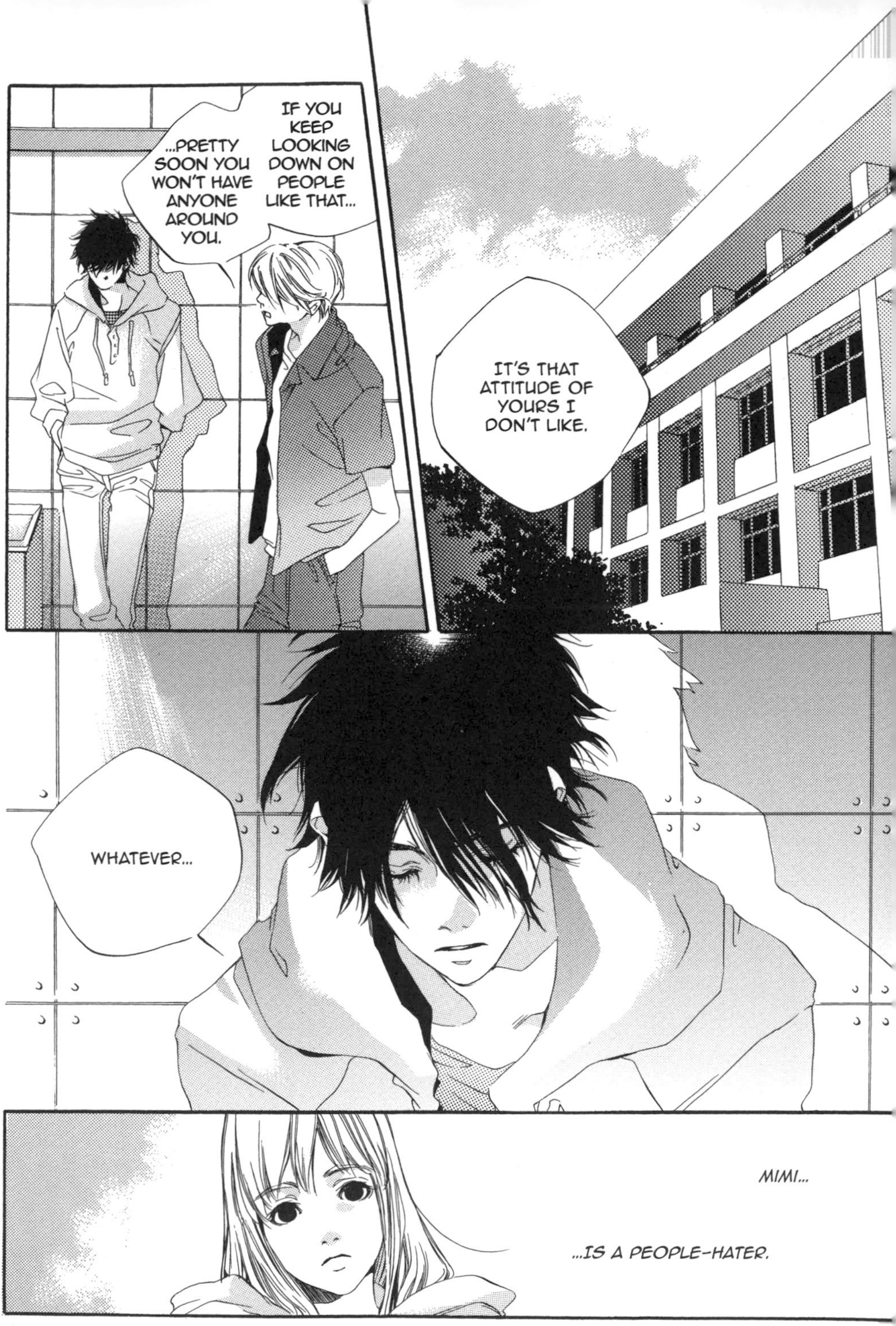
IT'S THAT ATTITUDE OF YOURS I DON'T LIKE.
IF YOU KEEP LOOKING DOWN ON PEOPLE LIKE THAT...
...PRETTY SOON YOU WON'T HAVE ANYONE AROUND YOU.
WHATEVER...
MIMI...
...IS A PEOPLE-HATER.

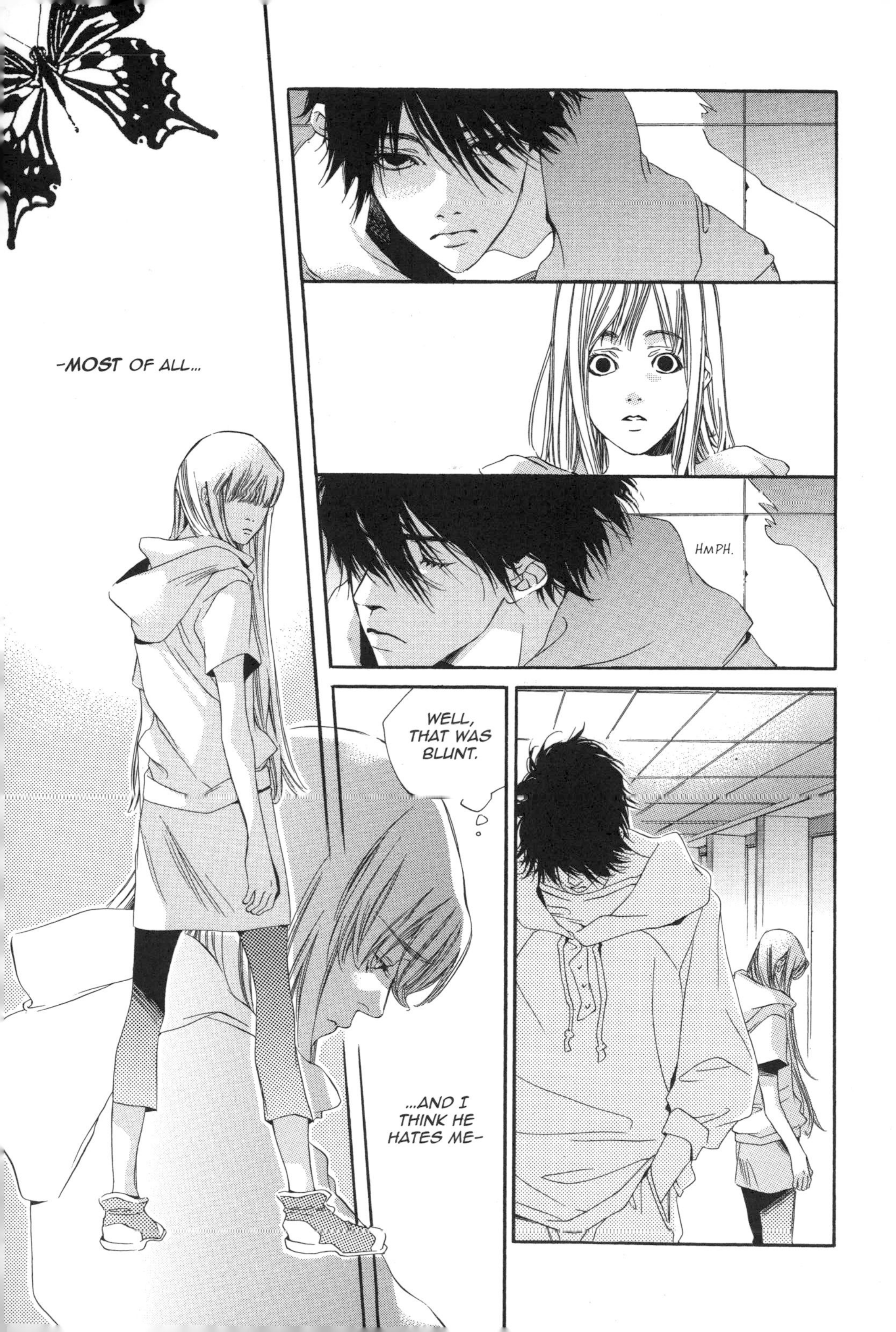
HMPH.
WELL, THAT WAS BLUNT.
-MOST OF ALL...
...AND I THINK HE HATES ME-

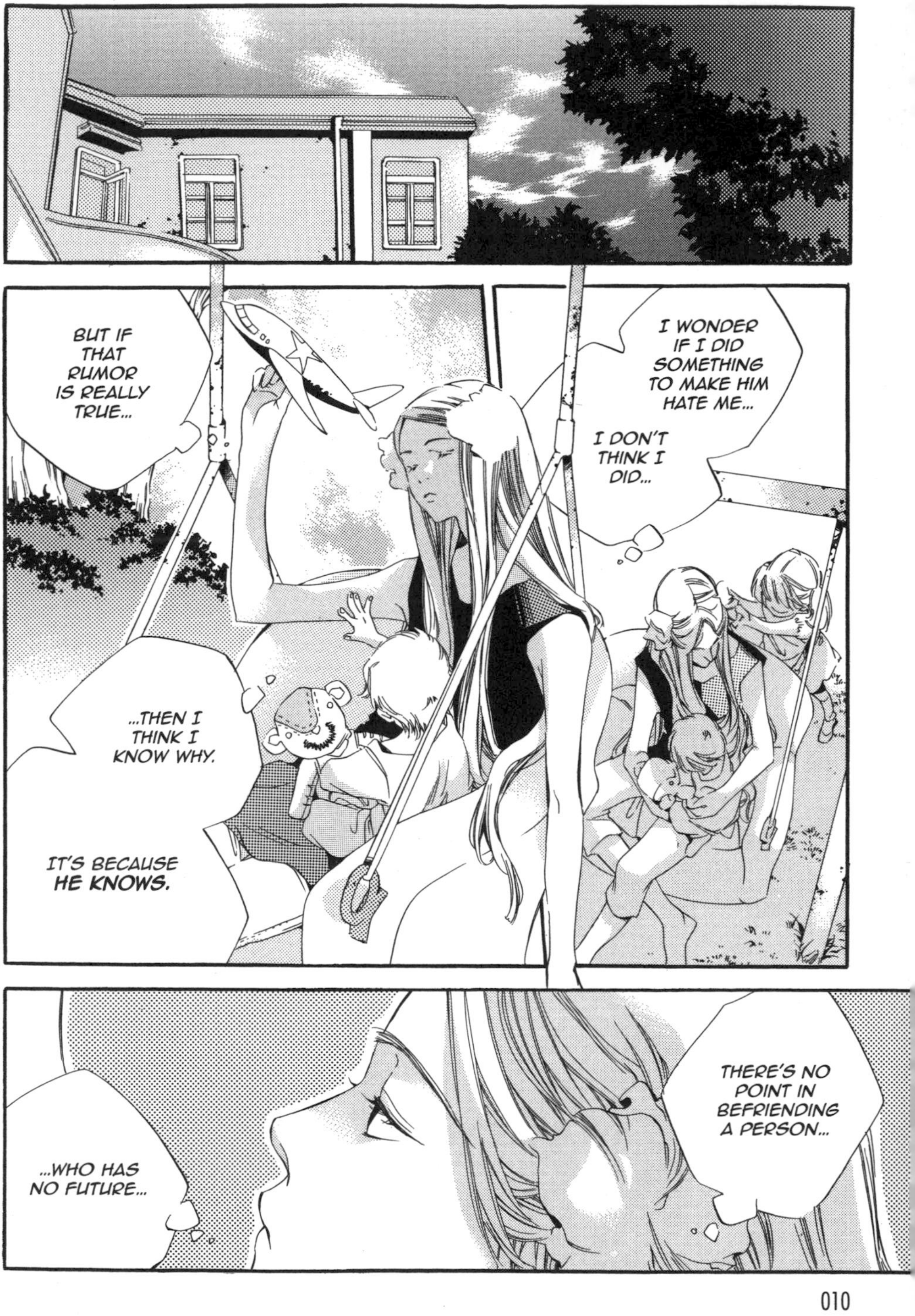
I WONDER IF I DID SOMETHING TO MAKE HIM HATE ME...
I DON'T THINK I DID...
BUT IF THAT RUMOR IS REALLY TRUE...
...THEN I THINK I KNOW WHY.
IT'S BECAUSE HE KNOWS.
THERE'S NO POINT IN BEFRIENDING A PERSON...
...WHO HAS NO FUTURE...

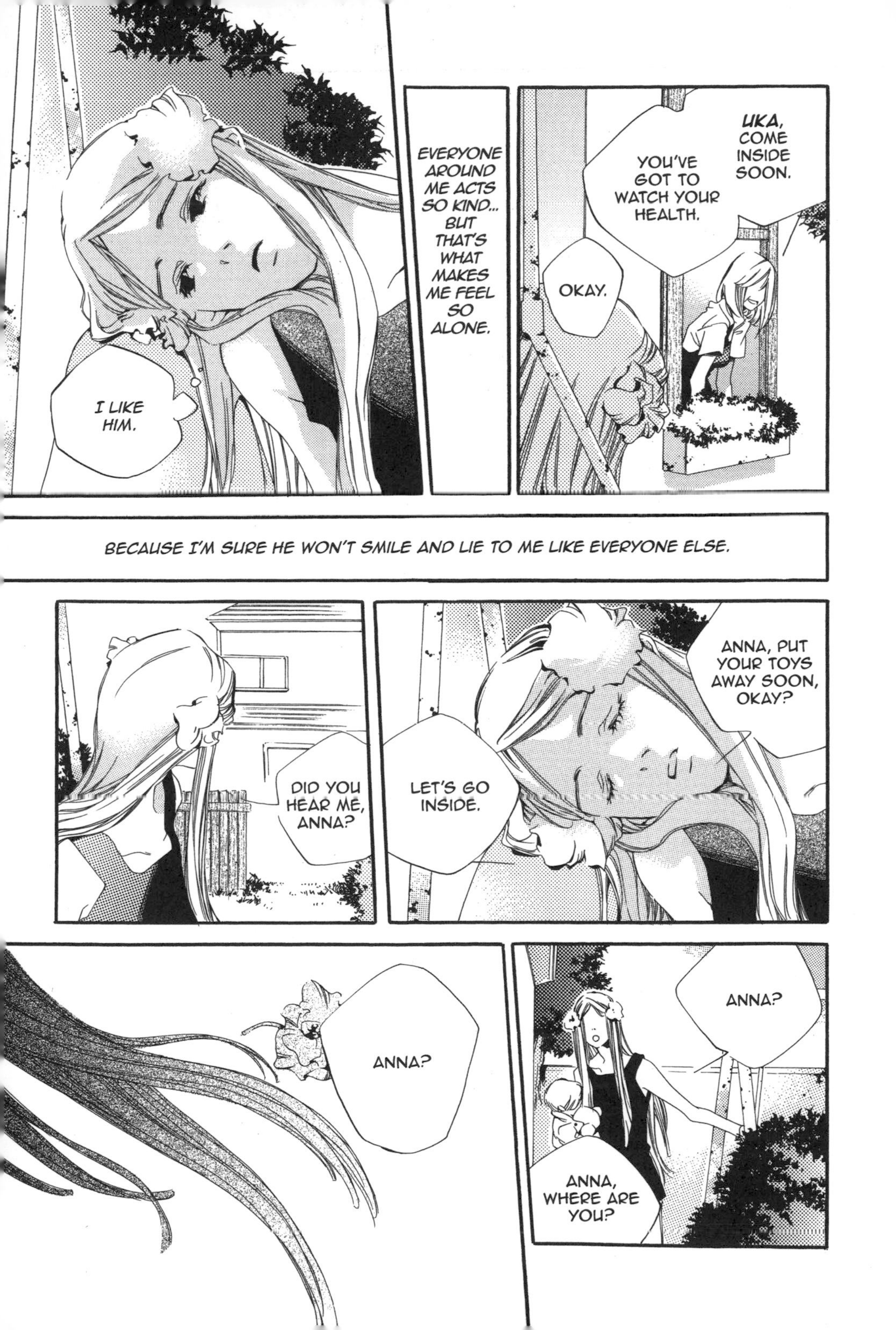
UKA, COME INSIDE SOON.
YOU'VE GOT TO WATCH YOUR HEALTH.
OKAY.
EVERYONE AROUND ME ACTS SO KIND... BUT THAT'S WHAT MAKES ME FEEL SO ALONE.
I LIKE HIM.
BECAUSE I'M SURE HE WON'T SMILE AND LIE TO ME LIKE EVERYONE ELSE.
ANNA, PUT YOUR TOYS AWAY SOON, OKAY?
LET'S GO INSIDE.
DID YOU HEAR ME, ANNA?
ANNA?
ANNA, WHERE ARE YOU?
ANNA?

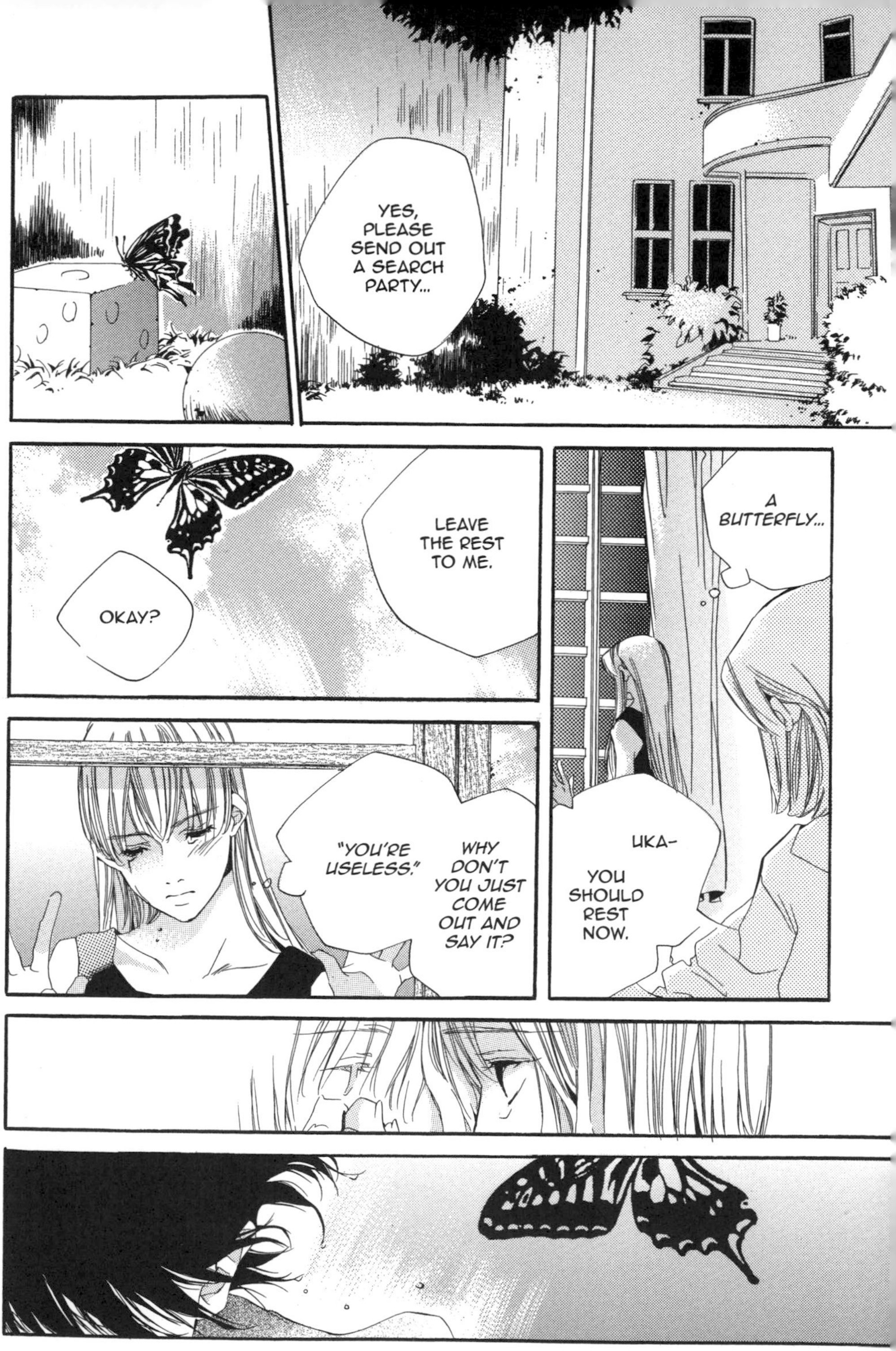
YES, PLEASE SEND OUT A SEARCH PARTY...
A BUTTERFLY...
UKA-
YOU SHOULD REST NOW.
LEAVE THE REST TO ME.
OKAY?
WHY DON'T YOU JUST COME OUT AND SAY IT?
"YOU'RE USELESS."

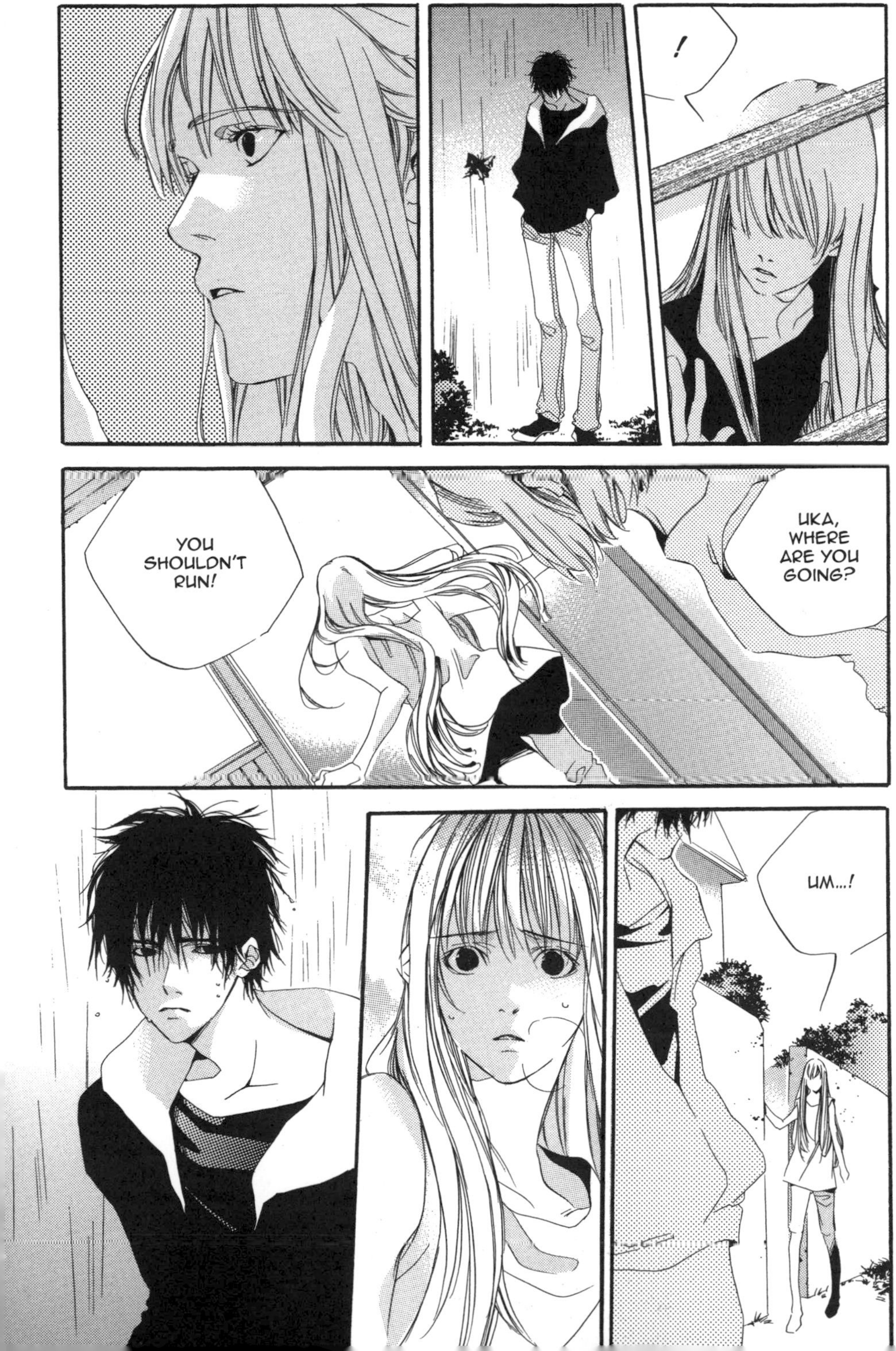
!
UKA, WHERE ARE YOU GOING?
YOU SHOULDN'T RUN!
UM...!

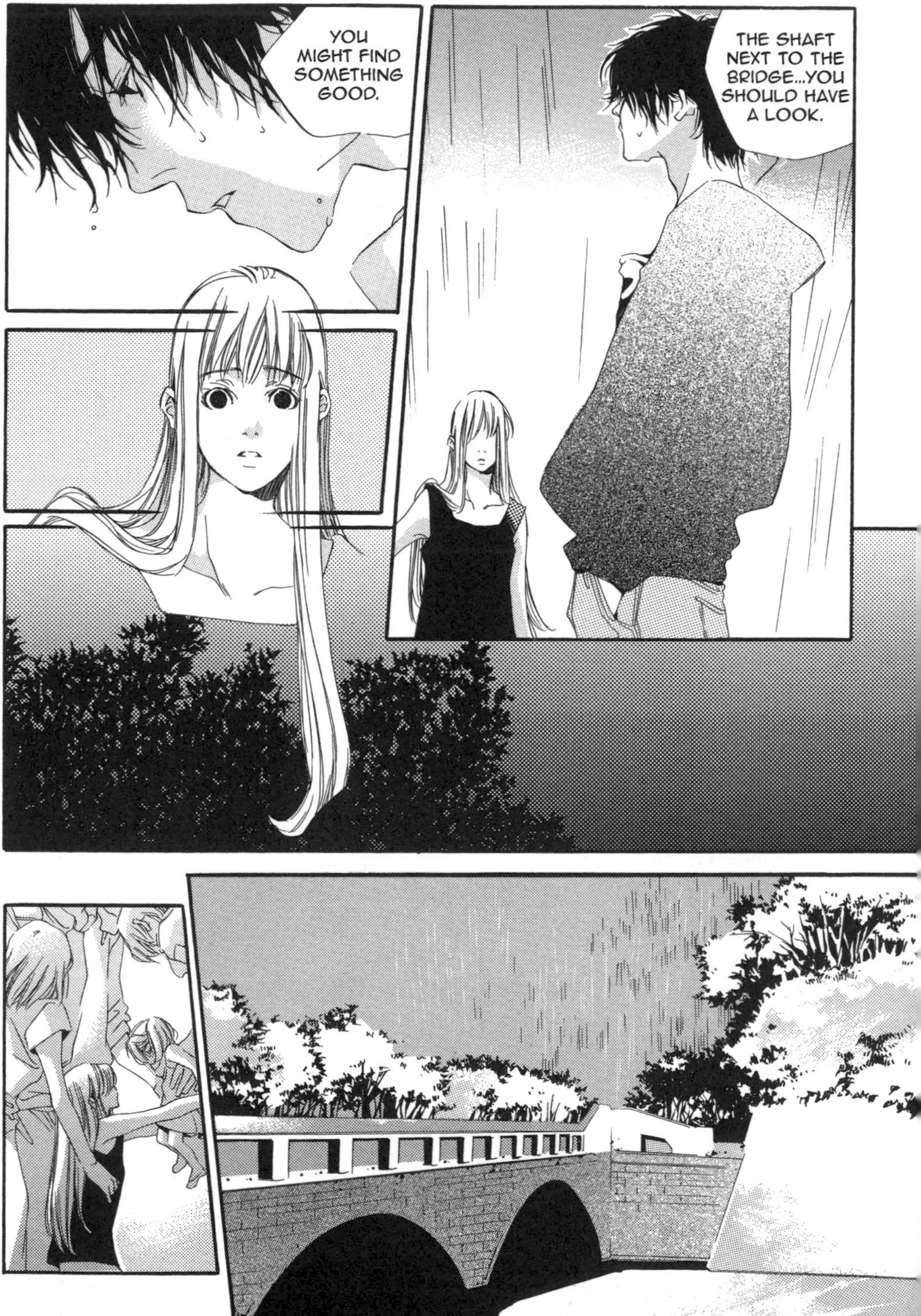
THE SHAFT NEXT TO THE BRIDGE...YOU SHOULD HAVE A LOOK.
YOU MIGHT FIND SOMETHING GOOD.

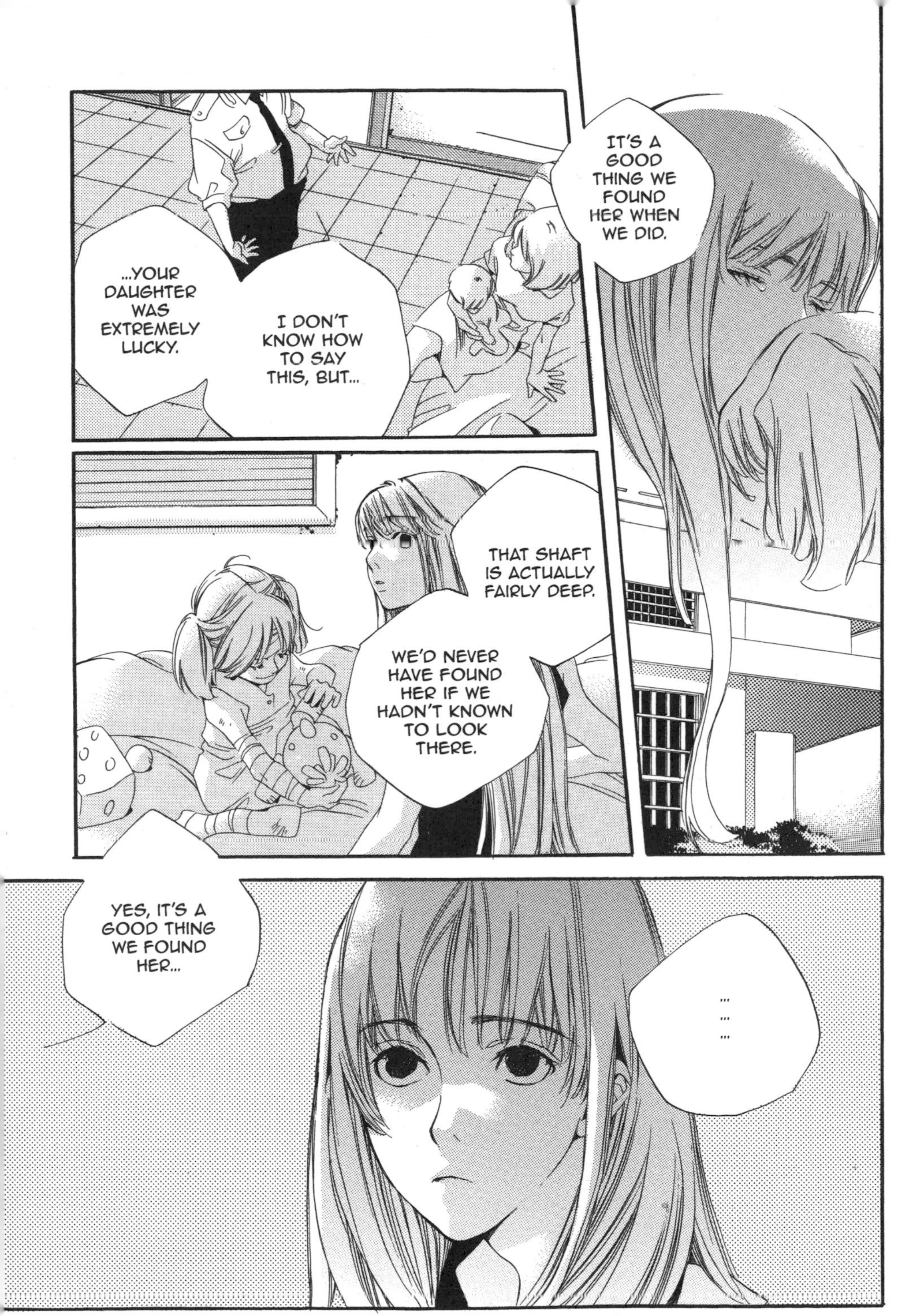
IT'S A GOOD THING WE FOUND HER WHEN WE DID.
I DON'T KNOW HOW TO SAY THIS, BUT...
...YOUR DAUGHTER WAS EXTREMELY LUCKY.
THAT SHAFT IS ACTUALLY FAIRLY DEEP.
WE'D NEVER HAVE FOUND HER IF WE HADN'T KNOWN TO LOOK THERE.
...
...
...
YES, IT'S A GOOD THING WE FOUND HER...

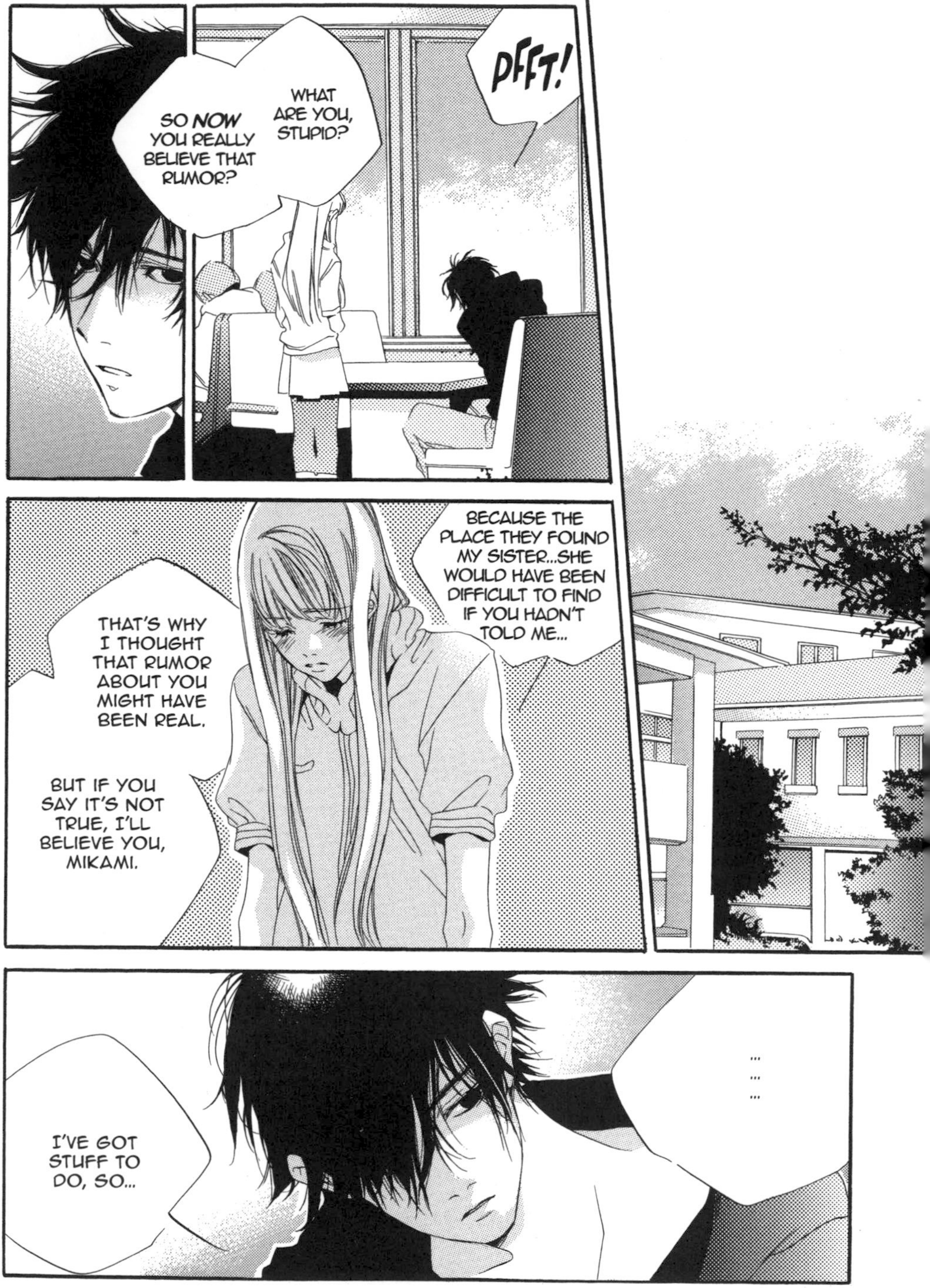
PFFT!
WHAT ARE YOU, STUPID?
SO NOW YOU REALLY BELIEVE THAT RUMOR?
BECAUSE THE PLACE THEY FOUND MY SISTER...SHE WOULD HAVE BEEN DIFFICULT TO FIND IF YOU HADN'T TOLD ME...
THAT'S WHY I THOUGHT THAT RUMOR ABOUT YOU MIGHT HAVE BEEN REAL.
BUT IF YOU SAY IT'S NOT TRUE, I'LL BELIEVE YOU, MIKAMI.
...
...
...
I'VE GOT STUFF TO DO, SO...

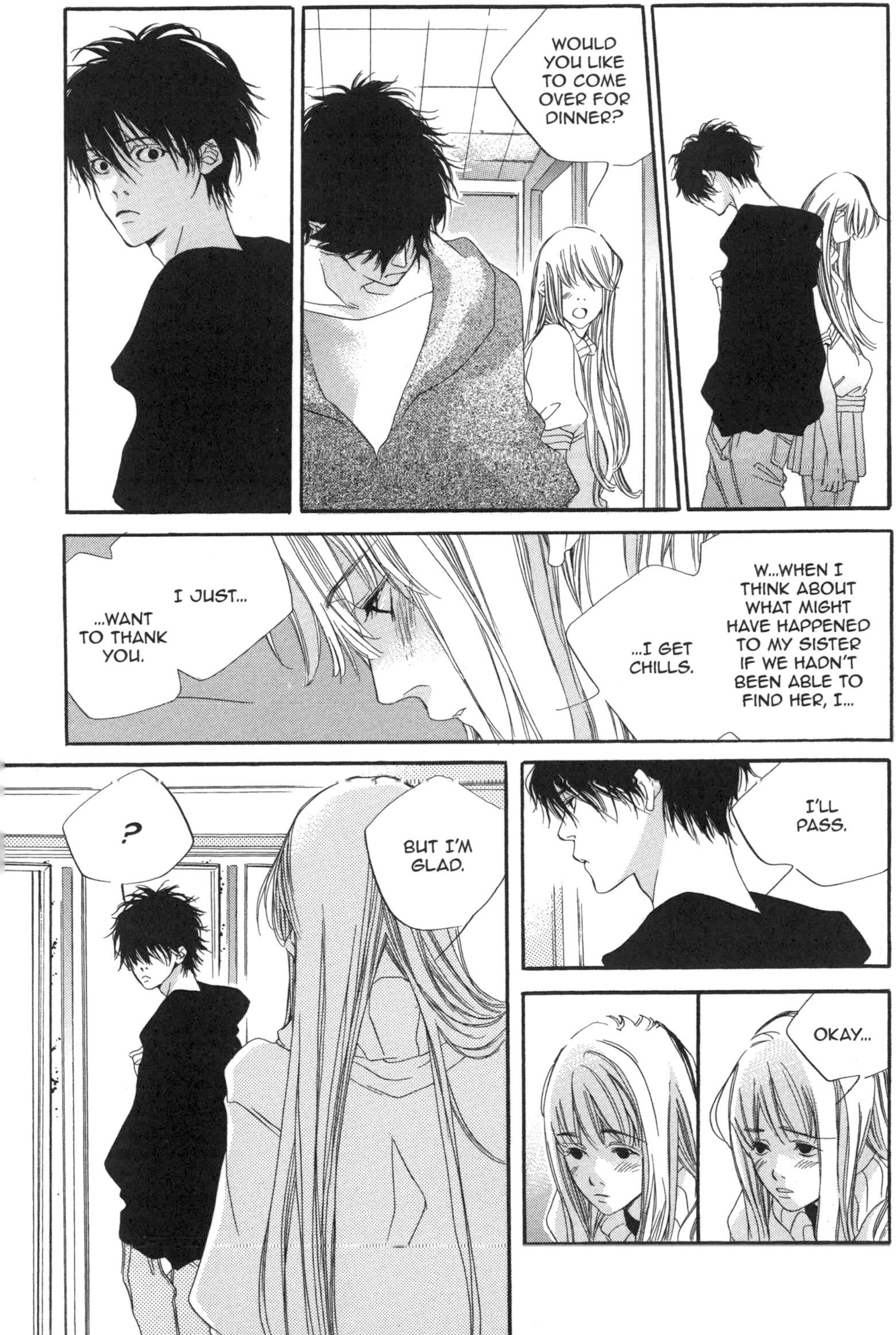
WOULD YOU LIKE TO COME OVER FOR DINNER?
W...WHEN I THINK ABOUT WHAT MIGHT HAVE HAPPENED TO MY SISTER IF WE HADN'T BEEN ABLE TO FIND HER, I...
...I GET CHILLS.
I JUST...
...WANT TO THANK YOU.
I'LL PASS.
OKAY...
BUT I'M GLAD.
?

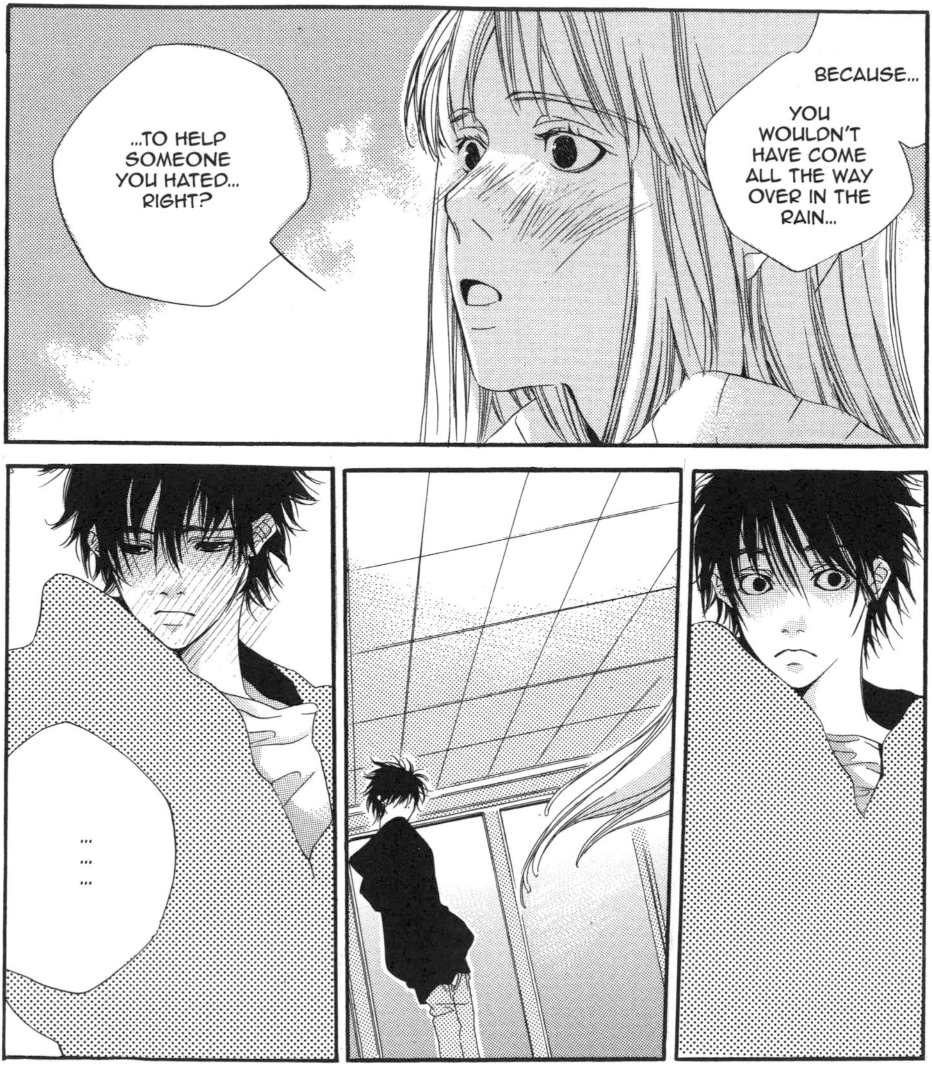
BECAUSE...
YOU WOULDN'T HAVE COME ALL THE WAY OVER IN THE RAIN...
...TO HELP SOMEONE YOU HATED... RIGHT?
... ...

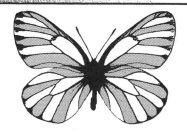

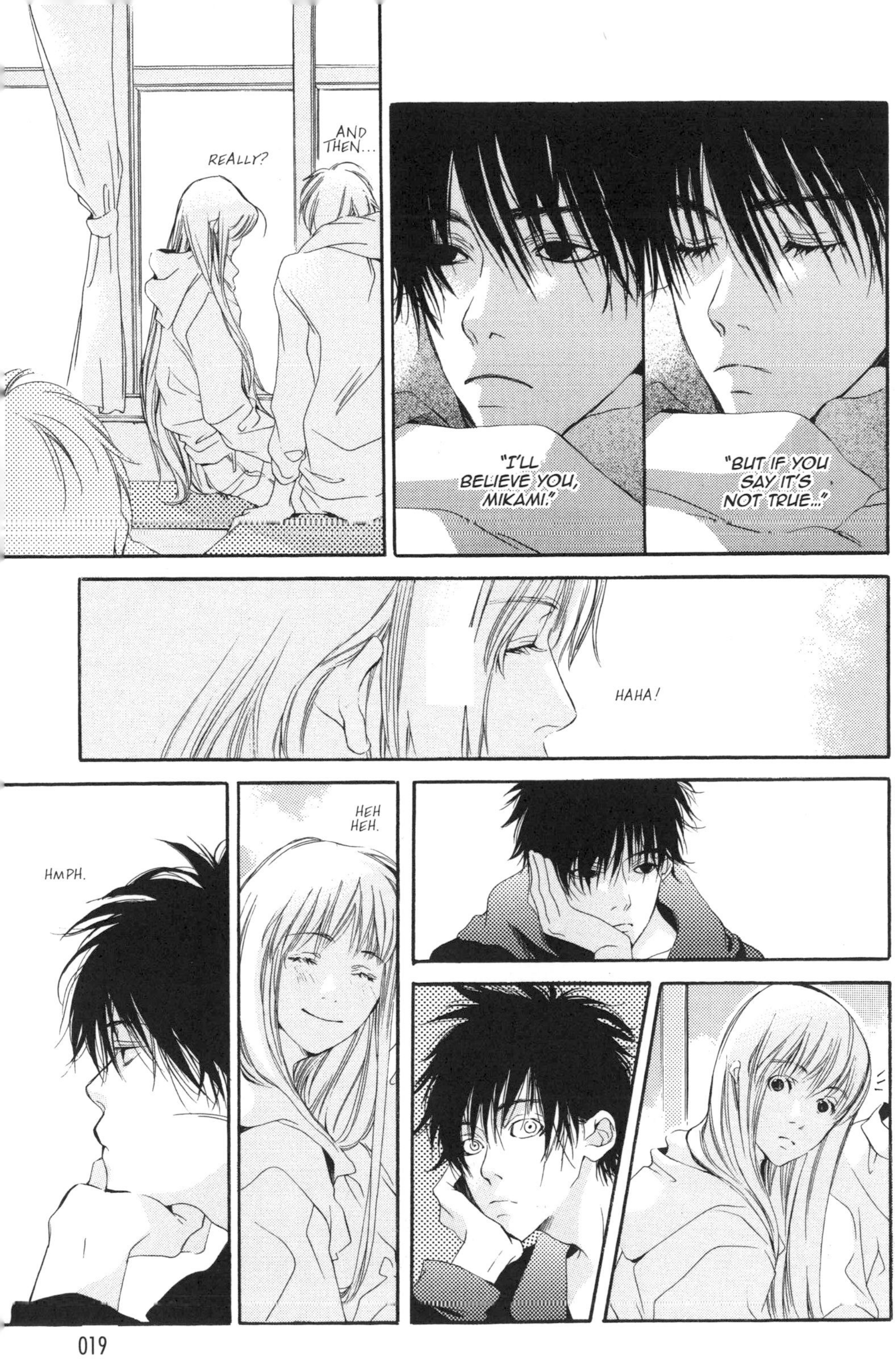
"BUT IF YOU SAY IT'S NOT TRUE..."
"I'LL BELIEVE YOU, MIKAMI."
AND THEN...
REALLY?
HAHA!
HEH HEH.
HMPH.

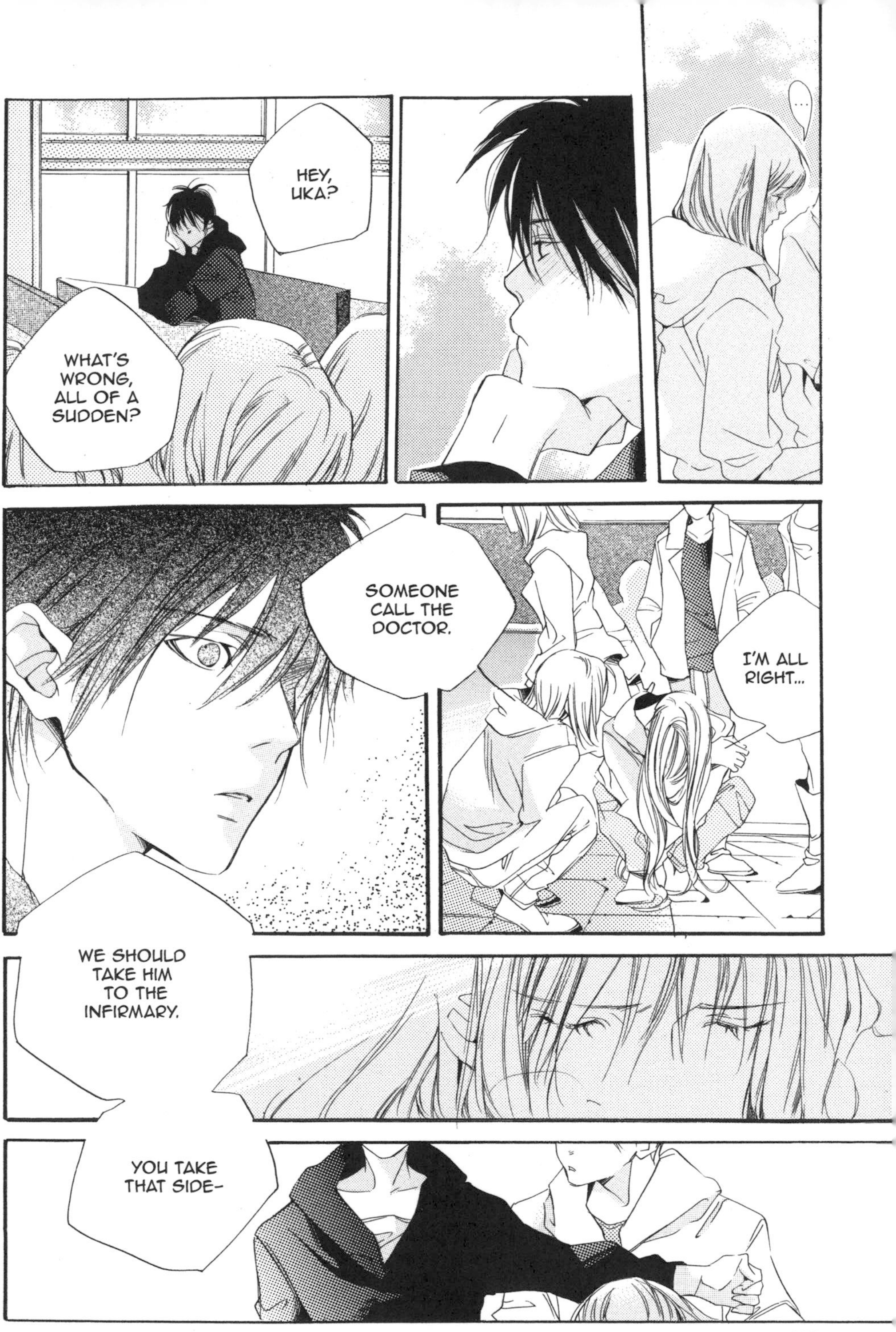
...
HEY, UKA?
WHAT'S WRONG, ALL OF A SUDDEN?
I'M ALL RIGHT...
SOMEONE CALL THE DOCTOR.
WE SHOULD TAKE HIM TO THE INFIRMARY.
YOU TAKE THAT SIDE-

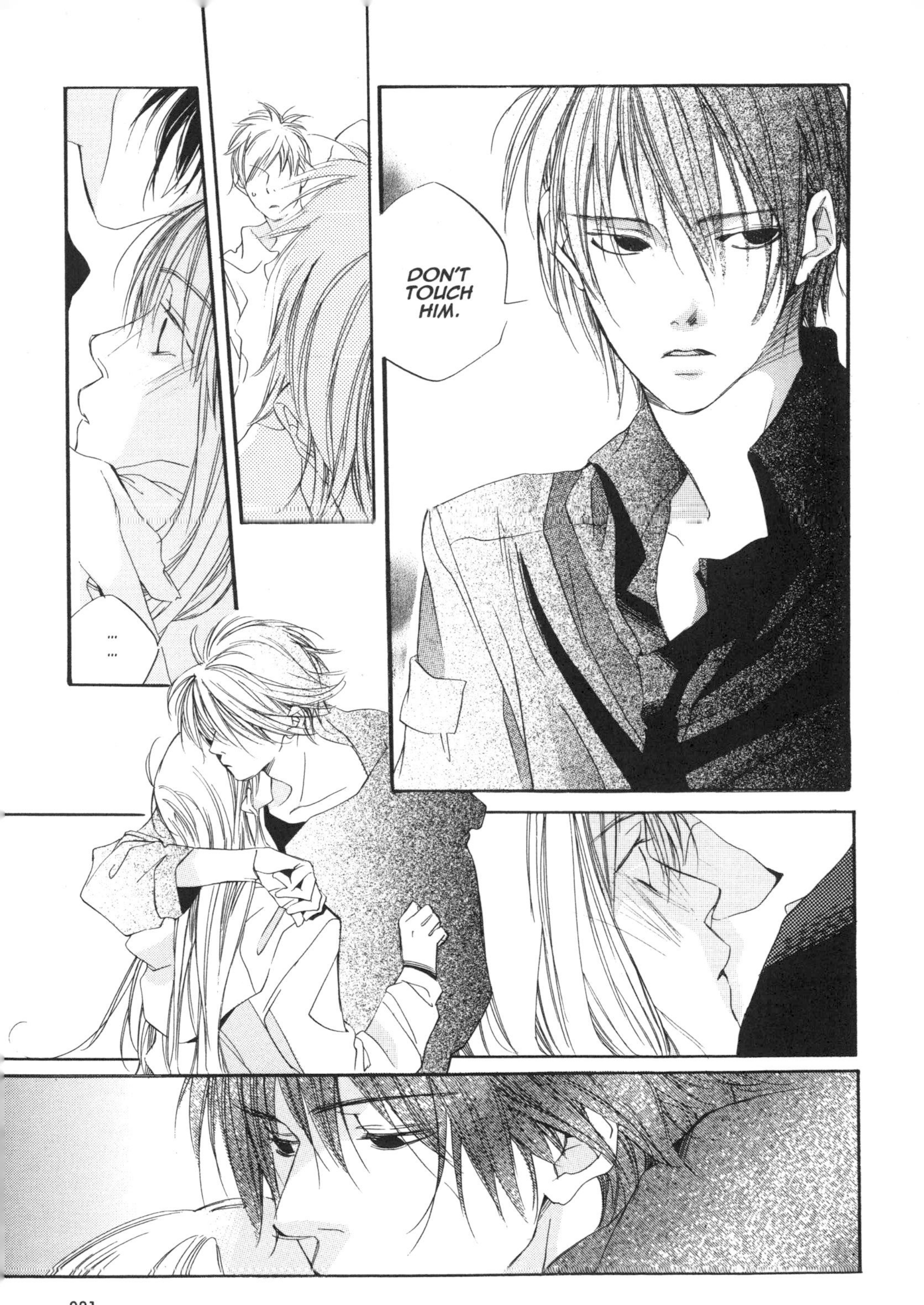
DON'T TOUCH HIM.
...
...

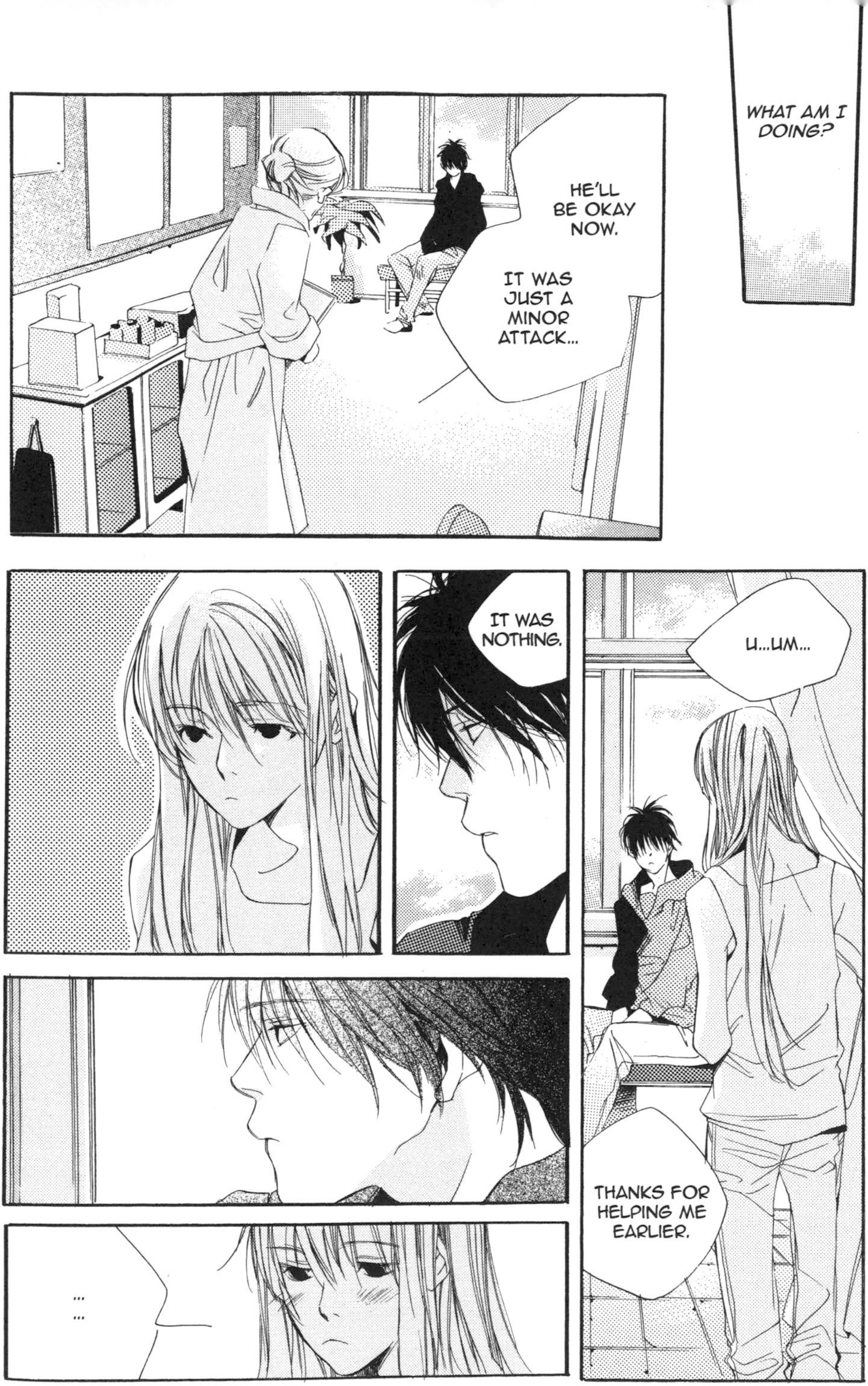
WHAT AM I DOING?
HE'LL BE OKAY NOW.
IT WAS JUST A MINOR ATTACK...
U...UM...
THANKS FOR HELPING ME EARLIER.
IT WAS NOTHING.
...
...

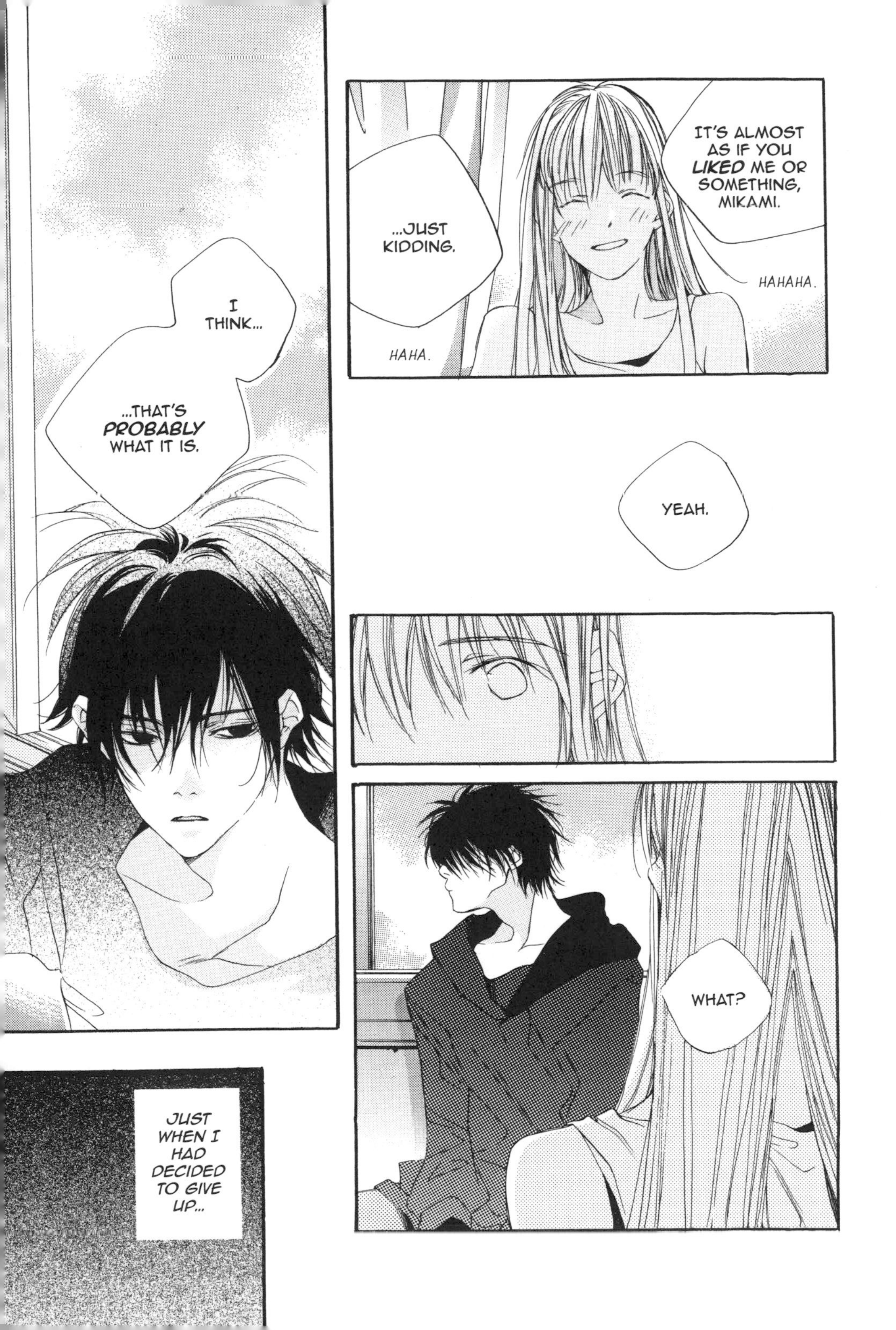

IT'S ALMOST AS IF YOU LIKED ME OR SOMETHING, MIKAMI.
HAHAHA.
...JUST KIDDING.
HAHA.
YEAH.
WHAT?
I THINK...
...THAT'S PROBABLY WHAT IT IS.
JUST WHEN I HAD DECIDED TO GIVE UP...

I WAS THE ONE WHO FIRST BEGAN NOTICING YOU.

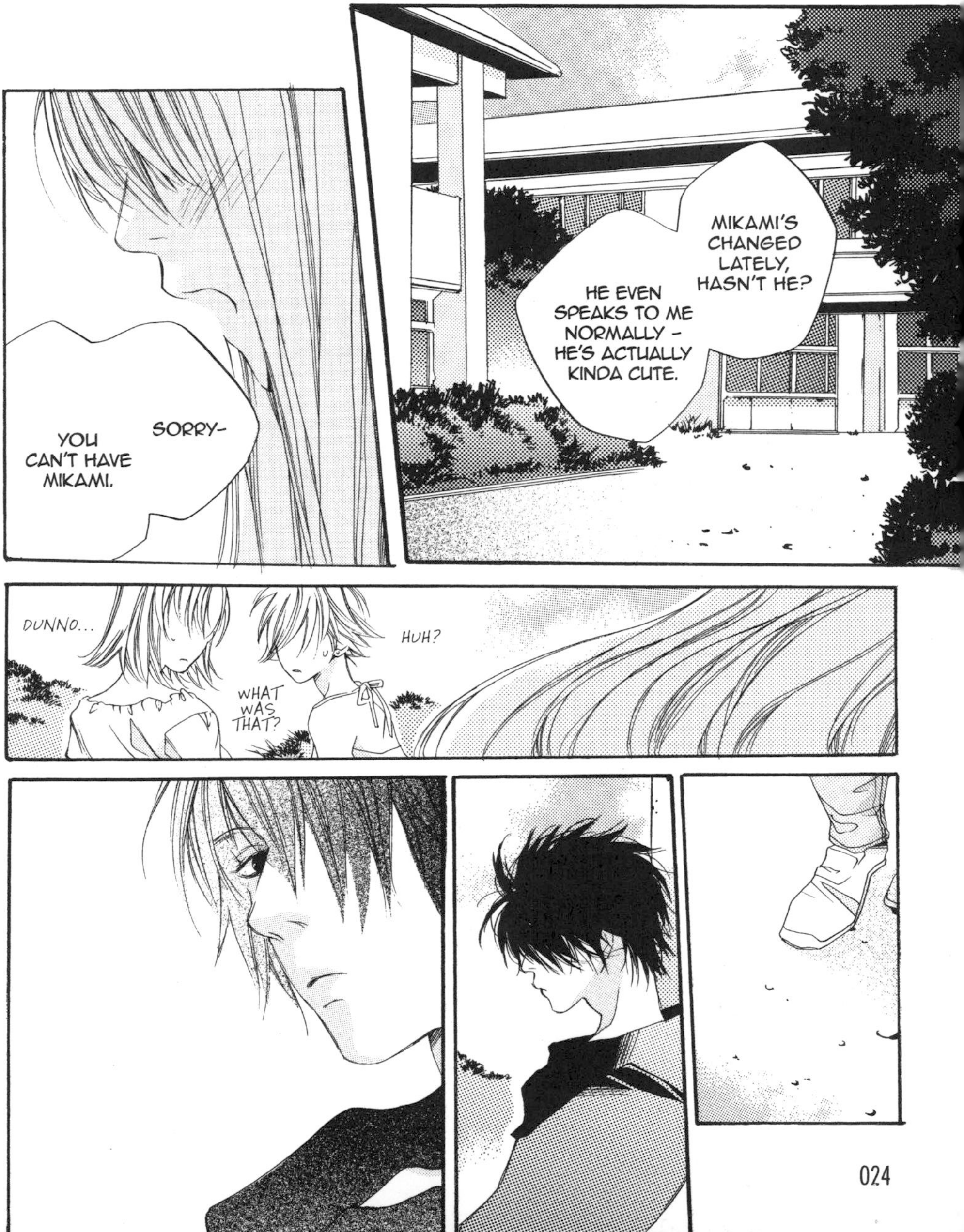
MIKAMI'S CHANGED LATELY, HASN'T HE?
HE EVEN SPEAKS TO ME NORMALLY - HE'S ACTUALLY KINDA CUTE.
SORRY-
YOU CAN'T HAVE MIKAMI.
HUH?
WHAT WAS THAT?
DUNNO...

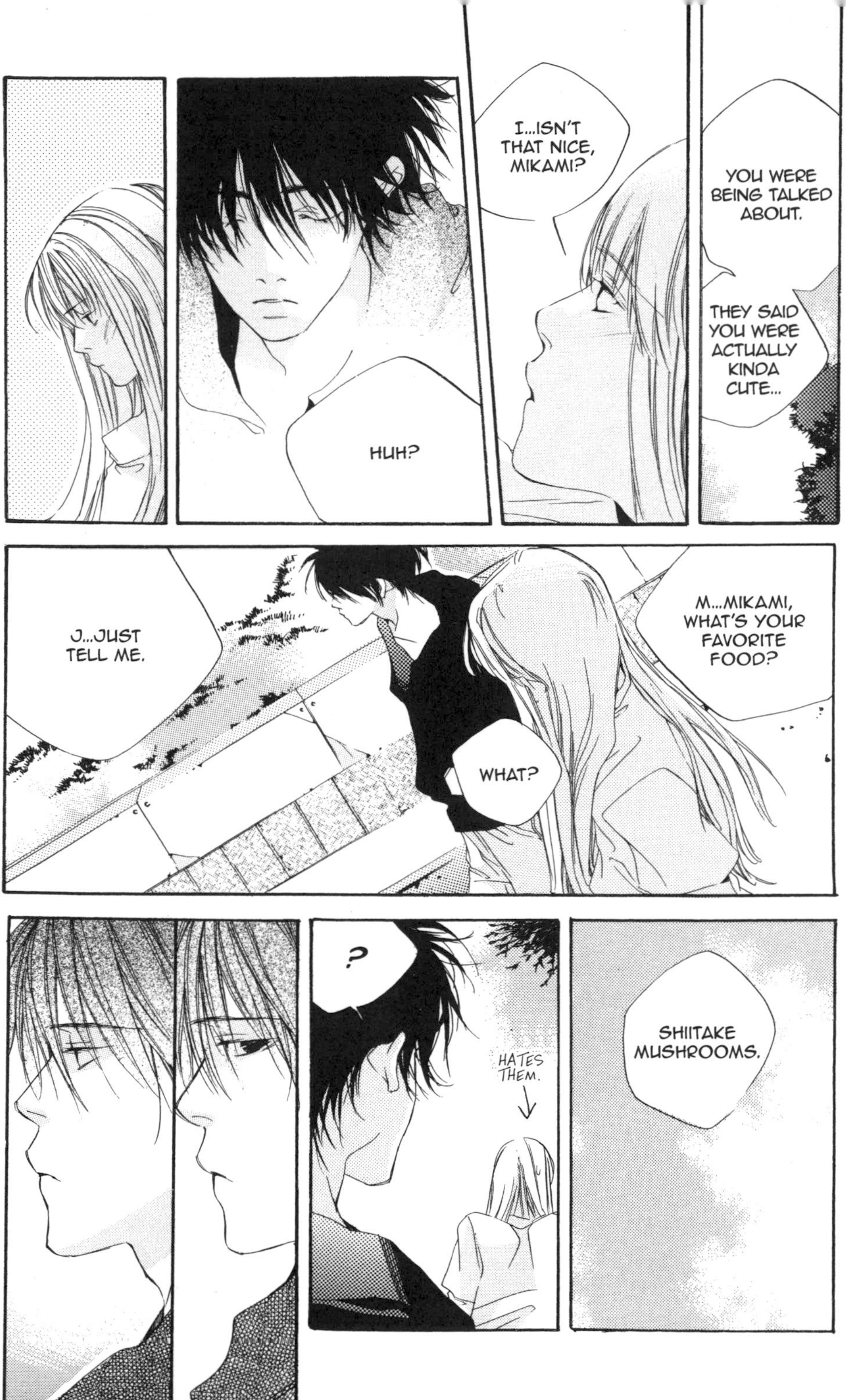
YOU WERE BEING TALKED ABOUT.
THEY SAID YOU WERE ACTUALLY KINDA CUTE...
I...ISN'T THAT NICE, MIKAMI?
HUH?
M...MIKAMI, WHAT'S YOUR FAVORITE FOOD?
WHAT?
J...JUST TELL ME.
SHIITAKE MUSHROOMS.
?
HATES THEM.

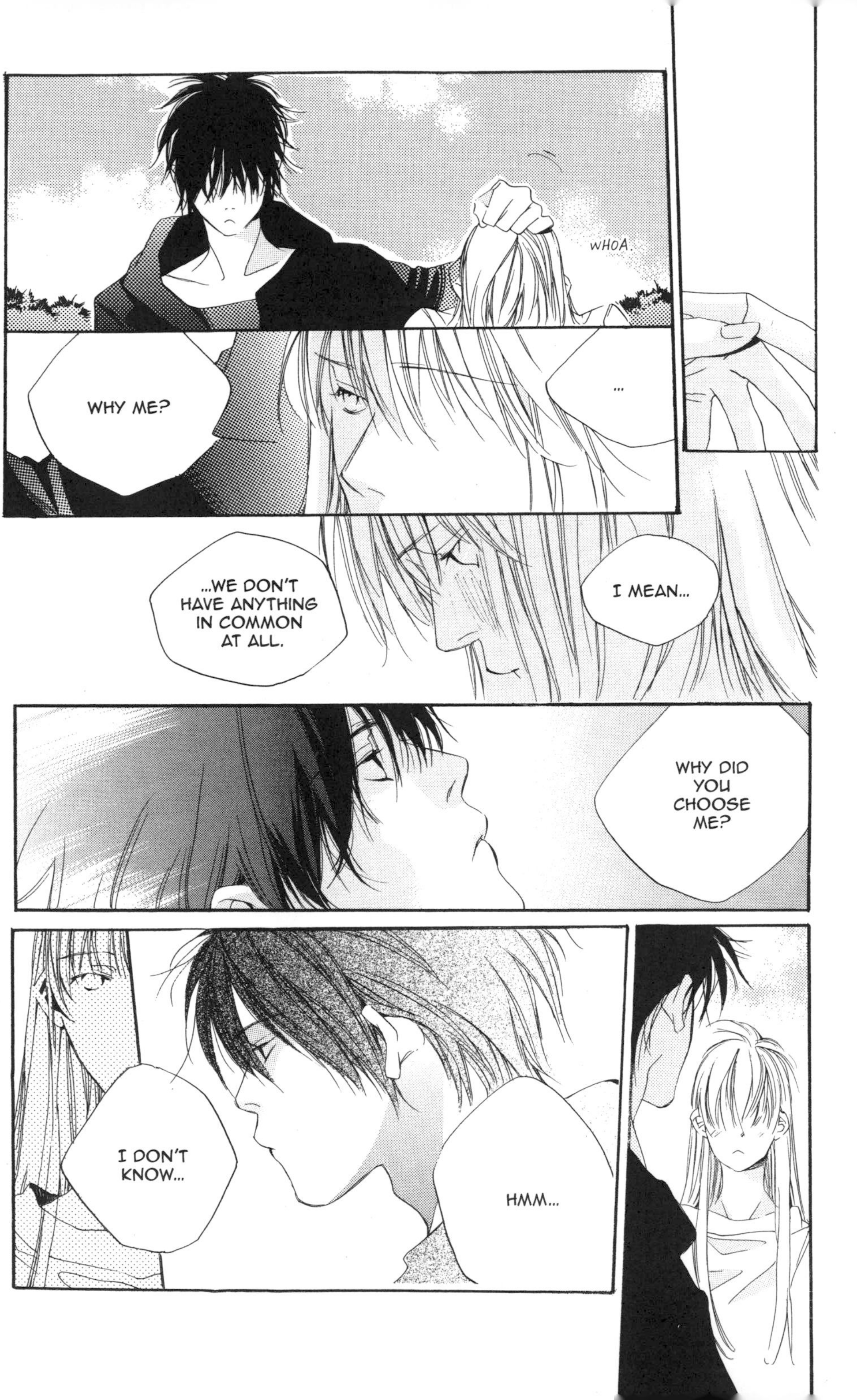
WHOA.
...
WHY ME?
I MEAN...
...WE DON'T HAVE ANYTHING IN COMMON AT ALL.
WHY DID YOU CHOOSE ME?
HMM...
I DON'T KNOW...

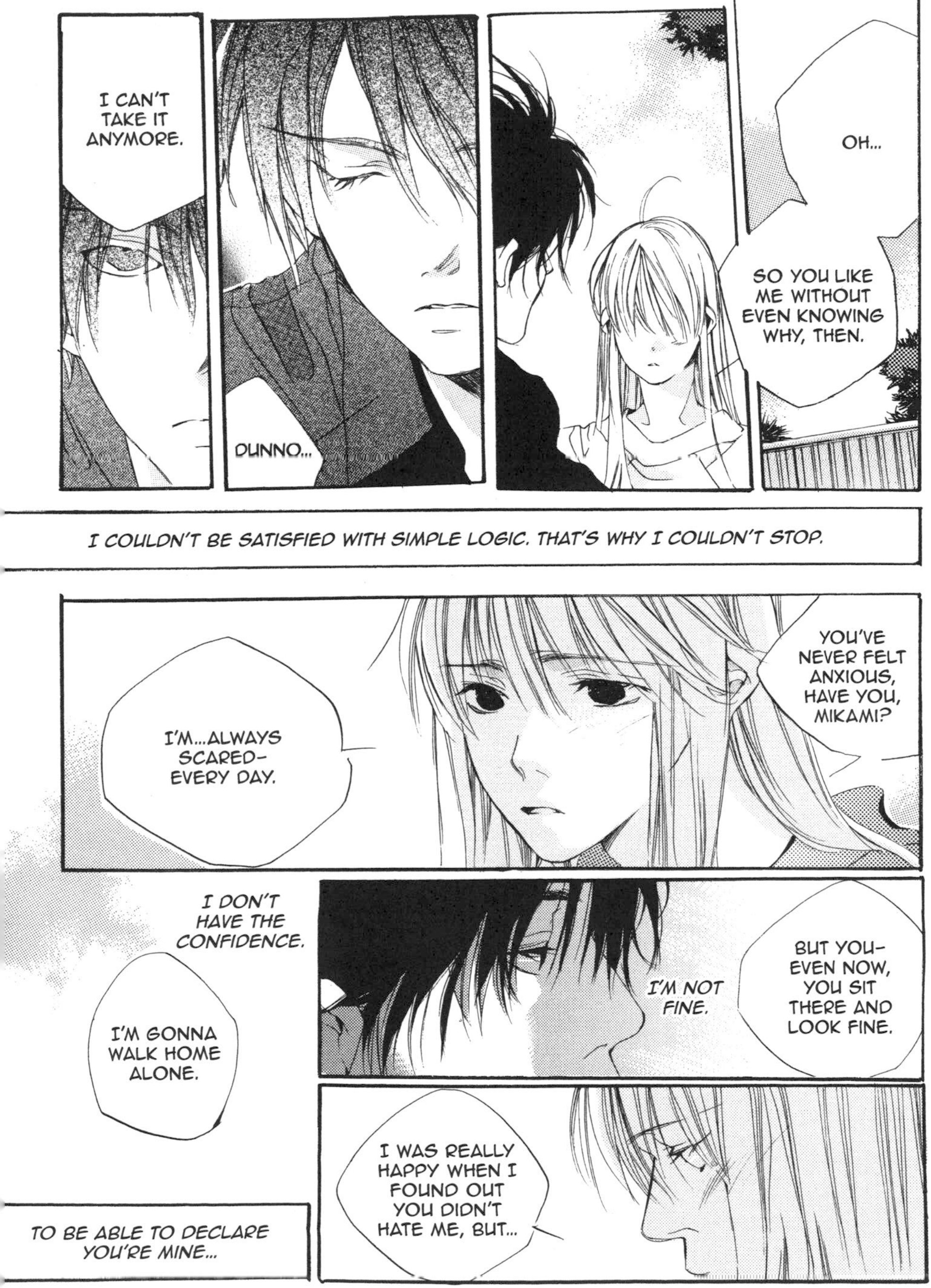
OH...
SO YOU LIKE ME WITHOUT EVEN KNOWING WHY, THEN.
DUNNO...
I CAN'T TAKE IT ANYMORE.
I COULDN'T BE SATISFIED WITH SIMPLE LOGIC. THAT'S WHY I COULDN'T STOP.
YOU'VE NEVER FELT ANXIOUS, HAVE YOU, MIKAMI?
I'M...ALWAYS SCARED- EVERY DAY.
BUT YOU- EVEN NOW, YOU SIT THERE AND LOOK FINE.
I'M NOT FINE.
I DON'T HAVE THE CONFIDENCE.
I'M GONNA WALK HOME ALONE.
I WAS REALLY HAPPY WHEN I FOUND OUT YOU DIDN'T HATE ME, BUT...
TO BE ABLE TO DECLARE YOU'RE MINE...

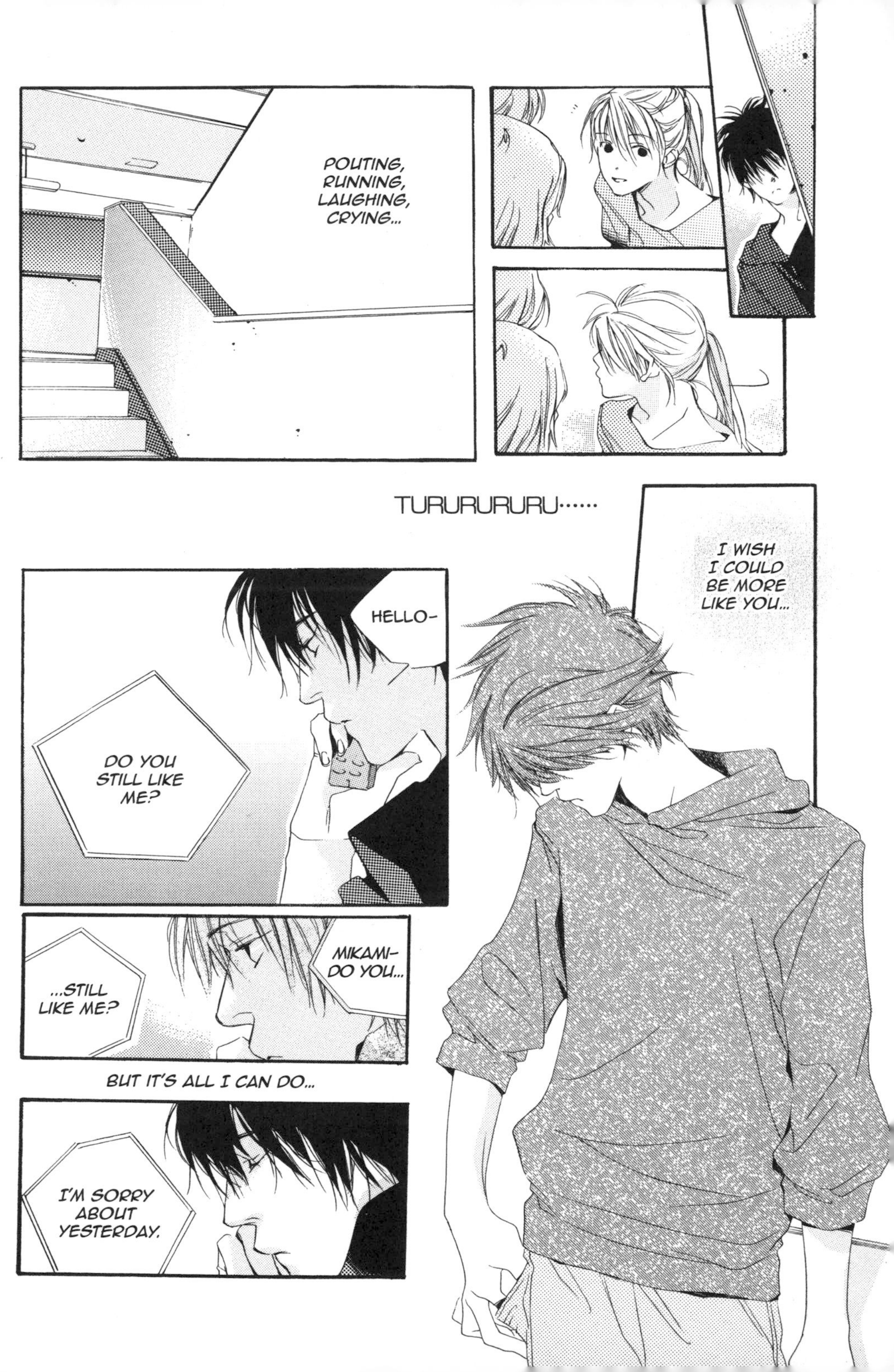
POUTING, RUNNING, LAUGHING, CRYING...
I WISH I COULD BE MORE LIKE YOU...
TURURURURU......
HELLO-
DO YOU STILL LIKE ME?
MIKAMI- DO YOU...
...STILL LIKE ME?
BUT IT'S ALL I CAN DO...
I'M SORRY ABOUT YESTERDAY.

...JUST TO NOD IN AGREEMENT...

YEAH.

TO BE HONEST—

...IT'S REALLY HARD FOR ME...

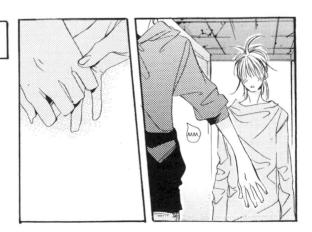

MM

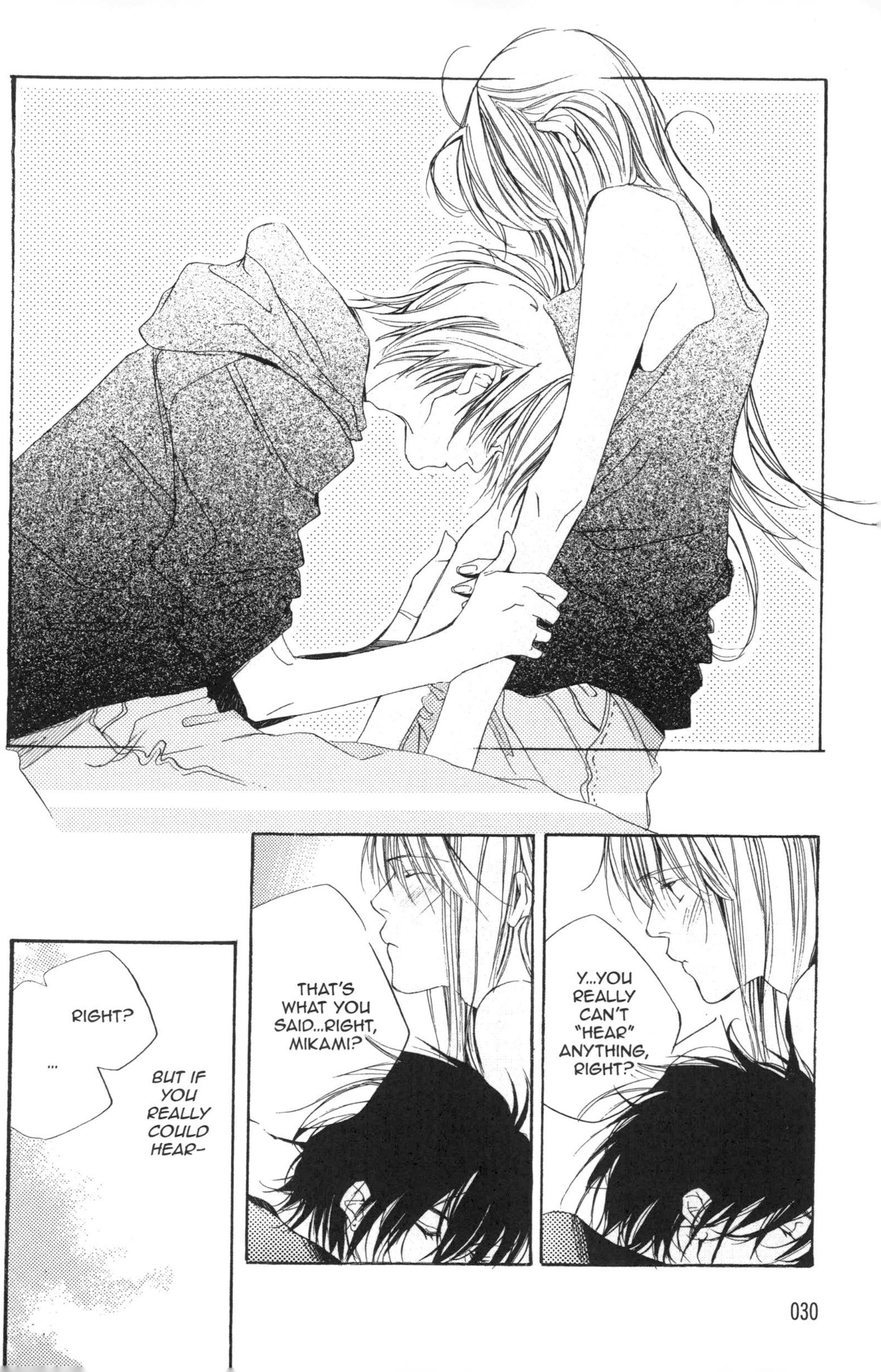
Y...YOU REALLY CAN'T "HEAR" ANYTHING, RIGHT?
THAT'S WHAT YOU SAID...RIGHT, MIKAMI?
RIGHT?
...
BUT IF YOU REALLY COULD HEAR-

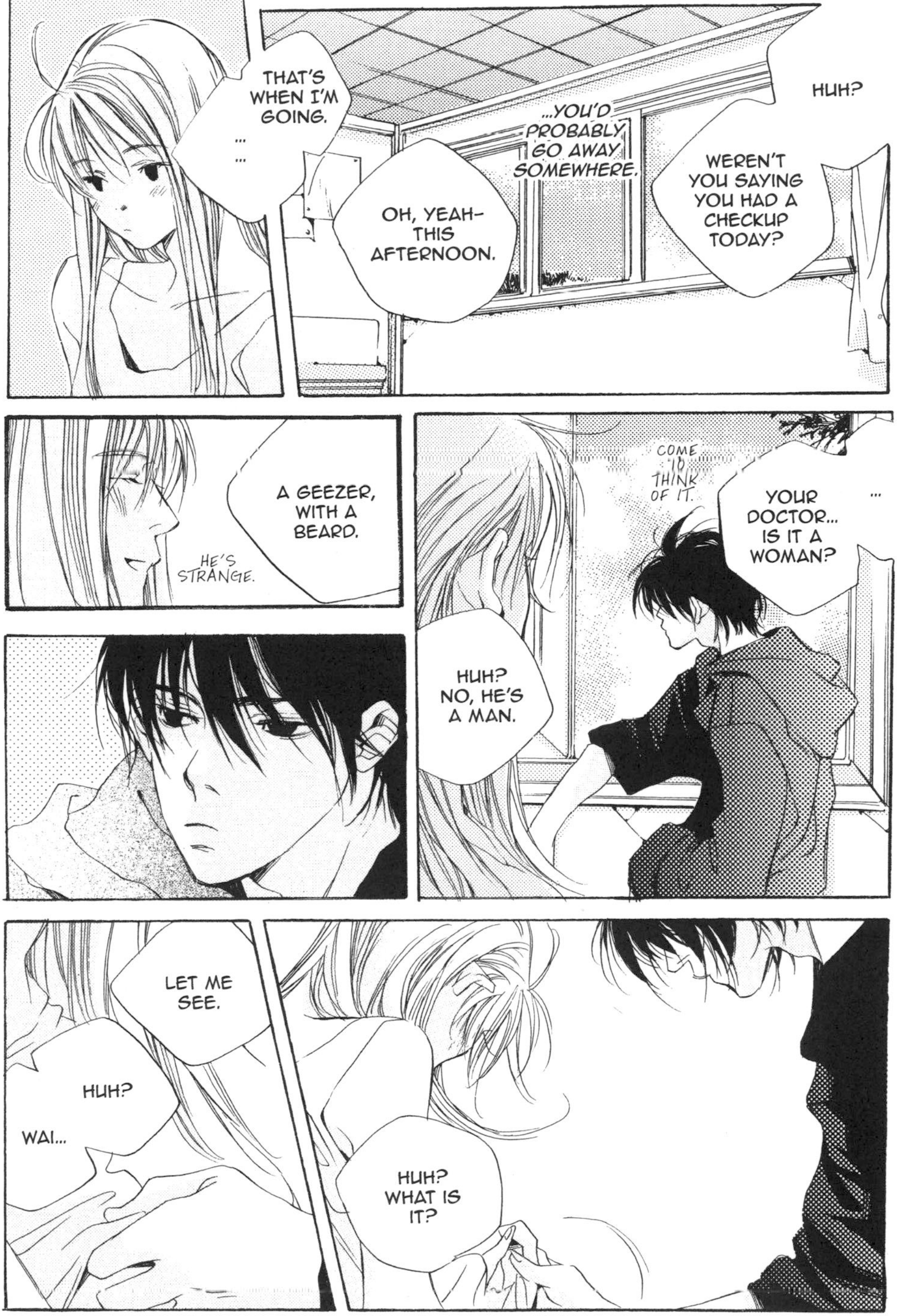

HUH?
WEREN'T YOU SAYING YOU HAD A CHECKUP TODAY?
OH, YEAH- THIS AFTERNOON.
...YOU'D PROBABLY GO AWAY SOMEWHERE.
THAT'S WHEN I'M GOING.
...
...
...
COME TO THINK OF IT.
YOUR DOCTOR... IS IT A WOMAN?
HUH? NO, HE'S A MAN.
A GEEZER, WITH A BEARD.
HE'S STRANGE.
HUH? WHAT IS IT?
LET ME SEE.
HUH?
WAI...

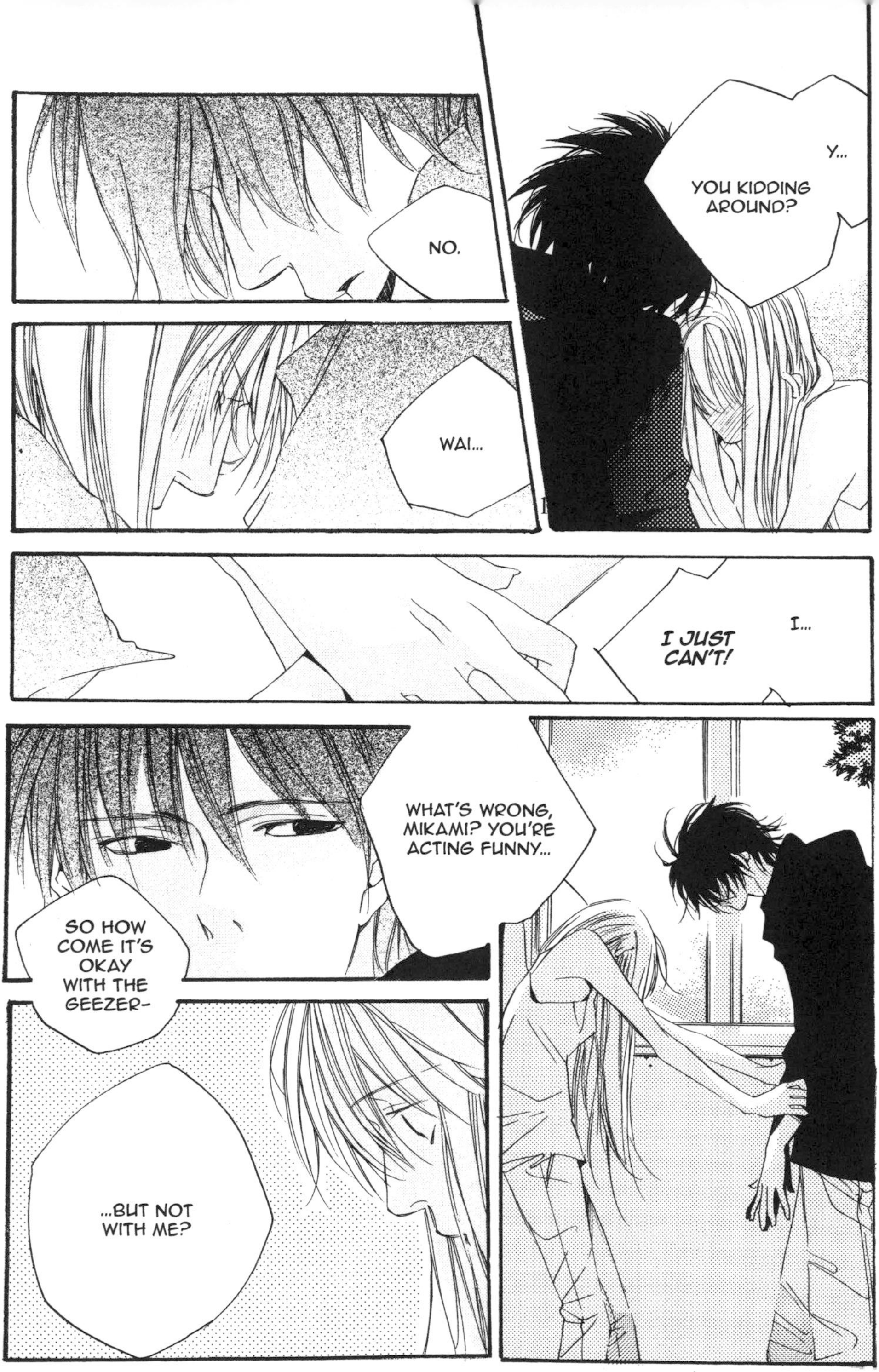
Y...
YOU KIDDING AROUND?
NO.
WAI...
I...
I JUST CAN'T!
WHAT'S WRONG, MIKAMI? YOU'RE ACTING FUNNY...
SO HOW COME IT'S OKAY WITH THE GEEZER-
...BUT NOT WITH ME?

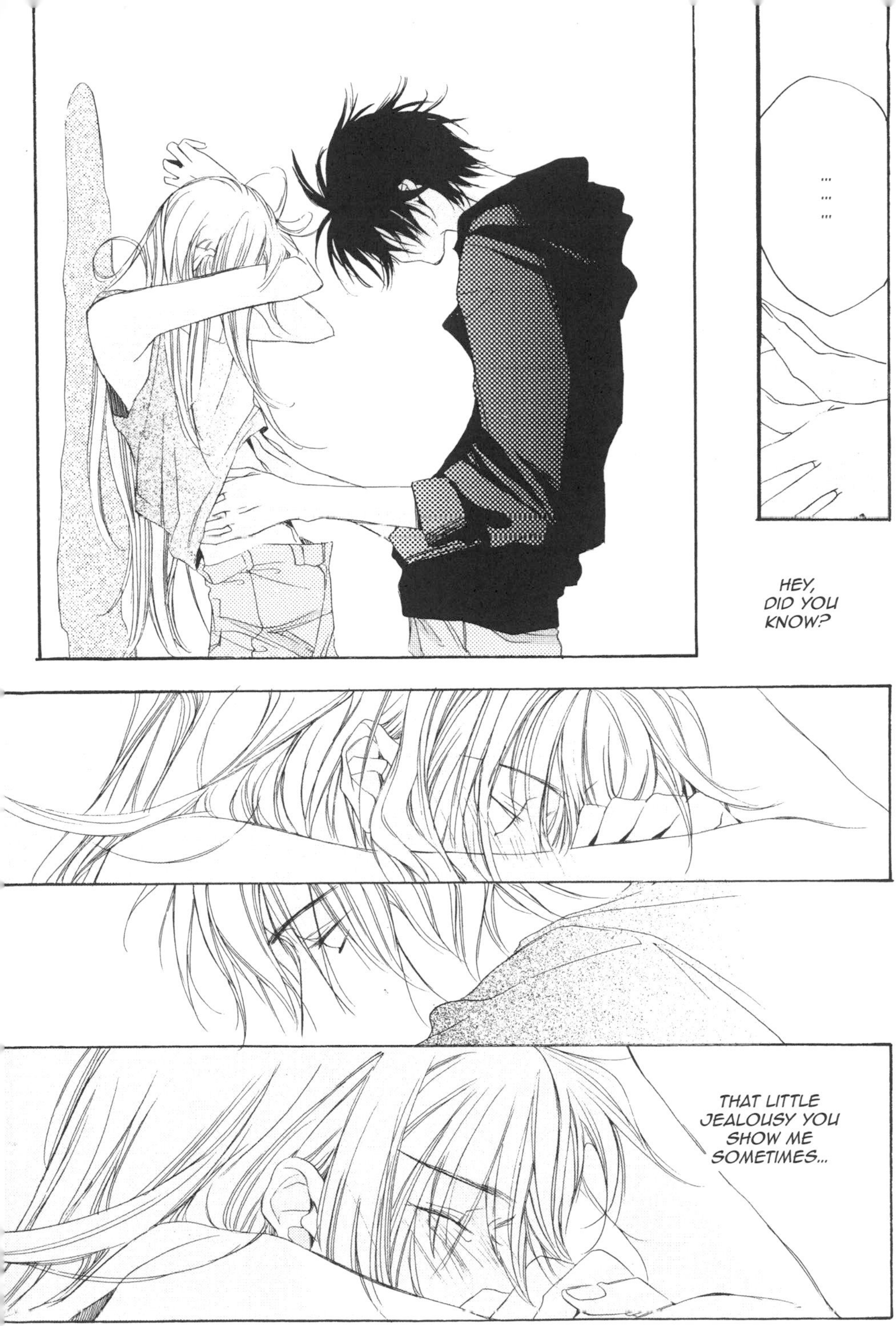
...
...
...
HEY, DID YOU KNOW?
THAT LITTLE JEALOUSY YOU SHOW ME SOMETIMES...

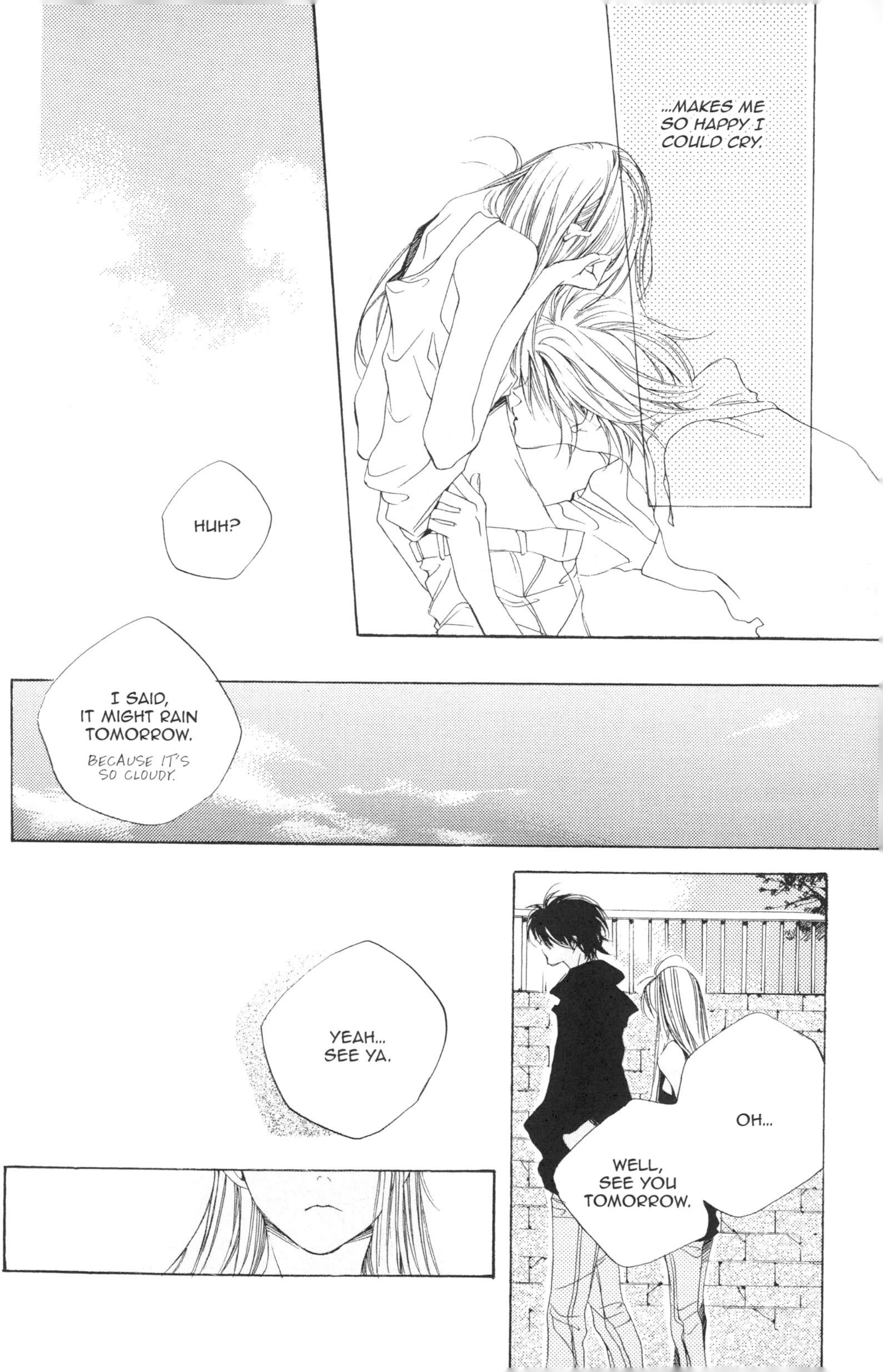
...MAKES ME SO HAPPY I COULD CRY.
HUH?
I SAID, IT MIGHT RAIN TOMORROW.
BECAUSE IT'S SO CLOUDY.
OH...
WELL, SEE YOU TOMORROW.
YEAH... SEE YA.

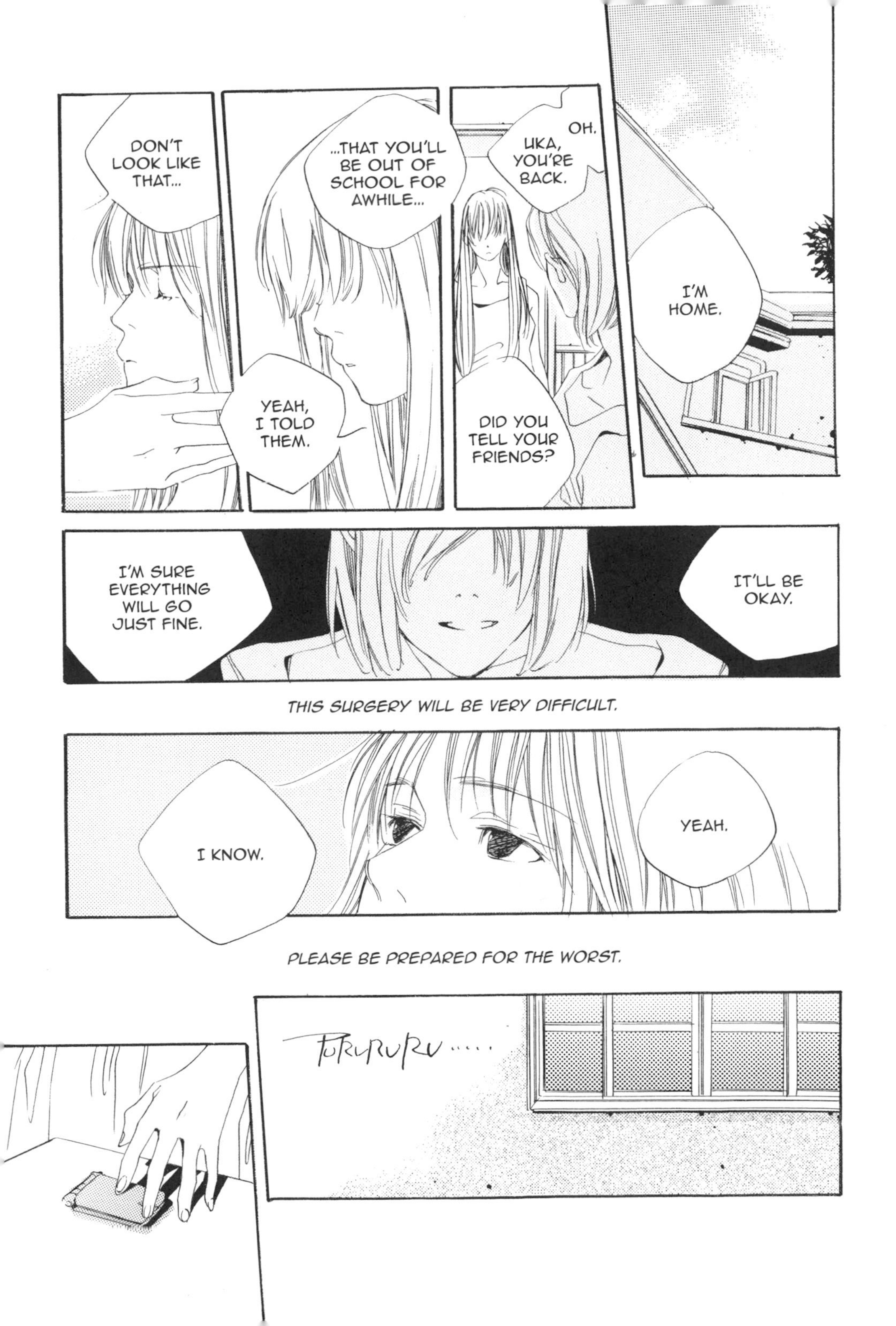
I'M HOME.
OH. UKA, YOU'RE BACK.
DID YOU TELL YOUR FRIENDS?
...THAT YOU'LL BE OUT OF SCHOOL FOR AWHILE...
YEAH, I TOLD THEM.
DON'T LOOK LIKE THAT...
IT'LL BE OKAY.
I'M SURE EVERYTHING WILL GO JUST FINE.
THIS SURGERY WILL BE VERY DIFFICULT.
YEAH.
I KNOW.
PLEASE BE PREPARED FOR THE WORST.
TURURURU.....

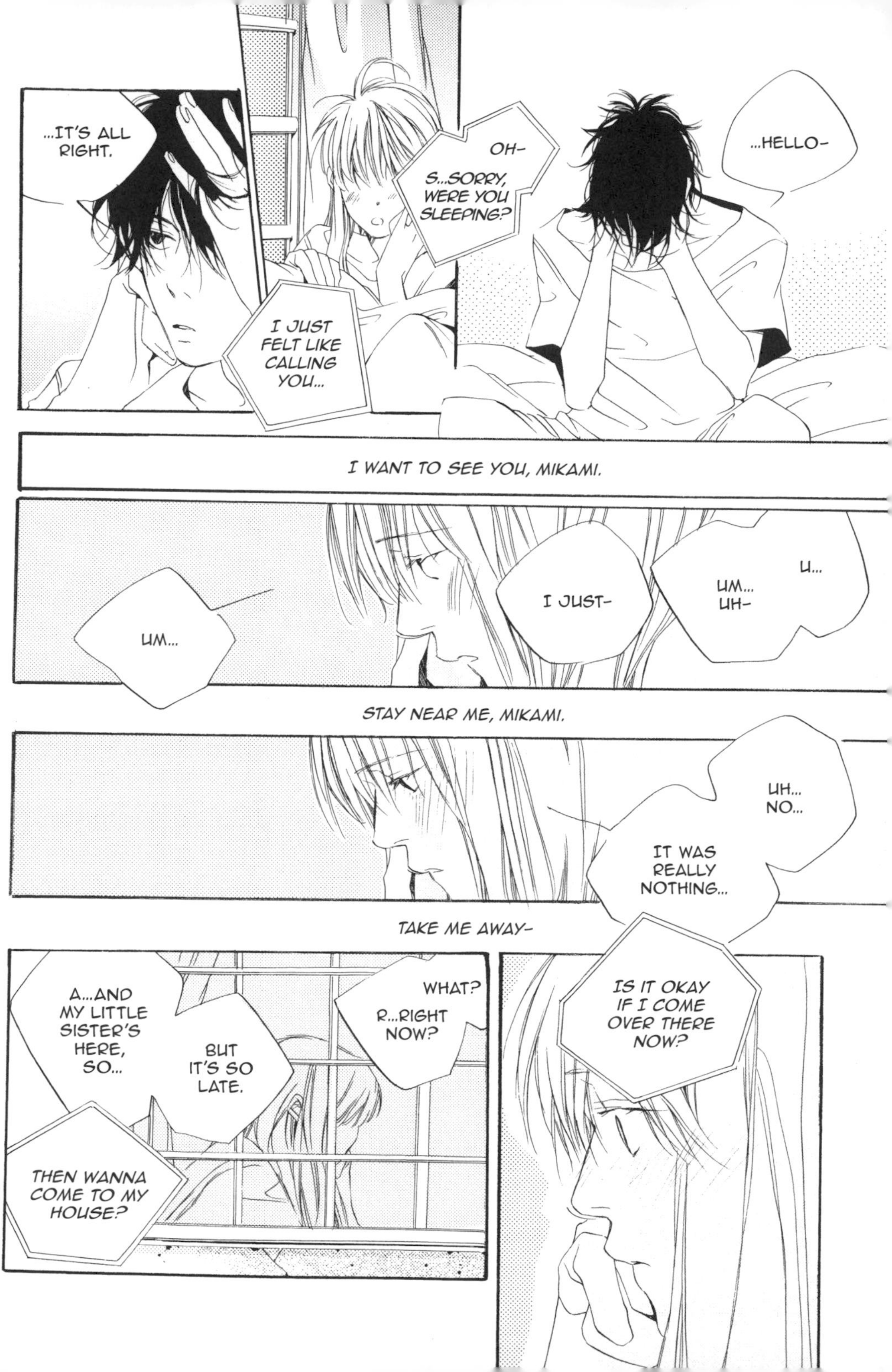
...HELLO-
OH-
S...SORRY, WERE YOU SLEEPING?
...IT'S ALL RIGHT.
I JUST FELT LIKE CALLING YOU...
I WANT TO SEE YOU, MIKAMI.
U...
UM... UH-
I JUST-
UM...
STAY NEAR ME, MIKAMI.
UH... NO...
IT WAS REALLY NOTHING...
TAKE ME AWAY-
IS IT OKAY IF I COME OVER THERE NOW?
WHAT?
R...RIGHT NOW?
BUT IT'S SO LATE.
A...AND MY LITTLE SISTER'S HERE, SO...
THEN WANNA COME TO MY HOUSE?

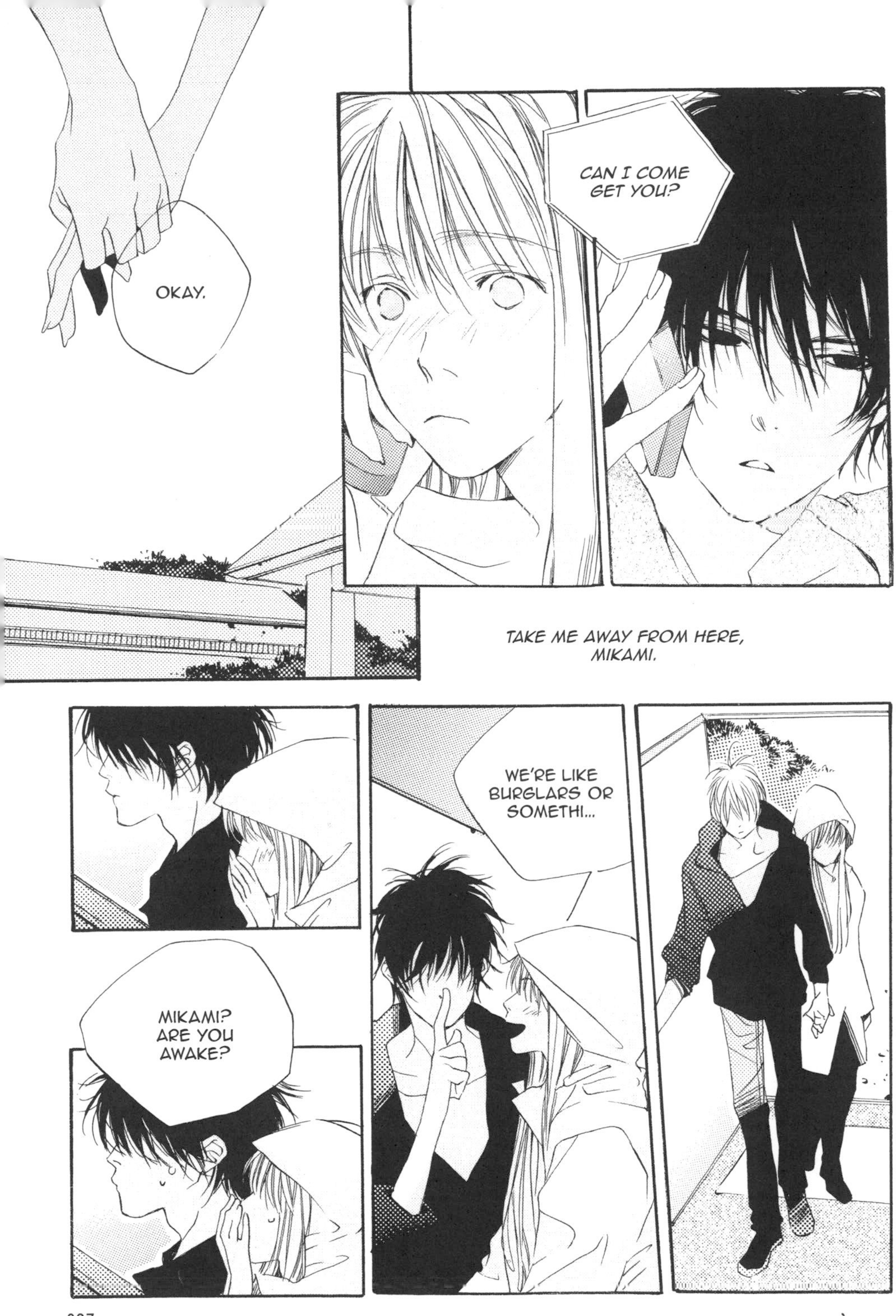
CAN I COME GET YOU?
OKAY.
TAKE ME AWAY FROM HERE, MIKAMI.
WE'RE LIKE BURGLARS OR SOMETHI...
MIKAMI? ARE YOU AWAKE?

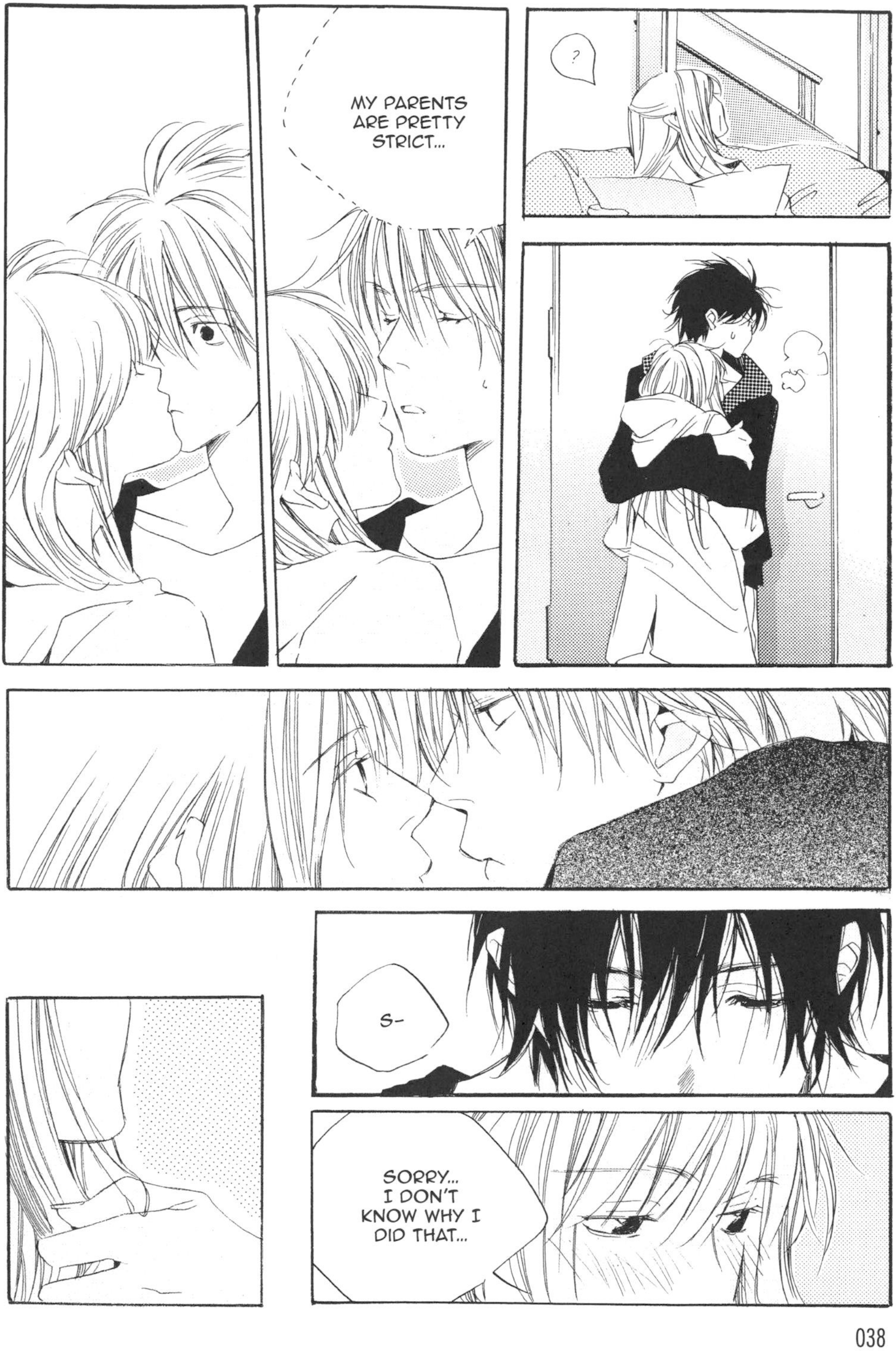
?
MY PARENTS ARE PRETTY STRICT...
S-
SORRY... I DON'T KNOW WHY I DID THAT...

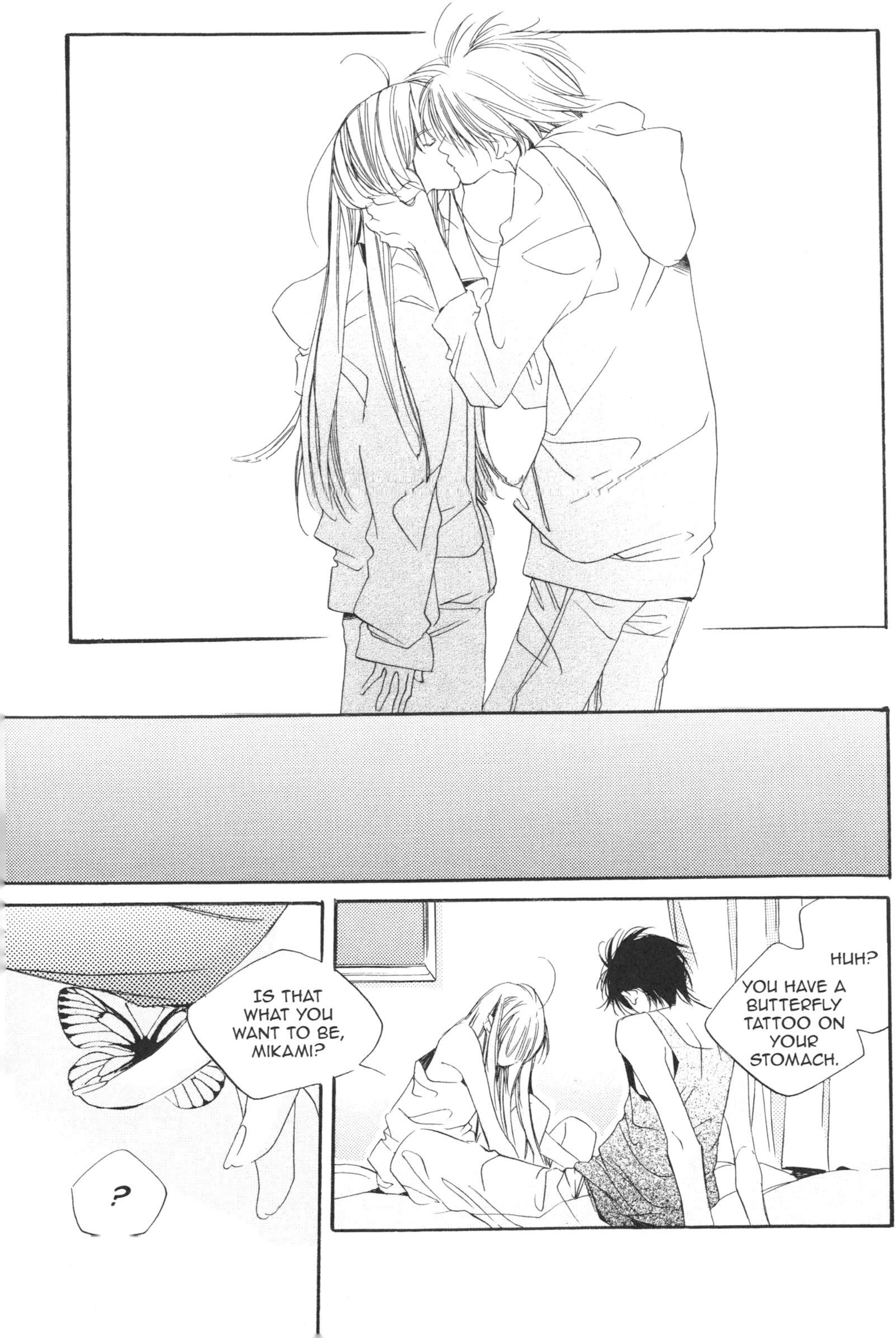
HUH?
YOU HAVE A BUTTERFLY TATTOO ON YOUR STOMACH.
IS THAT WHAT YOU WANT TO BE, MIKAMI?
?

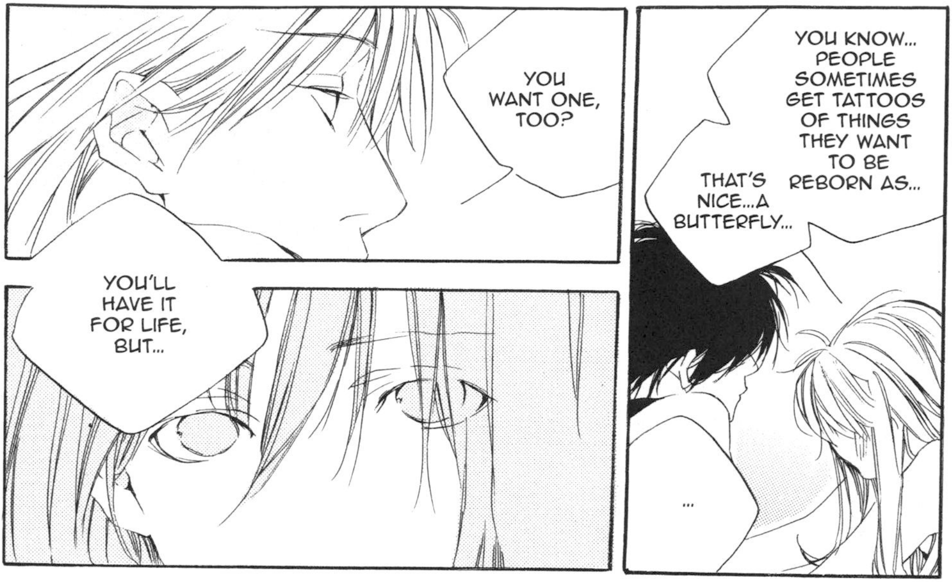
YOU KNOW... PEOPLE SOMETIMES GET TATTOOS OF THINGS THEY WANT TO BE REBORN AS...
THAT'S NICE...A BUTTERFLY...
...
YOU WANT ONE, TOO?
YOU'LL HAVE IT FOR LIFE, BUT...

THE REST OF YOUR LIFE,
THE SAME BUTTERFLY AS ME...

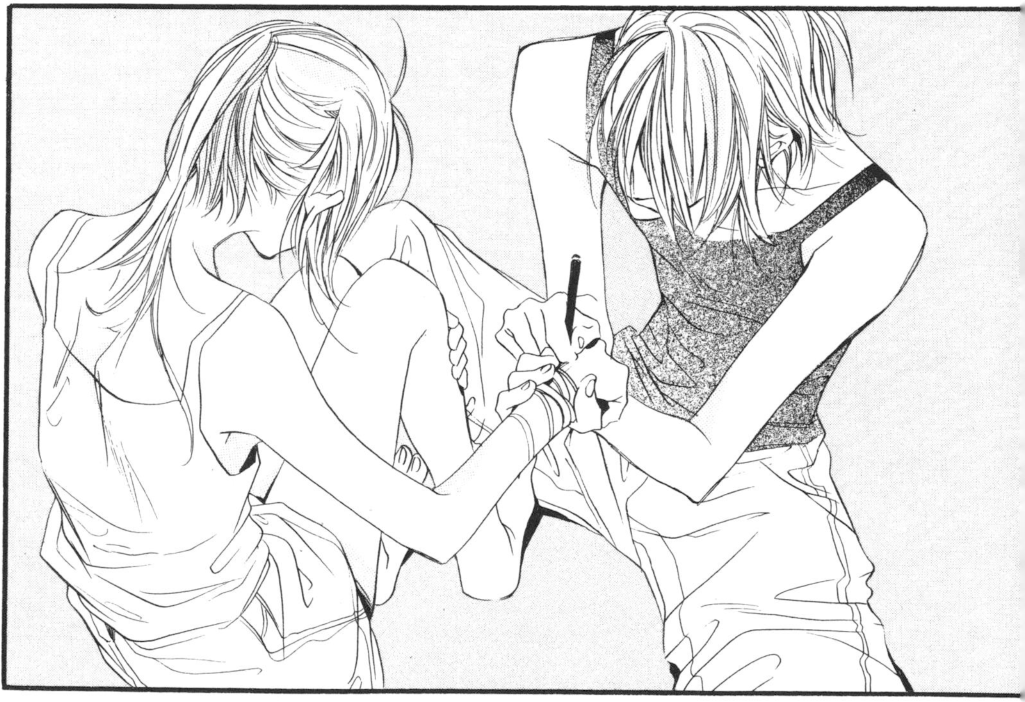

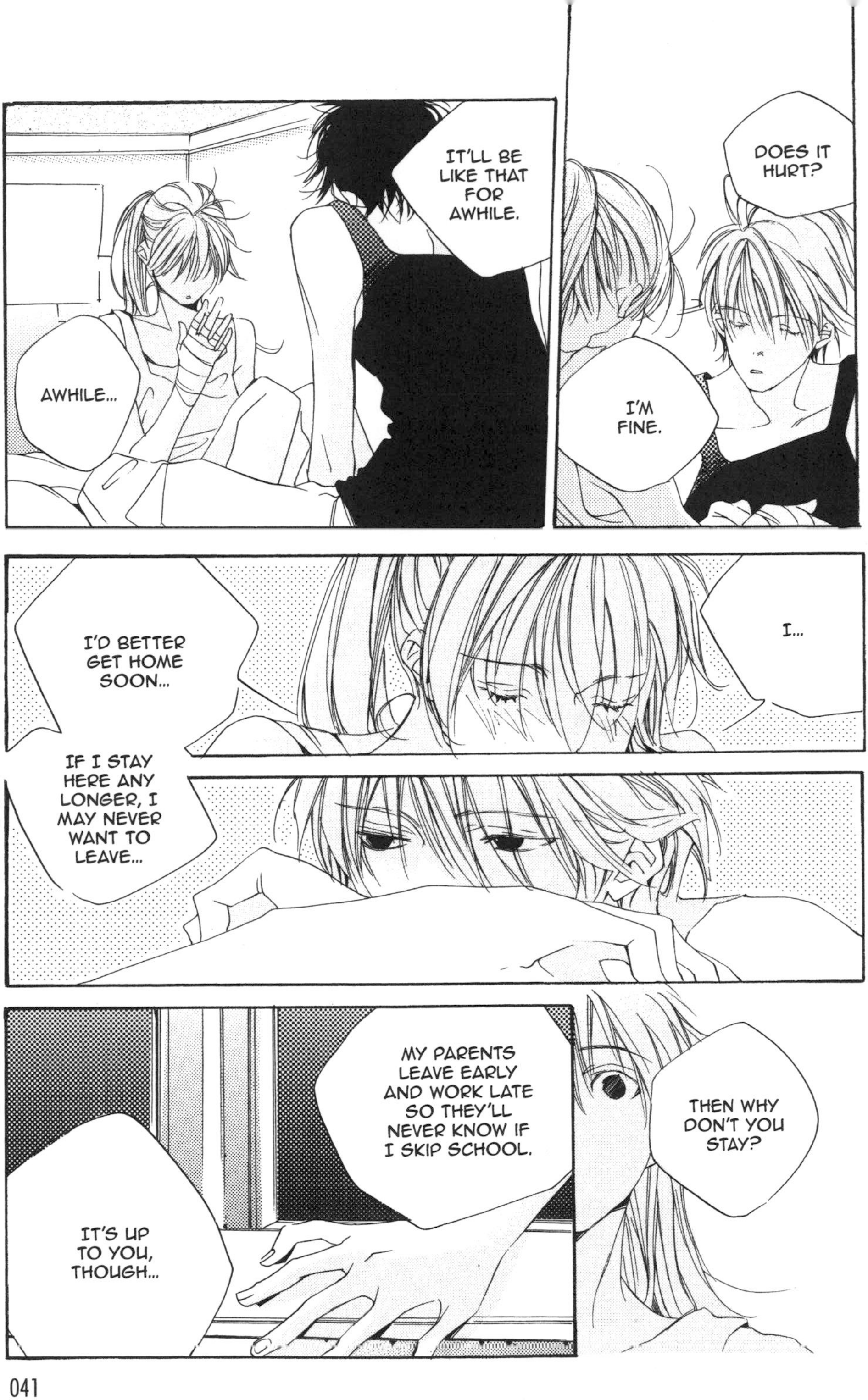
DOES IT HURT?
I'M FINE.
IT'LL BE LIKE THAT FOR AWHILE.
AWHILE...
I...
I'D BETTER GET HOME SOON...
IF I STAY HERE ANY LONGER, I MAY NEVER WANT TO LEAVE...
THEN WHY DON'T YOU STAY?
MY PARENTS LEAVE EARLY AND WORK LATE SO THEY'LL NEVER KNOW IF I SKIP SCHOOL.
IT'S UP TO YOU, THOUGH...

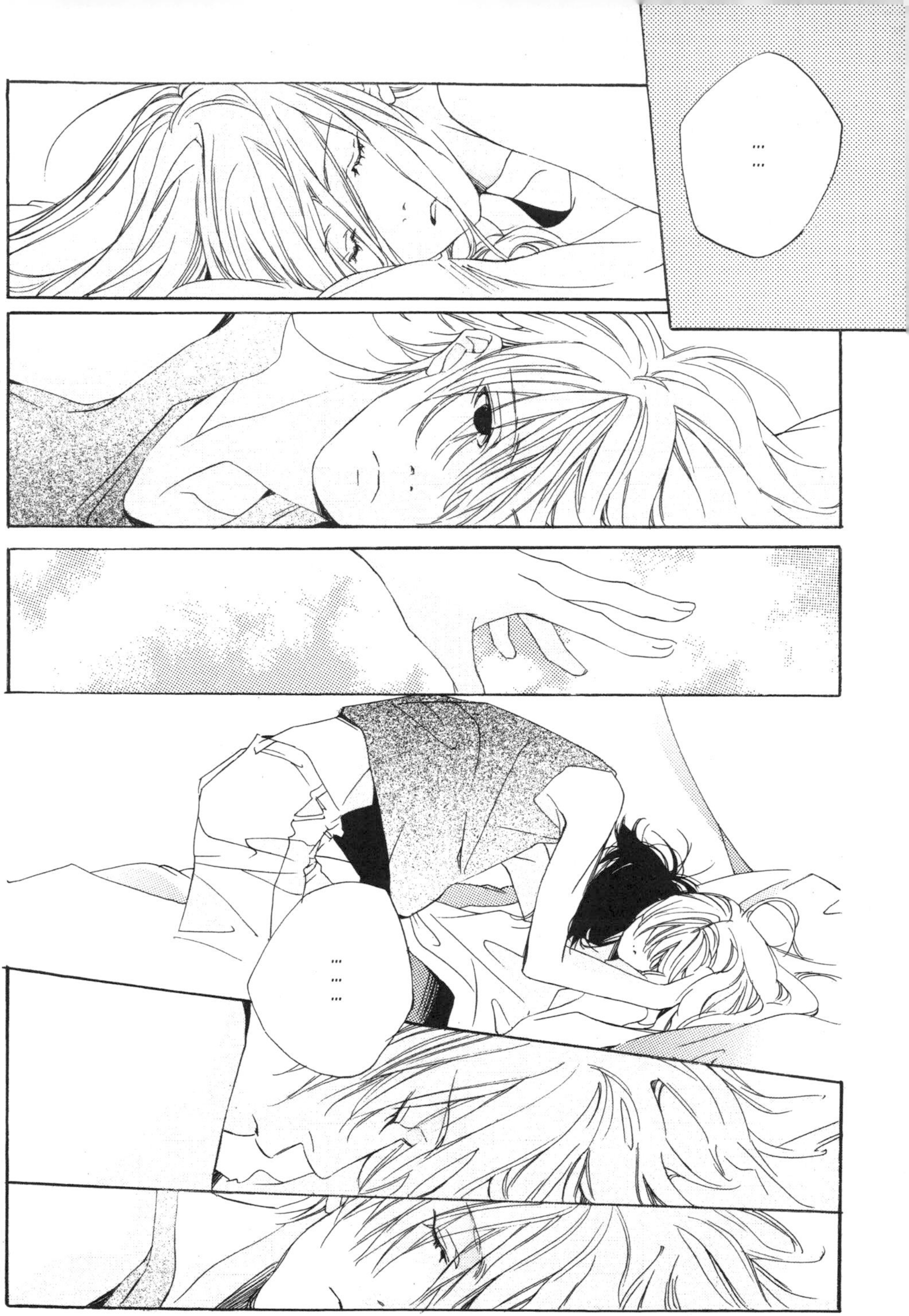
...
...
...
...
...

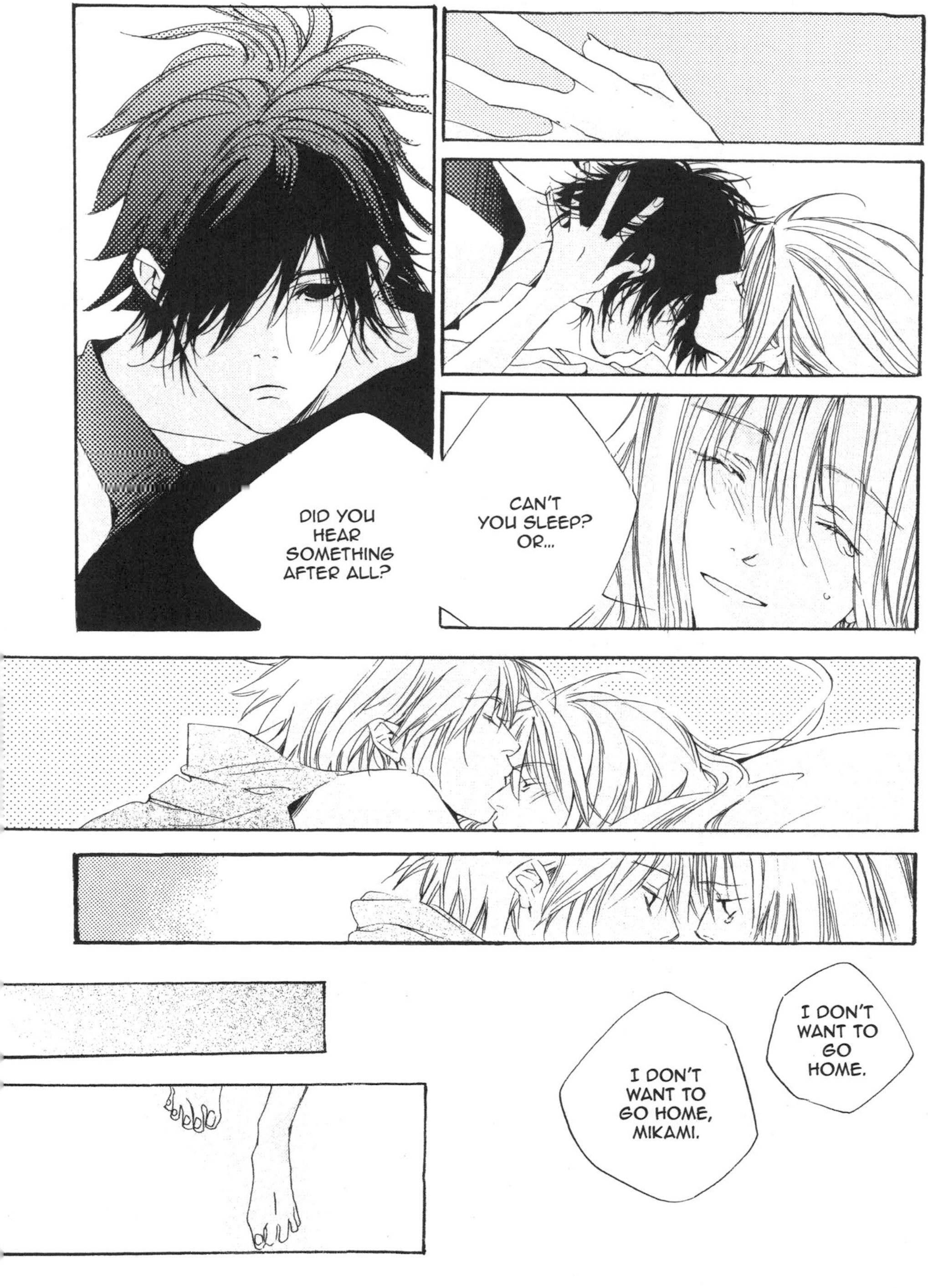
CAN'T YOU SLEEP? OR...
DID YOU HEAR SOMETHING AFTER ALL?
I DON'T WANT TO GO HOME.
I DON'T WANT TO GO HOME, MIKAMI.

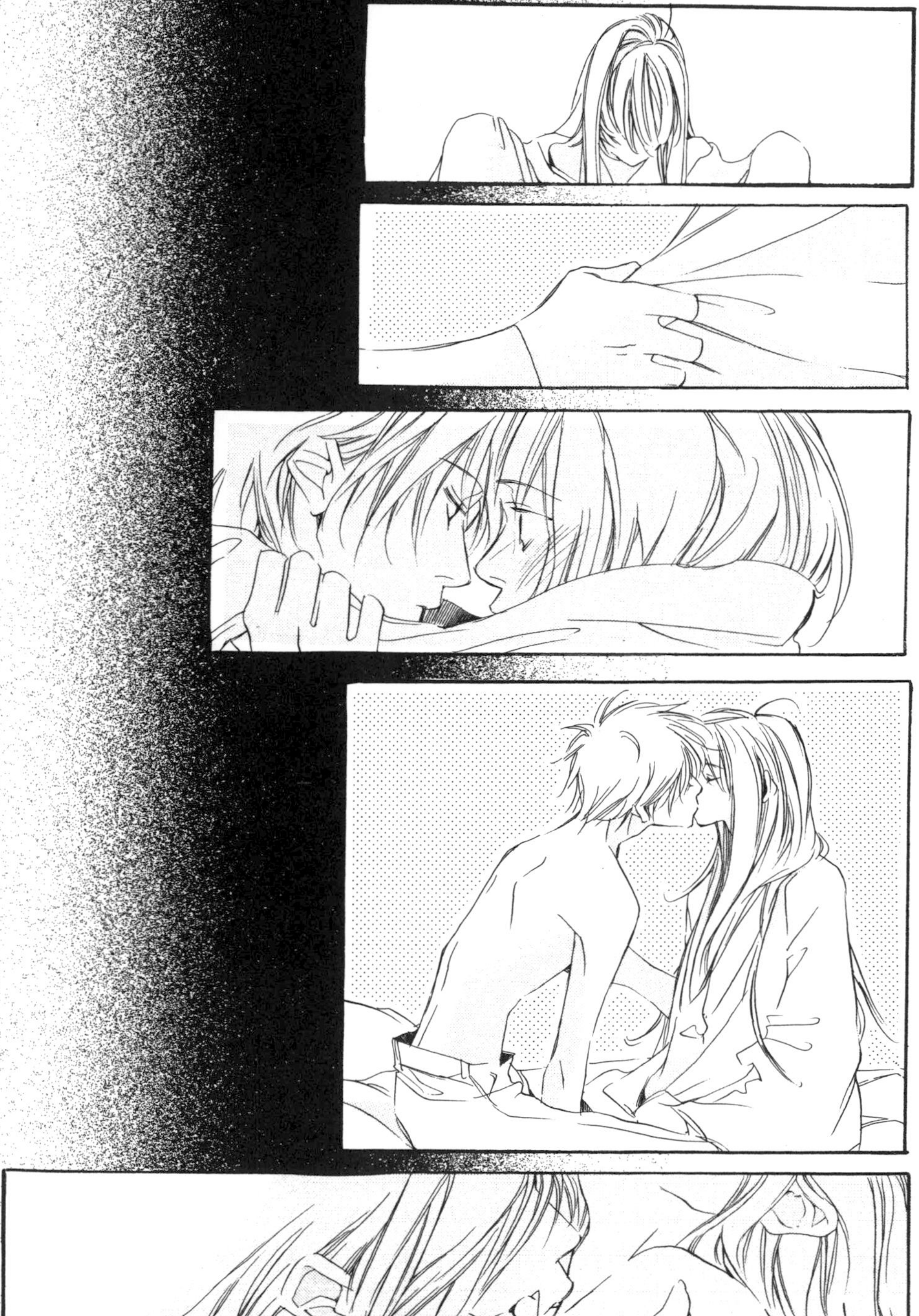

I WONDER WHY MIKAMI CAN HEAR IT?

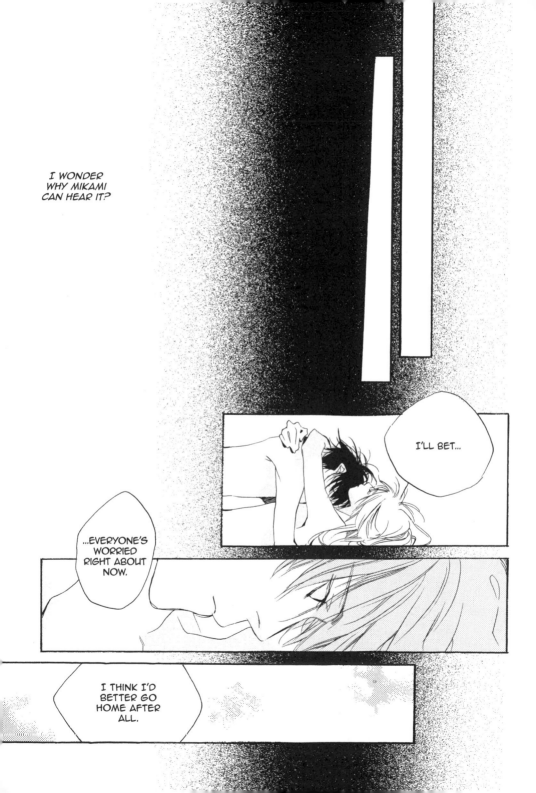

I'LL BET...

...EVERYONE'S WORRIED RIGHT ABOUT NOW.

I THINK I'D BETTER GO HOME AFTER ALL.

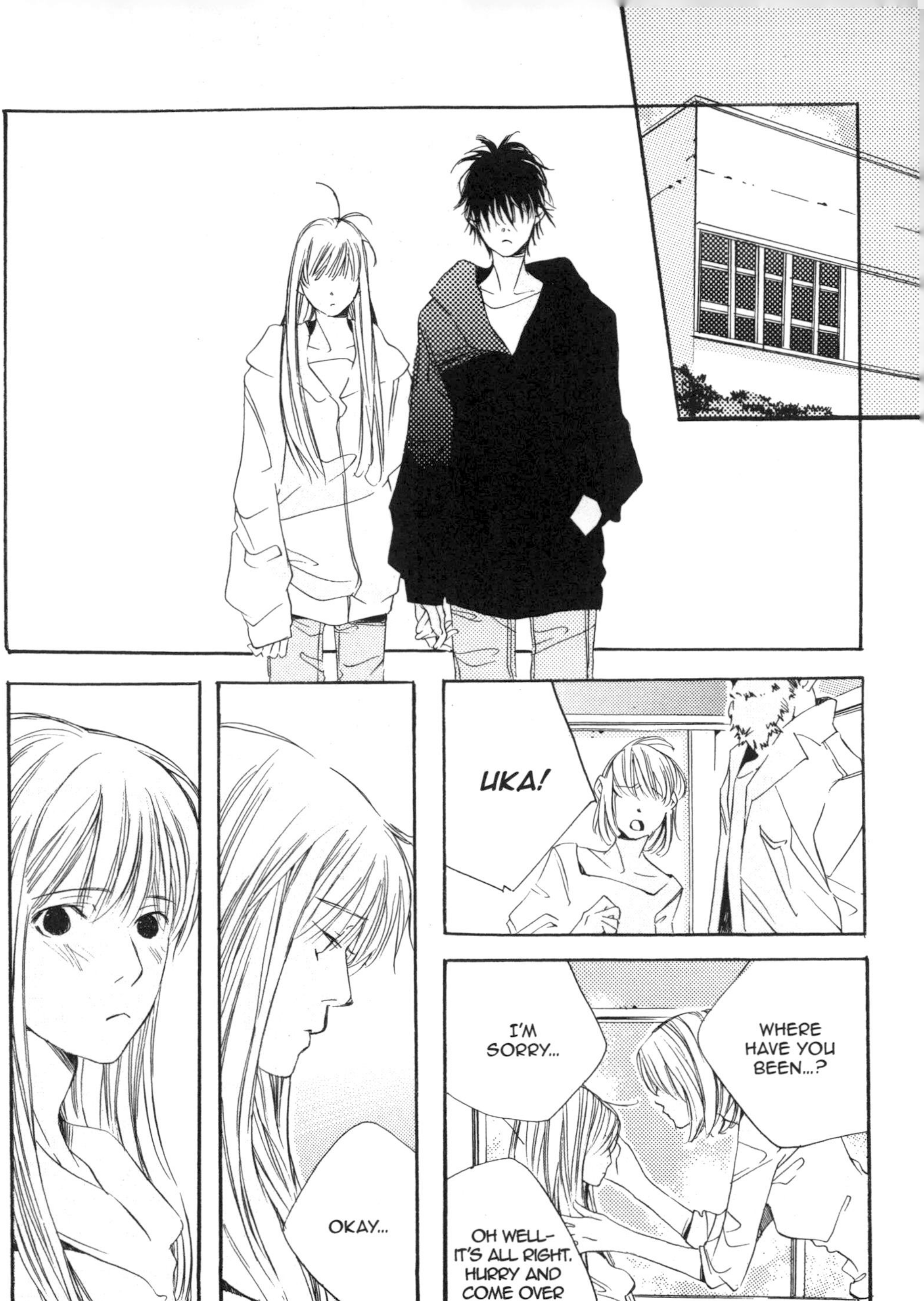
UKA!
WHERE HAVE YOU BEEN...?
I'M SORRY...
OH WELL- IT'S ALL RIGHT. HURRY AND COME OVER HERE.
OKAY...

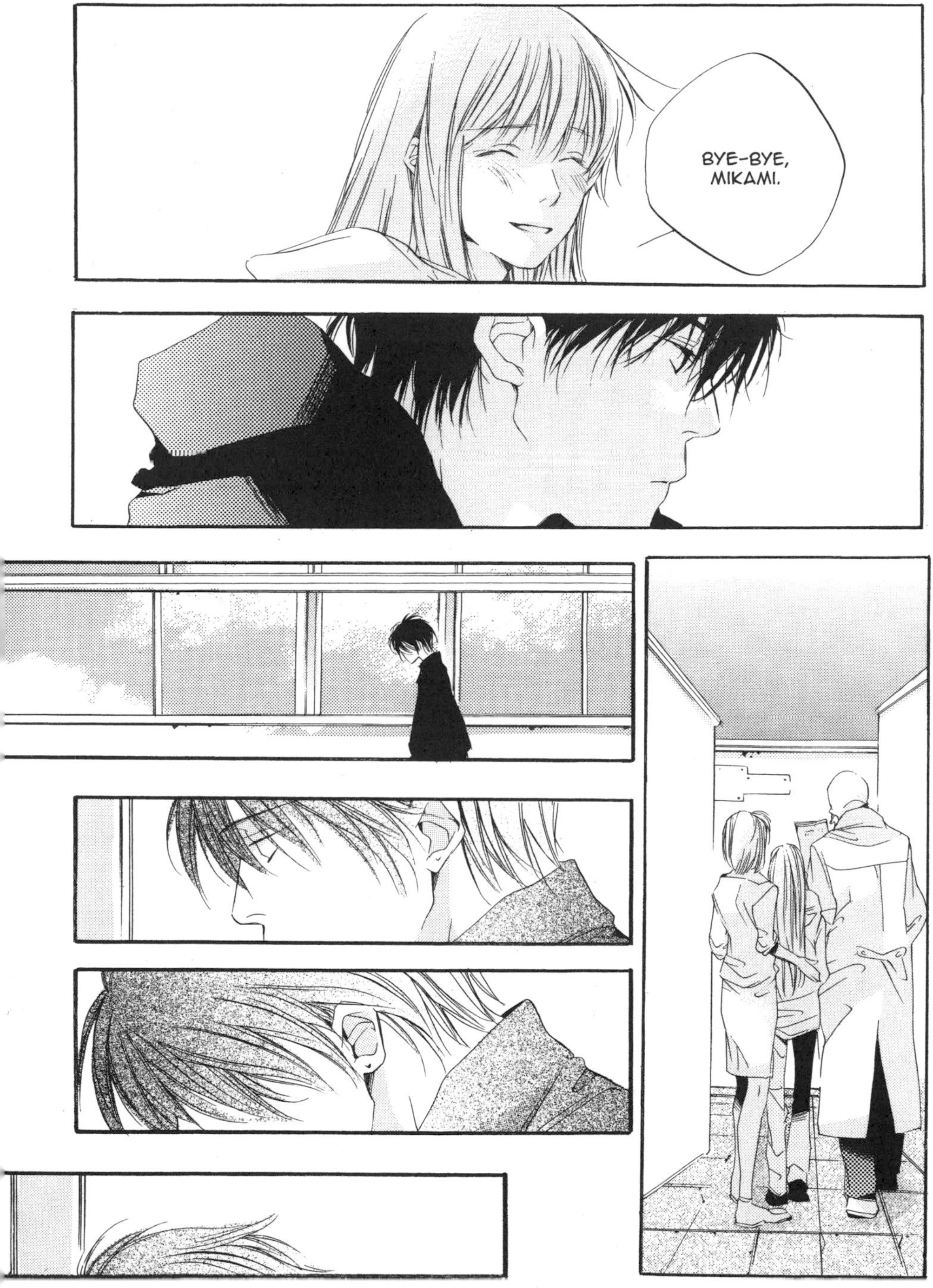
BYE-BYE, MIKAMI.

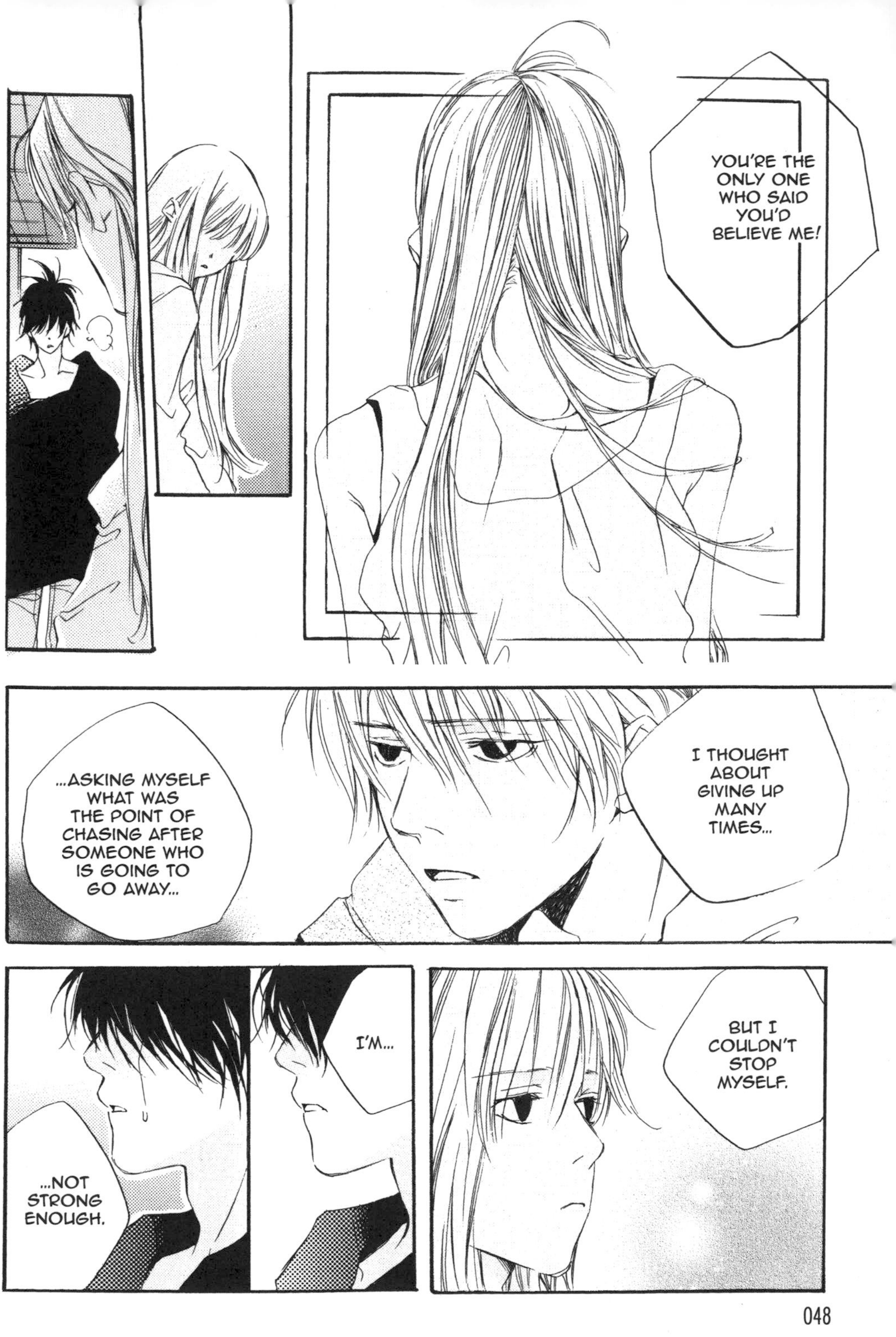
YOU'RE THE ONLY ONE WHO SAID YOU'D BELIEVE ME!
I THOUGHT ABOUT GIVING UP MANY TIMES...
...ASKING MYSELF WHAT WAS THE POINT OF CHASING AFTER SOMEONE WHO IS GOING TO GO AWAY...
BUT I COULDN'T STOP MYSELF.
I'M...
...NOT STRONG ENOUGH.

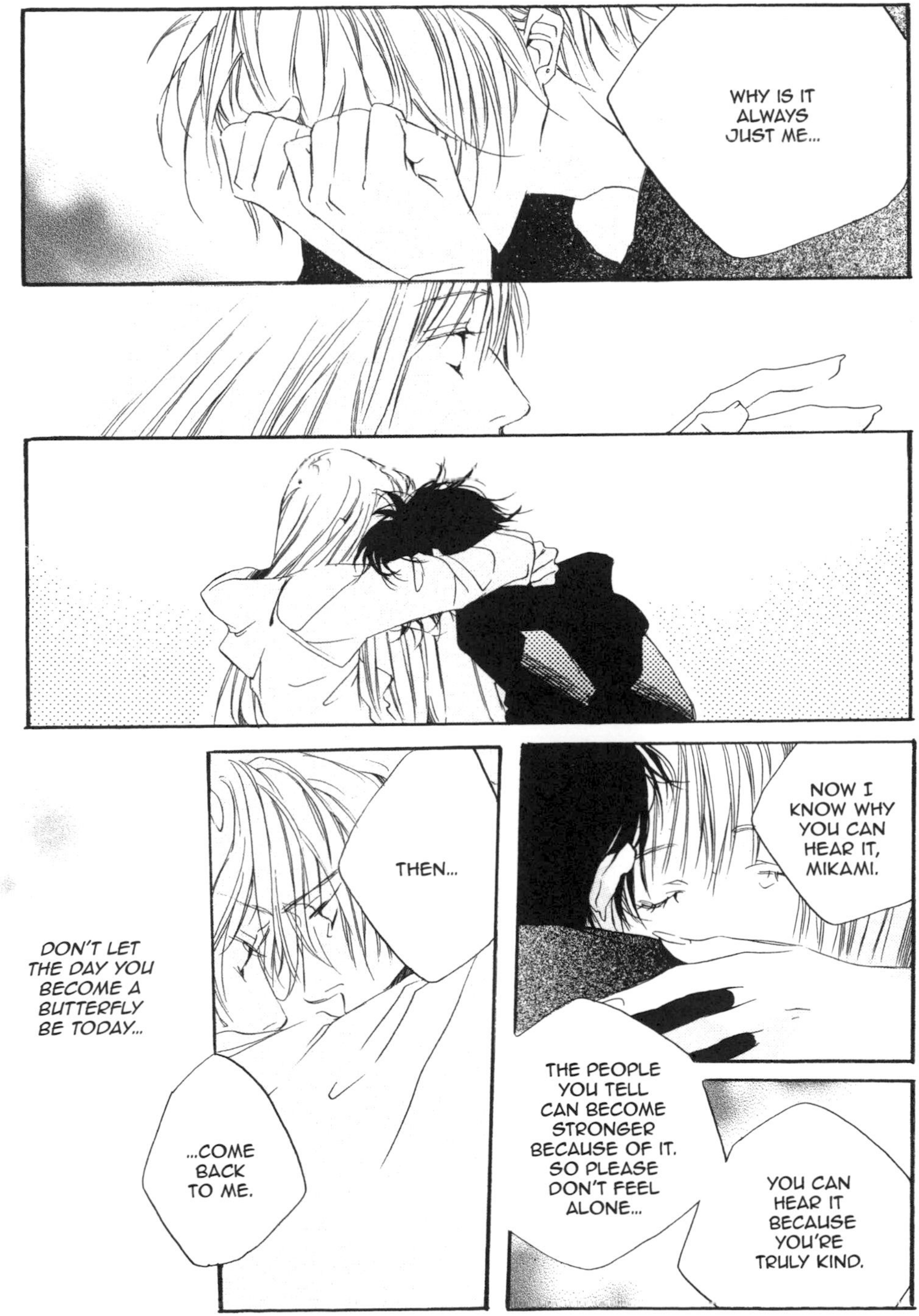
WHY IS IT ALWAYS JUST ME...
NOW I KNOW WHY YOU CAN HEAR IT, MIKAMI.
YOU CAN HEAR IT BECAUSE YOU'RE TRULY KIND.
THE PEOPLE YOU TELL CAN BECOME STRONGER BECAUSE OF IT. SO PLEASE DON'T FEEL ALONE...
THEN...
...COME BACK TO ME.
DON'T LET THE DAY YOU BECOME A BUTTERFLY BE TODAY...

OH LOOK, MIKAMI- A BUTTERFLY.

SEE?

...YEAH.

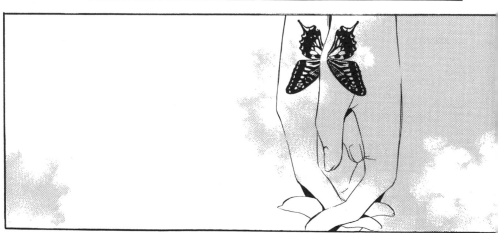

THE DAY I BECOME A BUTTERFLY / END

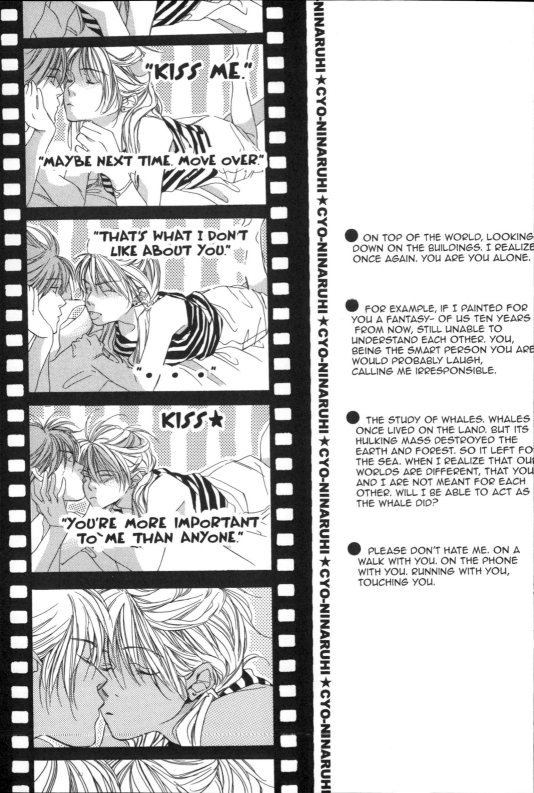

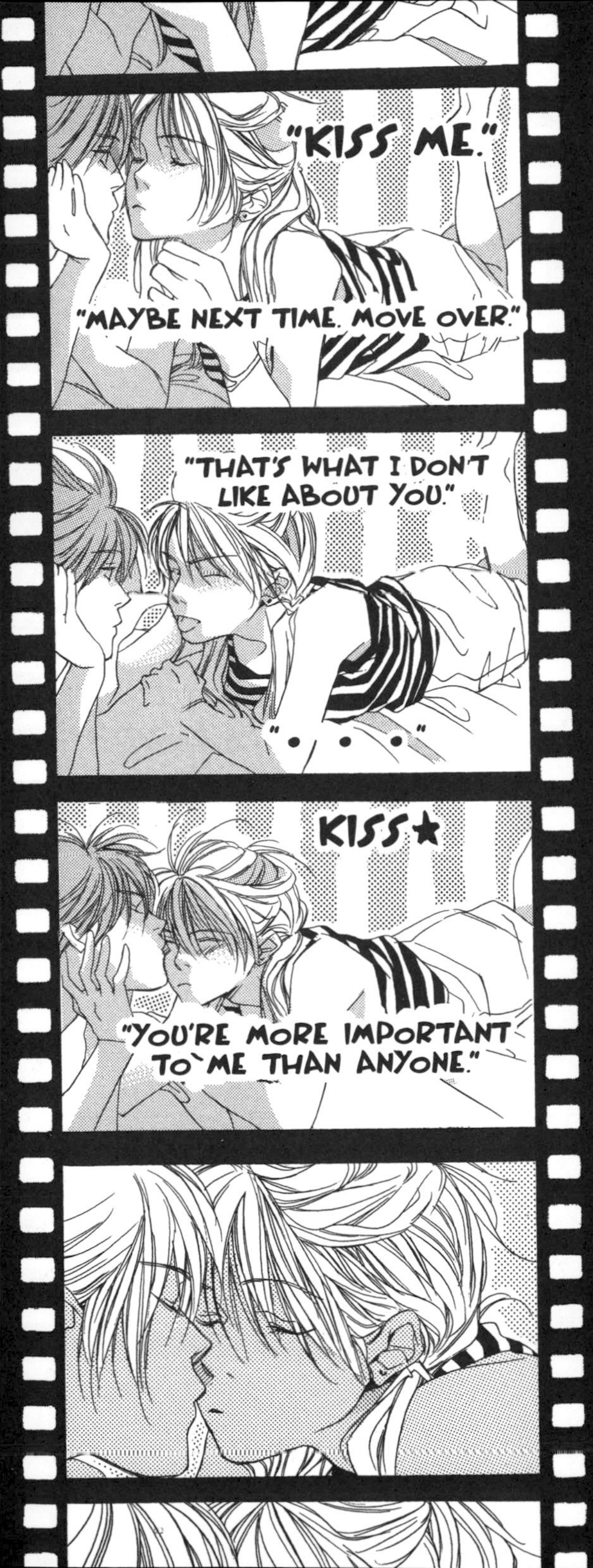
"KISS ME."
"MAYBE NEXT TIME. MOVE OVER."
"THAT'S WHAT I DON'T LIKE ABOUT YOU."
". . ."
KISS★
"YOU'RE MORE IMPORTANT TO`ME THAN ANYONE."

NINARUHI★CYO-NINARUHI★CYO-NINARUHI★CYO-NINARUHI★CYO-NINARUHI★CYO-NINARUHI★CYO-NINARUHI

● ON TOP OF THE WORLD, LOOKING DOWN ON THE BUILDINGS. I REALIZE ONCE AGAIN. YOU ARE YOU ALONE.

● FOR EXAMPLE, IF I PAINTED FOR YOU A FANTASY- OF US TEN YEARS FROM NOW, STILL UNABLE TO UNDERSTAND EACH OTHER. YOU, BEING THE SMART PERSON YOU ARE WOULD PROBABLY LAUGH, CALLING ME IRRESPONSIBLE.

● THE STUDY OF WHALES. WHALES ONCE LIVED ON THE LAND. BUT ITS HULKING MASS DESTROYED THE EARTH AND FOREST. SO IT LEFT FO THE SEA. WHEN I REALIZE THAT OU WORLDS ARE DIFFERENT, THAT YOU AND I ARE NOT MEANT FOR EACH OTHER. WILL I BE ABLE TO ACT AS THE WHALE DID?

● PLEASE DON'T HATE ME. ON A WALK WITH YOU. ON THE PHONE WITH YOU. RUNNING WITH YOU, TOUCHING YOU.

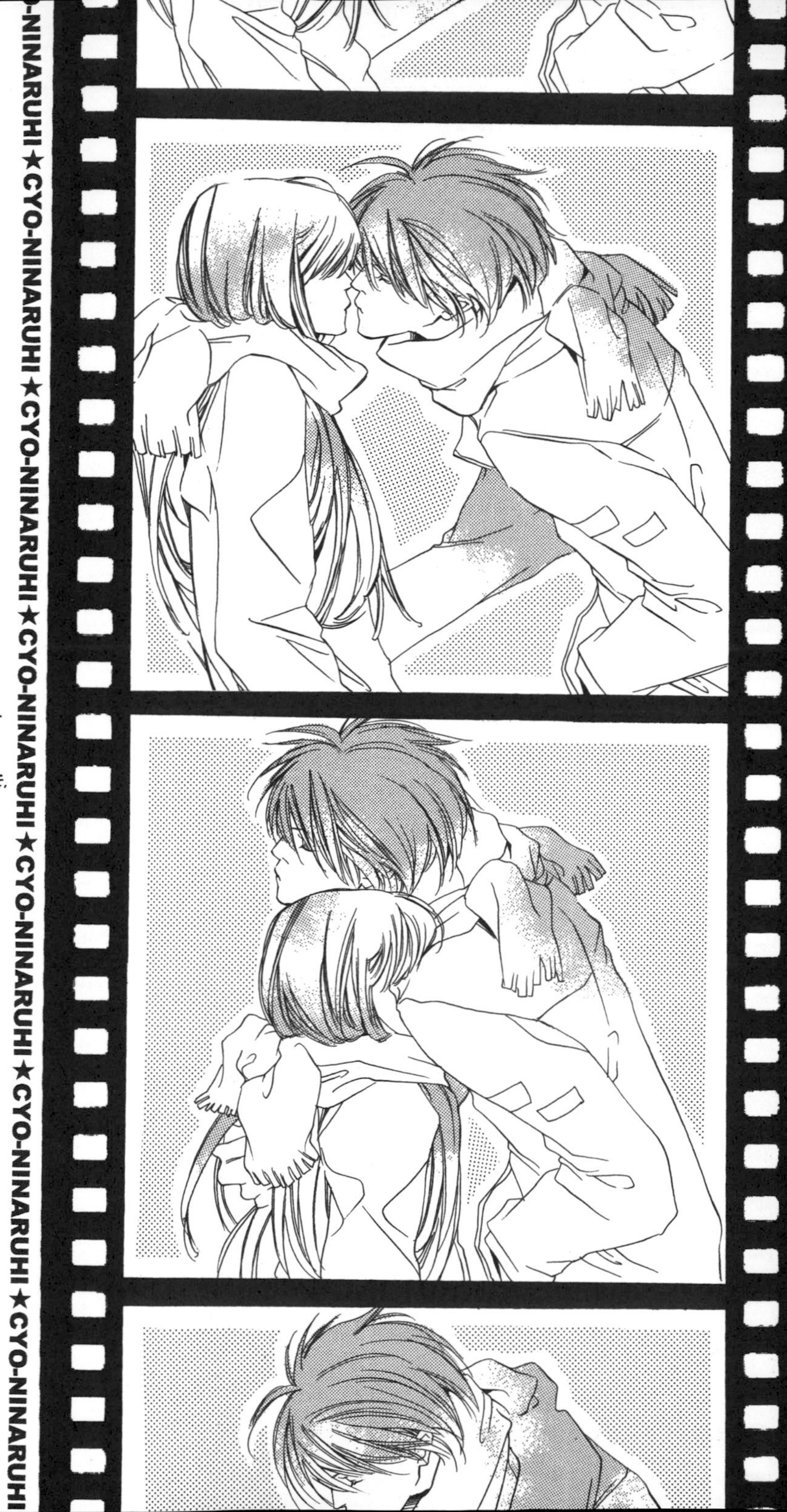
O-NINARUHI★CYO-NINARUHI★CYO-NINARUHI★CYO-NINARUHI★CYO-NINARUHI★CYO-NINARUHI★CYO-NINARUHI★CYO-NINARUHI

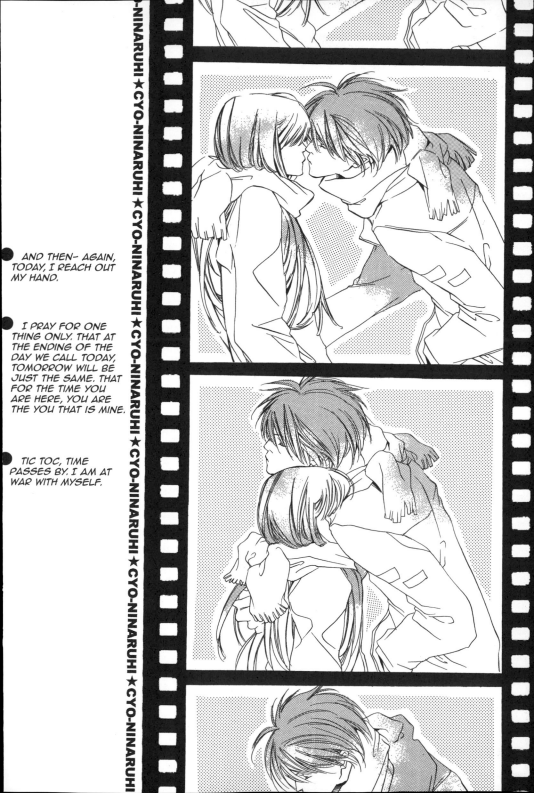

AND THEN- AGAIN, TODAY, I REACH OUT MY HAND.

I PRAY FOR ONE THING ONLY. THAT AT THE ENDING OF THE DAY WE CALL TODAY, TOMORROW WILL BE JUST THE SAME. THAT FOR THE TIME YOU ARE HERE, YOU ARE THE YOU THAT IS MINE.

TIC TOC, TIME PASSES BY. I AM AT WAR WITH MYSELF.

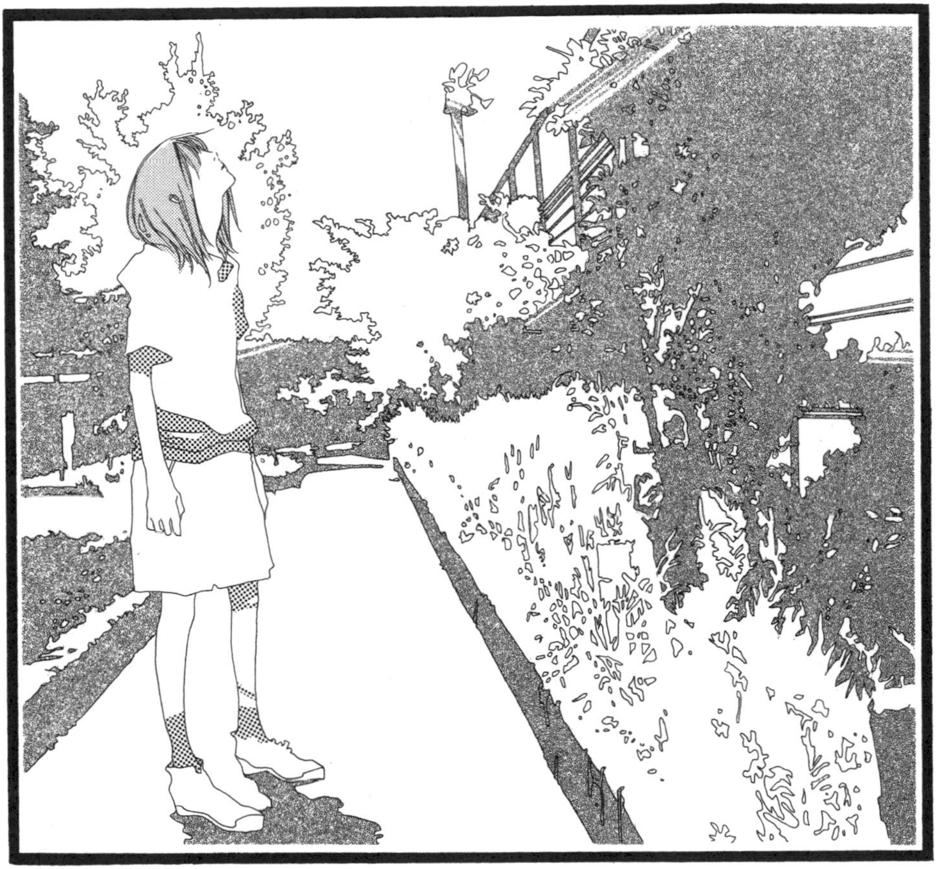

YOU AT THE END

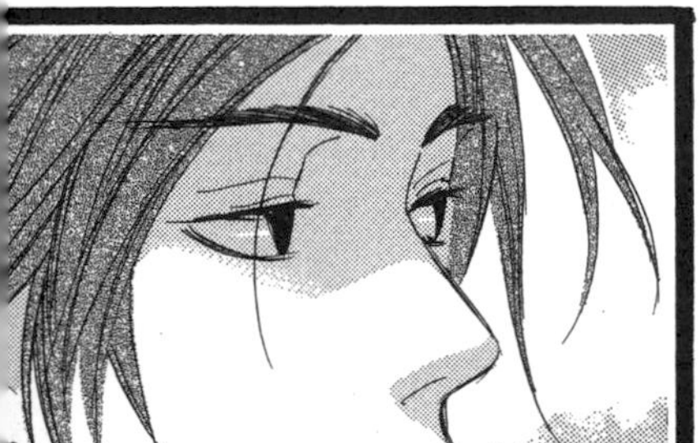

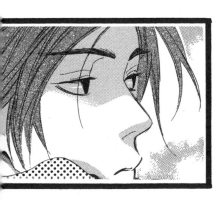

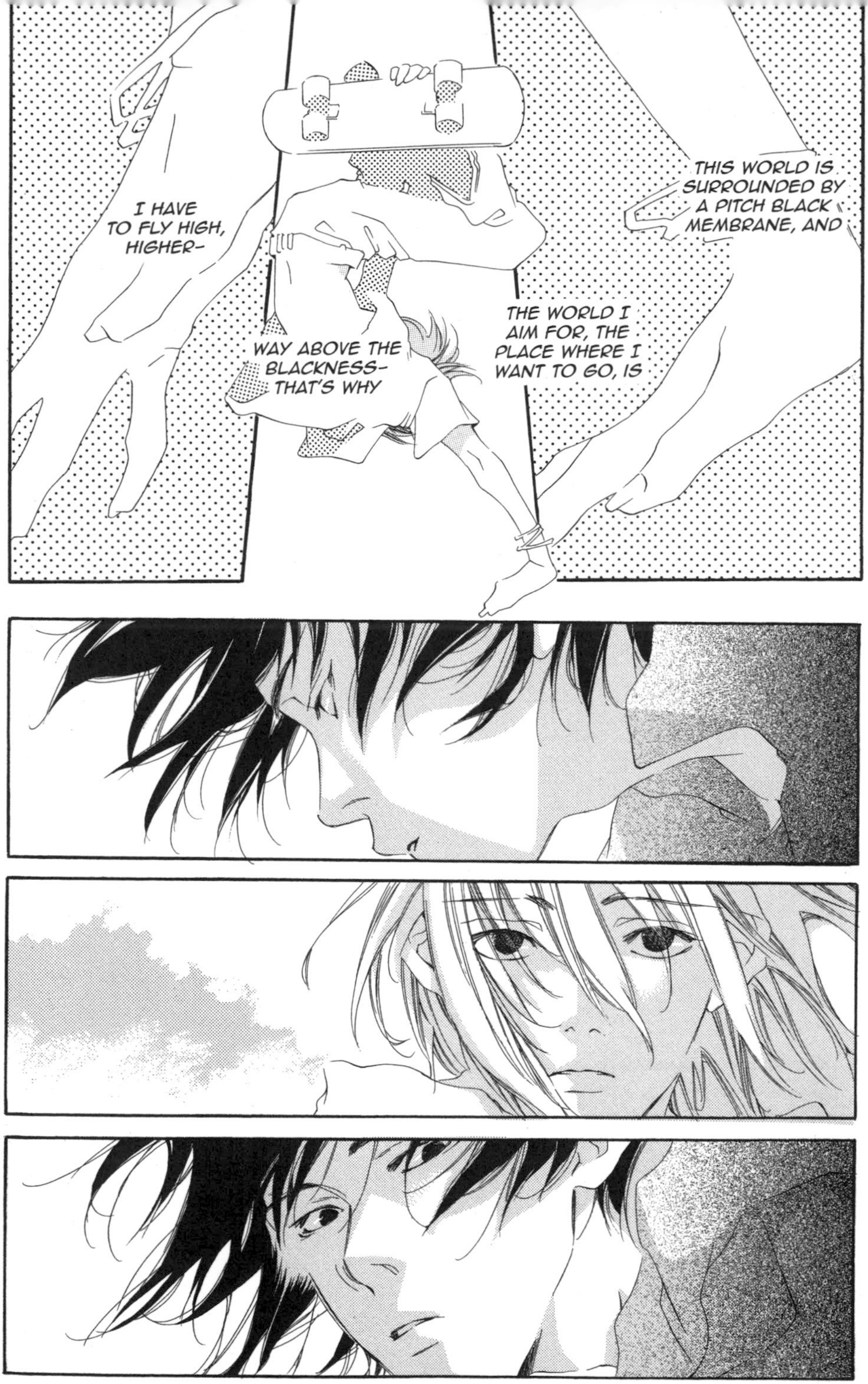
THIS WORLD IS SURROUNDED BY A PITCH BLACK MEMBRANE, AND
THE WORLD I AIM FOR, THE PLACE WHERE I WANT TO GO, IS
WAY ABOVE THE BLACKNESS- THAT'S WHY
I HAVE TO FLY HIGH, HIGHER-

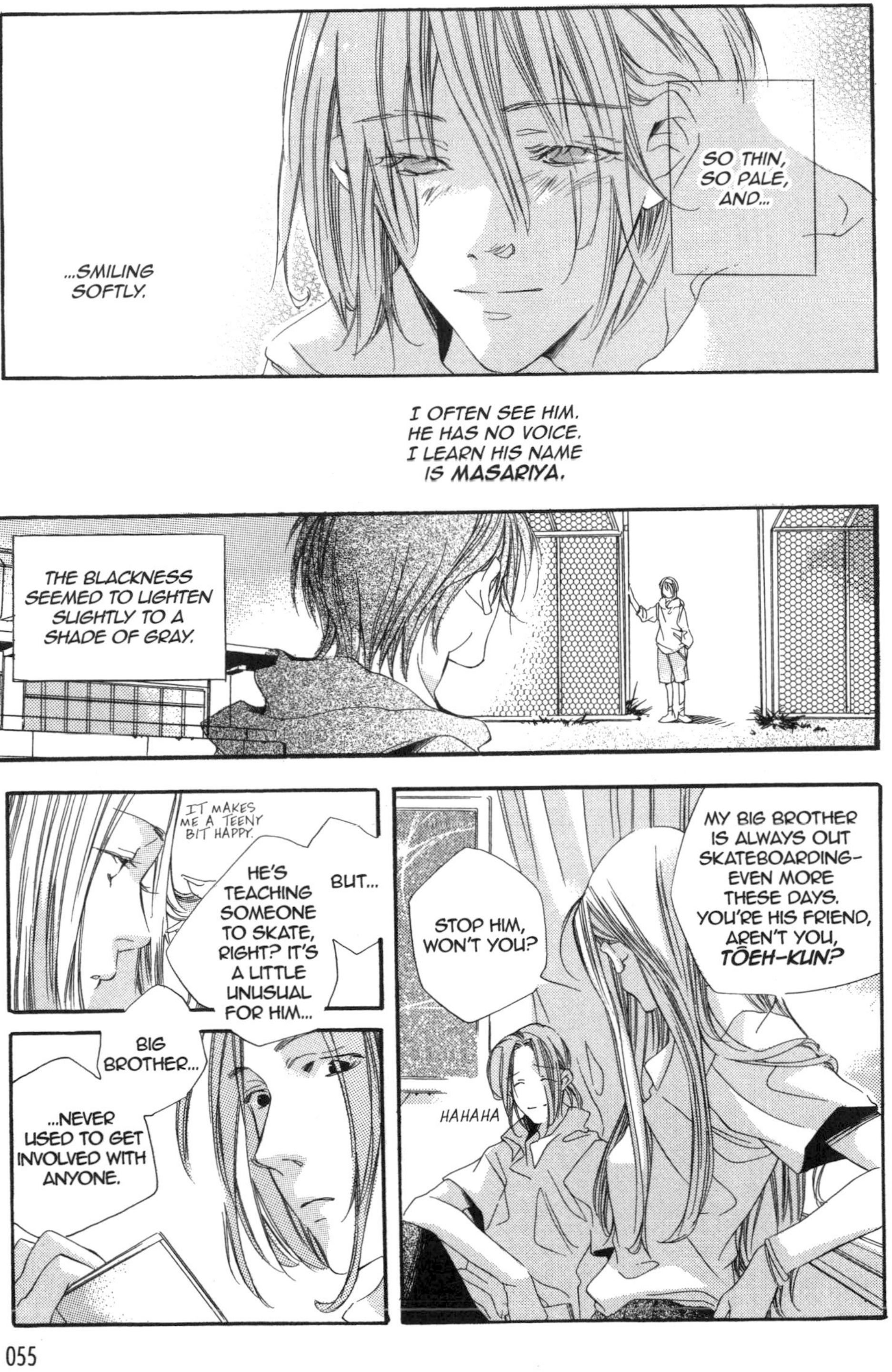

SO THIN, SO PALE, AND...
...SMILING SOFTLY.
I OFTEN SEE HIM. HE HAS NO VOICE. I LEARN HIS NAME IS MASARIYA.
THE BLACKNESS SEEMED TO LIGHTEN SLIGHTLY TO A SHADE OF GRAY.
MY BIG BROTHER IS ALWAYS OUT SKATEBOARDING-EVEN MORE THESE DAYS. YOU'RE HIS FRIEND, AREN'T YOU, TŌEH-KUN?
STOP HIM, WON'T YOU?
HAHAHA
HE'S TEACHING SOMEONE TO SKATE, RIGHT? IT'S A LITTLE UNUSUAL FOR HIM...
BUT...
IT MAKES ME A TEENY BIT HAPPY.
BIG BROTHER...
...NEVER USED TO GET INVOLVED WITH ANYONE.

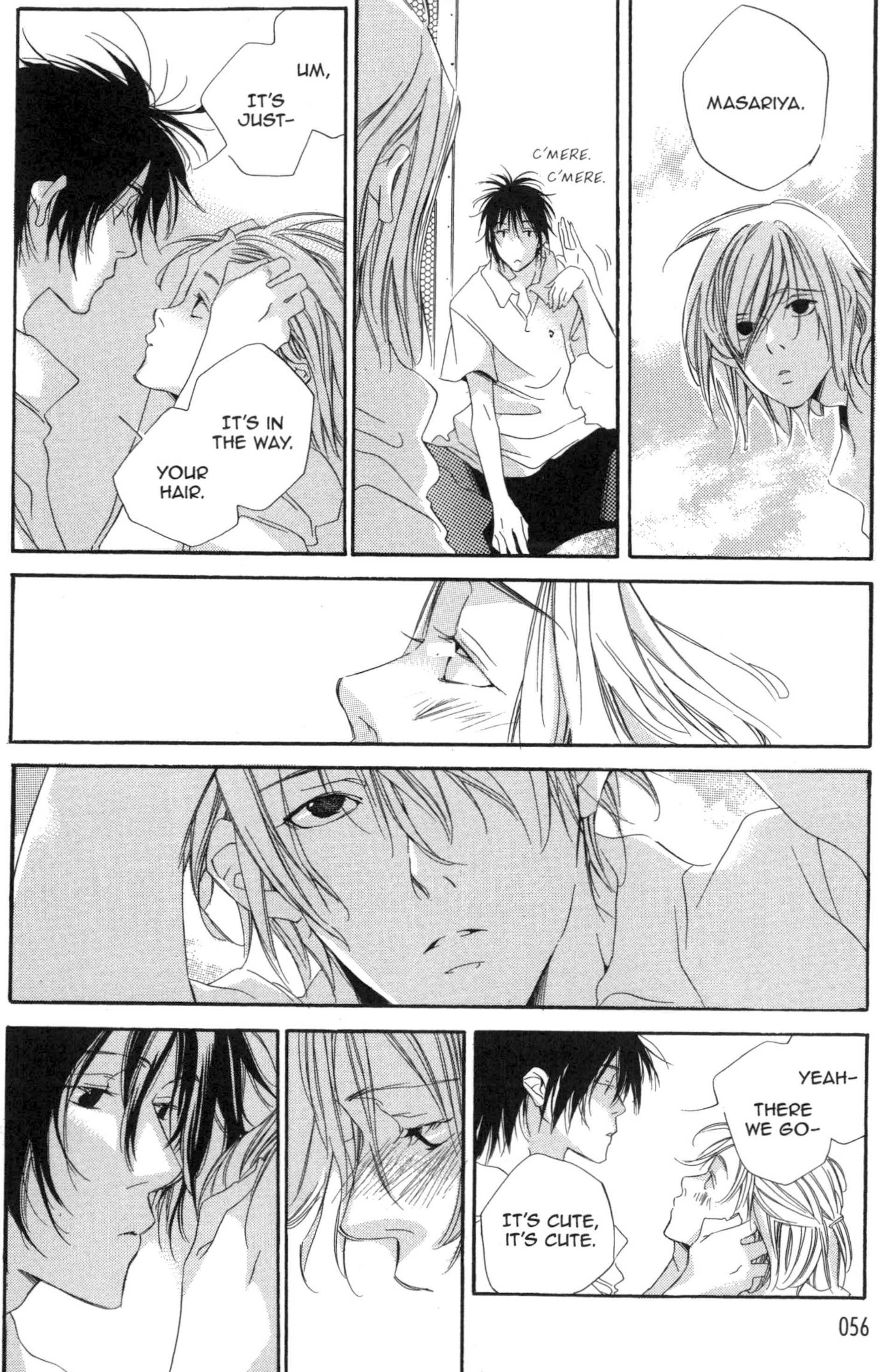
MASARIYA.
C'MERE. C'MERE.
UM, IT'S JUST-
IT'S IN THE WAY.
YOUR HAIR.
YEAH- THERE WE GO-
IT'S CUTE, IT'S CUTE.

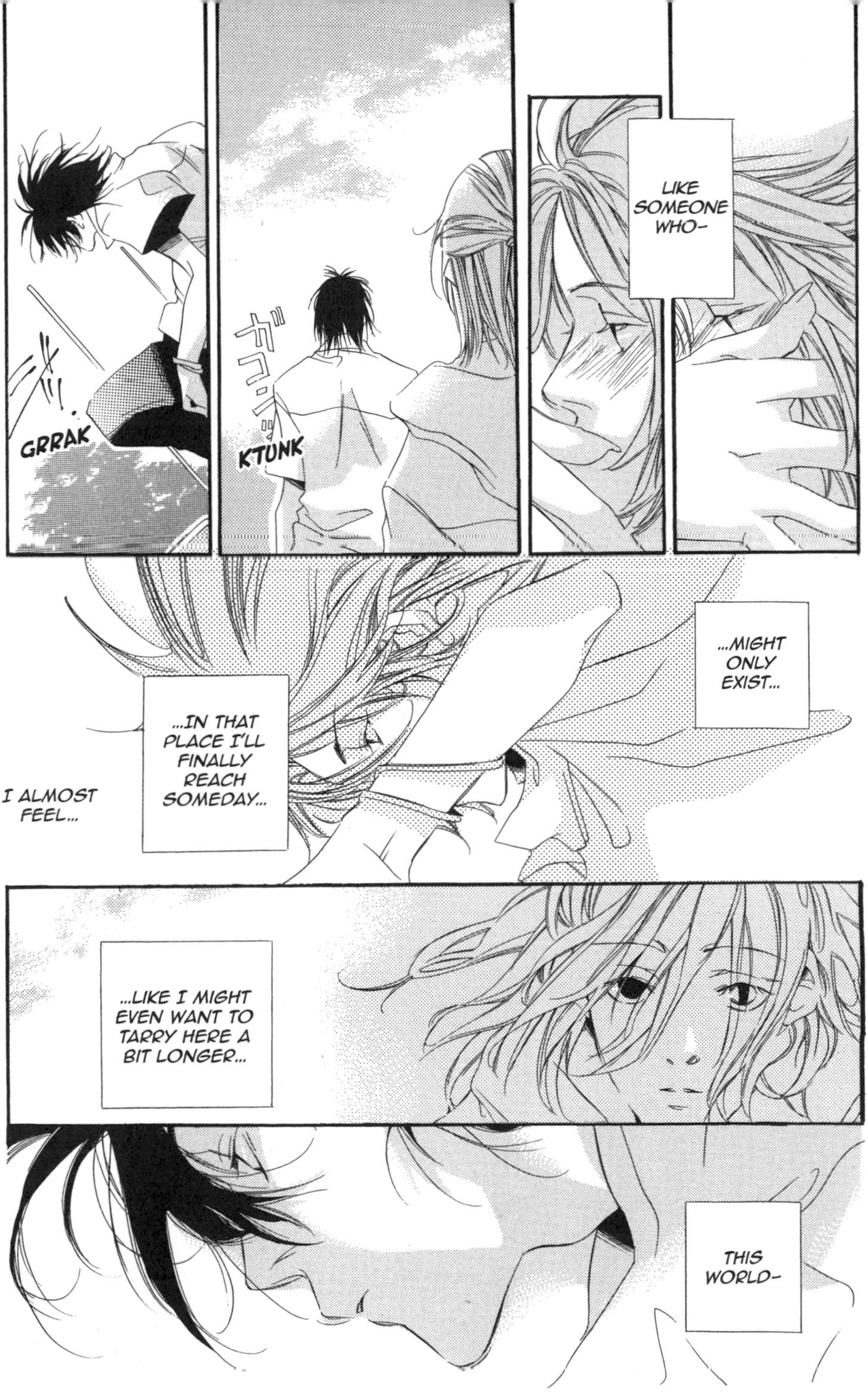
LIKE SOMEONE WHO-
KTUNK
GRRAK
...MIGHT ONLY EXIST...
...IN THAT PLACE I'LL FINALLY REACH SOMEDAY...
I ALMOST FEEL...
...LIKE I MIGHT EVEN WANT TO TARRY HERE A BIT LONGER...
THIS WORLD-

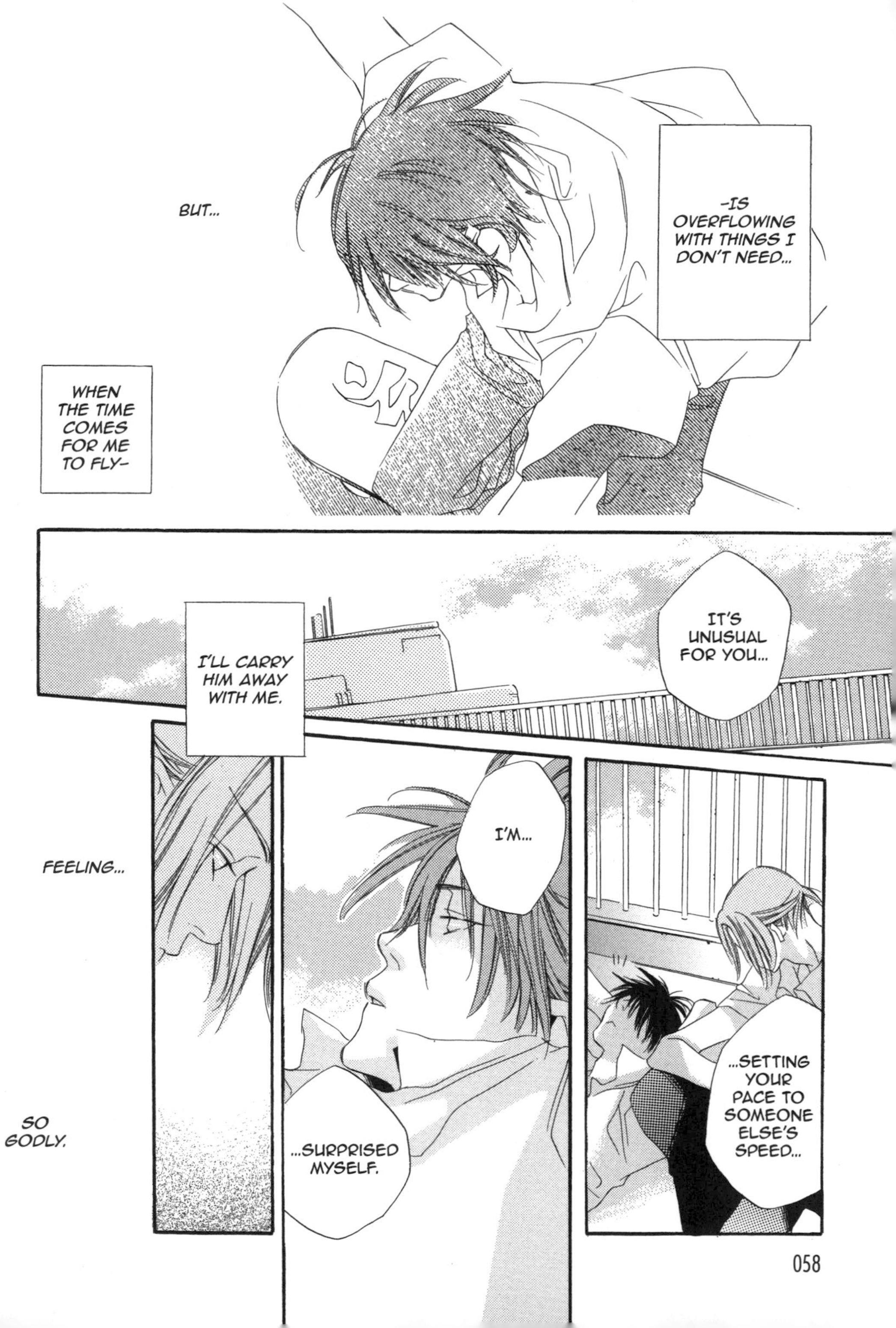
-IS OVERFLOWING WITH THINGS I DON'T NEED...
BUT...
WHEN THE TIME COMES FOR ME TO FLY-
IT'S UNUSUAL FOR YOU...
I'LL CARRY HIM AWAY WITH ME.
...SETTING YOUR PACE TO SOMEONE ELSE'S SPEED...
I'M...
...SURPRISED MYSELF.
FEELING...
SO GODLY.

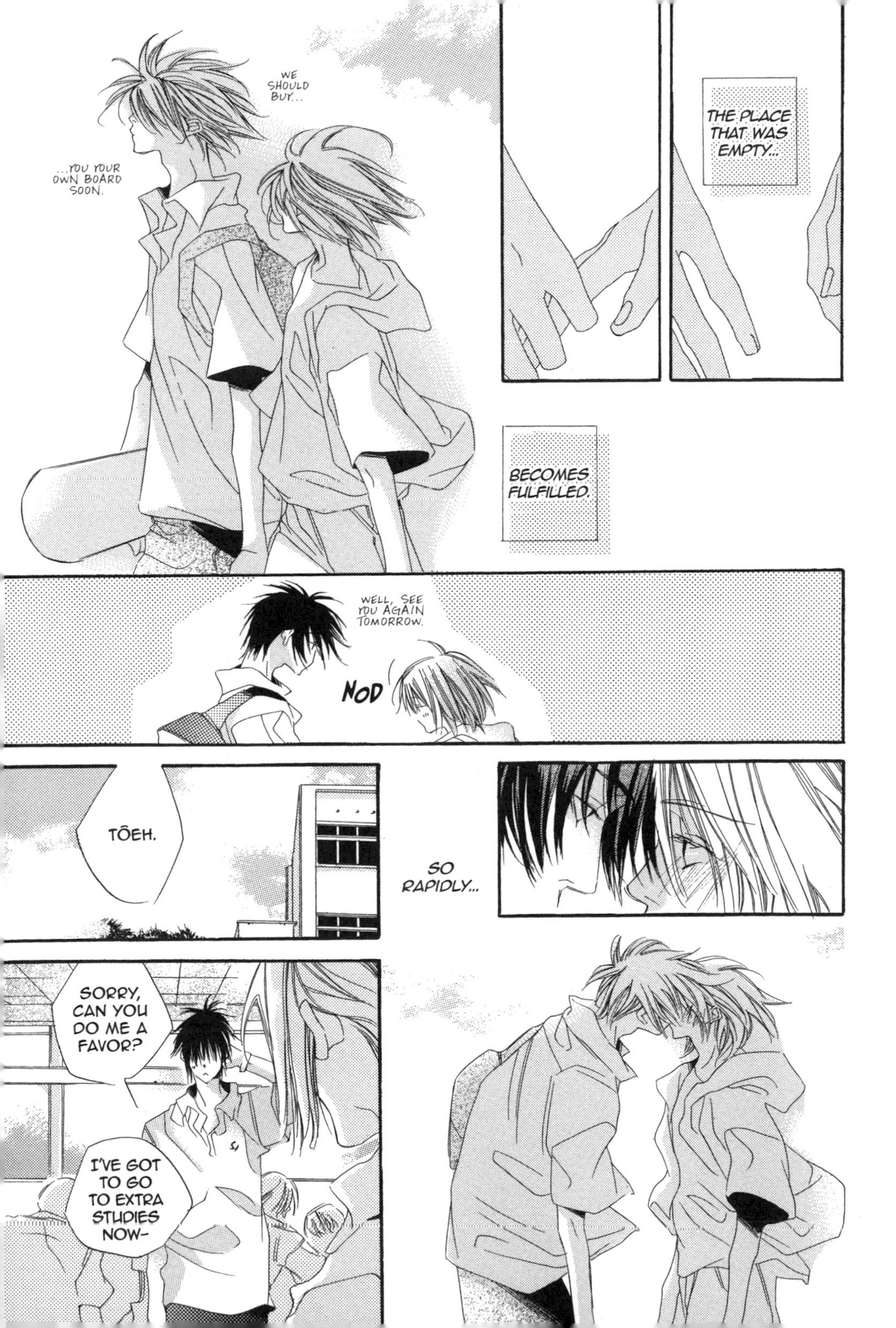
THE PLACE THAT WAS EMPTY...
BECOMES FULFILLED.
WE SHOULD BUY...
...YOU YOUR OWN BOARD SOON.
WELL, SEE YOU AGAIN TOMORROW.
NOD
SO RAPIDLY...
TÔEH.
SORRY, CAN YOU DO ME A FAVOR?
I'VE GOT TO GO TO EXTRA STUDIES NOW-

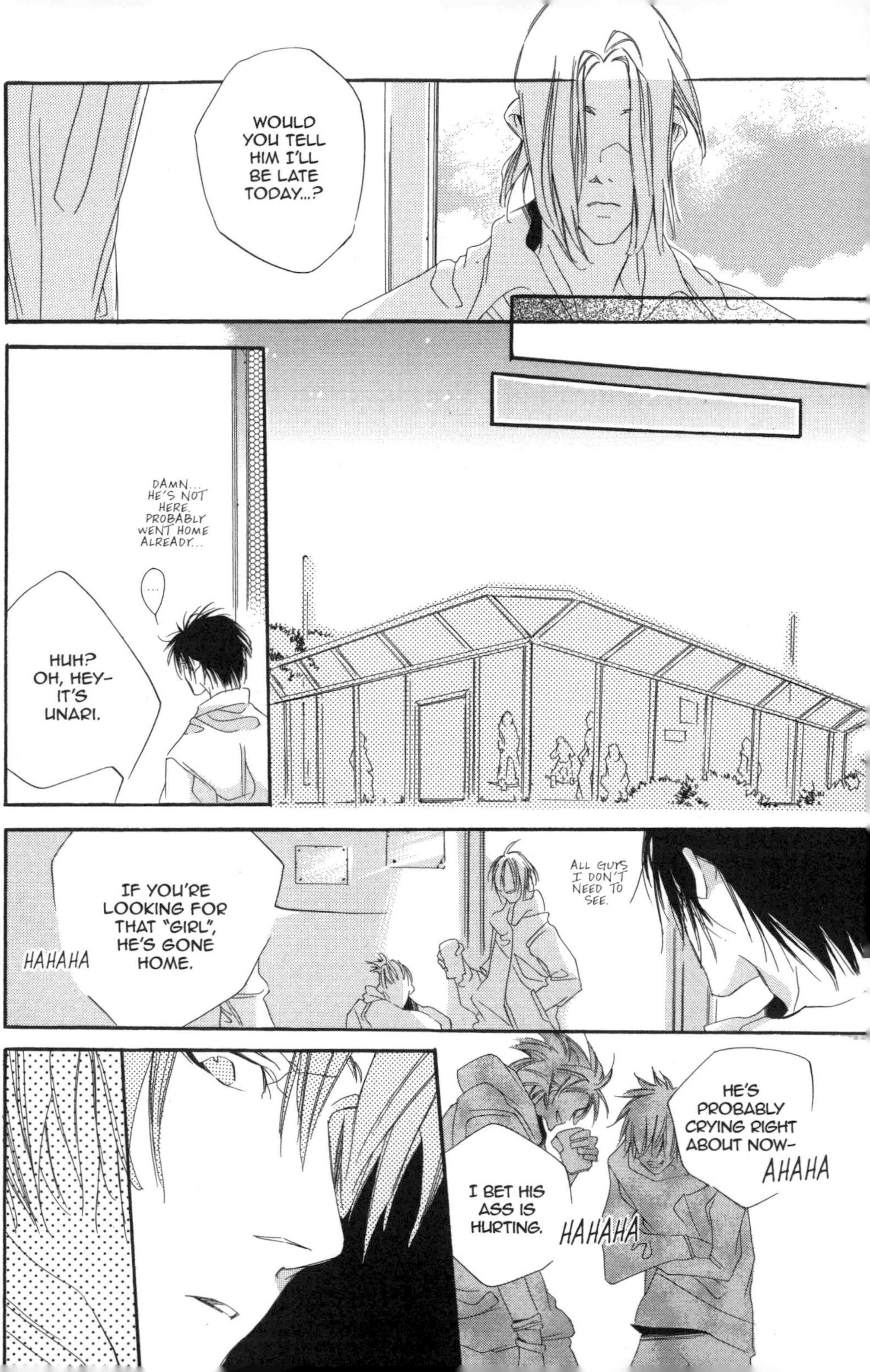
WOULD YOU TELL HIM I'LL BE LATE TODAY...?
DAMN... HE'S NOT HERE. PROBABLY WENT HOME ALREADY...
...
HUH? OH, HEY- IT'S UNARI.
ALL GUYS I DON'T NEED TO SEE.
IF YOU'RE LOOKING FOR THAT "GIRL", HE'S GONE HOME.
HAHAHA
HE'S PROBABLY CRYING RIGHT ABOUT NOW-
AHAHA
I BET HIS ASS IS HURTING.
HAHAHA

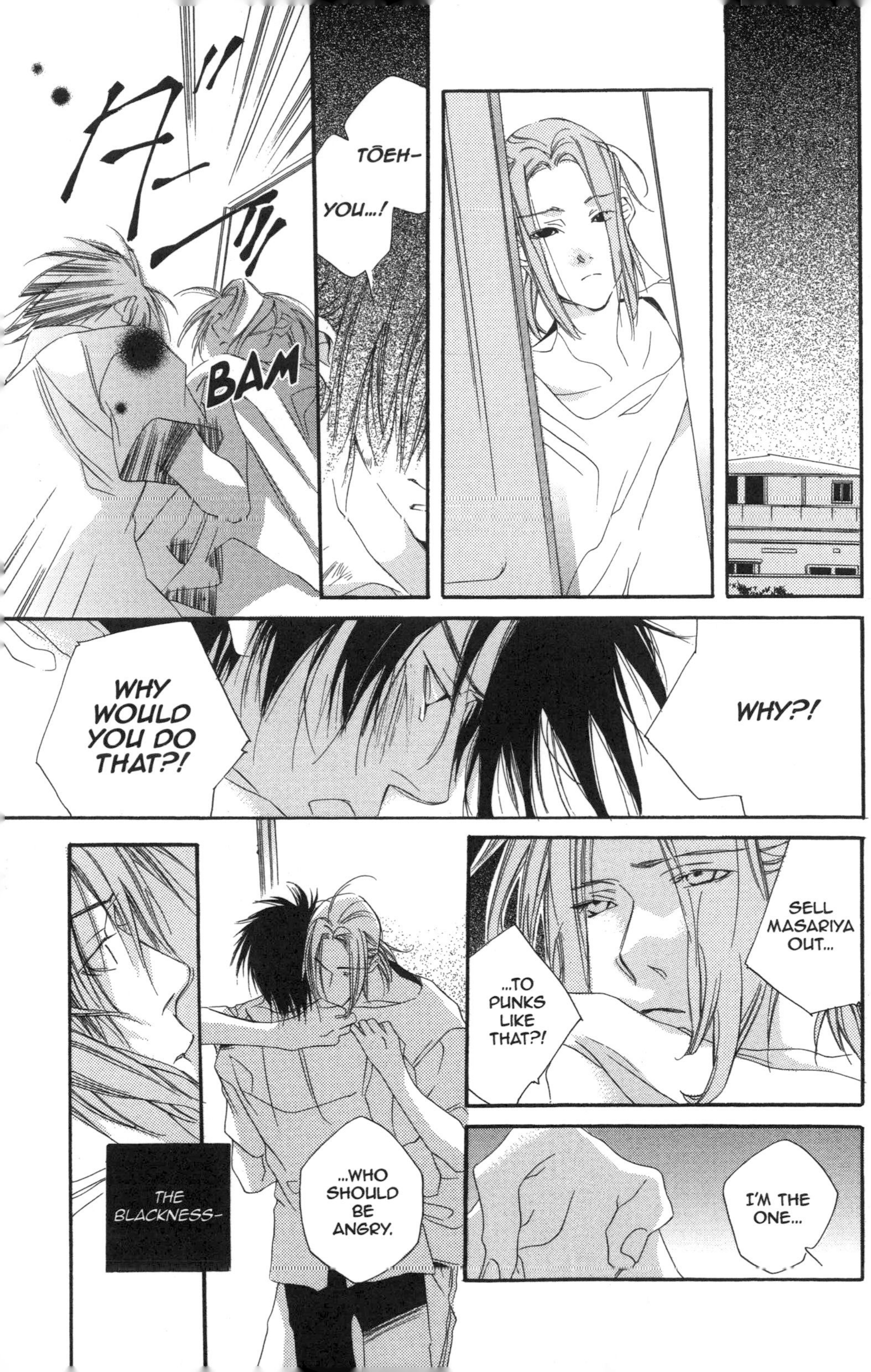
TŌEH-
YOU...!
BAM
WHY?!
WHY WOULD YOU DO THAT?!
SELL MASARIYA OUT...
...TO PUNKS LIKE THAT?!
I'M THE ONE...
...WHO SHOULD BE ANGRY.
THE BLACKNESS-

WHY DO YOU THINK I'VE STAYED NEAR YOU...

...ALL THIS TIME?

...A PART OF IT, TOO?

AM I...

I'M STEPPING OUT FOR A WHILE, OKAY?

UNARI HAS COME TO VISIT YOU—

MASARIYA!

I'M SORRY. HE'S SHUT HIMSELF UP IN HIS ROOM EVER SINCE YESTERDAY...

I'M...

KCHAK.

...COMING IN.

DASH

PLEASE... OPEN UP, MASARIYA.

I BOUGHT YOU A BOARD.

I'M SORRY, MASARIYA.

I'M SORRY!

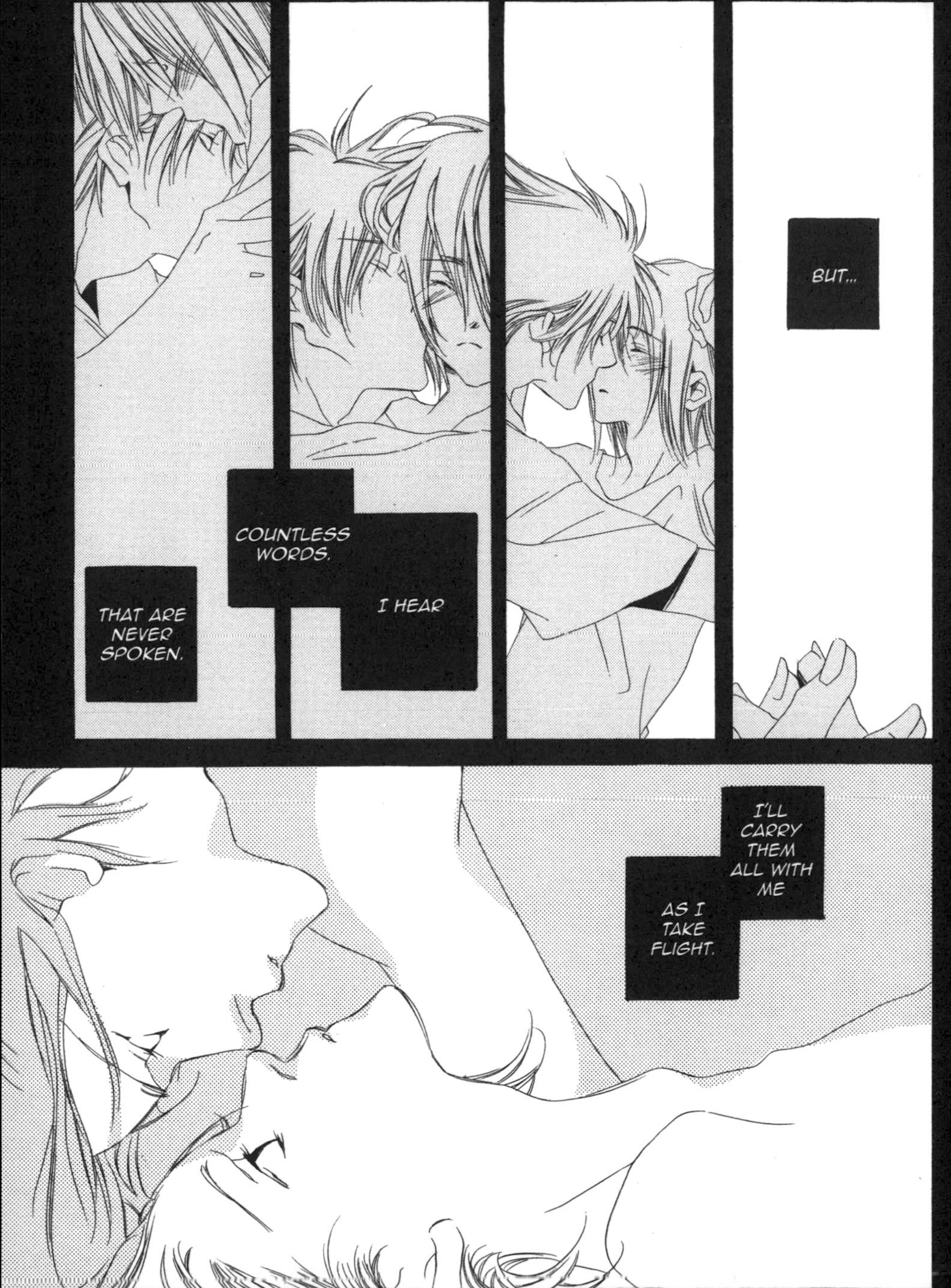
BUT...
I HEAR
COUNTLESS WORDS.
THAT ARE NEVER SPOKEN.
I'LL CARRY THEM ALL WITH ME
AS I TAKE FLIGHT.

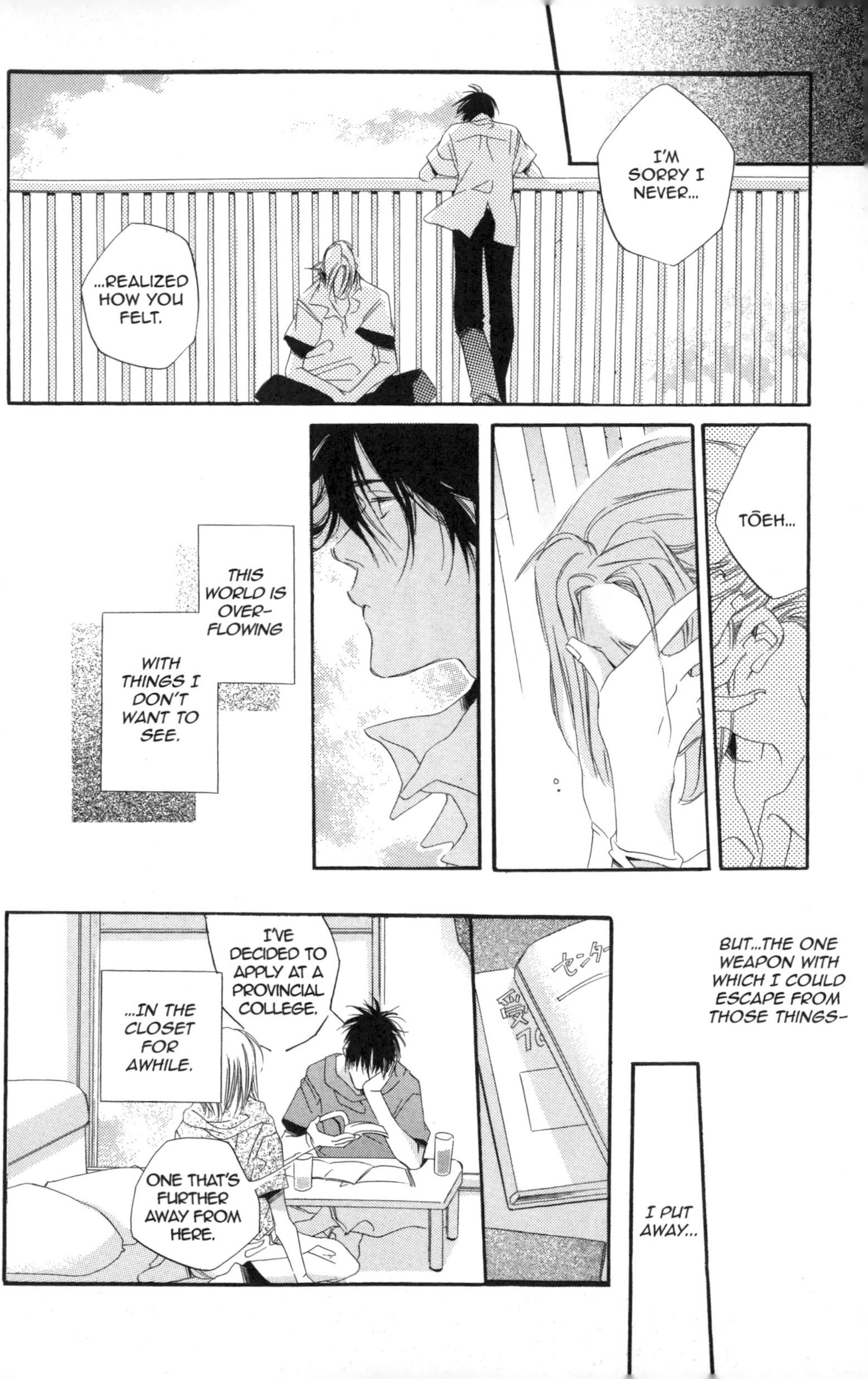
I'M SORRY I NEVER...
...REALIZED HOW YOU FELT.
TŌEH...
THIS WORLD IS OVER-FLOWING
WITH THINGS I DON'T WANT TO SEE.
BUT...THE ONE WEAPON WITH WHICH I COULD ESCAPE FROM THOSE THINGS-
I PUT AWAY...
...IN THE CLOSET FOR AWHILE.
I'VE DECIDED TO APPLY AT A PROVINCIAL COLLEGE.
ONE THAT'S FURTHER AWAY FROM HERE.

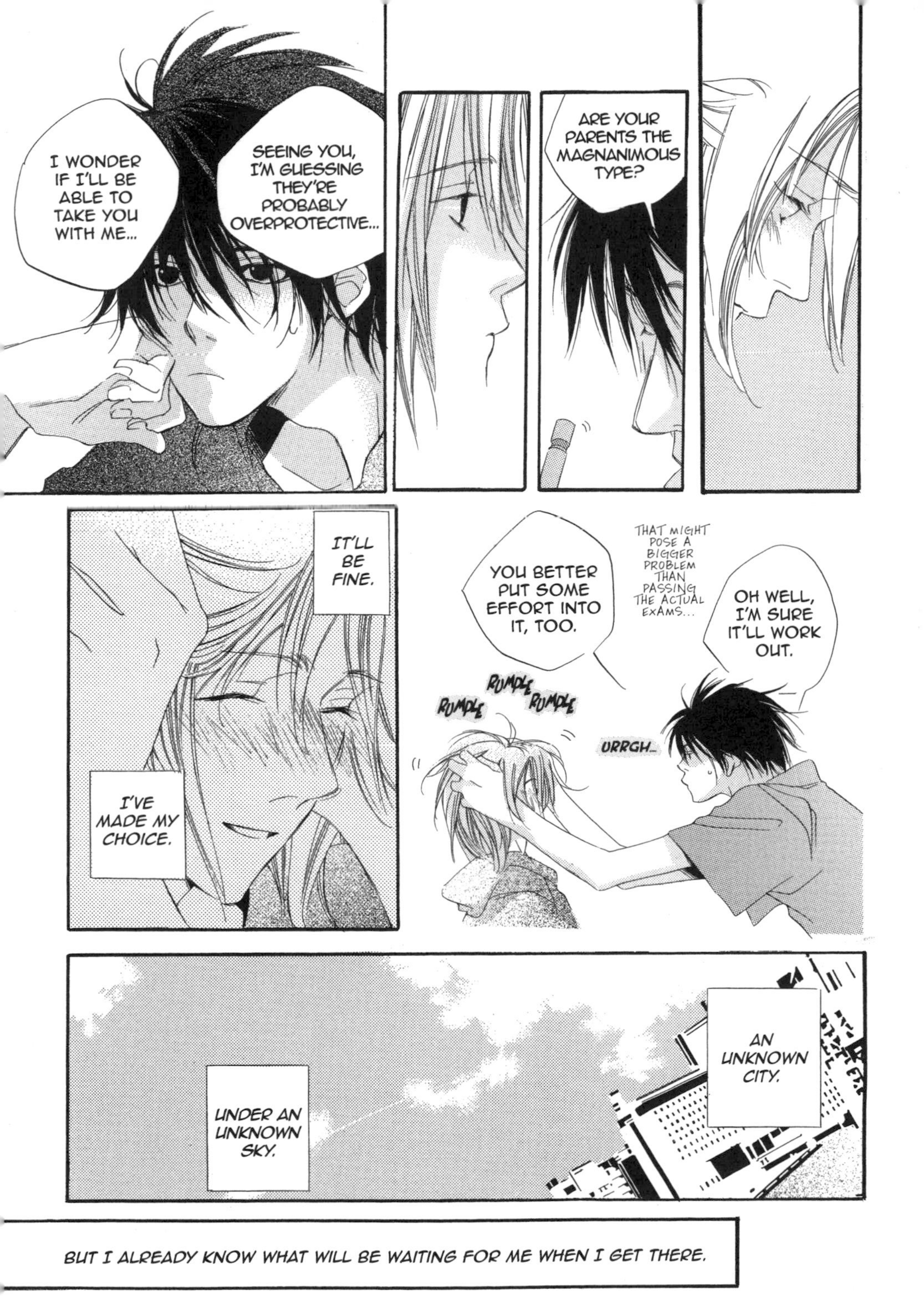
ARE YOUR PARENTS THE MAGNANIMOUS TYPE?
SEEING YOU, I'M GUESSING THEY'RE PROBABLY OVERPROTECTIVE...
I WONDER IF I'LL BE ABLE TO TAKE YOU WITH ME...
OH WELL, I'M SURE IT'LL WORK OUT.
THAT MIGHT POSE A BIGGER PROBLEM THAN PASSING THE ACTUAL EXAMS...
YOU BETTER PUT SOME EFFORT INTO IT, TOO.
RUMPLE RUMPLE
RUMPLE
URRGH...
IT'LL BE FINE.
I'VE MADE MY CHOICE.
AN UNKNOWN CITY.
UNDER AN UNKNOWN SKY.
BUT I ALREADY KNOW WHAT WILL BE WAITING FOR ME WHEN I GET THERE.

*DO YOU KNOW
ABOUT THE
WRETCHED SIDE
OF ME?*

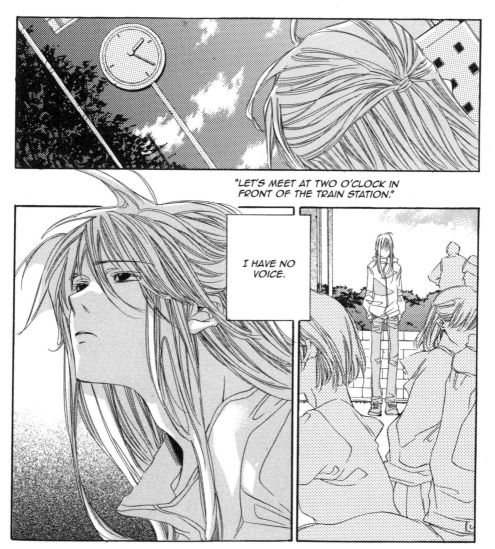

*"LET'S MEET AT TWO O'CLOCK IN
FRONT OF THE TRAIN STATION."*

I HAVE NO
VOICE.

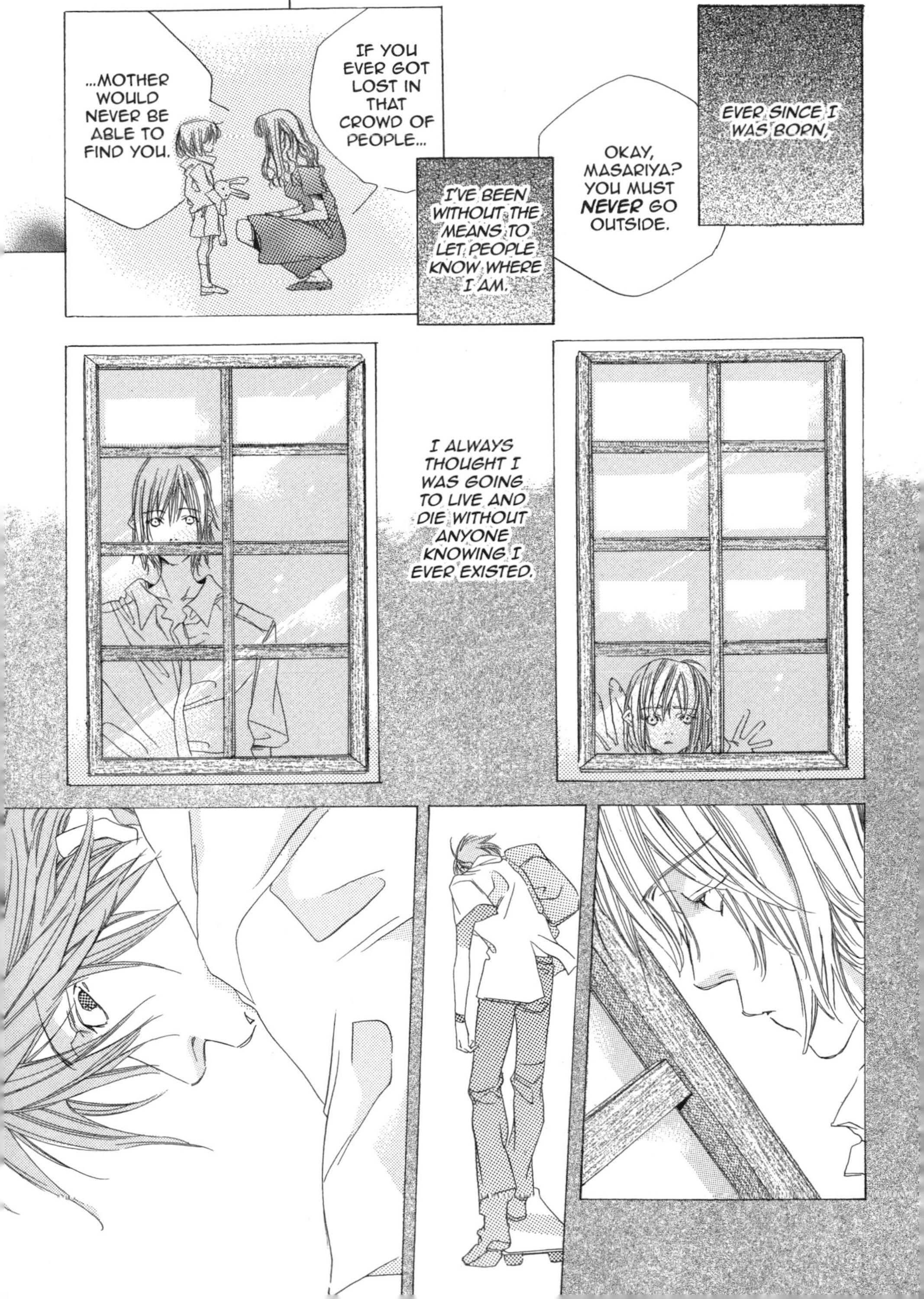
EVER SINCE I WAS BORN,
OKAY, MASARIYA? YOU MUST **NEVER** GO OUTSIDE.
I'VE BEEN WITHOUT THE MEANS TO LET PEOPLE KNOW WHERE I AM.
IF YOU EVER GOT LOST IN THAT CROWD OF PEOPLE...
...MOTHER WOULD NEVER BE ABLE TO FIND YOU.
I ALWAYS THOUGHT I WAS GOING TO LIVE AND DIE WITHOUT ANYONE KNOWING I EVER EXISTED.

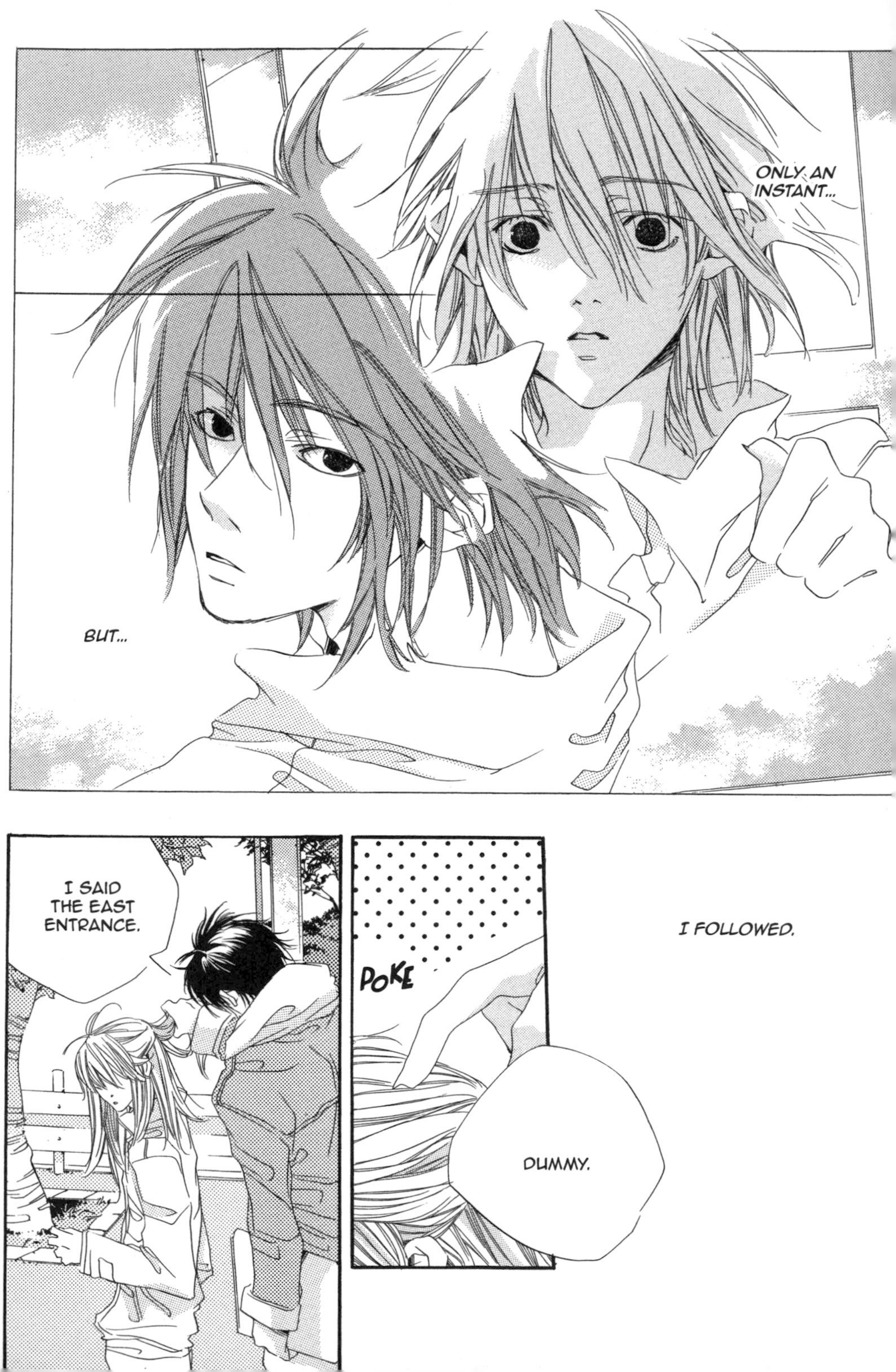
ONLY AN INSTANT...
BUT...
I FOLLOWED.
POKE
DUMMY.
I SAID THE EAST ENTRANCE.

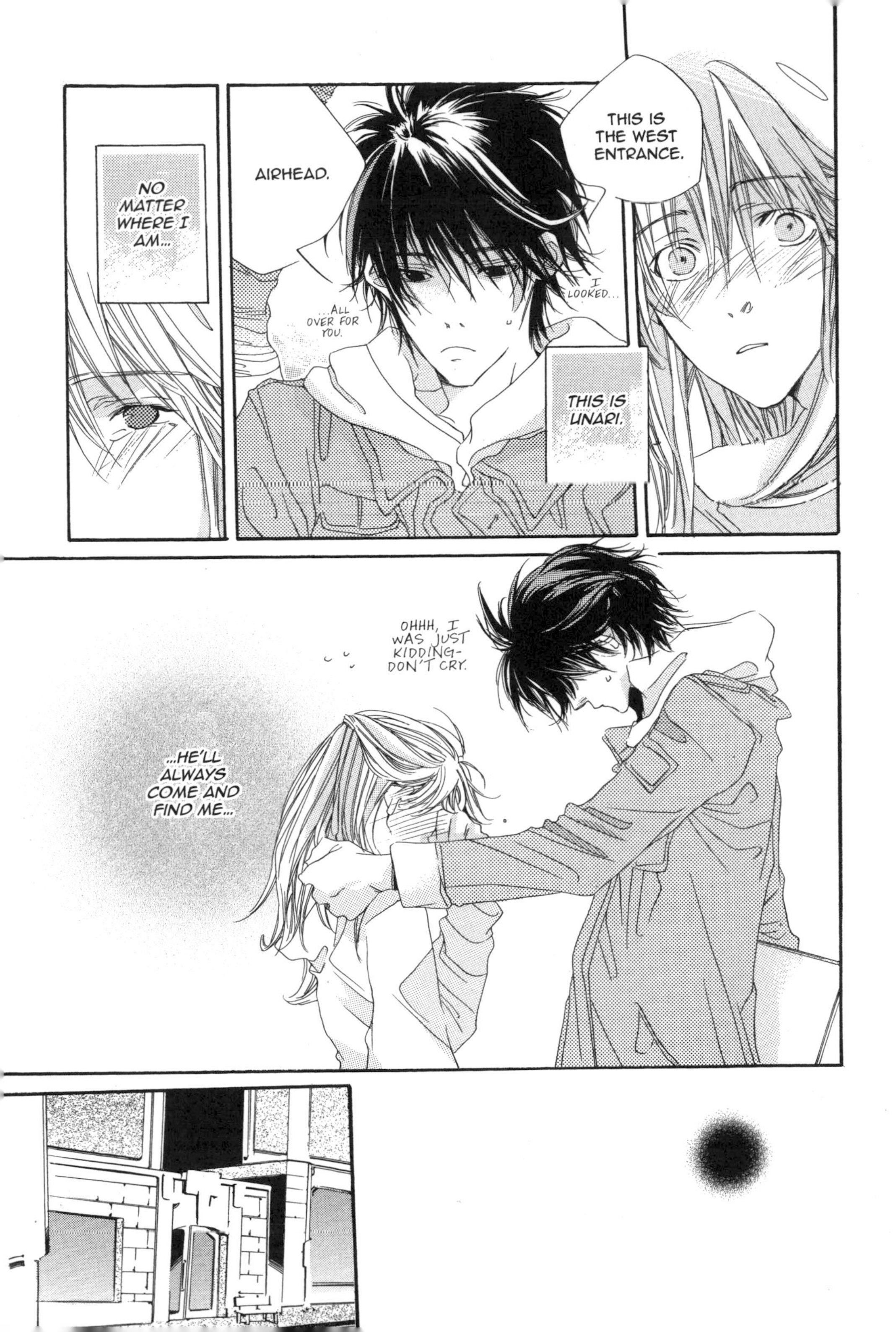
THIS IS THE WEST ENTRANCE.
I LOOKED...
...ALL OVER FOR YOU.
AIRHEAD.
THIS IS UNARI.
NO MATTER WHERE I AM...
OHHH, I WAS JUST KIDDING-DON'T CRY.
...HE'LL ALWAYS COME AND FIND ME...

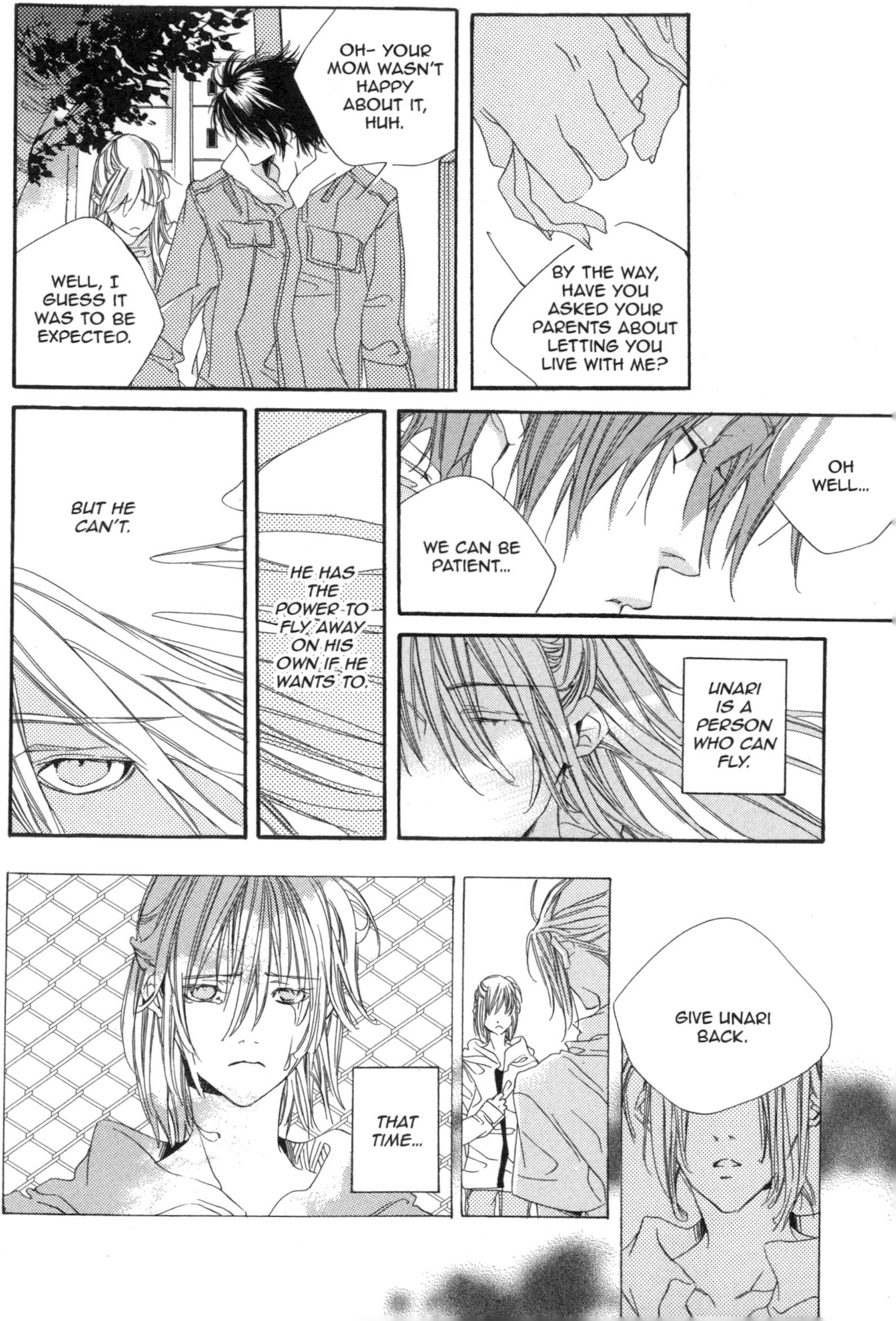
BY THE WAY, HAVE YOU ASKED YOUR PARENTS ABOUT LETTING YOU LIVE WITH ME?
OH- YOUR MOM WASN'T HAPPY ABOUT IT, HUH.
WELL, I GUESS IT WAS TO BE EXPECTED.
OH WELL...
WE CAN BE PATIENT...
UNARI IS A PERSON WHO CAN FLY.
HE HAS THE POWER TO FLY AWAY ON HIS OWN IF HE WANTS TO.
BUT HE CAN'T.
GIVE UNARI BACK.
THAT TIME...

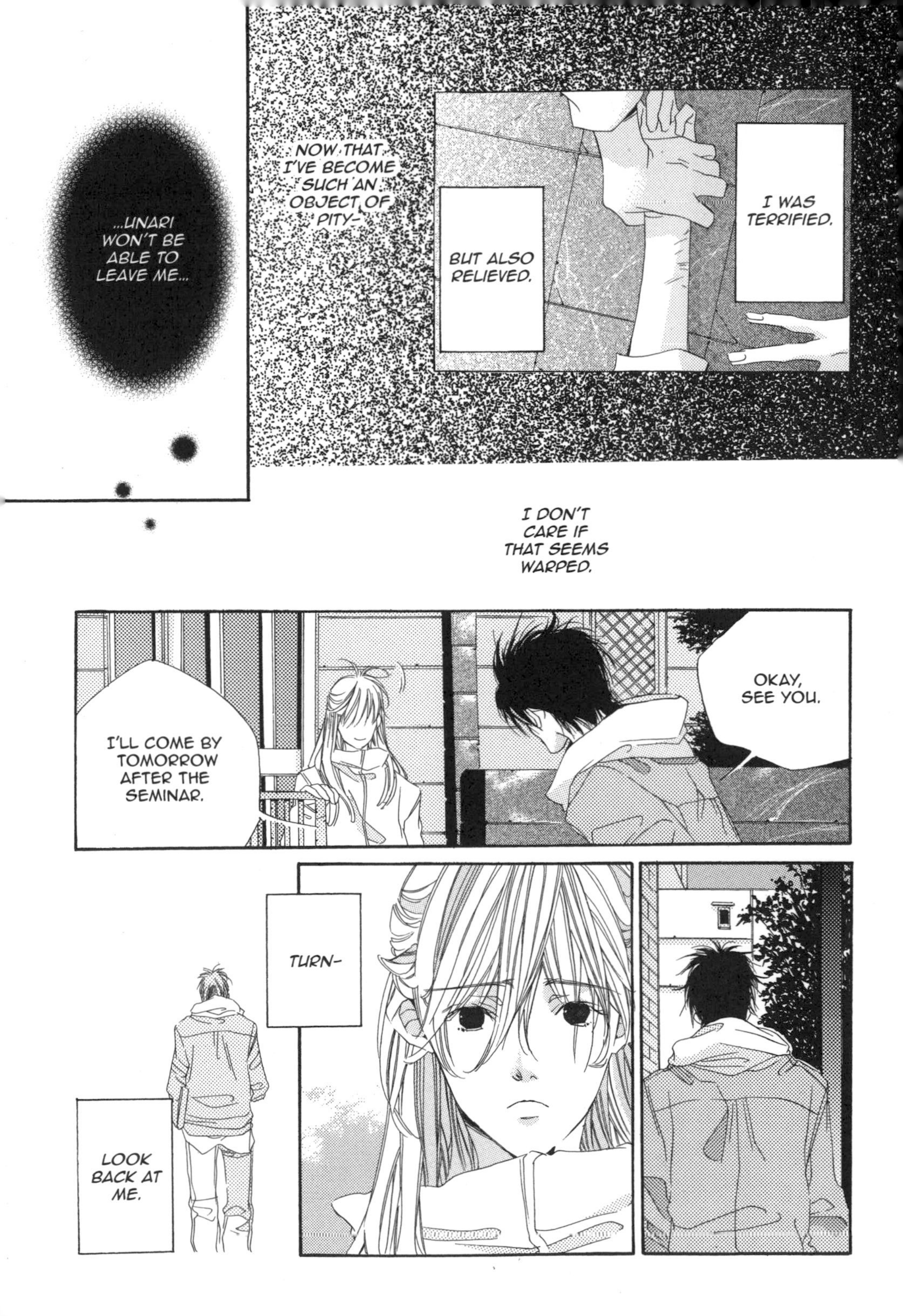
I WAS TERRIFIED.
BUT ALSO RELIEVED.
NOW THAT I'VE BECOME SUCH AN OBJECT OF PITY-
...UNARI WON'T BE ABLE TO LEAVE ME...
I DON'T CARE IF THAT SEEMS WARPED.
OKAY, SEE YOU.
I'LL COME BY TOMORROW AFTER THE SEMINAR.
TURN-
LOOK BACK AT ME.

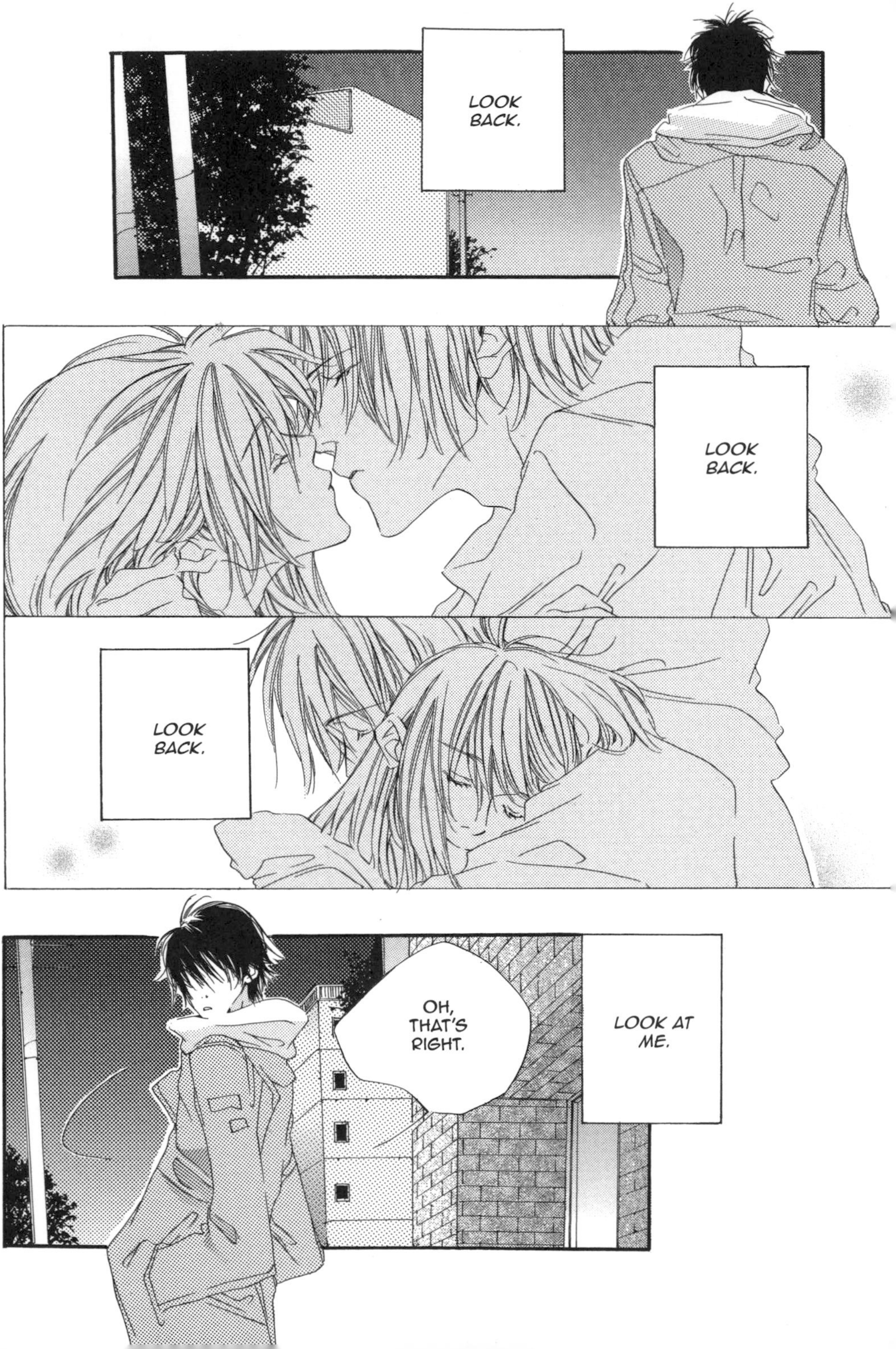
LOOK BACK.
LOOK BACK.
LOOK BACK.
LOOK AT ME.
OH, THAT'S RIGHT.

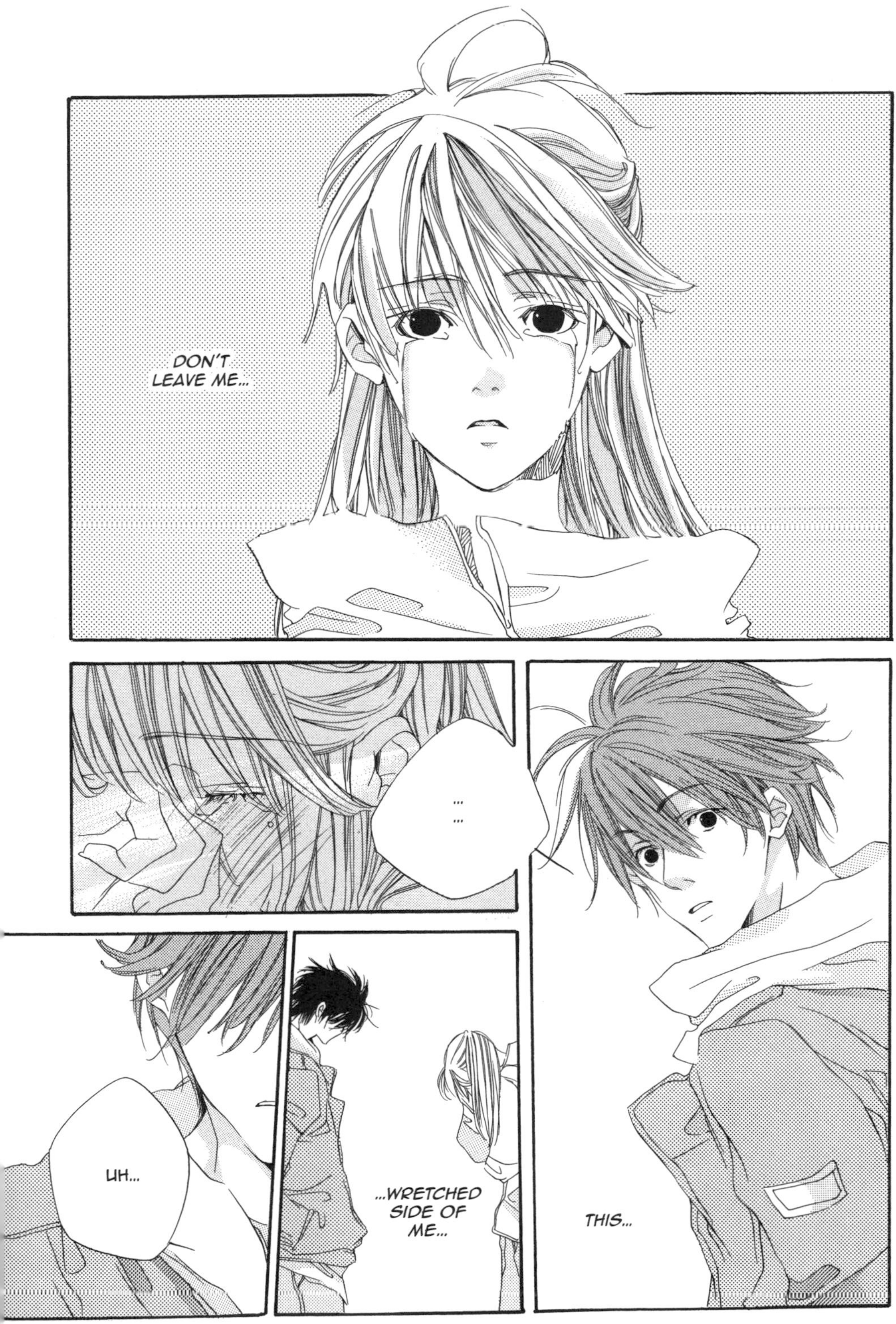

DON'T LEAVE ME...
THIS...
... ...
...WRETCHED SIDE OF ME...
UH...

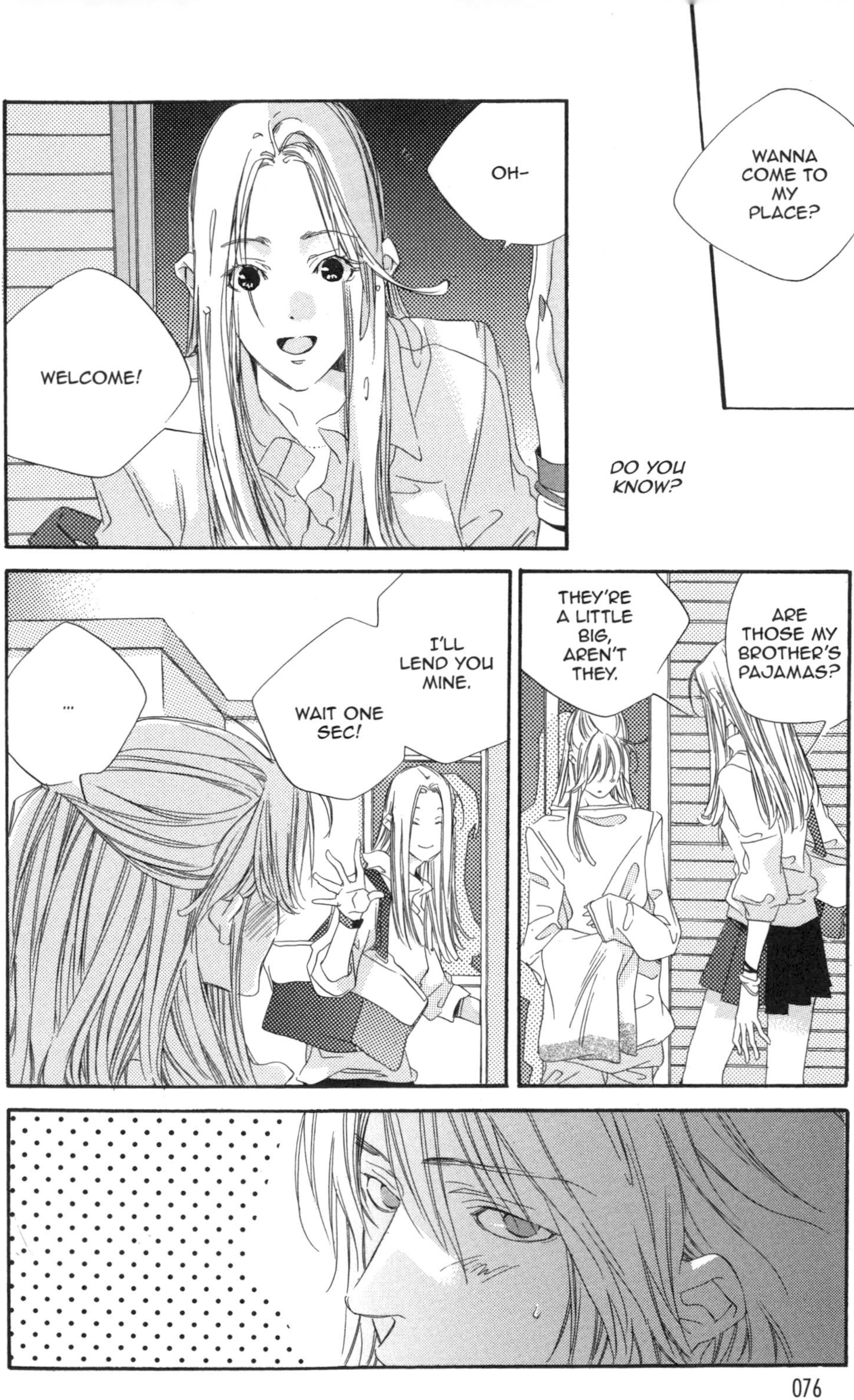
WANNA COME TO MY PLACE?
DO YOU KNOW?
OH-
WELCOME!
ARE THOSE MY BROTHER'S PAJAMAS?
THEY'RE A LITTLE BIG, AREN'T THEY.
I'LL LEND YOU MINE.
WAIT ONE SEC!
...

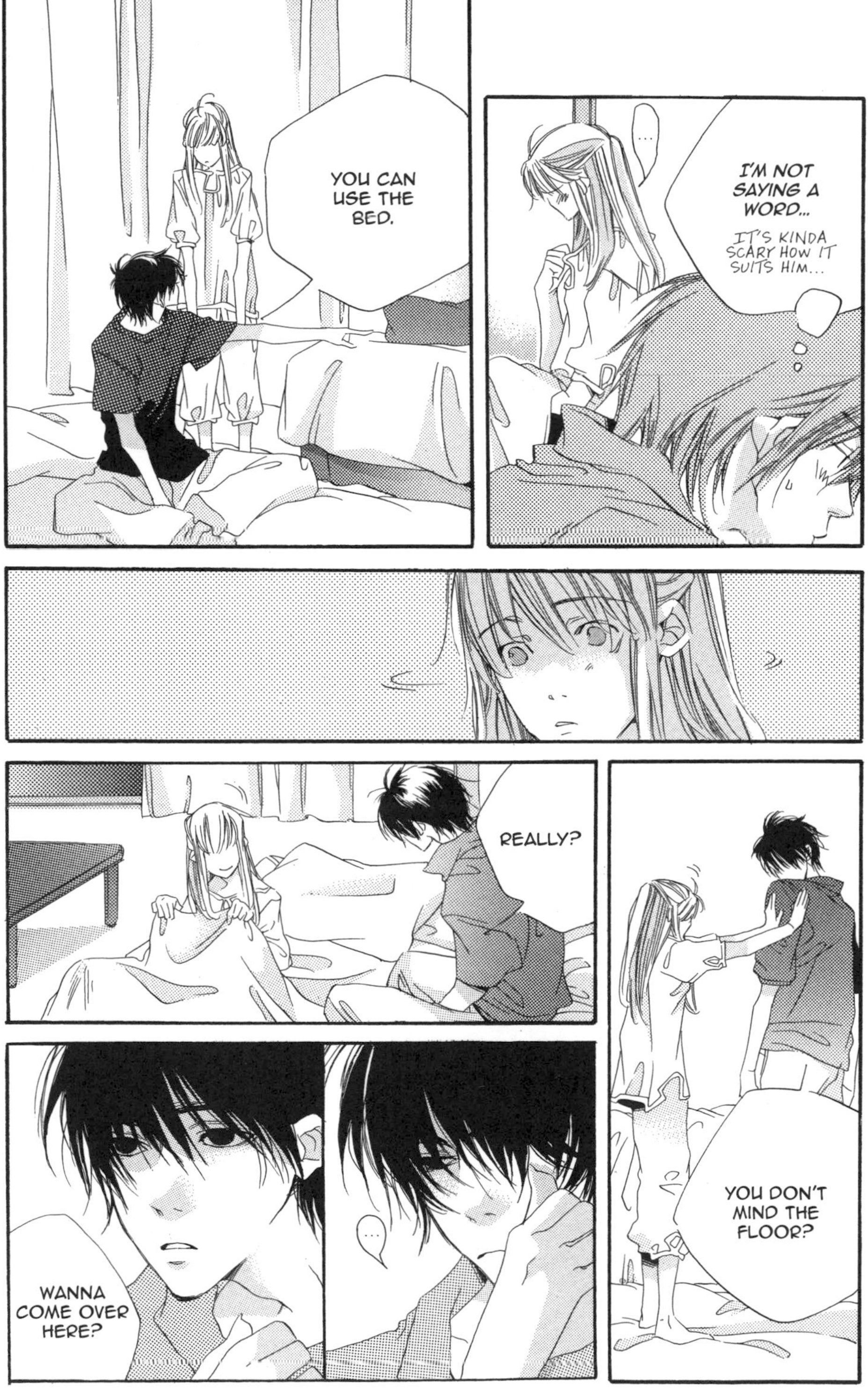
...
I'M NOT SAYING A WORD...
IT'S KINDA SCARY HOW IT SUITS HIM...
YOU CAN USE THE BED.
YOU DON'T MIND THE FLOOR?
REALLY?
...
WANNA COME OVER HERE?

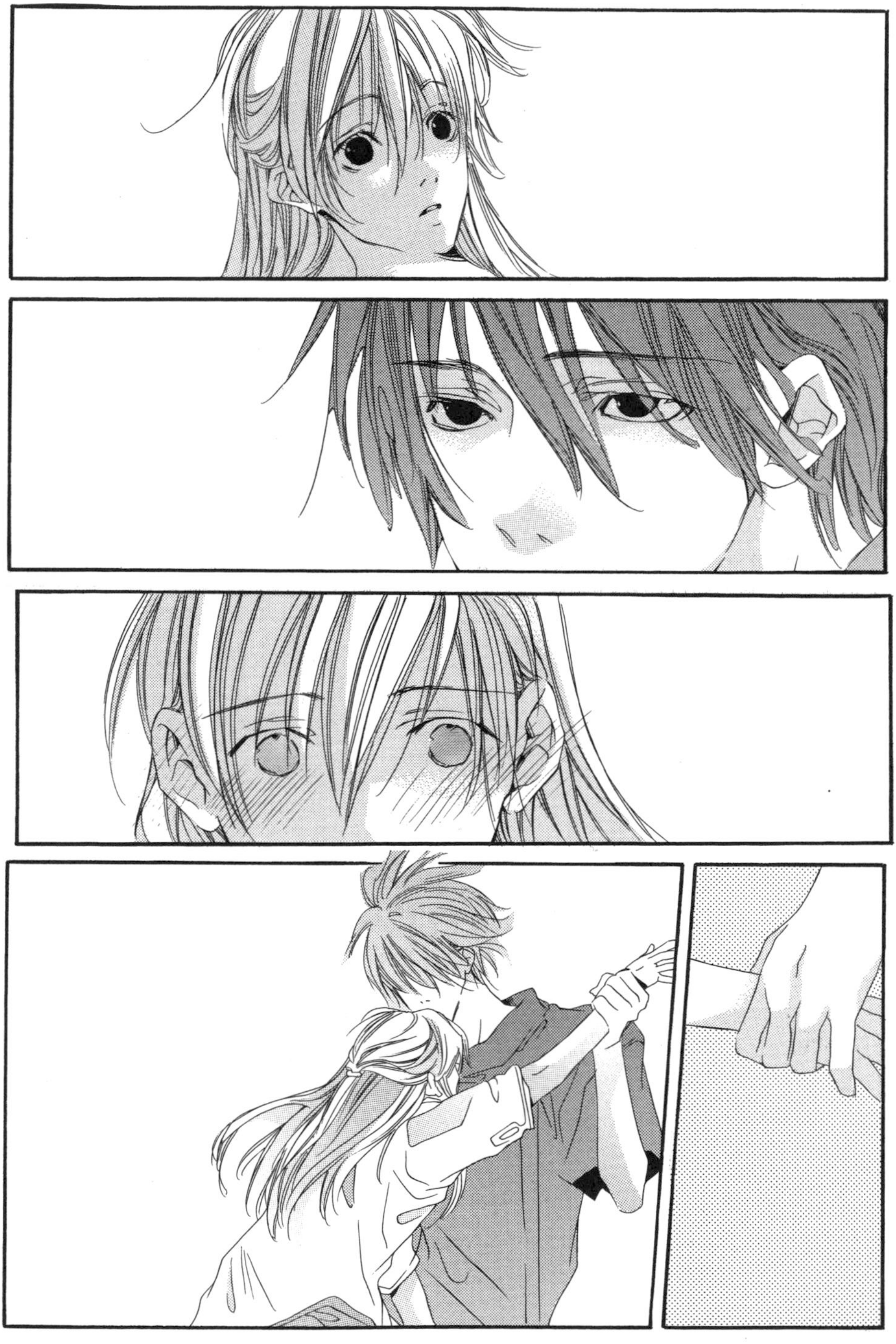

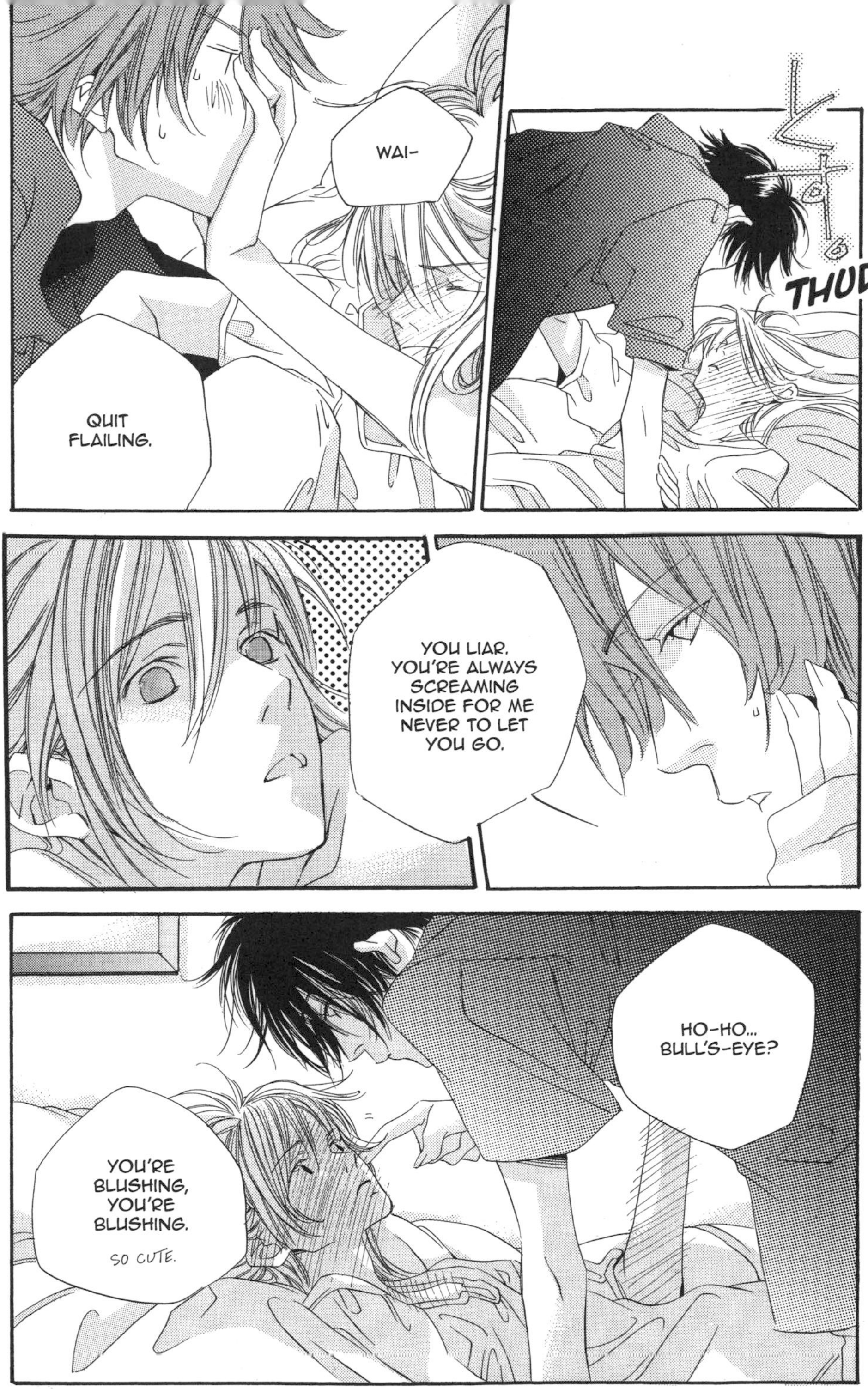
THUD
WAI-
QUIT FLAILING.
YOU LIAR. YOU'RE ALWAYS SCREAMING INSIDE FOR ME NEVER TO LET YOU GO.
HO-HO... BULL'S-EYE?
YOU'RE BLUSHING, YOU'RE BLUSHING.
SO CUTE.

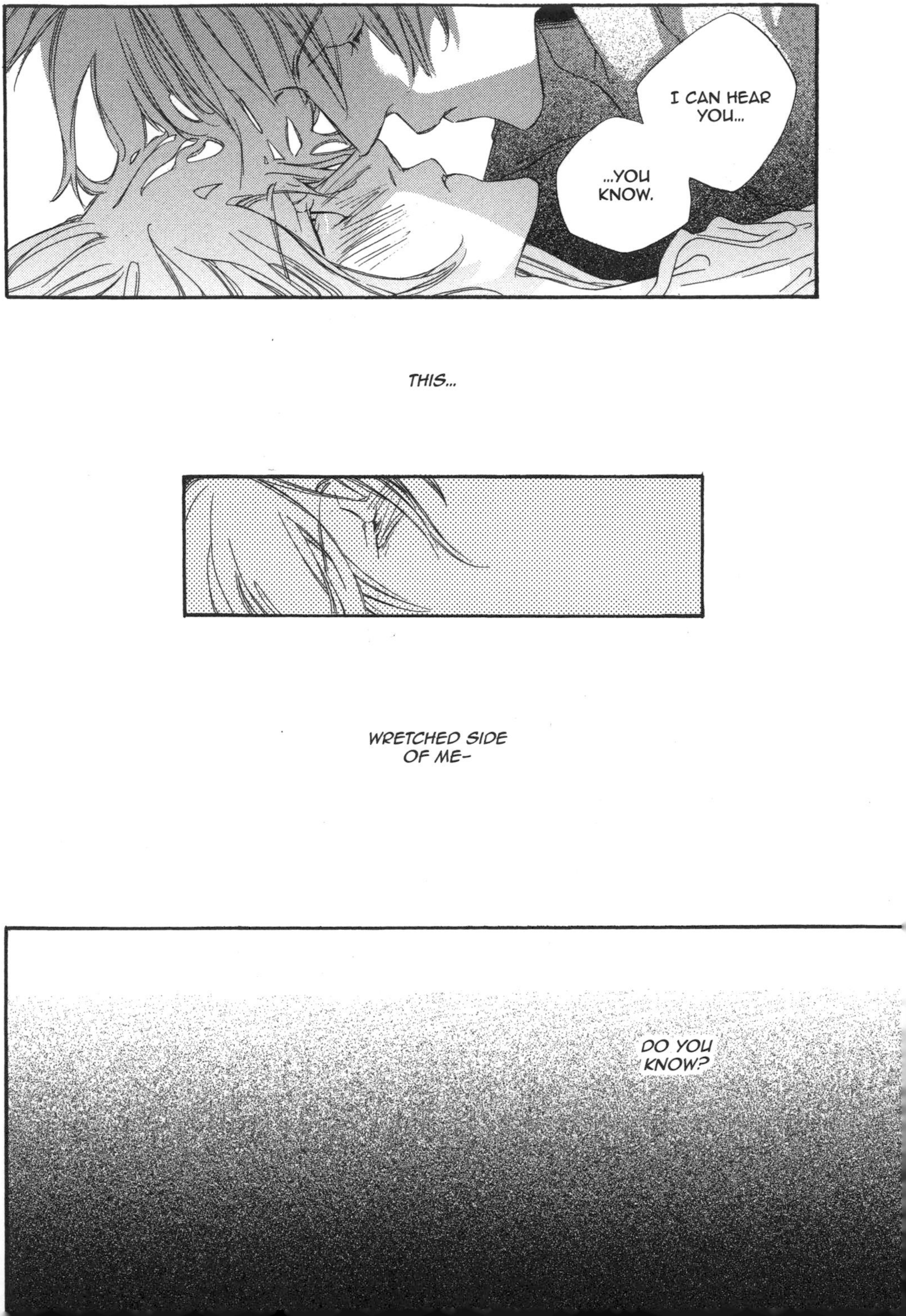
I CAN HEAR YOU...
...YOU KNOW.
THIS...
WRETCHED SIDE OF ME-
DO YOU KNOW?

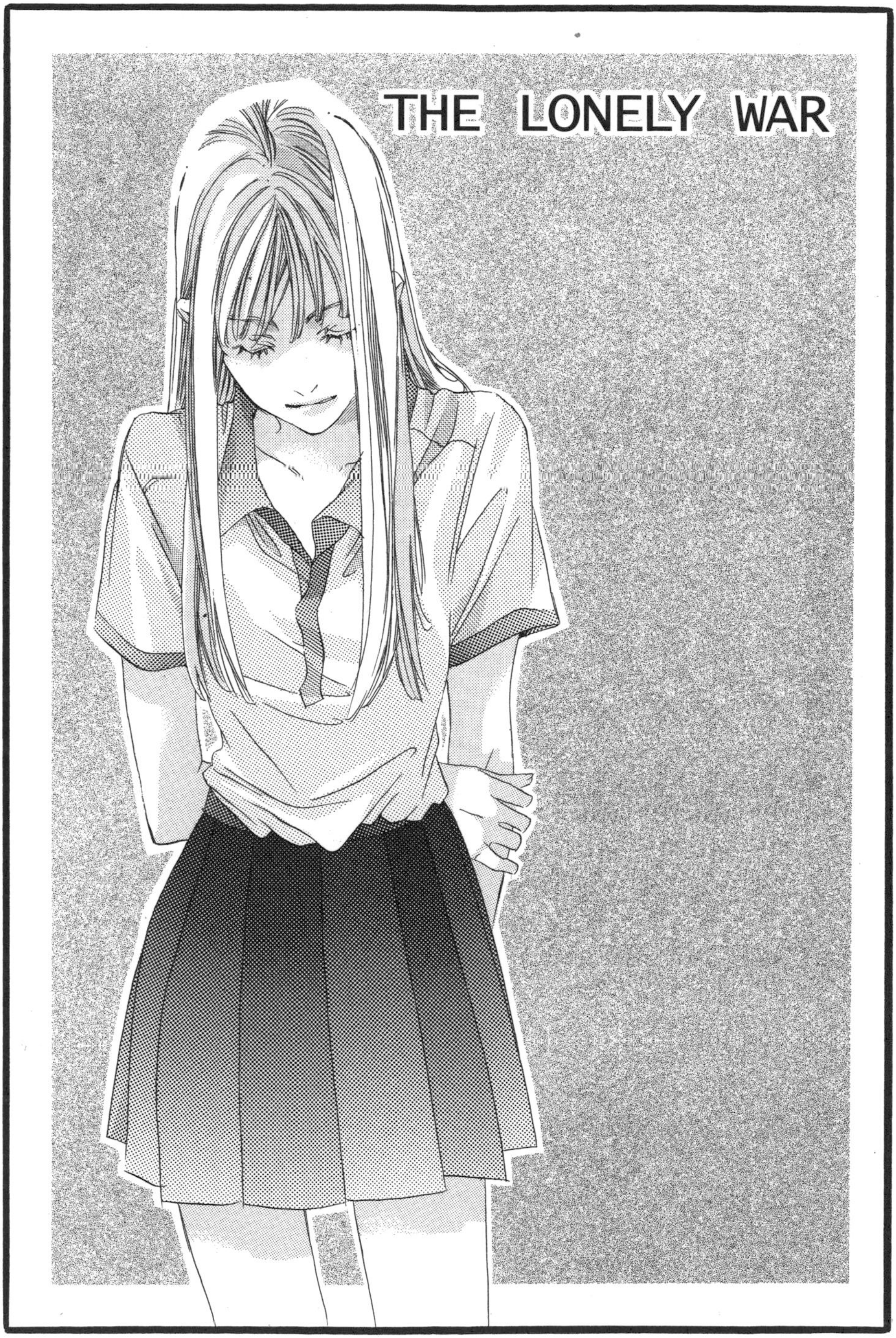
THE LONELY WAR

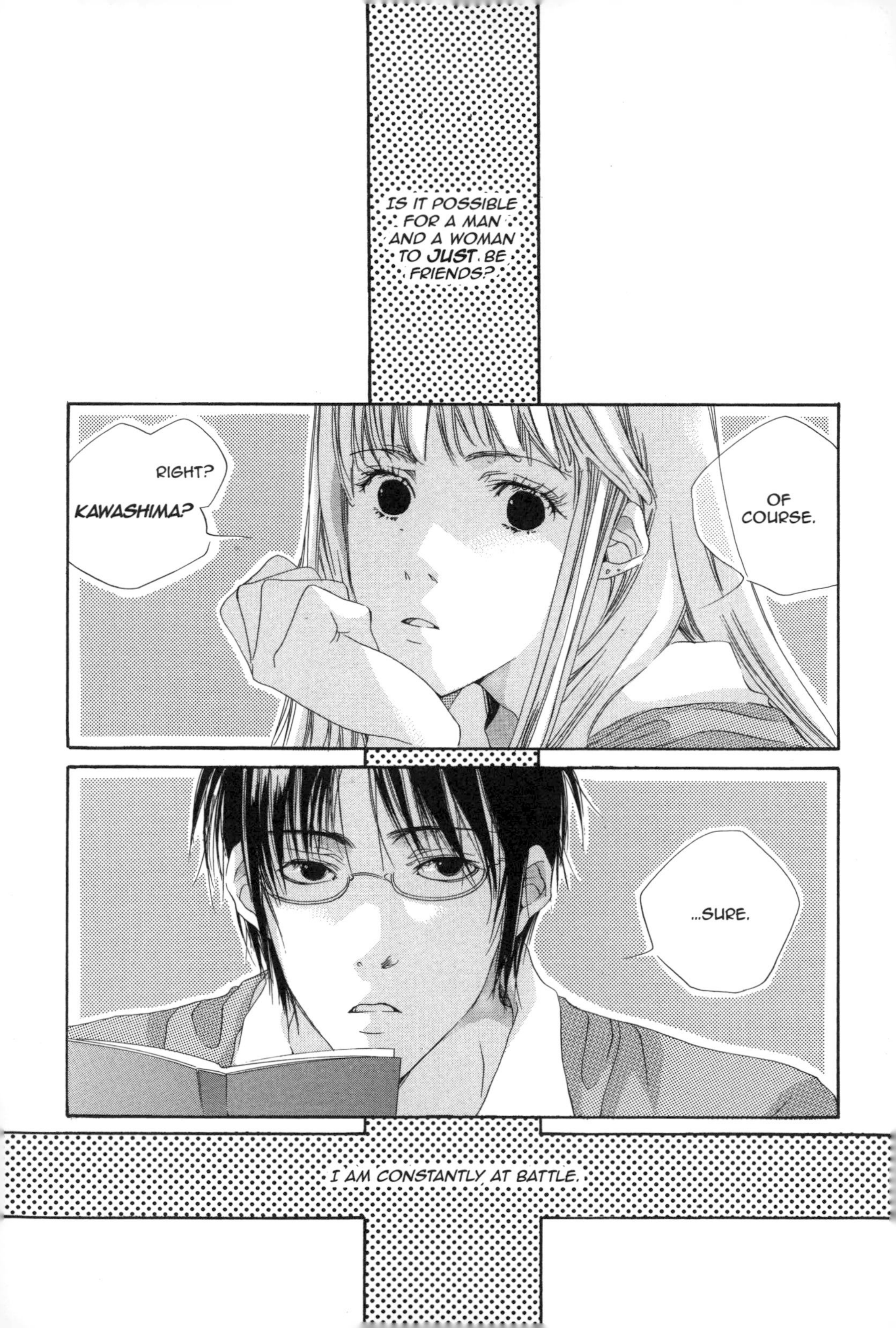
IS IT POSSIBLE FOR A MAN AND A WOMAN TO JUST BE FRIENDS?
OF COURSE.
RIGHT? KAWASHIMA?
...SURE.
I AM CONSTANTLY AT BATTLE.

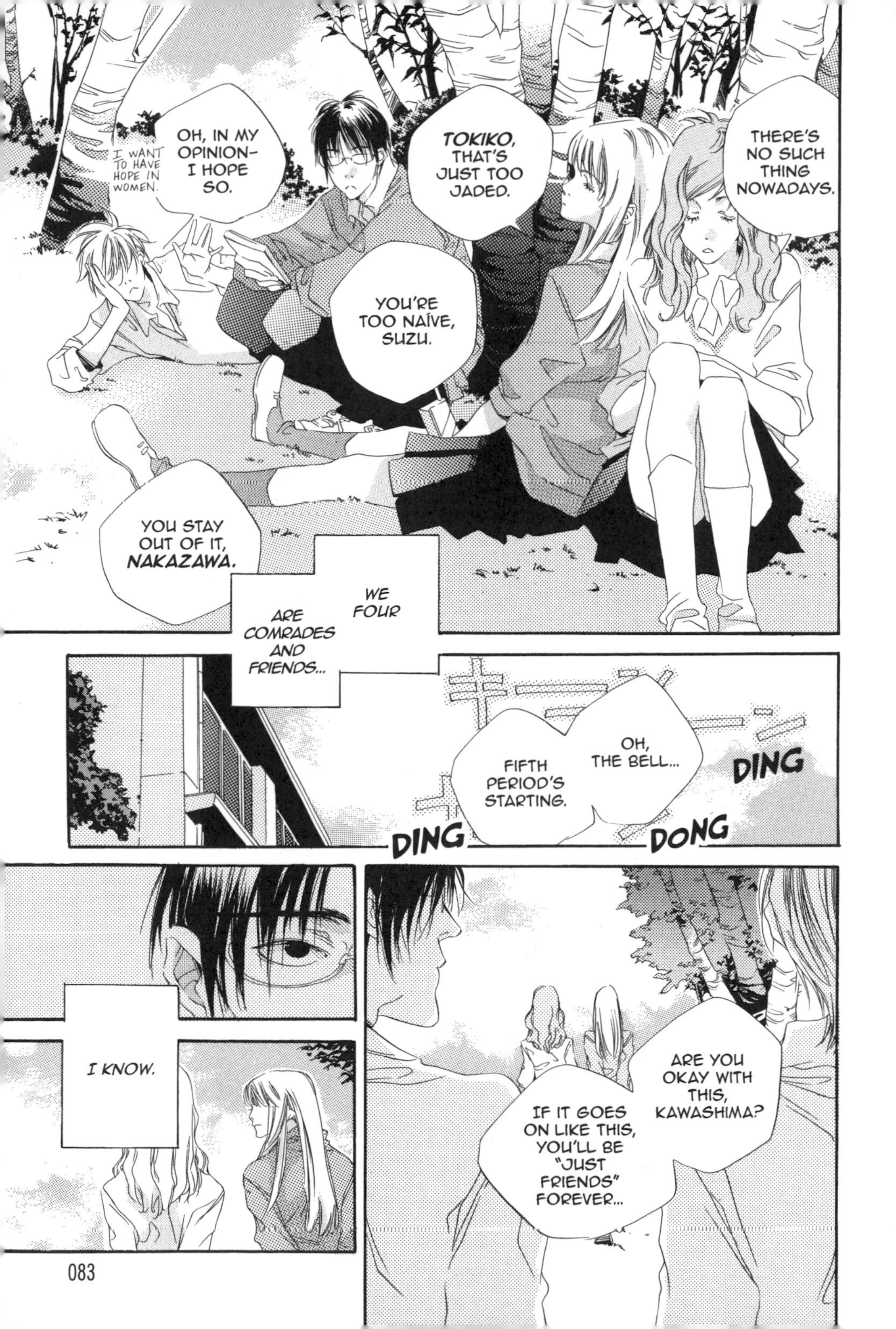
THERE'S NO SUCH THING NOWADAYS.
TOKIKO, THAT'S JUST TOO JADED.
YOU'RE TOO NAÏVE, SUZU.
OH, IN MY OPINION- I HOPE SO.
I WANT TO HAVE HOPE IN WOMEN.
YOU STAY OUT OF IT, NAKAZAWA.
WE FOUR ARE COMRADES AND FRIENDS...
DING
OH, THE BELL...
FIFTH PERIOD'S STARTING.
DING
DONG
ARE YOU OKAY WITH THIS, KAWASHIMA?
IF IT GOES ON LIKE THIS, YOU'LL BE "JUST FRIENDS" FOREVER...
I KNOW.

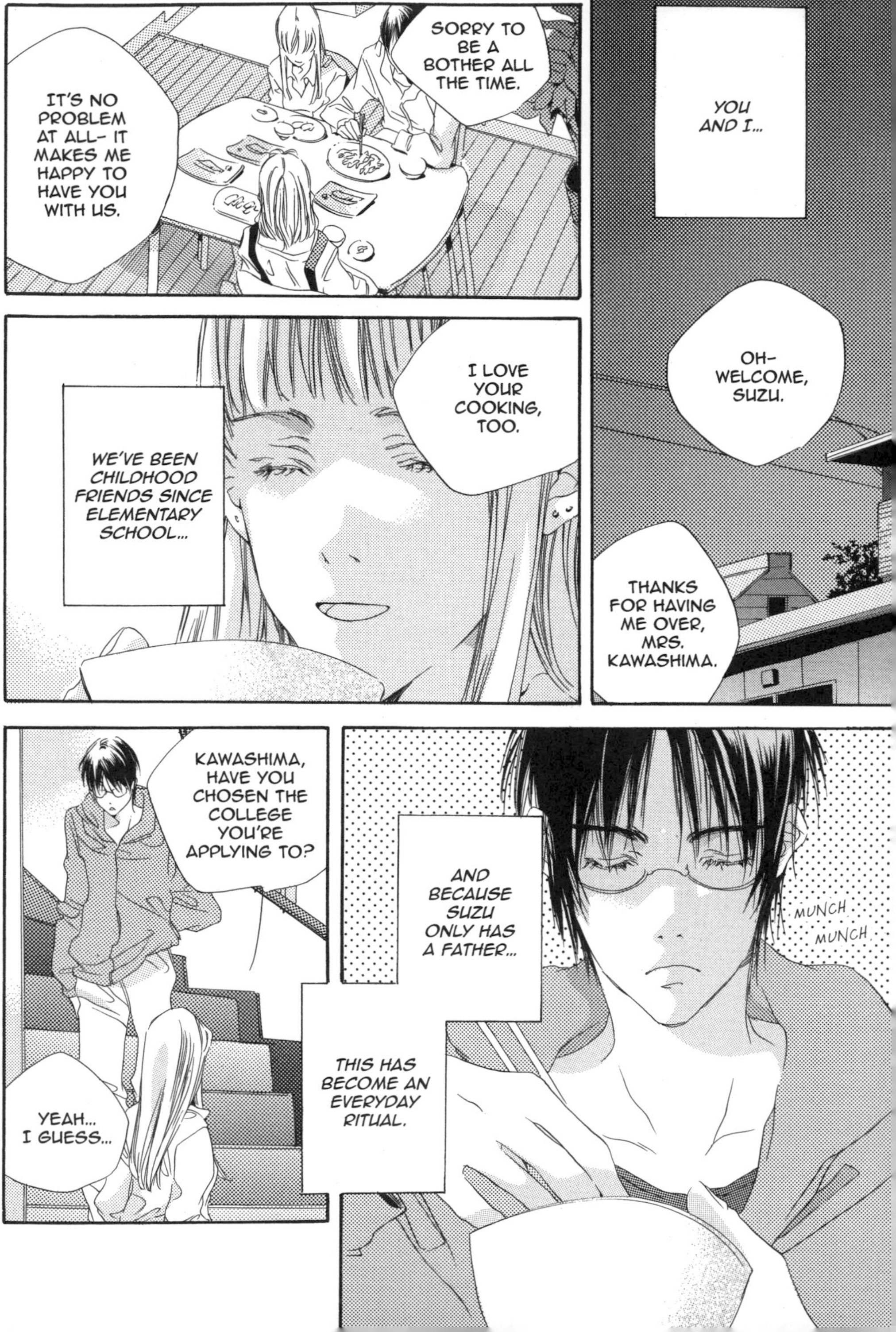
YOU AND I...
OH- WELCOME, SUZU.
THANKS FOR HAVING ME OVER, MRS. KAWASHIMA.
SORRY TO BE A BOTHER ALL THE TIME.
IT'S NO PROBLEM AT ALL- IT MAKES ME HAPPY TO HAVE YOU WITH US.
I LOVE YOUR COOKING, TOO.
WE'VE BEEN CHILDHOOD FRIENDS SINCE ELEMENTARY SCHOOL...
MUNCH MUNCH
AND BECAUSE SUZU ONLY HAS A FATHER...
THIS HAS BECOME AN EVERYDAY RITUAL.
KAWASHIMA, HAVE YOU CHOSEN THE COLLEGE YOU'RE APPLYING TO?
YEAH... I GUESS...

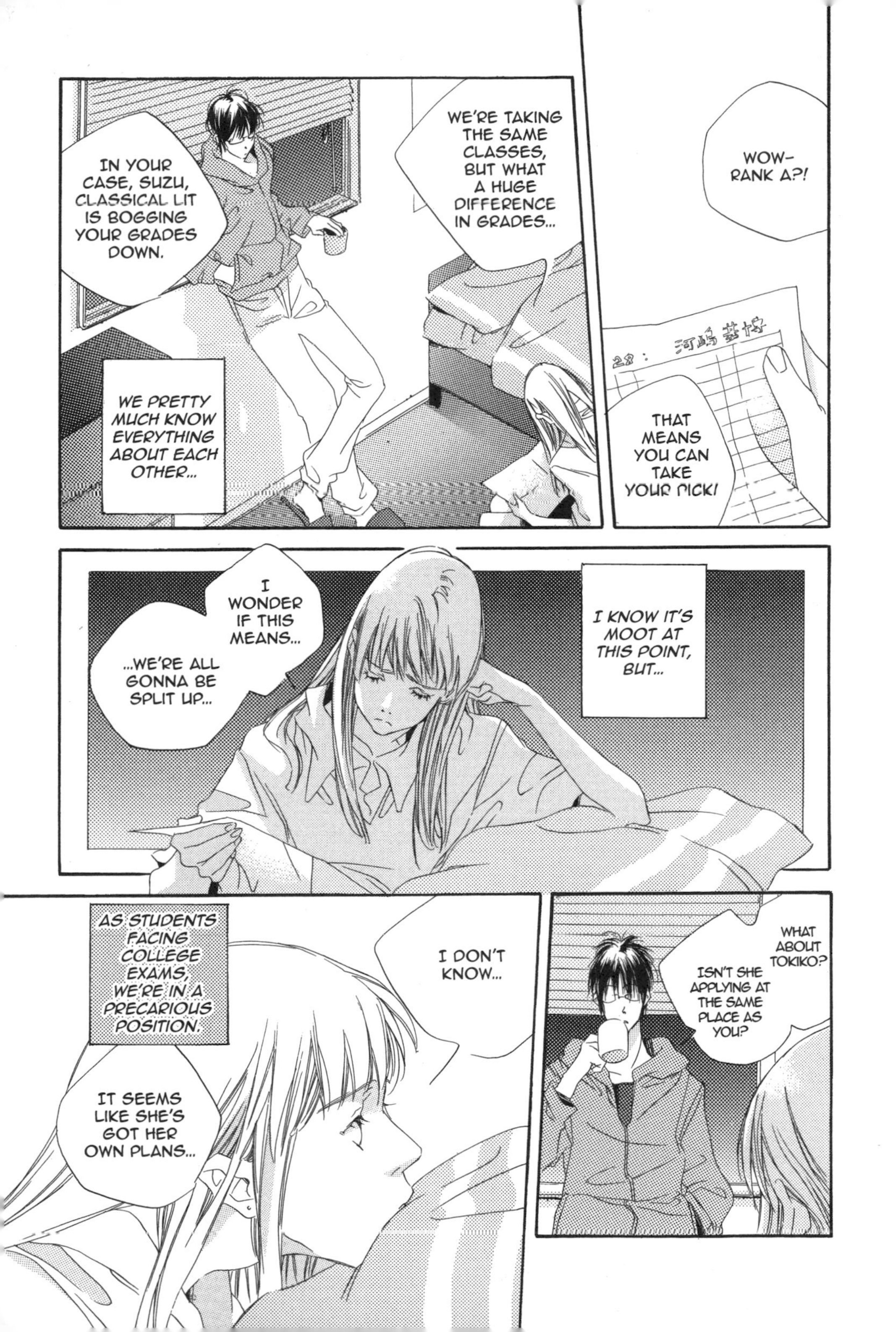
WOW-RANK A?!
THAT MEANS YOU CAN TAKE YOUR PICK!
WE'RE TAKING THE SAME CLASSES, BUT WHAT A HUGE DIFFERENCE IN GRADES...
IN YOUR CASE, SUZU, CLASSICAL LIT IS BOGGING YOUR GRADES DOWN.
WE PRETTY MUCH KNOW EVERYTHING ABOUT EACH OTHER...
I KNOW IT'S MOOT AT THIS POINT, BUT...
I WONDER IF THIS MEANS...
...WE'RE ALL GONNA BE SPLIT UP...
WHAT ABOUT TOKIKO?
ISN'T SHE APPLYING AT THE SAME PLACE AS YOU?
I DON'T KNOW...
AS STUDENTS FACING COLLEGE EXAMS, WE'RE IN A PRECARIOUS POSITION.
IT SEEMS LIKE SHE'S GOT HER OWN PLANS...

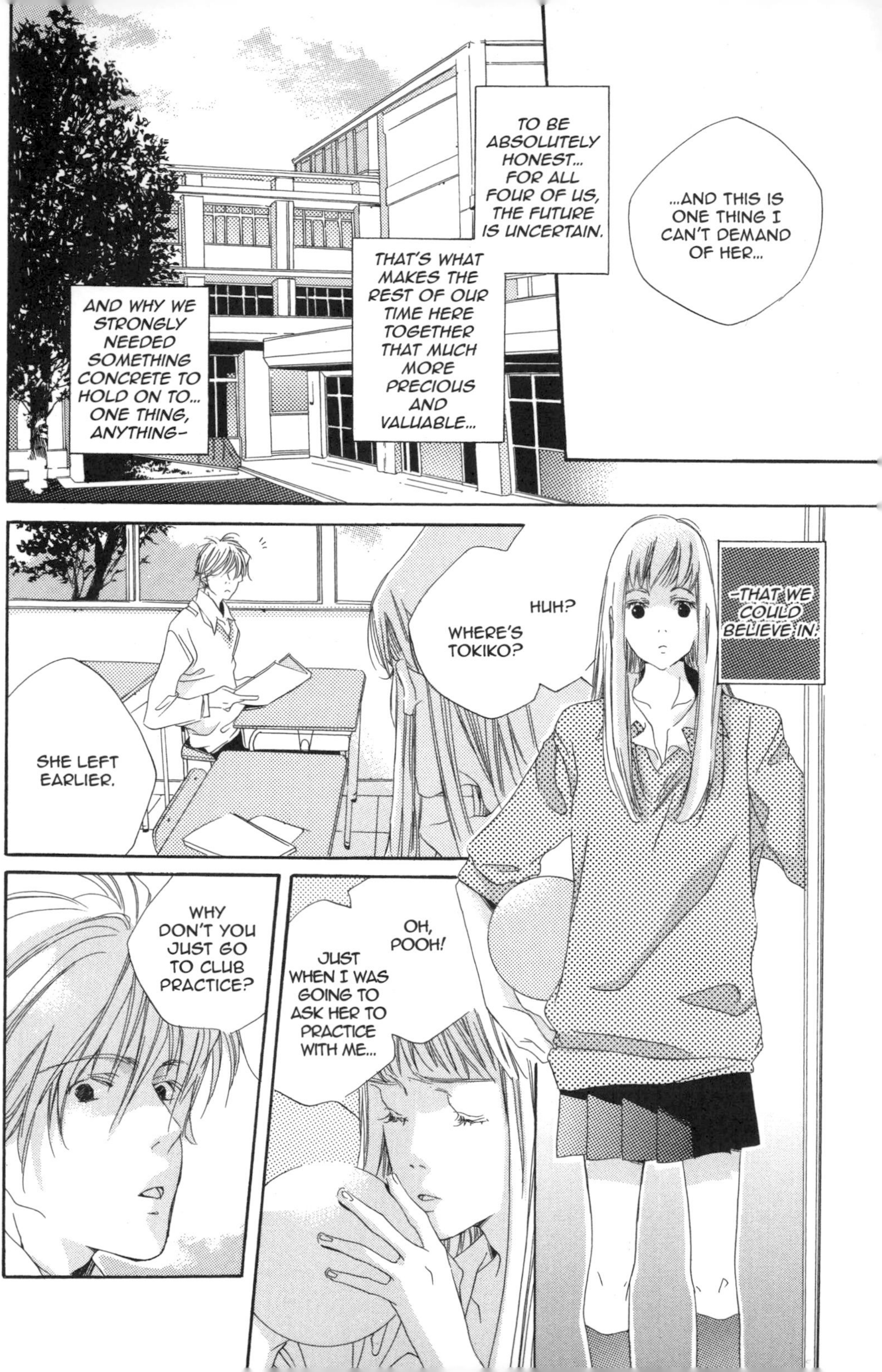
...AND THIS IS ONE THING I CAN'T DEMAND OF HER...
TO BE ABSOLUTELY HONEST... FOR ALL FOUR OF US, THE FUTURE IS UNCERTAIN.
THAT'S WHAT MAKES THE REST OF OUR TIME HERE TOGETHER THAT MUCH MORE PRECIOUS AND VALUABLE...
AND WHY WE STRONGLY NEEDED SOMETHING CONCRETE TO HOLD ON TO... ONE THING, ANYTHING-
-THAT WE COULD BELIEVE IN.
HUH?
WHERE'S TOKIKO?
SHE LEFT EARLIER.
OH, POOH!
JUST WHEN I WAS GOING TO ASK HER TO PRACTICE WITH ME...
WHY DON'T YOU JUST GO TO CLUB PRACTICE?

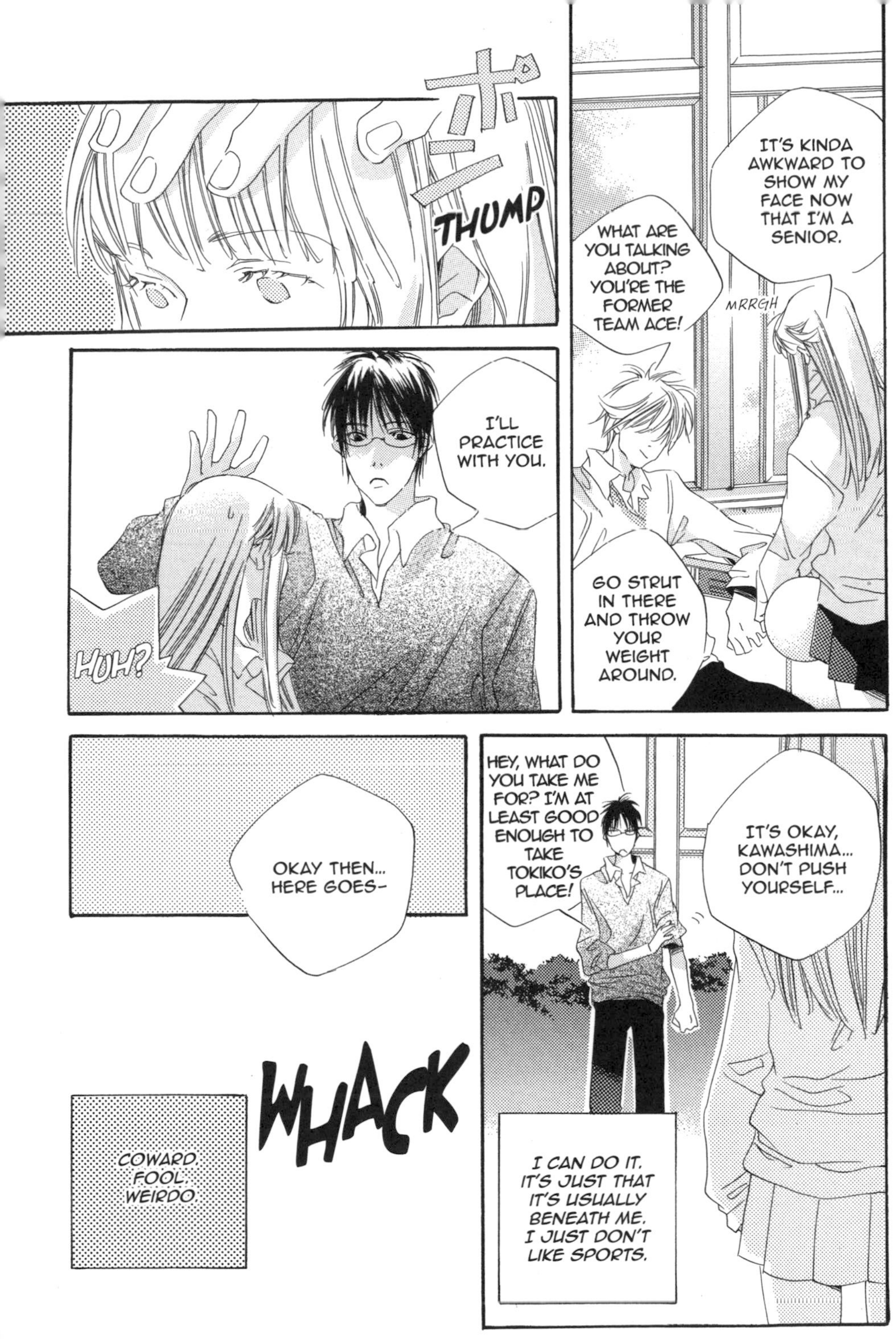
IT'S KINDA AWKWARD TO SHOW MY FACE NOW THAT I'M A SENIOR.
WHAT ARE YOU TALKING ABOUT? YOU'RE THE FORMER TEAM ACE!
MRRGH
GO STRUT IN THERE AND THROW YOUR WEIGHT AROUND.
ポン
THUMP
I'LL PRACTICE WITH YOU.
HUH?
IT'S OKAY, KAWASHIMA... DON'T PUSH YOURSELF...
HEY, WHAT DO YOU TAKE ME FOR? I'M AT LEAST GOOD ENOUGH TO TAKE TOKIKO'S PLACE!
I CAN DO IT. IT'S JUST THAT IT'S USUALLY BENEATH ME. I JUST DON'T LIKE SPORTS.
OKAY THEN... HERE GOES-
WHACK
COWARD. FOOL. WEIRDO.

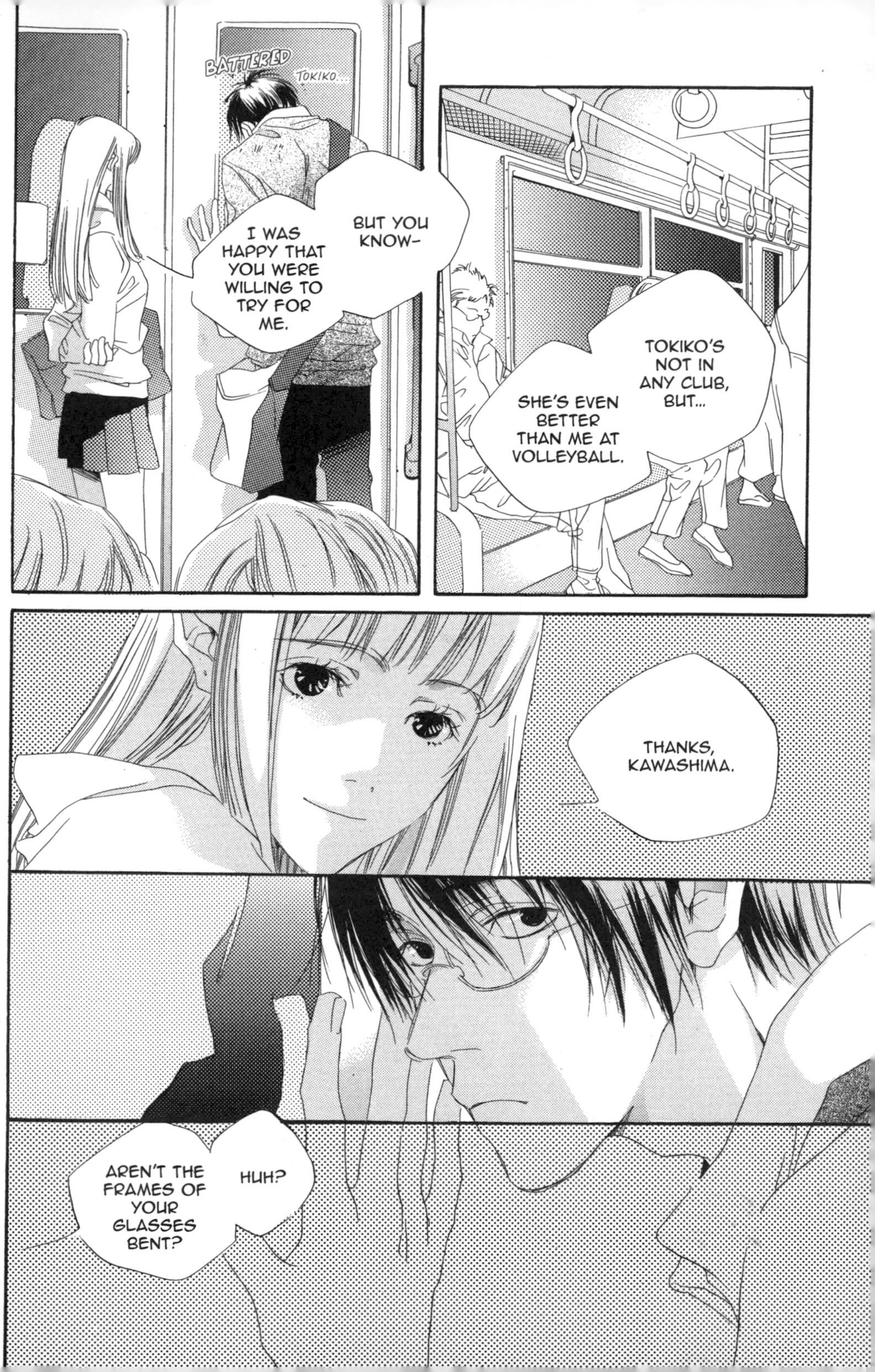
TOKIKO'S NOT IN ANY CLUB, BUT...
SHE'S EVEN BETTER THAN ME AT VOLLEYBALL.
BATTERED
TOKIKO...
BUT YOU KNOW-
I WAS HAPPY THAT YOU WERE WILLING TO TRY FOR ME.
THANKS, KAWASHIMA.
HUH?
AREN'T THE FRAMES OF YOUR GLASSES BENT?

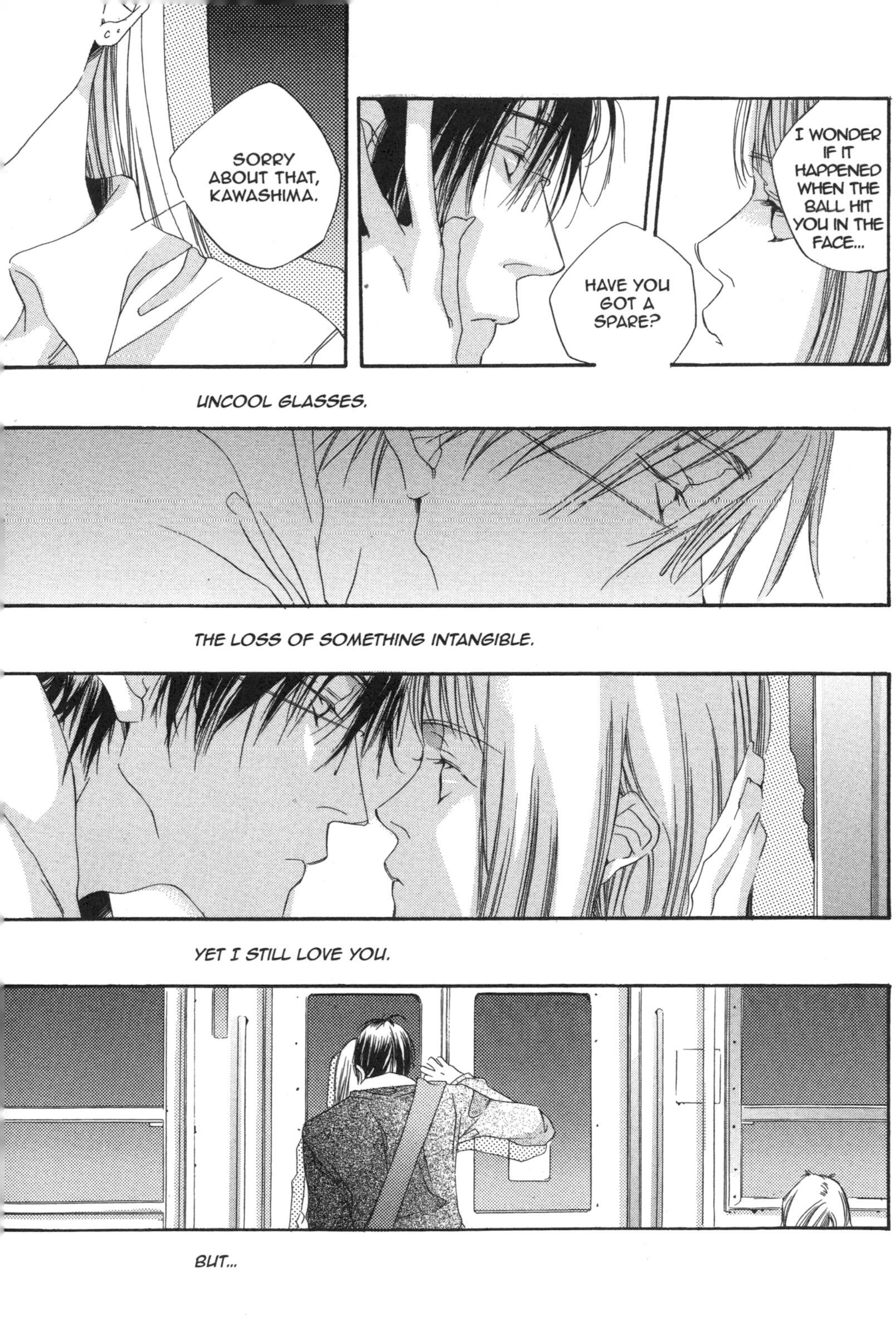
I WONDER IF IT HAPPENED WHEN THE BALL HIT YOU IN THE FACE...
HAVE YOU GOT A SPARE?
SORRY ABOUT THAT, KAWASHIMA.
UNCOOL GLASSES.
THE LOSS OF SOMETHING INTANGIBLE.
YET I STILL LOVE YOU.
BUT...

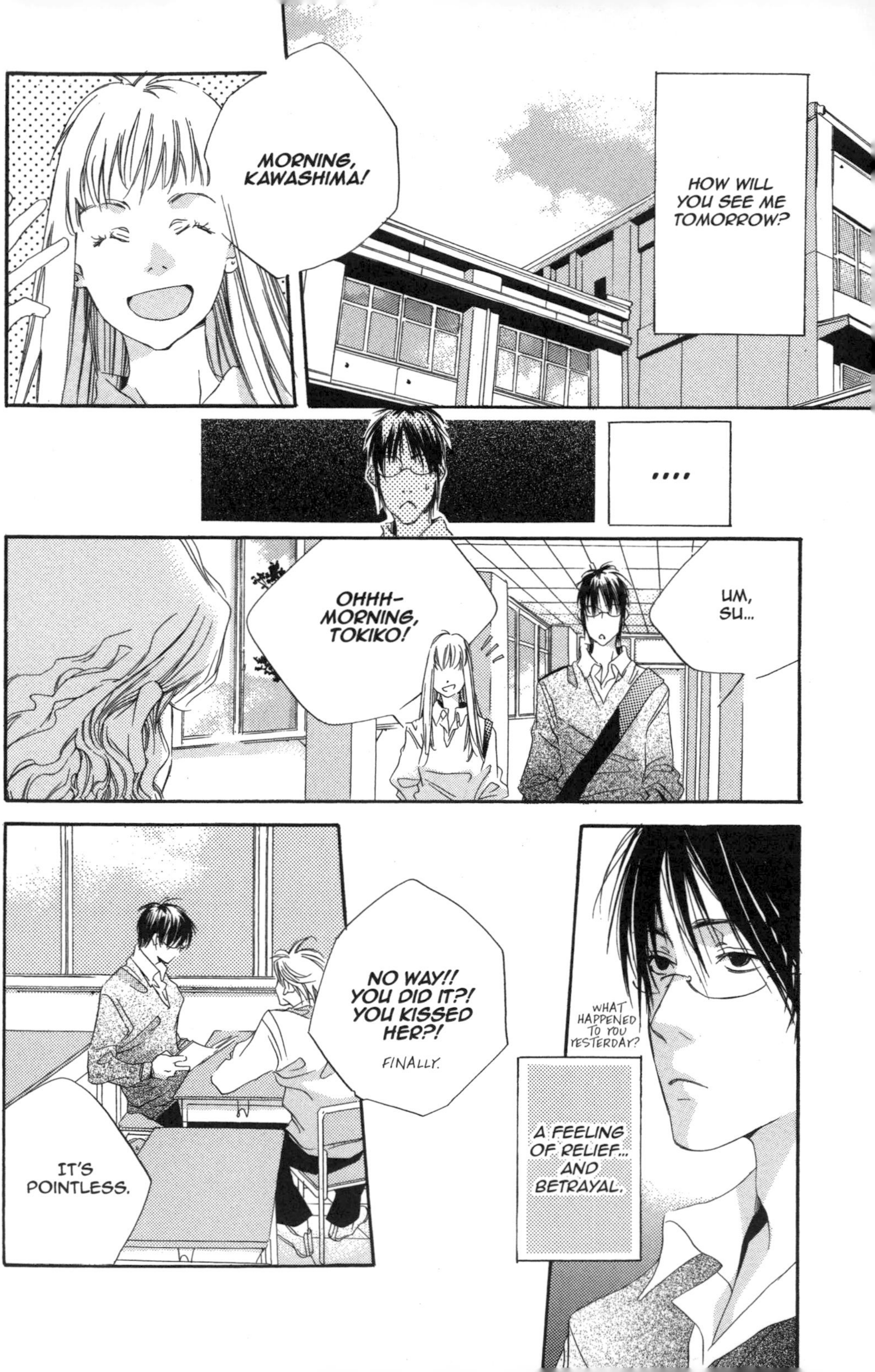
HOW WILL YOU SEE ME TOMORROW?
MORNING, KAWASHIMA!
....
UM, SU...
OHHH- MORNING, TOKIKO!
WHAT HAPPENED TO YOU YESTERDAY?
A FEELING OF RELIEF... AND BETRAYAL.
NO WAY!! YOU DID IT?! YOU KISSED HER?!
FINALLY.
IT'S POINTLESS.

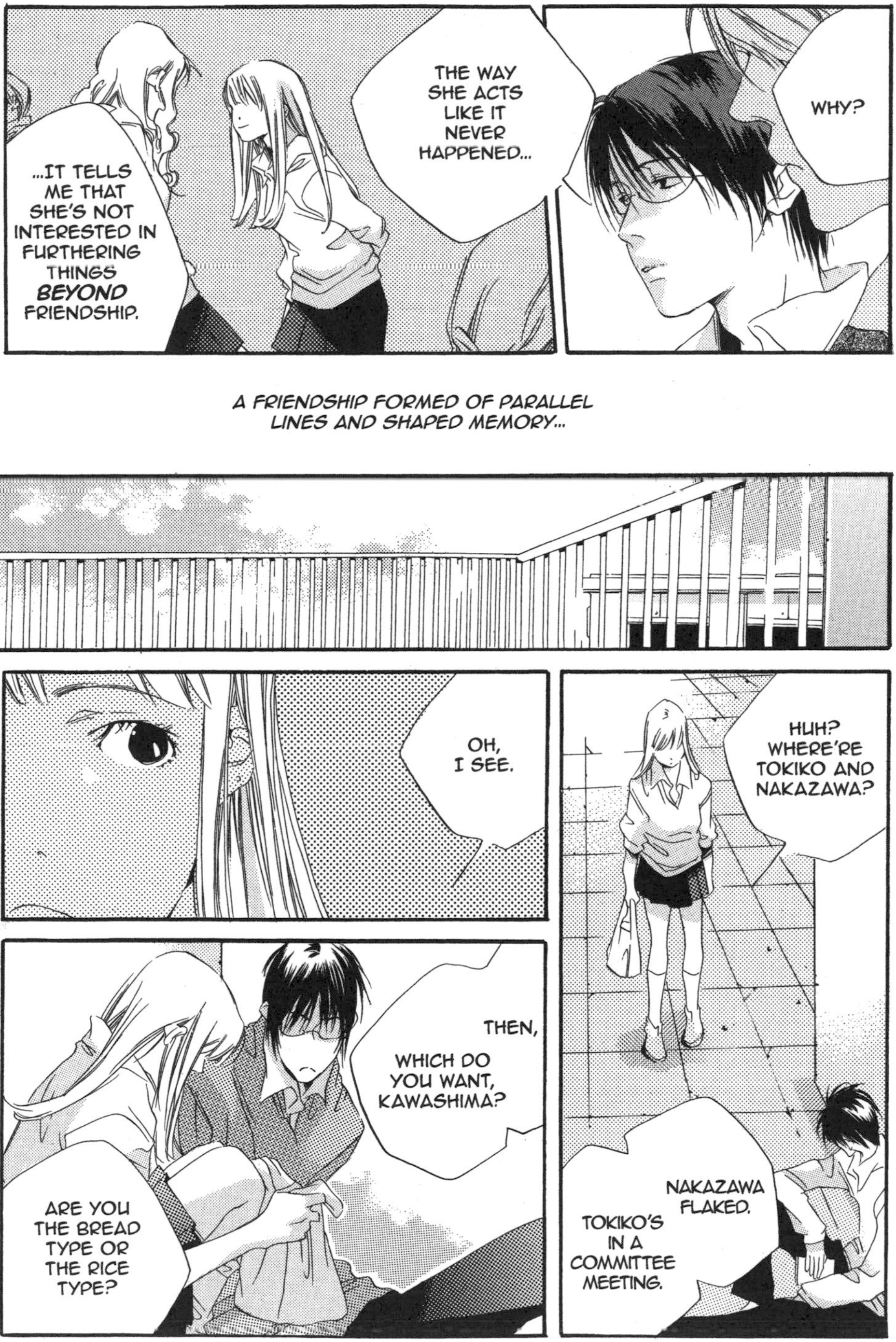
WHY?
THE WAY SHE ACTS LIKE IT NEVER HAPPENED...
...IT TELLS ME THAT SHE'S NOT INTERESTED IN FURTHERING THINGS ***BEYOND*** FRIENDSHIP.
A FRIENDSHIP FORMED OF PARALLEL LINES AND SHAPED MEMORY...
HUH? WHERE'RE TOKIKO AND NAKAZAWA?
NAKAZAWA FLAKED.
TOKIKO'S IN A COMMITTEE MEETING.
OH, I SEE.
THEN,
WHICH DO YOU WANT, KAWASHIMA?
ARE YOU THE BREAD TYPE OR THE RICE TYPE?

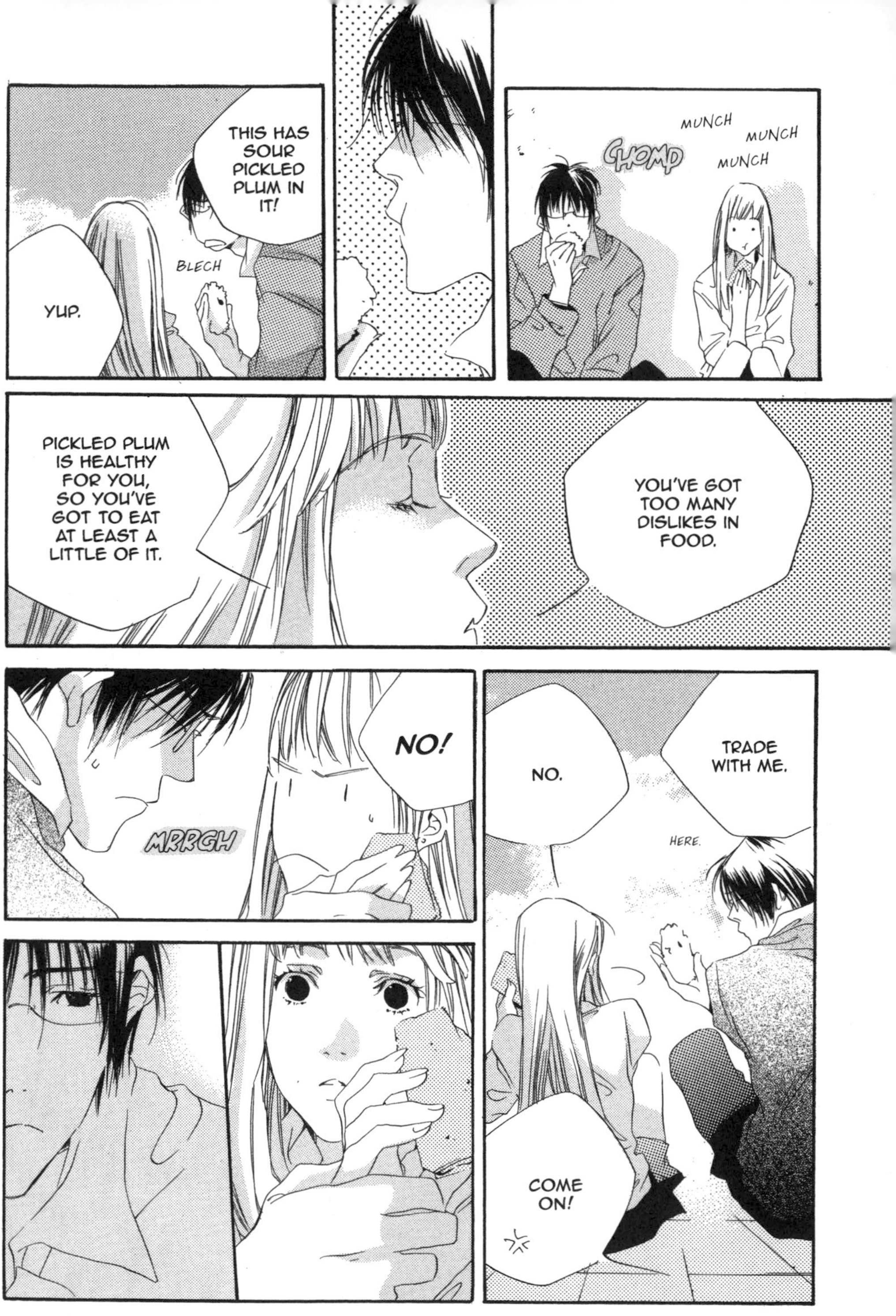
CHOMP
MUNCH
MUNCH
MUNCH
THIS HAS SOUR PICKLED PLUM IN IT!
BLECH
YUP.
YOU'VE GOT TOO MANY DISLIKES IN FOOD.
PICKLED PLUM IS HEALTHY FOR YOU, SO YOU'VE GOT TO EAT AT LEAST A LITTLE OF IT.
TRADE WITH ME.
HERE.
NO.
COME ON!
NO!
MRRGH

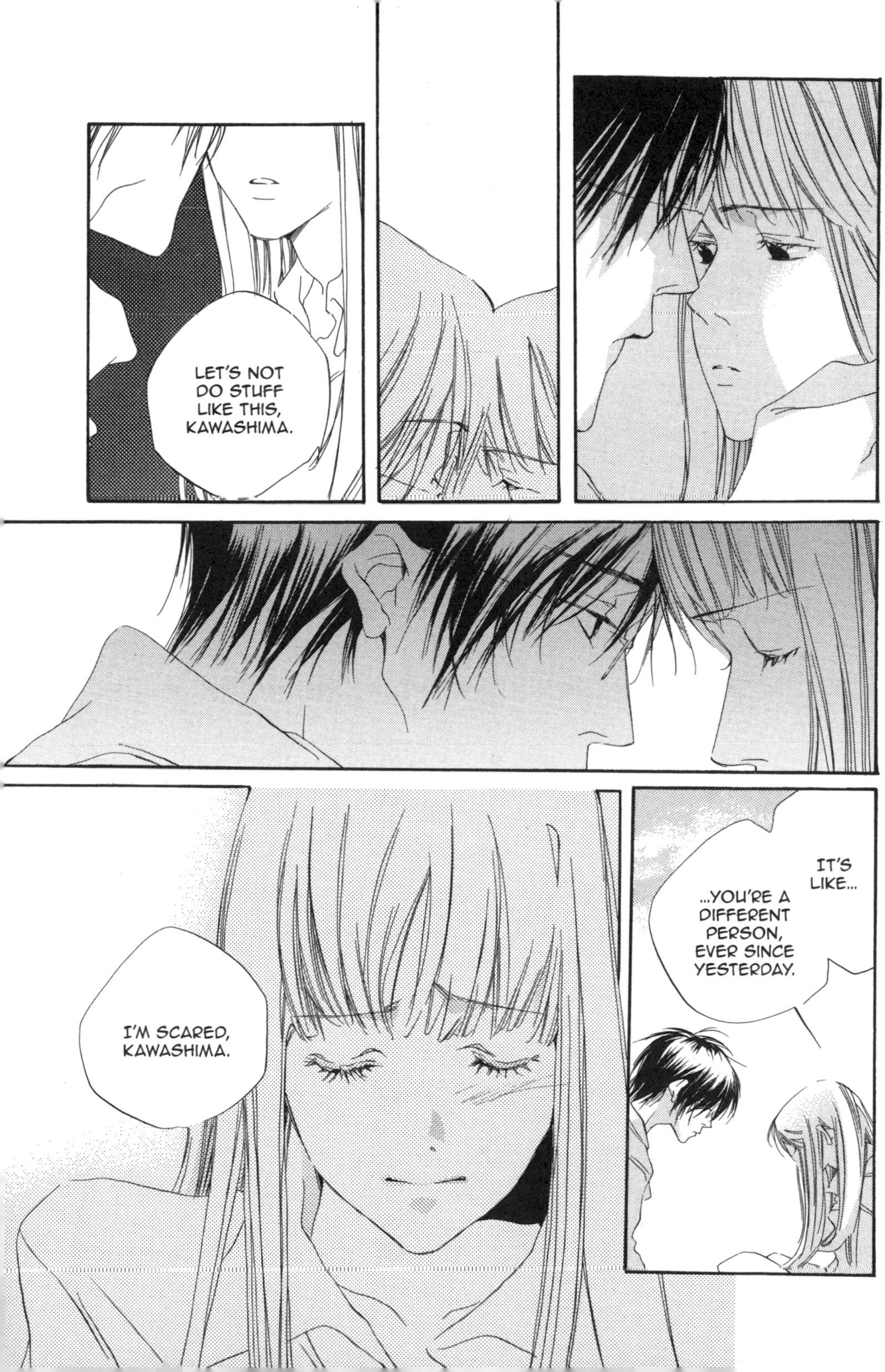
LET'S NOT DO STUFF LIKE THIS, KAWASHIMA.
IT'S LIKE...
...YOU'RE A DIFFERENT PERSON, EVER SINCE YESTERDAY.
I'M SCARED, KAWASHIMA.

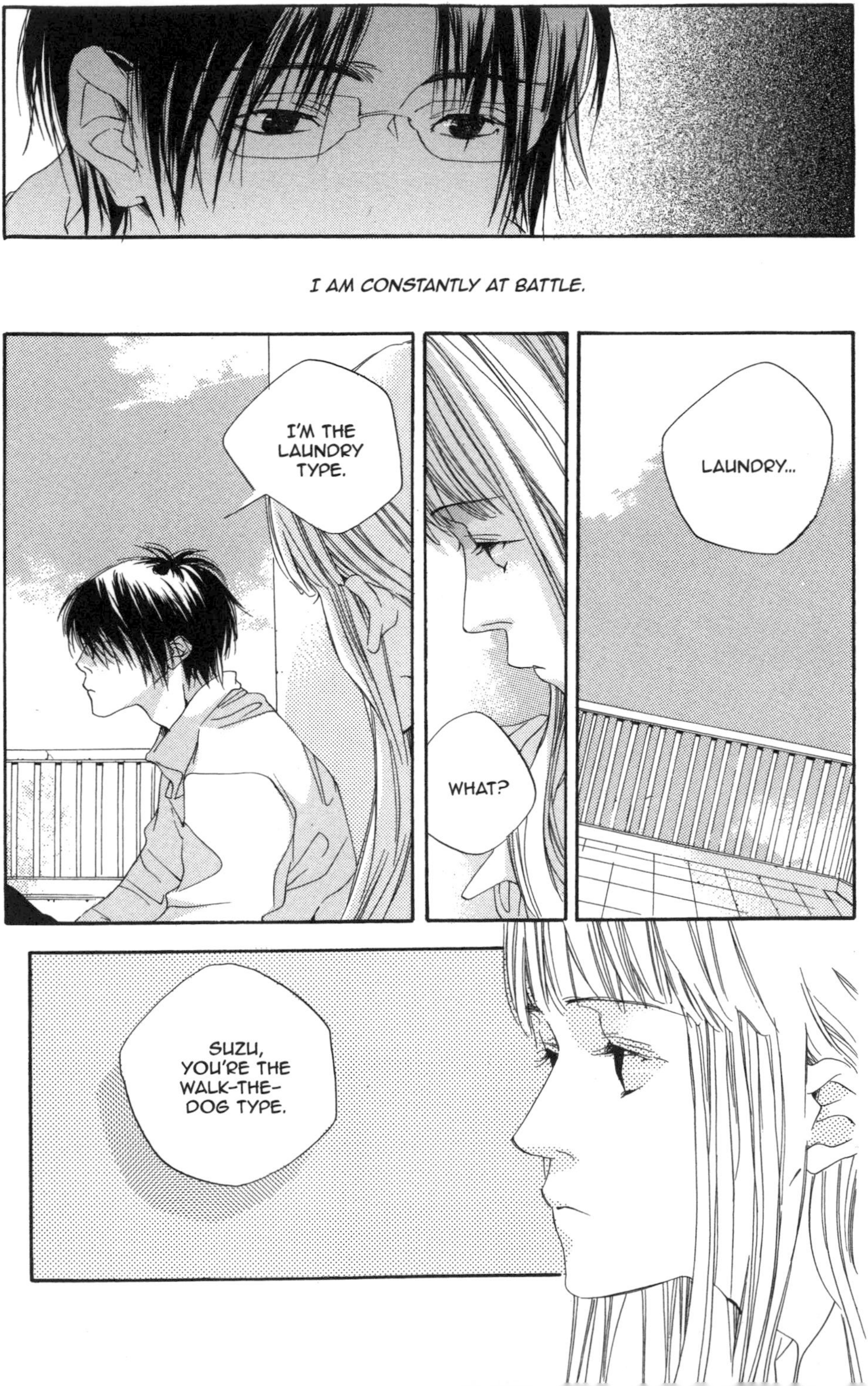
I AM CONSTANTLY AT BATTLE.
LAUNDRY...
WHAT?
I'M THE LAUNDRY TYPE.
SUZU, YOU'RE THE WALK-THE-DOG TYPE.

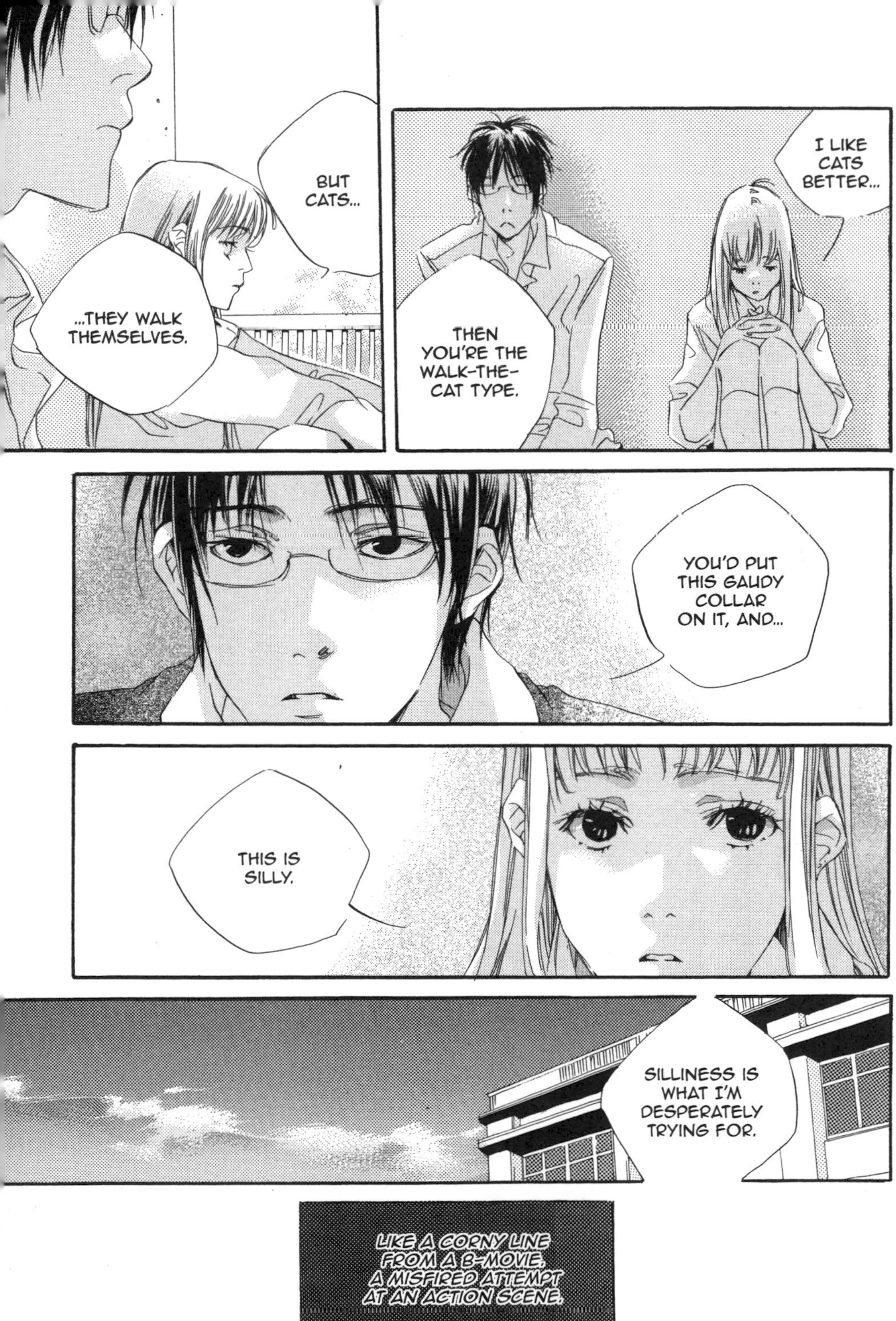
I LIKE CATS BETTER...
THEN YOU'RE THE WALK-THE-CAT TYPE.
BUT CATS...
...THEY WALK THEMSELVES.
YOU'D PUT THIS GAUDY COLLAR ON IT, AND...
THIS IS SILLY.
SILLINESS IS WHAT I'M DESPERATELY TRYING FOR.
LIKE A CORNY LINE FROM A B-MOVIE, A MISFIRED ATTEMPT AT AN ACTION SCENE.

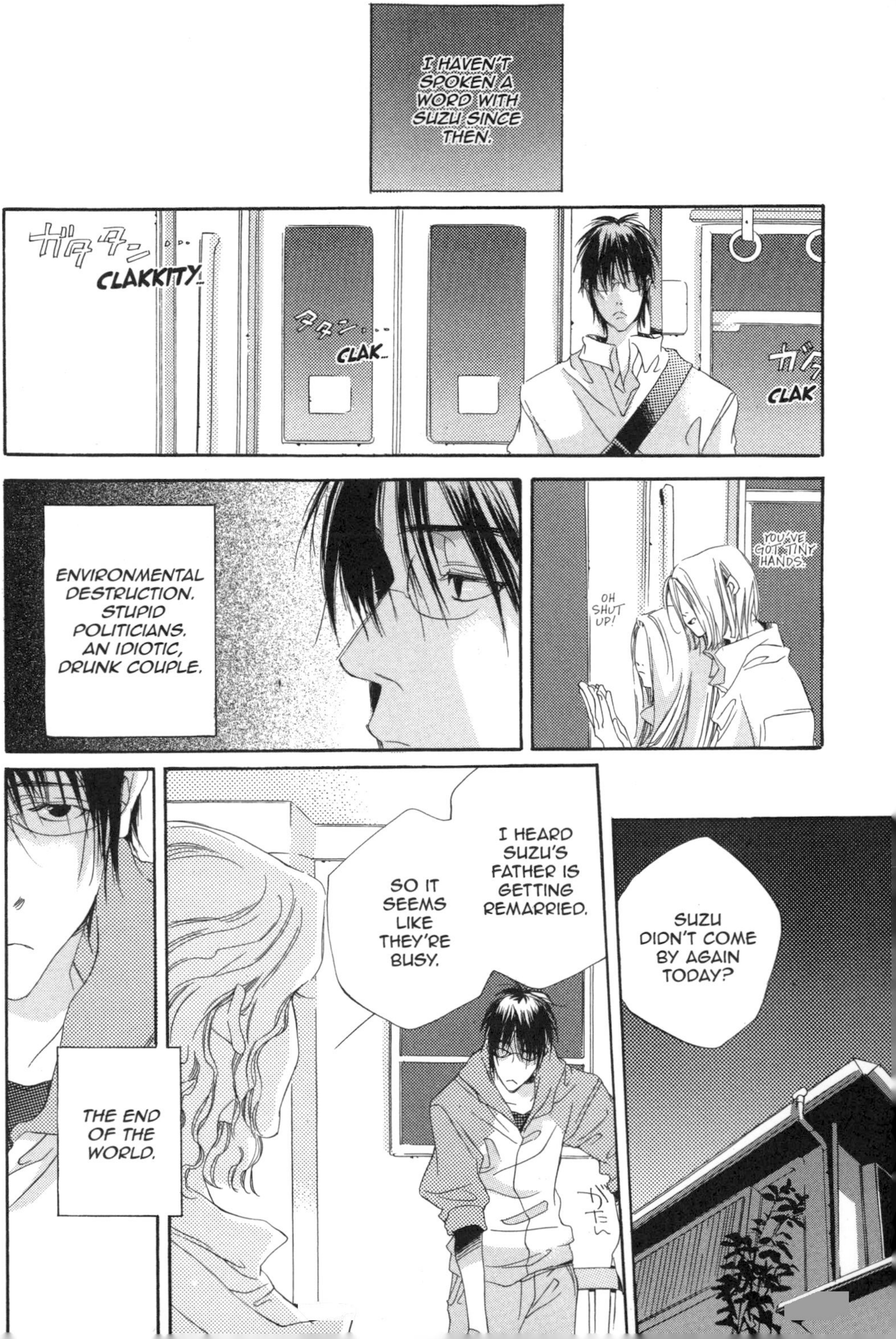
I HAVEN'T SPOKEN A WORD WITH SUZU SINCE THEN.
ガタ
CLAK
タタン...
CLAK...
ガタタン...
CLAKKITY...
YOU'VE GOT TINY HANDS.
OH SHUT UP!
ENVIRONMENTAL DESTRUCTION. STUPID POLITICIANS. AN IDIOTIC, DRUNK COUPLE.
SUZU DIDN'T COME BY AGAIN TODAY?
I HEARD SUZU'S FATHER IS GETTING REMARRIED.
SO IT SEEMS LIKE THEY'RE BUSY.
かたん
THE END OF THE WORLD.

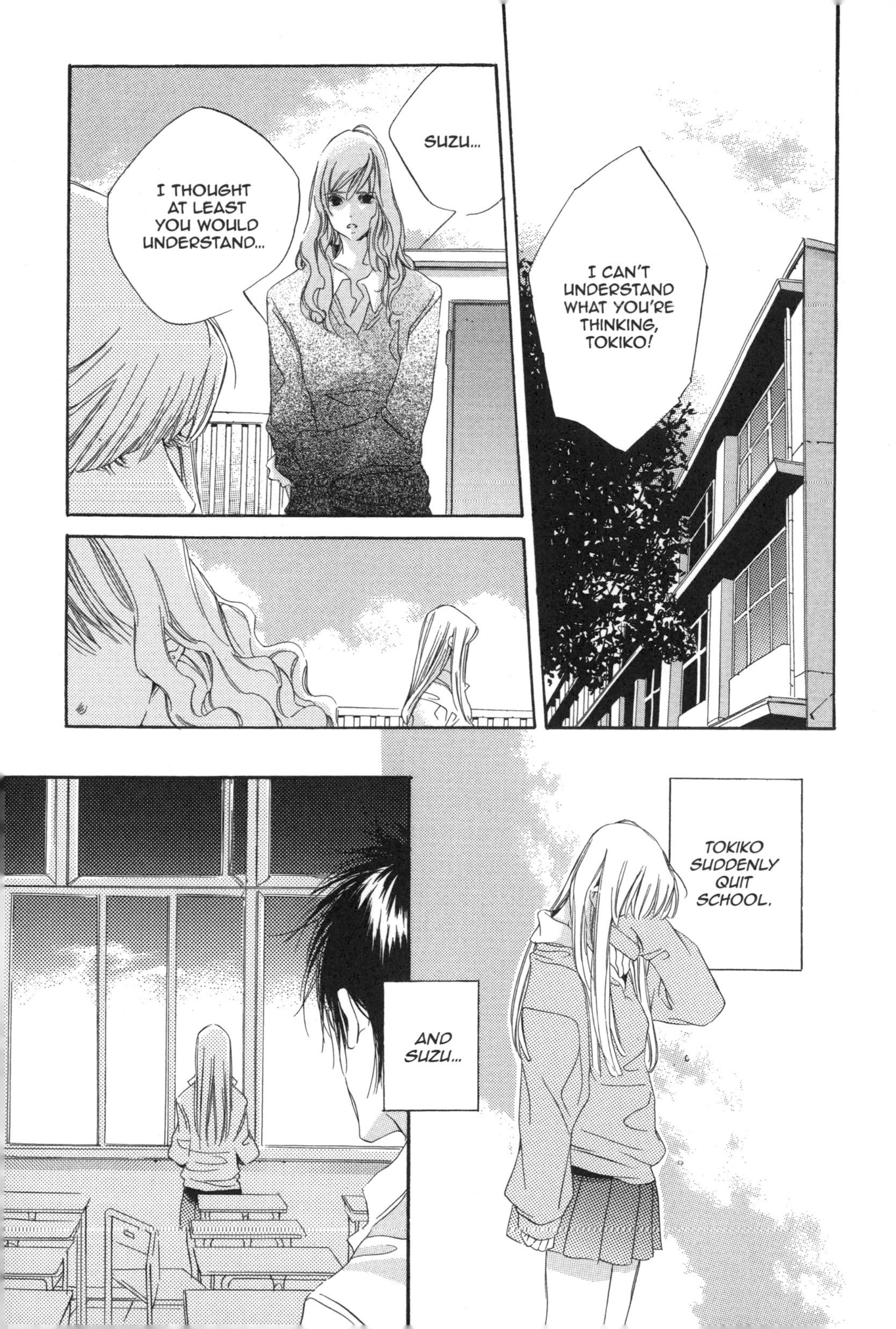
I CAN'T UNDERSTAND WHAT YOU'RE THINKING, TOKIKO!
SUZU...
I THOUGHT AT LEAST YOU WOULD UNDERSTAND...
TOKIKO SUDDENLY QUIT SCHOOL.
AND SUZU...

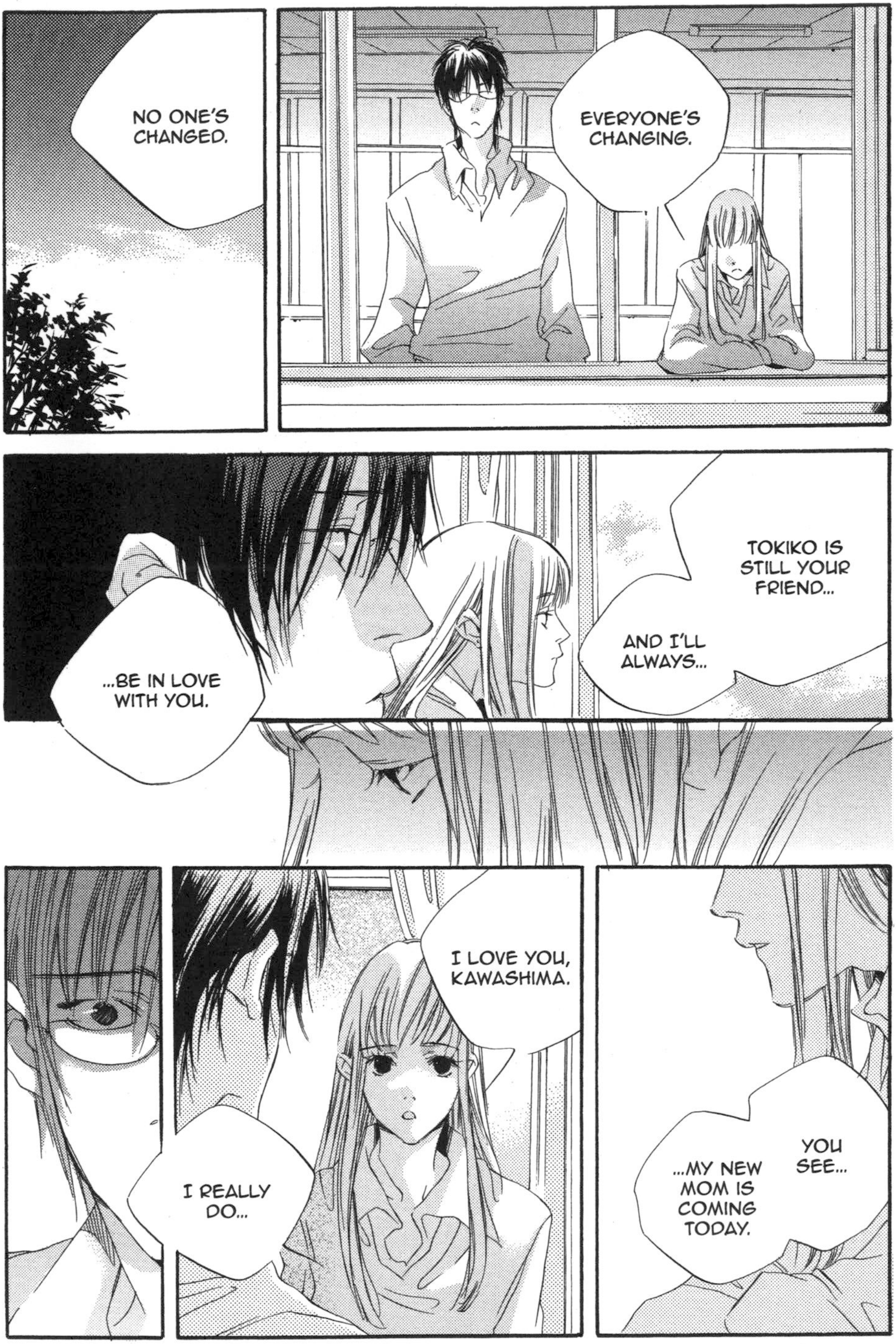
EVERYONE'S CHANGING.
NO ONE'S CHANGED.
TOKIKO IS STILL YOUR FRIEND...
AND I'LL ALWAYS...
...BE IN LOVE WITH YOU.
YOU SEE...
...MY NEW MOM IS COMING TODAY.
I LOVE YOU, KAWASHIMA.
I REALLY DO...

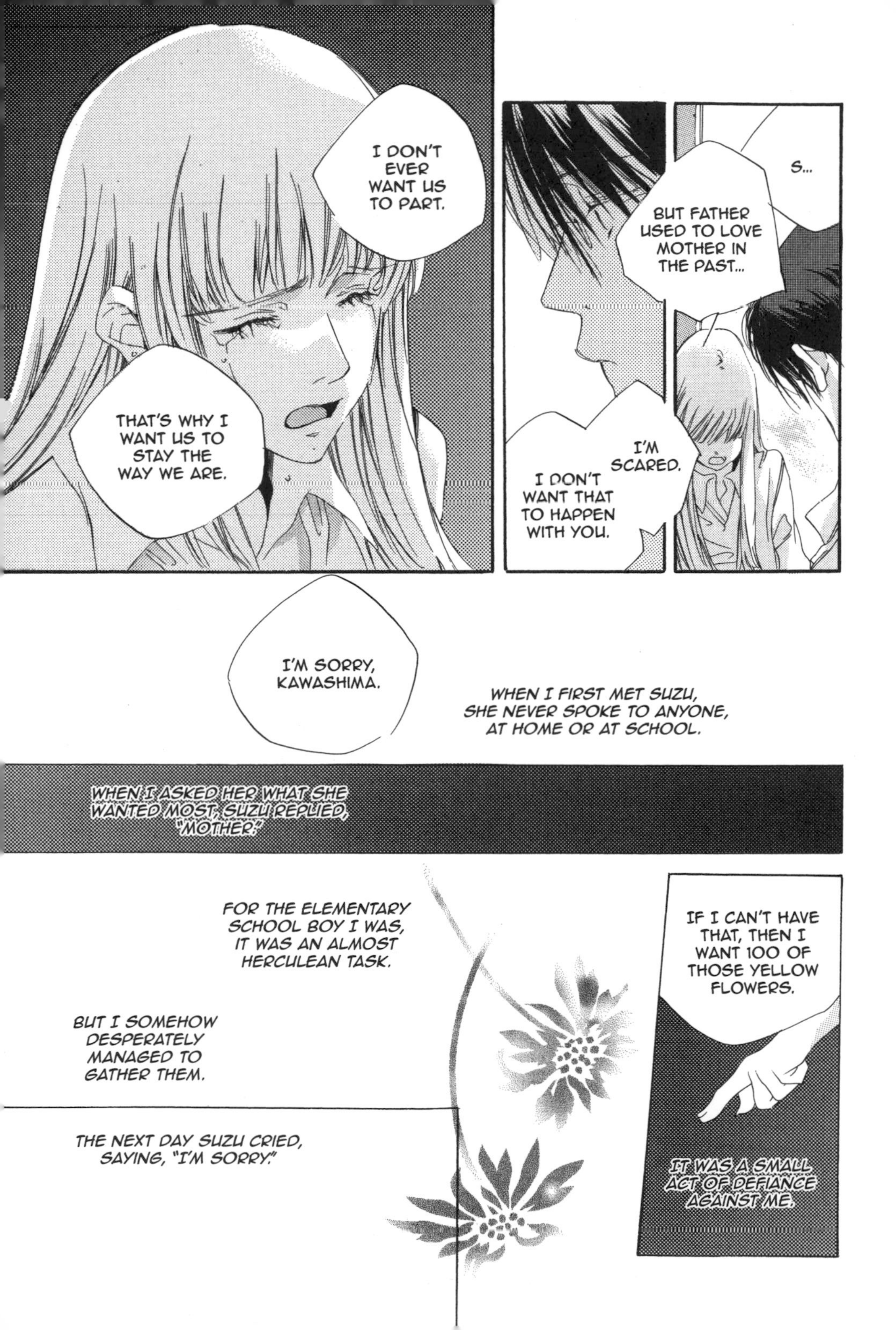
S...
BUT FATHER USED TO LOVE MOTHER IN THE PAST...
I'M SCARED.
I DON'T WANT THAT TO HAPPEN WITH YOU.
I DON'T EVER WANT US TO PART.
THAT'S WHY I WANT US TO STAY THE WAY WE ARE.
I'M SORRY, KAWASHIMA.
WHEN I FIRST MET SUZU, SHE NEVER SPOKE TO ANYONE, AT HOME OR AT SCHOOL.
WHEN I ASKED HER WHAT SHE WANTED MOST, SUZU REPLIED, "MOTHER."
IF I CAN'T HAVE THAT, THEN I WANT 100 OF THOSE YELLOW FLOWERS.
IT WAS A SMALL ACT OF DEFIANCE AGAINST ME.
FOR THE ELEMENTARY SCHOOL BOY I WAS, IT WAS AN ALMOST HERCULEAN TASK.
BUT I SOMEHOW DESPERATELY MANAGED TO GATHER THEM.
THE NEXT DAY SUZU CRIED, SAYING, "I'M SORRY."

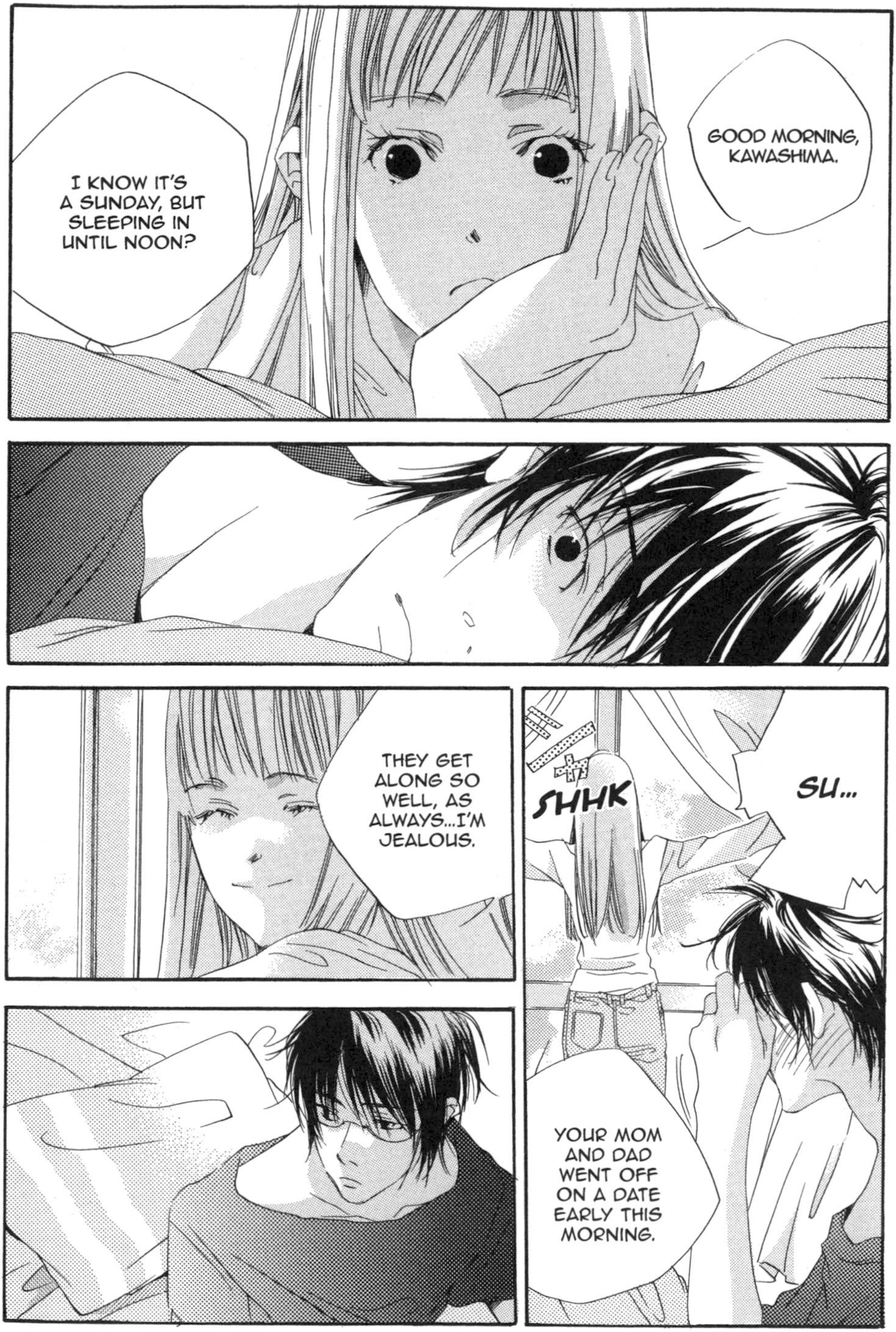
GOOD MORNING, KAWASHIMA.
I KNOW IT'S A SUNDAY, BUT SLEEPING IN UNTIL NOON?
SU...
SHHK
YOUR MOM AND DAD WENT OFF ON A DATE EARLY THIS MORNING.
THEY GET ALONG SO WELL, AS ALWAYS...I'M JEALOUS.

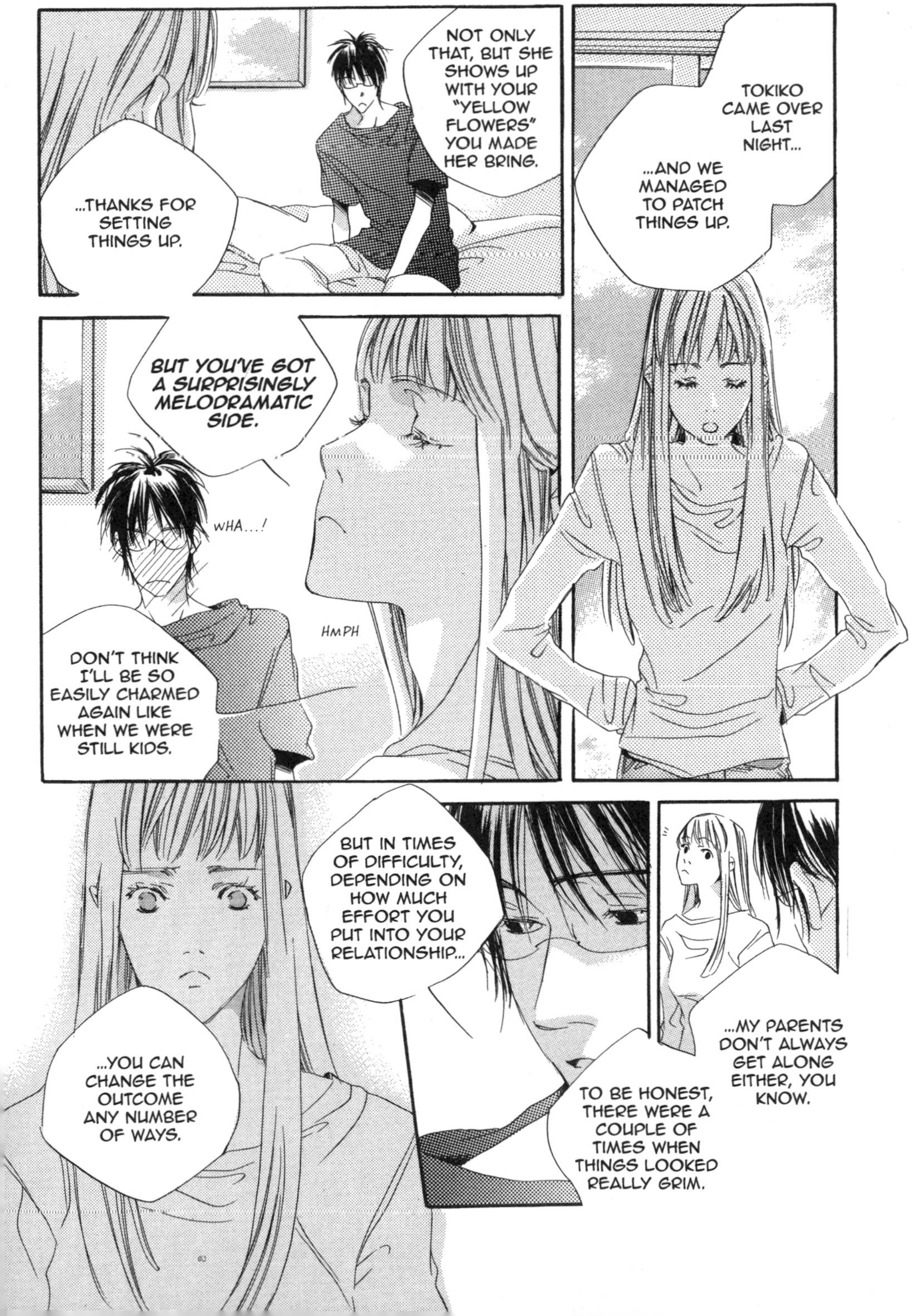
TOKIKO CAME OVER LAST NIGHT...
...AND WE MANAGED TO PATCH THINGS UP.
NOT ONLY THAT, BUT SHE SHOWS UP WITH YOUR "YELLOW FLOWERS" YOU MADE HER BRING.
...THANKS FOR SETTING THINGS UP.
BUT YOU'VE GOT A SURPRISINGLY MELODRAMATIC SIDE.
WHA...!
HMPH
DON'T THINK I'LL BE SO EASILY CHARMED AGAIN LIKE WHEN WE WERE STILL KIDS.
...MY PARENTS DON'T ALWAYS GET ALONG EITHER, YOU KNOW.
TO BE HONEST, THERE WERE A COUPLE OF TIMES WHEN THINGS LOOKED REALLY GRIM.
BUT IN TIMES OF DIFFICULTY, DEPENDING ON HOW MUCH EFFORT YOU PUT INTO YOUR RELATIONSHIP...
...YOU CAN CHANGE THE OUTCOME ANY NUMBER OF WAYS.

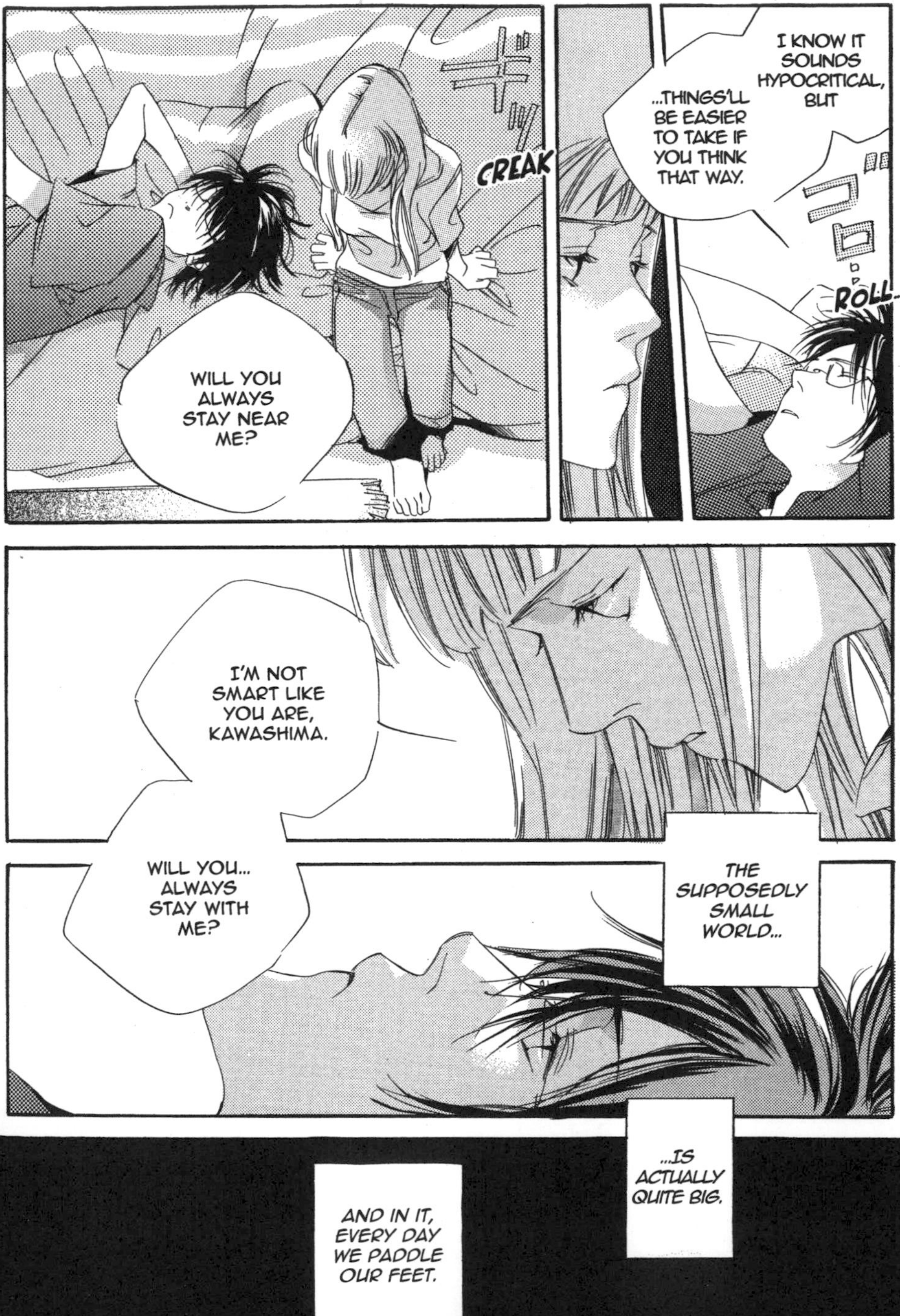

I KNOW IT SOUNDS HYPOCRITICAL, BUT
...THINGS'LL BE EASIER TO TAKE IF YOU THINK THAT WAY.
ROLL...
CREAK
WILL YOU ALWAYS STAY NEAR ME?
I'M NOT SMART LIKE YOU ARE, KAWASHIMA.
THE SUPPOSEDLY SMALL WORLD...
WILL YOU... ALWAYS STAY WITH ME?
...IS ACTUALLY QUITE BIG.
AND IN IT, EVERY DAY WE PADDLE OUR FEET.

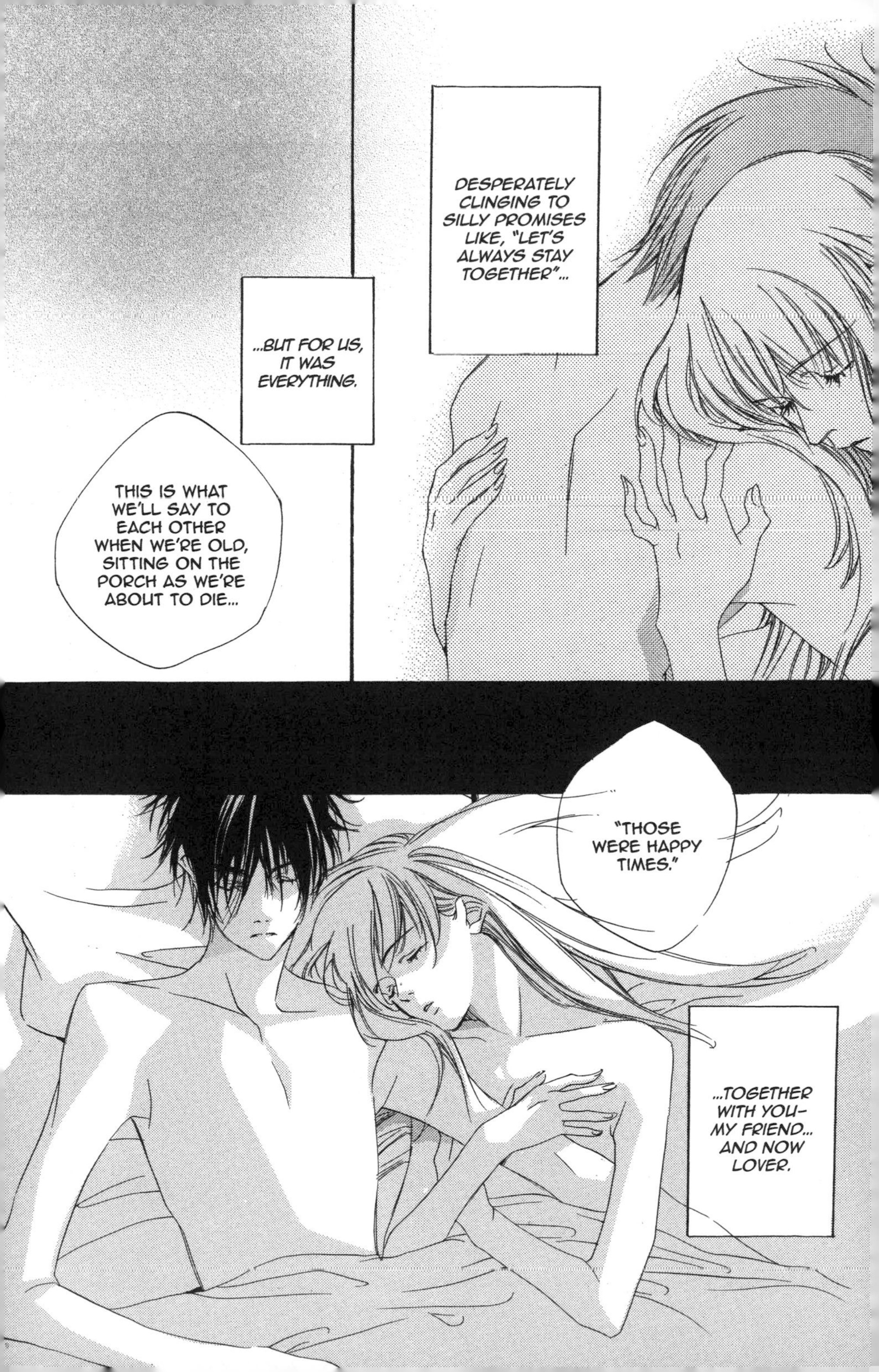
DESPERATELY CLINGING TO SILLY PROMISES LIKE, "LET'S ALWAYS STAY TOGETHER"...
...BUT FOR US, IT WAS EVERYTHING.
THIS IS WHAT WE'LL SAY TO EACH OTHER WHEN WE'RE OLD, SITTING ON THE PORCH AS WE'RE ABOUT TO DIE...
"THOSE WERE HAPPY TIMES."
...TOGETHER WITH YOU-MY FRIEND... AND NOW LOVER.

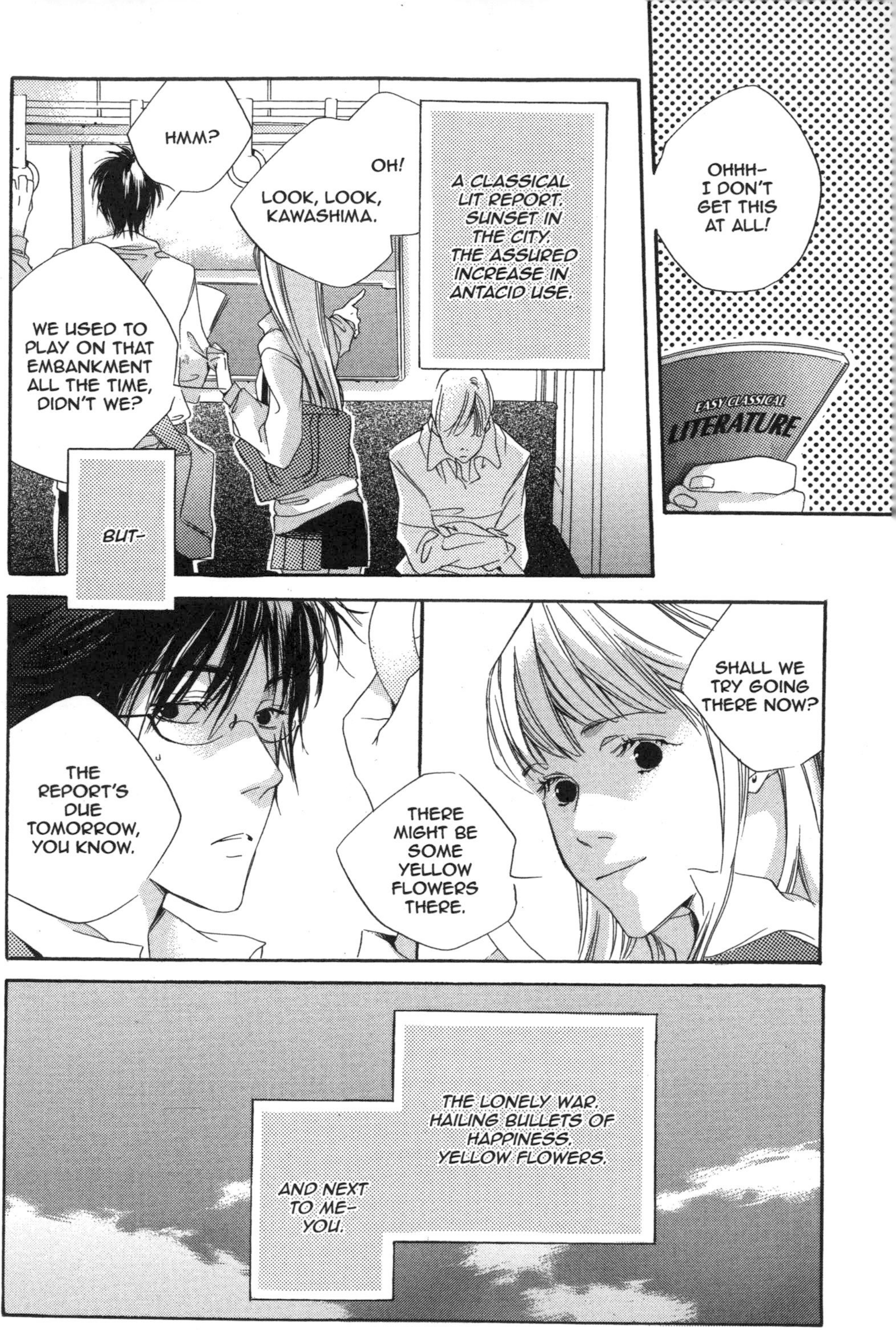
OHHH- I DON'T GET THIS AT ALL!
EASY CLASSICAL LITERATURE
A CLASSICAL LIT REPORT. SUNSET IN THE CITY. THE ASSURED INCREASE IN ANTACID USE.
OH!
LOOK, LOOK, KAWASHIMA.
HMM?
WE USED TO PLAY ON THAT EMBANKMENT ALL THE TIME, DIDN'T WE?
BUT-
SHALL WE TRY GOING THERE NOW?
THERE MIGHT BE SOME YELLOW FLOWERS THERE.
THE REPORT'S DUE TOMORROW, YOU KNOW.
THE LONELY WAR. HAILING BULLETS OF HAPPINESS. YELLOW FLOWERS.
AND NEXT TO ME- YOU.

THE LONELY WAR / END

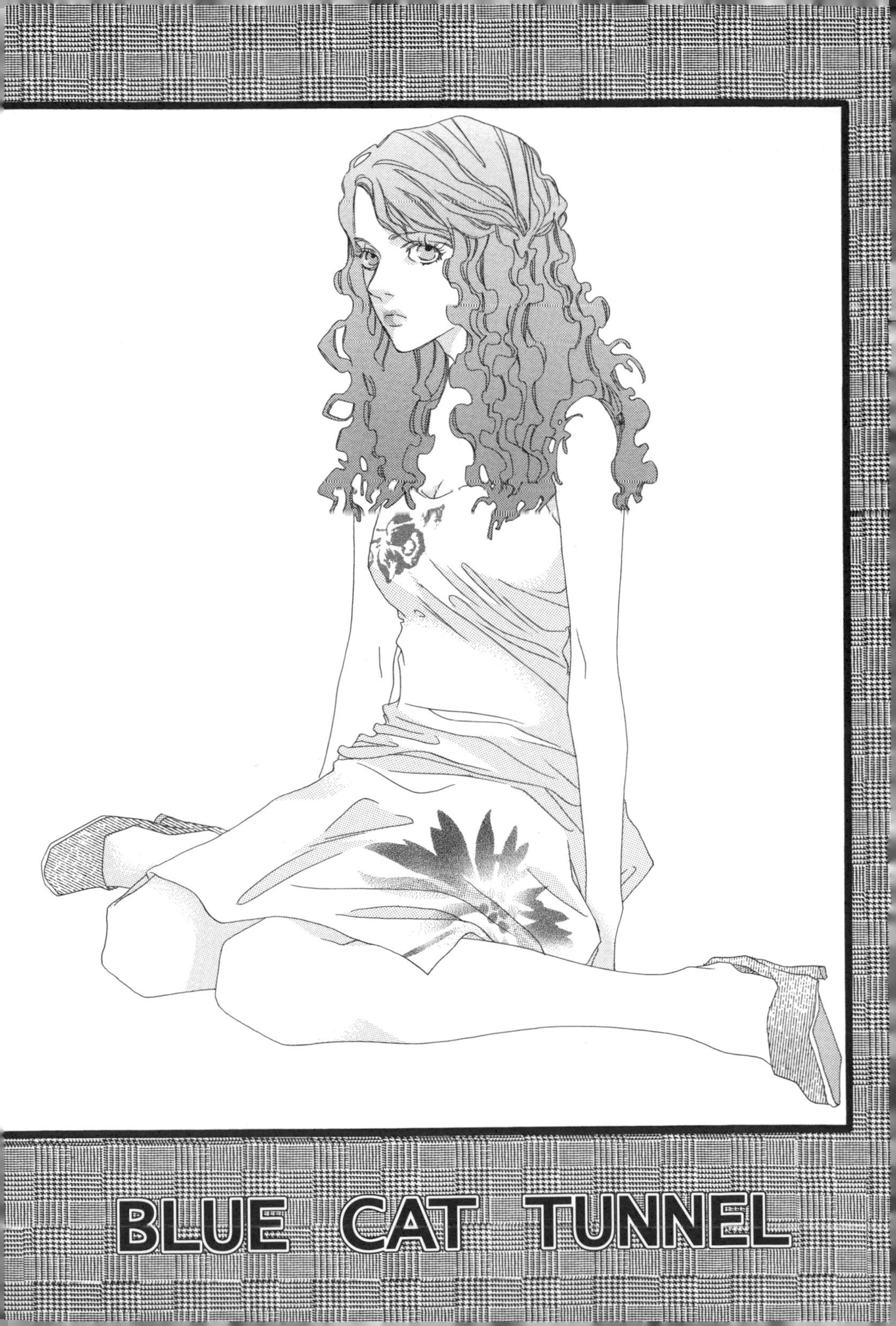

BLUE CAT TUNNEL

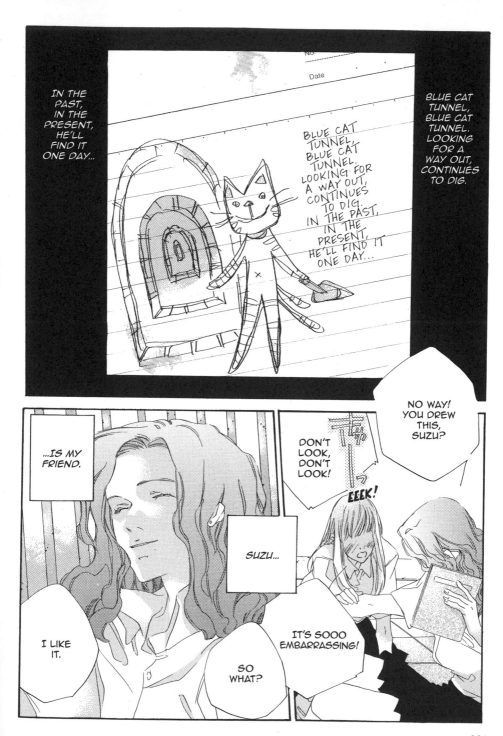

IN THE PAST, IN THE PRESENT, HE'LL FIND IT ONE DAY...

BLUE CAT TUNNEL, BLUE CAT TUNNEL. LOOKING FOR A WAY OUT, CONTINUES TO DIG. IN THE PAST, IN THE PRESENT, HE'LL FIND IT ONE DAY...

BLUE CAT TUNNEL, BLUE CAT TUNNEL. LOOKING FOR A WAY OUT, CONTINUES TO DIG.

NO WAY! YOU DREW THIS, SUZU?

DON'T LOOK, DON'T LOOK!

EEEK!

...IS MY FRIEND.

SUZU...

I LIKE IT.

SO WHAT?

IT'S SOOO EMBARRASSING!

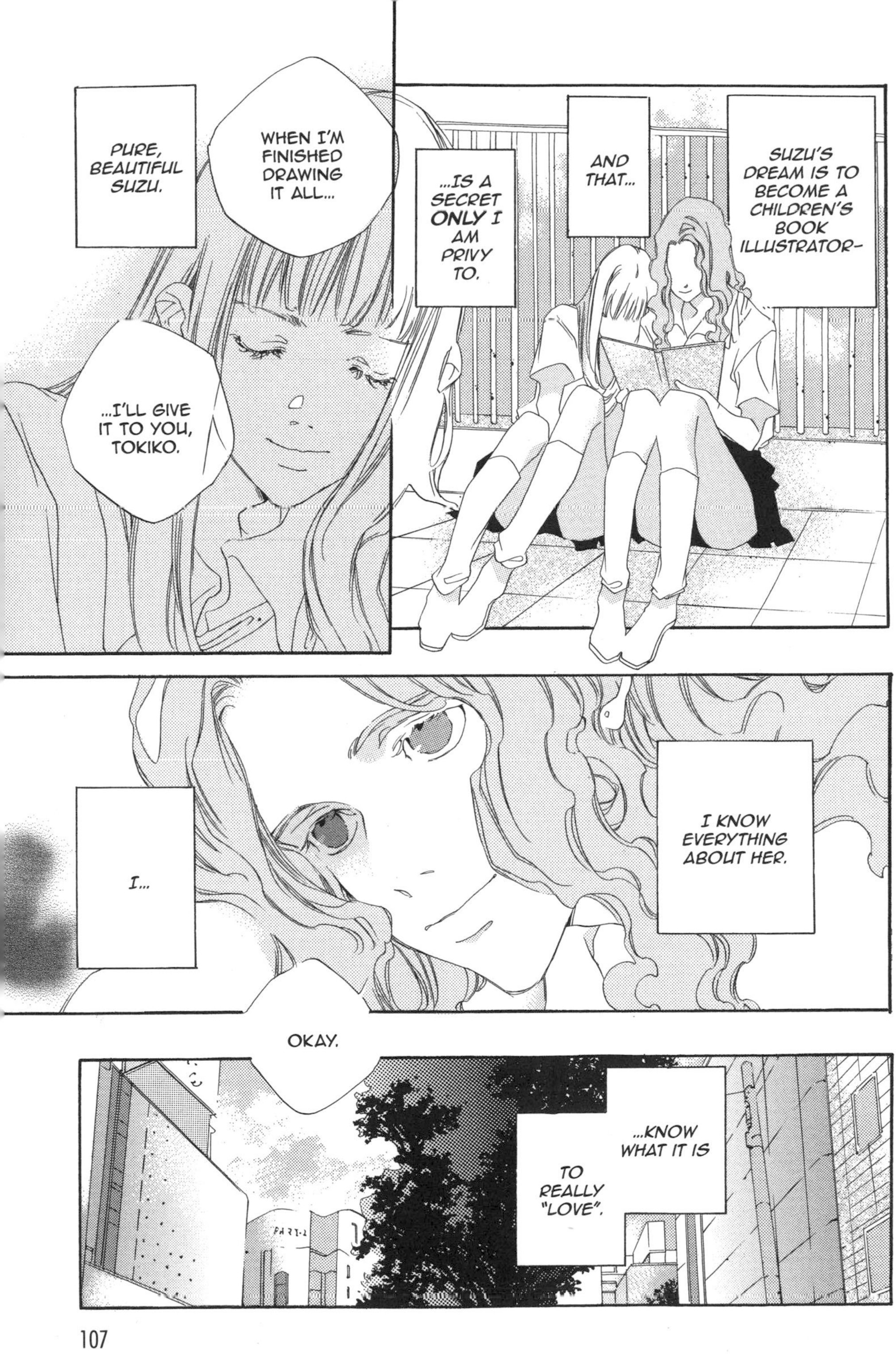
SUZU'S DREAM IS TO BECOME A CHILDREN'S BOOK ILLUSTRATOR-
AND THAT...
...IS A SECRET ONLY I AM PRIVY TO.
WHEN I'M FINISHED DRAWING IT ALL...
PURE, BEAUTIFUL SUZU.
...I'LL GIVE IT TO YOU, TOKIKO.
I KNOW EVERYTHING ABOUT HER.
I...
OKAY.
...KNOW WHAT IT IS
TO REALLY "LOVE".

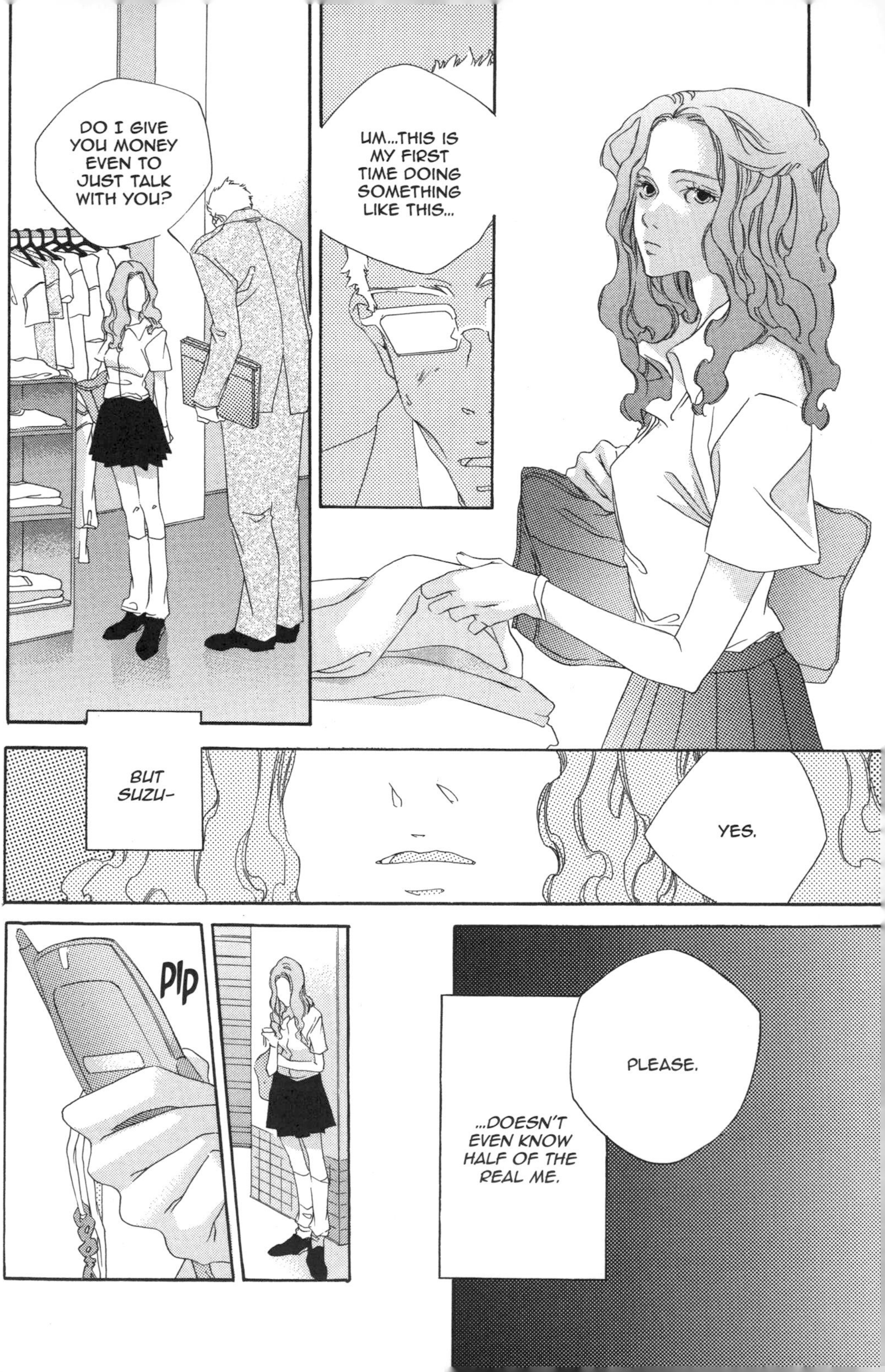
UM...THIS IS MY FIRST TIME DOING SOMETHING LIKE THIS...
DO I GIVE YOU MONEY EVEN TO JUST TALK WITH YOU?
YES.
BUT SUZU-
PLEASE.
...DOESN'T EVEN KNOW HALF OF THE REAL ME.
PIP

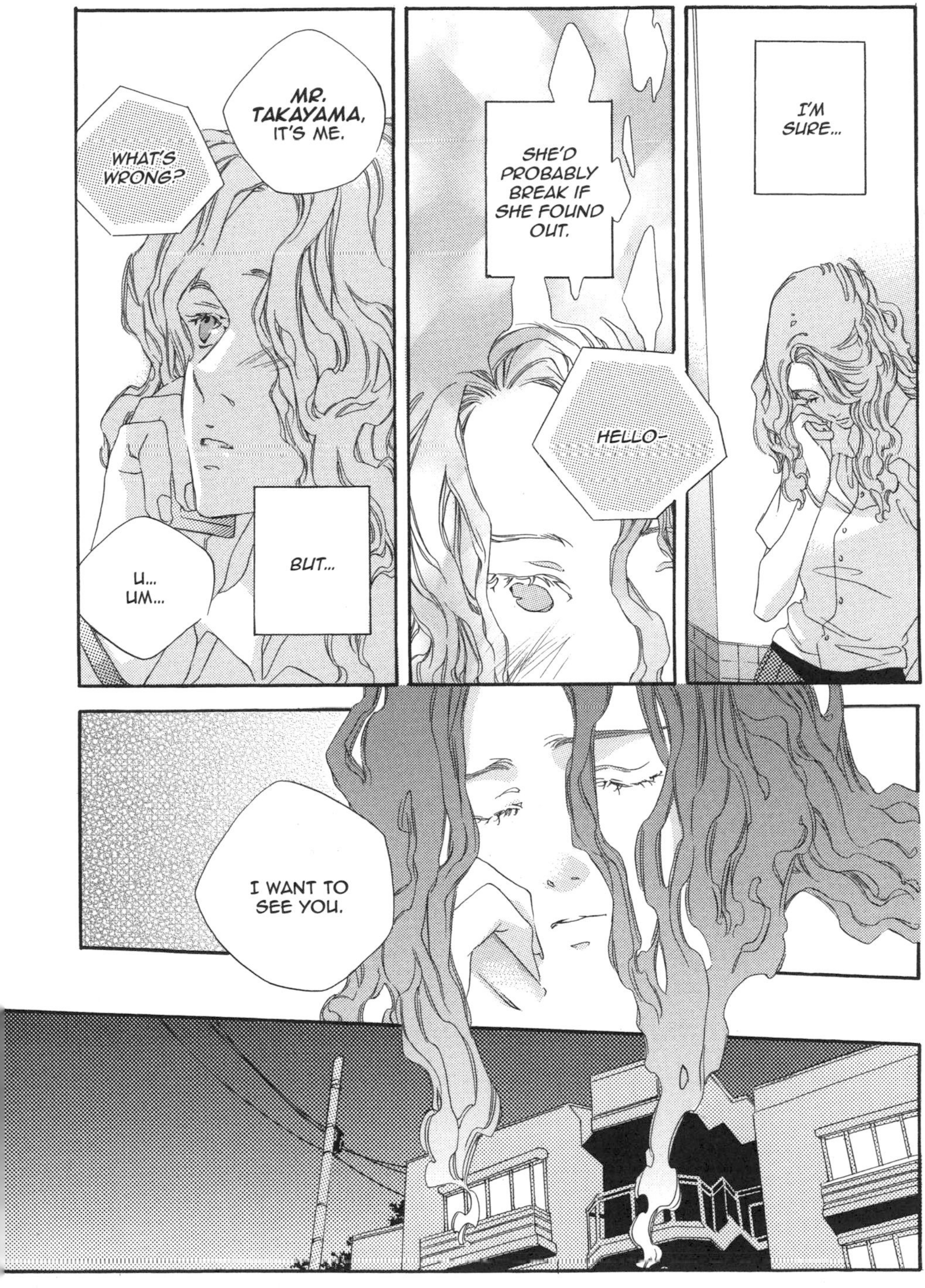
I'M SURE...
SHE'D PROBABLY BREAK IF SHE FOUND OUT.
HELLO-
MR. TAKAYAMA, IT'S ME.
WHAT'S WRONG?
BUT...
U... UM...
I WANT TO SEE YOU.

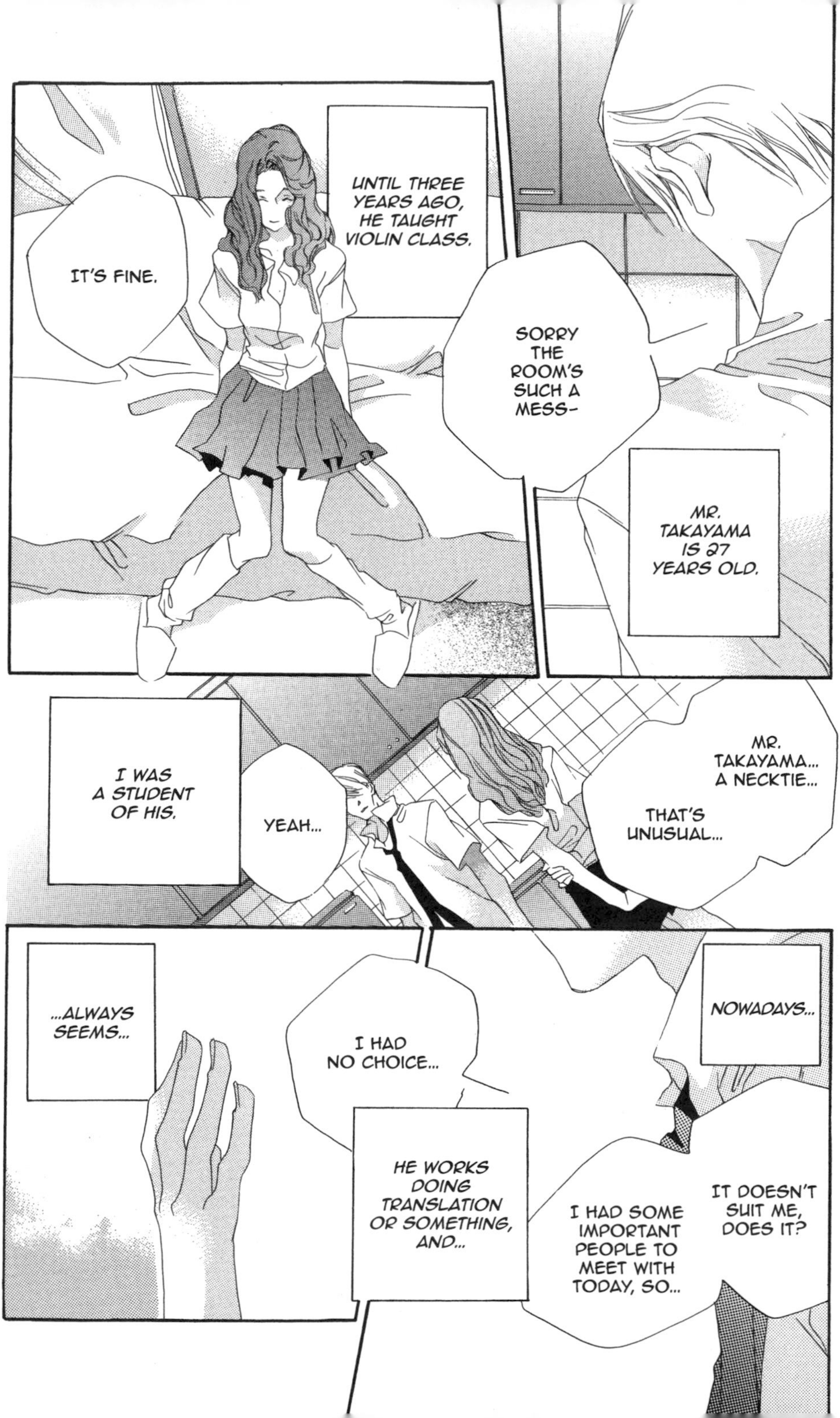
SORRY THE ROOM'S SUCH A MESS-
MR. TAKAYAMA IS 27 YEARS OLD.
UNTIL THREE YEARS AGO, HE TAUGHT VIOLIN CLASS.
IT'S FINE.
MR. TAKAYAMA... A NECKTIE...
THAT'S UNUSUAL...
YEAH...
I WAS A STUDENT OF HIS.
NOWADAYS...
I HAD NO CHOICE...
IT DOESN'T SUIT ME, DOES IT?
I HAD SOME IMPORTANT PEOPLE TO MEET WITH TODAY, SO...
HE WORKS DOING TRANSLATION OR SOMETHING, AND...
...ALWAYS SEEMS...

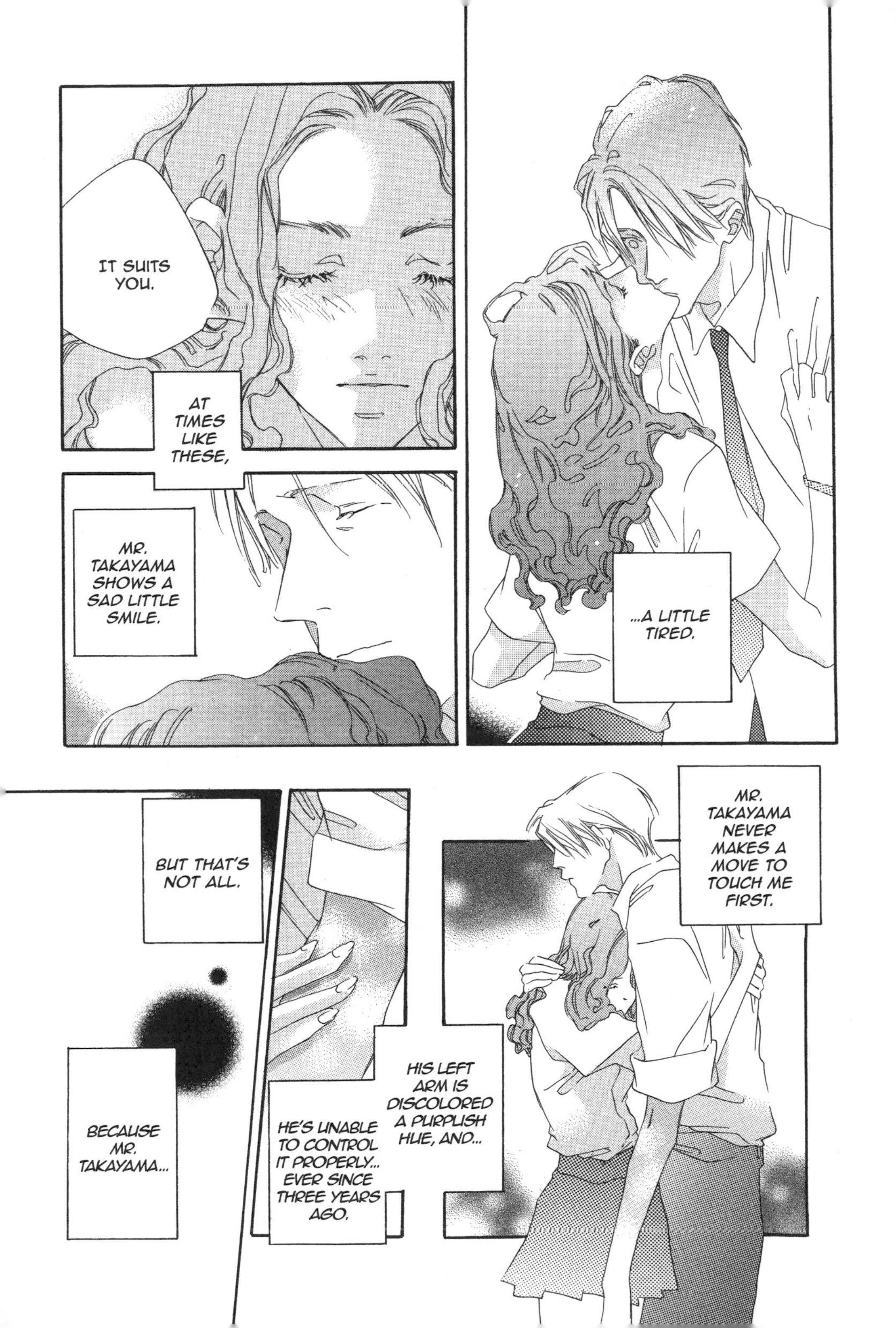
...A LITTLE TIRED.
IT SUITS YOU.
AT TIMES LIKE THESE,
MR. TAKAYAMA SHOWS A SAD LITTLE SMILE.
MR. TAKAYAMA NEVER MAKES A MOVE TO TOUCH ME FIRST.
HIS LEFT ARM IS DISCOLORED A PURPLISH HUE, AND...
HE'S UNABLE TO CONTROL IT PROPERLY... EVER SINCE THREE YEARS AGO.
BUT THAT'S NOT ALL.
BECAUSE MR. TAKAYAMA...

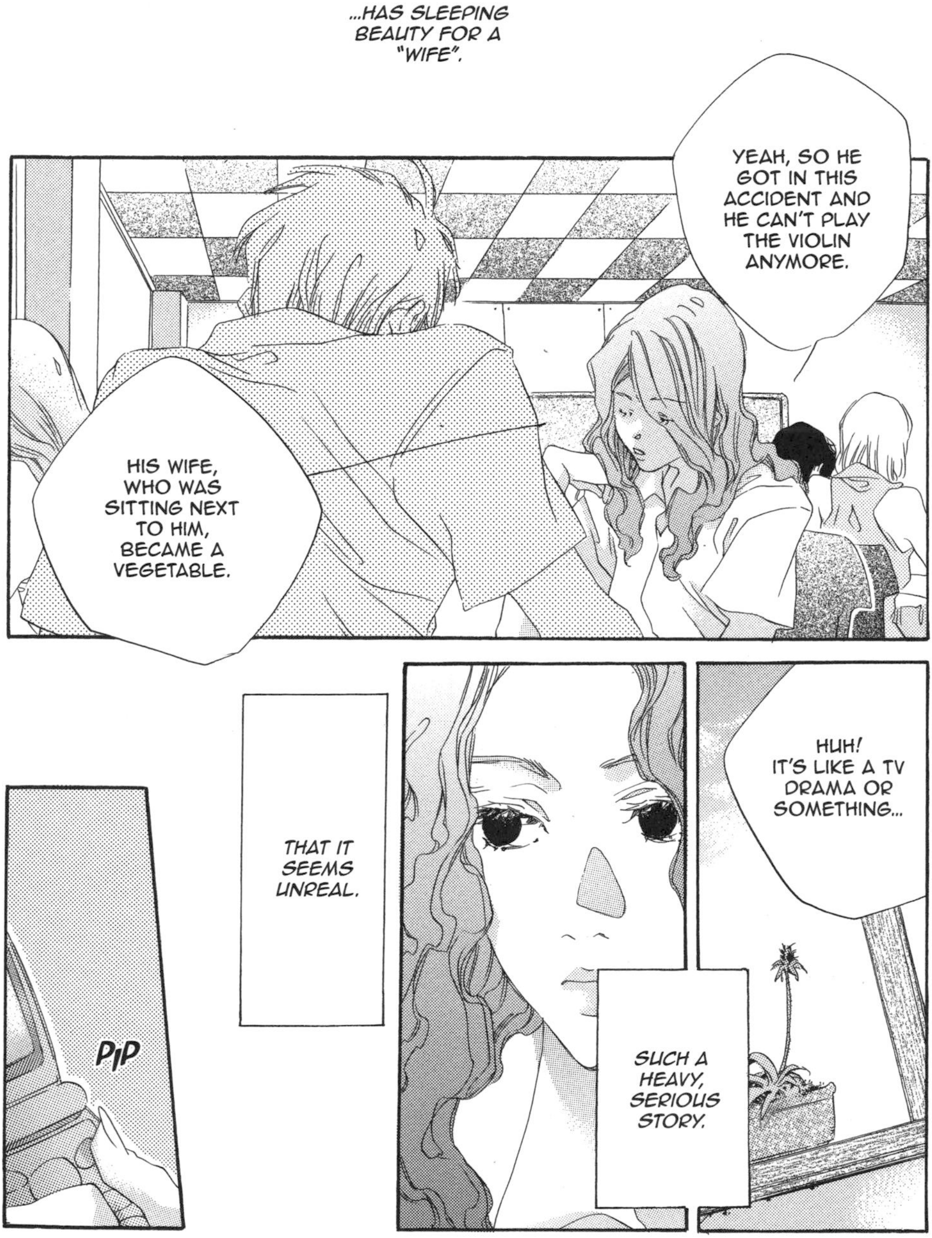
...HAS SLEEPING BEAUTY FOR A "WIFE".
YEAH, SO HE GOT IN THIS ACCIDENT AND HE CAN'T PLAY THE VIOLIN ANYMORE.
HIS WIFE, WHO WAS SITTING NEXT TO HIM, BECAME A VEGETABLE.
HUH! IT'S LIKE A TV DRAMA OR SOMETHING...
SUCH A HEAVY, SERIOUS STORY.
THAT IT SEEMS UNREAL.
PIP

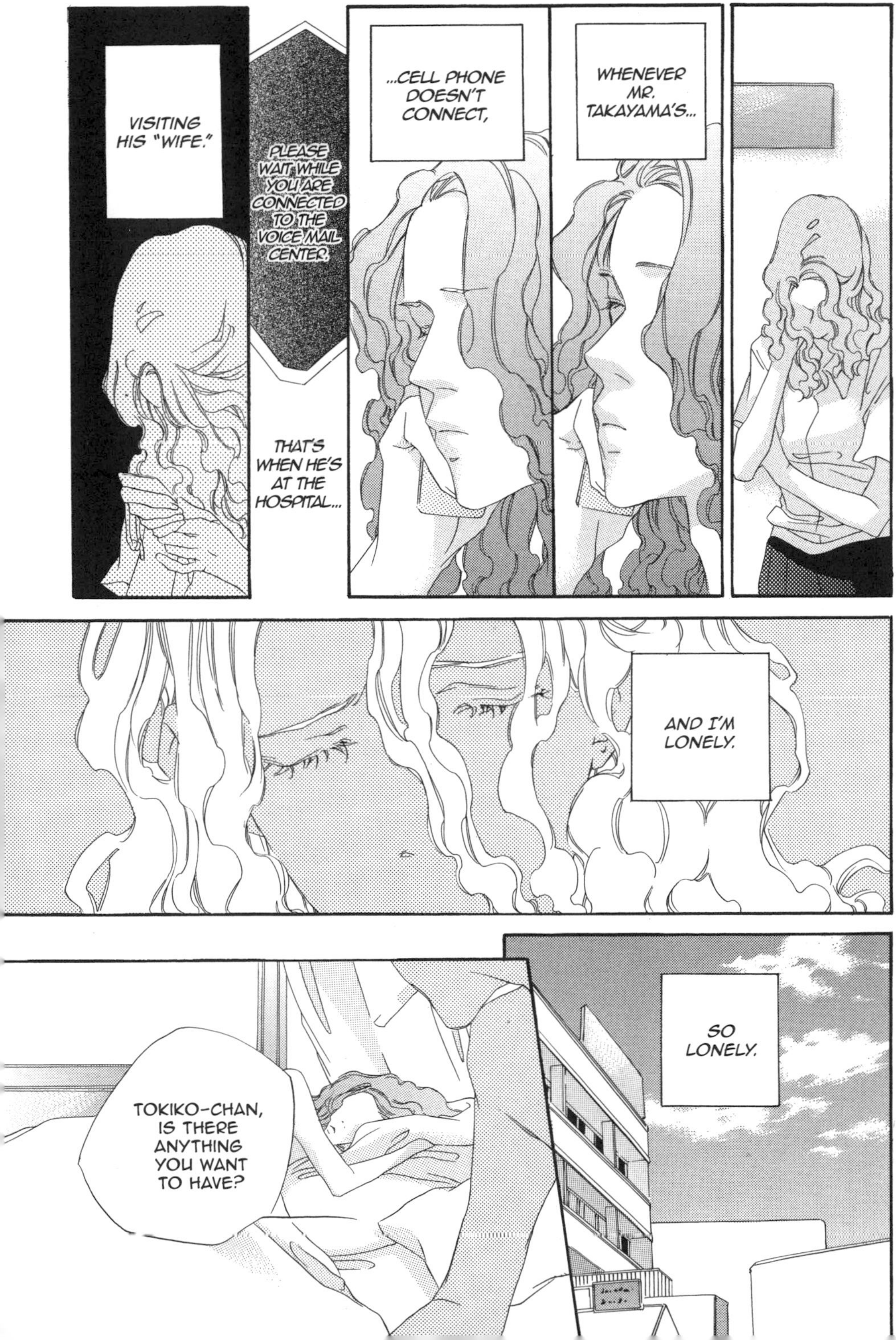
WHENEVER MR. TAKAYAMA'S...
...CELL PHONE DOESN'T CONNECT,
PLEASE WAIT WHILE YOU ARE CONNECTED TO THE VOICE MAIL CENTER.
THAT'S WHEN HE'S AT THE HOSPITAL...
VISITING HIS "WIFE."
AND I'M LONELY.
SO LONELY.
TOKIKO-CHAN, IS THERE ANYTHING YOU WANT TO HAVE?

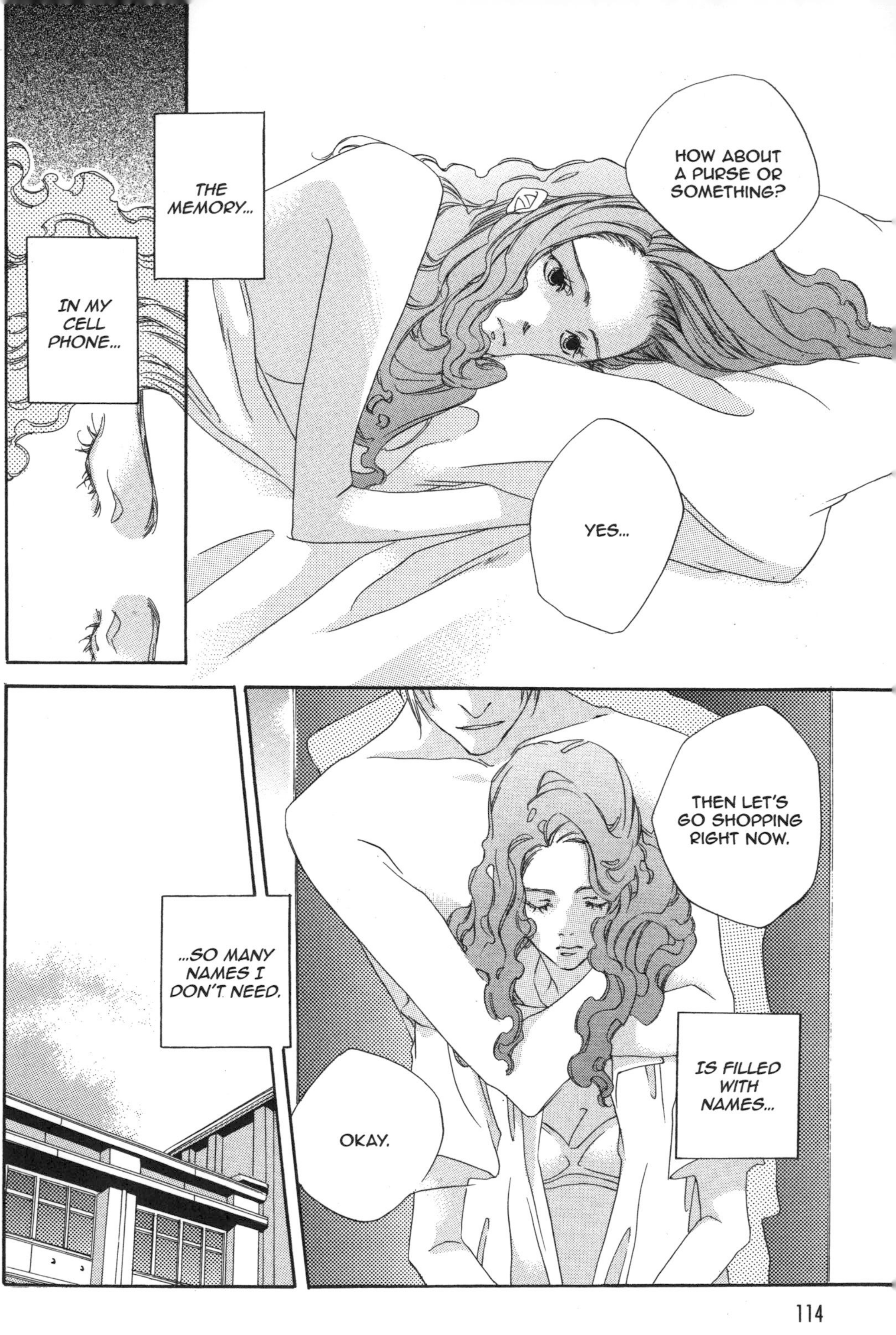
HOW ABOUT A PURSE OR SOMETHING?
THE MEMORY...
YES...
IN MY CELL PHONE...
THEN LET'S GO SHOPPING RIGHT NOW.
IS FILLED WITH NAMES...
OKAY.
...SO MANY NAMES I DON'T NEED.

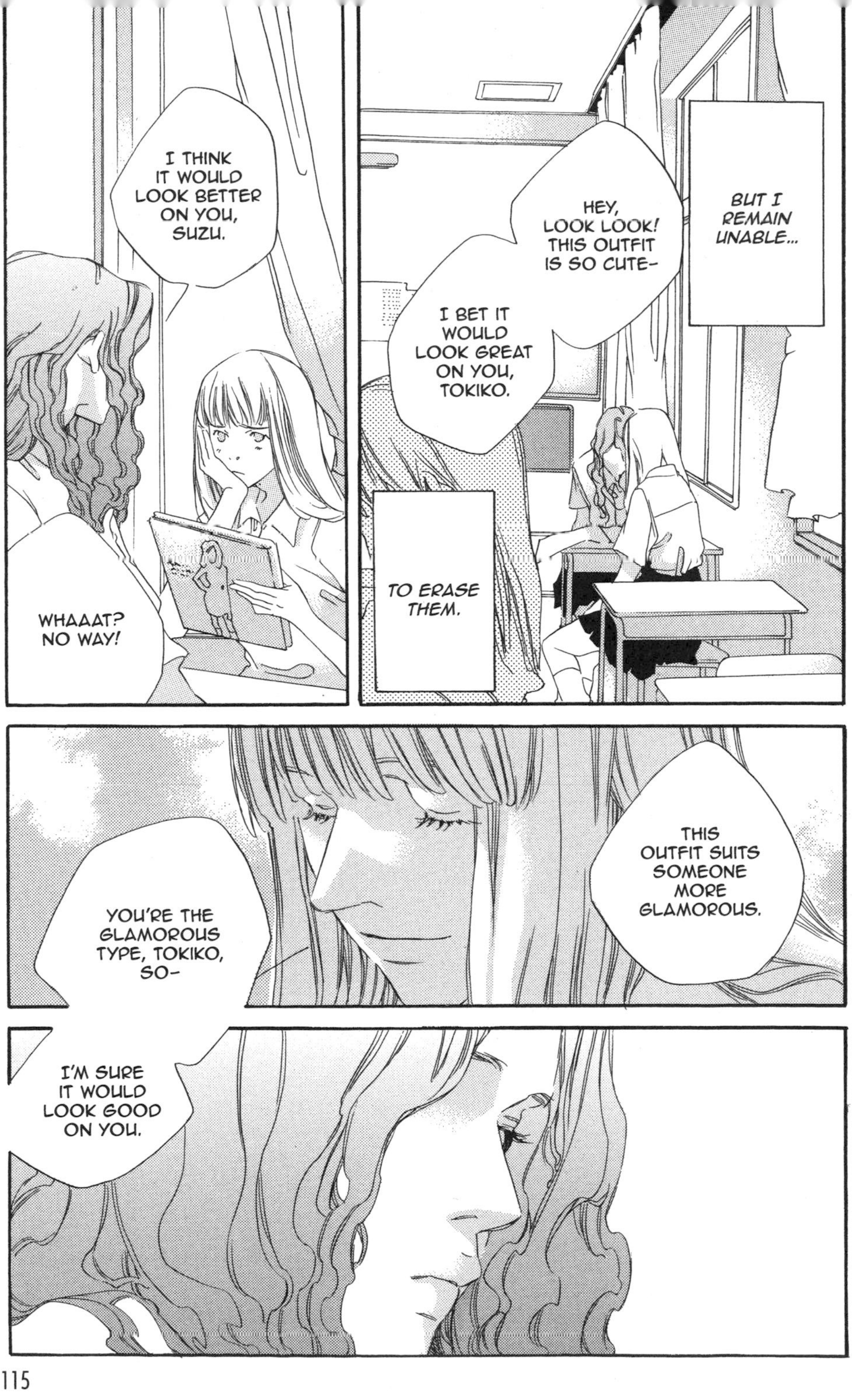
BUT I REMAIN UNABLE...
HEY, LOOK LOOK! THIS OUTFIT IS SO CUTE-
I BET IT WOULD LOOK GREAT ON YOU, TOKIKO.
TO ERASE THEM.
I THINK IT WOULD LOOK BETTER ON YOU, SUZU.
WHAAAT? NO WAY!
THIS OUTFIT SUITS SOMEONE MORE GLAMOROUS.
YOU'RE THE GLAMOROUS TYPE, TOKIKO, SO-
I'M SURE IT WOULD LOOK GOOD ON YOU.

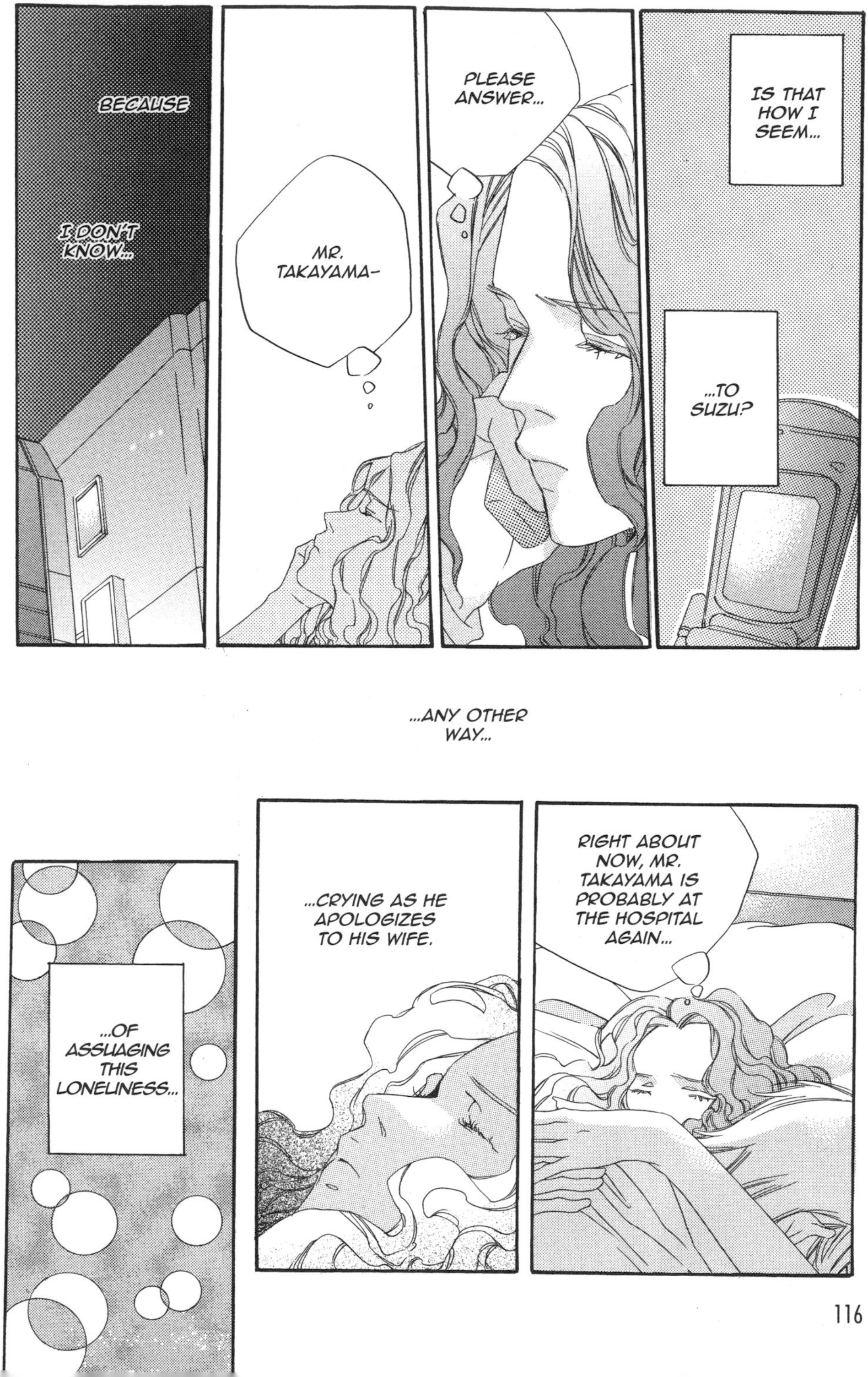
IS THAT HOW I SEEM...
...TO SUZU?
PLEASE ANSWER...
MR. TAKAYAMA-
BECAUSE
I DON'T KNOW...
...ANY OTHER WAY...
RIGHT ABOUT NOW, MR. TAKAYAMA IS PROBABLY AT THE HOSPITAL AGAIN...
...CRYING AS HE APOLOGIZES TO HIS WIFE.
...OF ASSUAGING THIS LONELINESS...

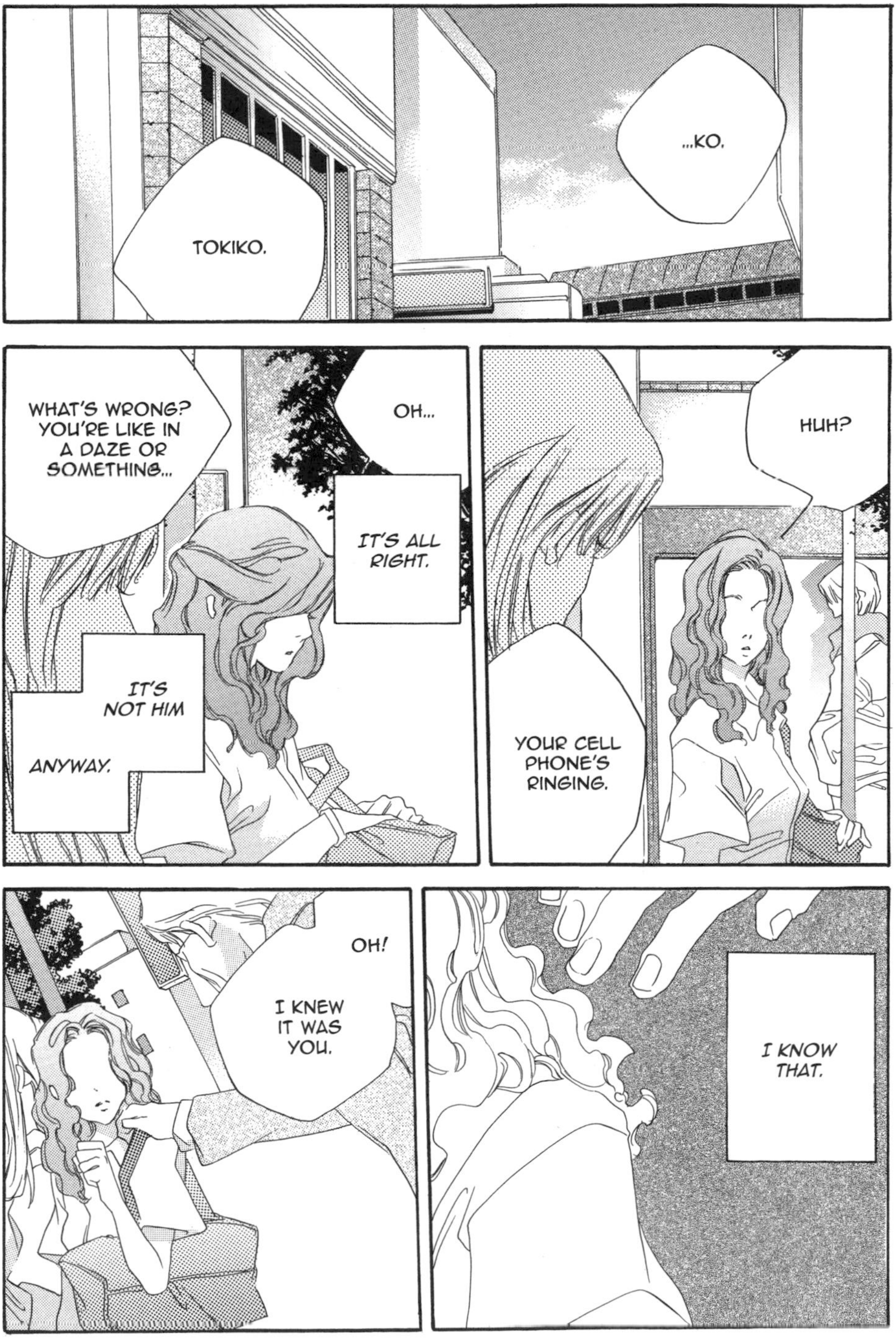
...KO.
TOKIKO.
HUH?
YOUR CELL PHONE'S RINGING.
OH...
WHAT'S WRONG? YOU'RE LIKE IN A DAZE OR SOMETHING...
IT'S ALL RIGHT.
IT'S NOT HIM ANYWAY.
I KNOW THAT.
OH!
I KNEW IT WAS YOU.

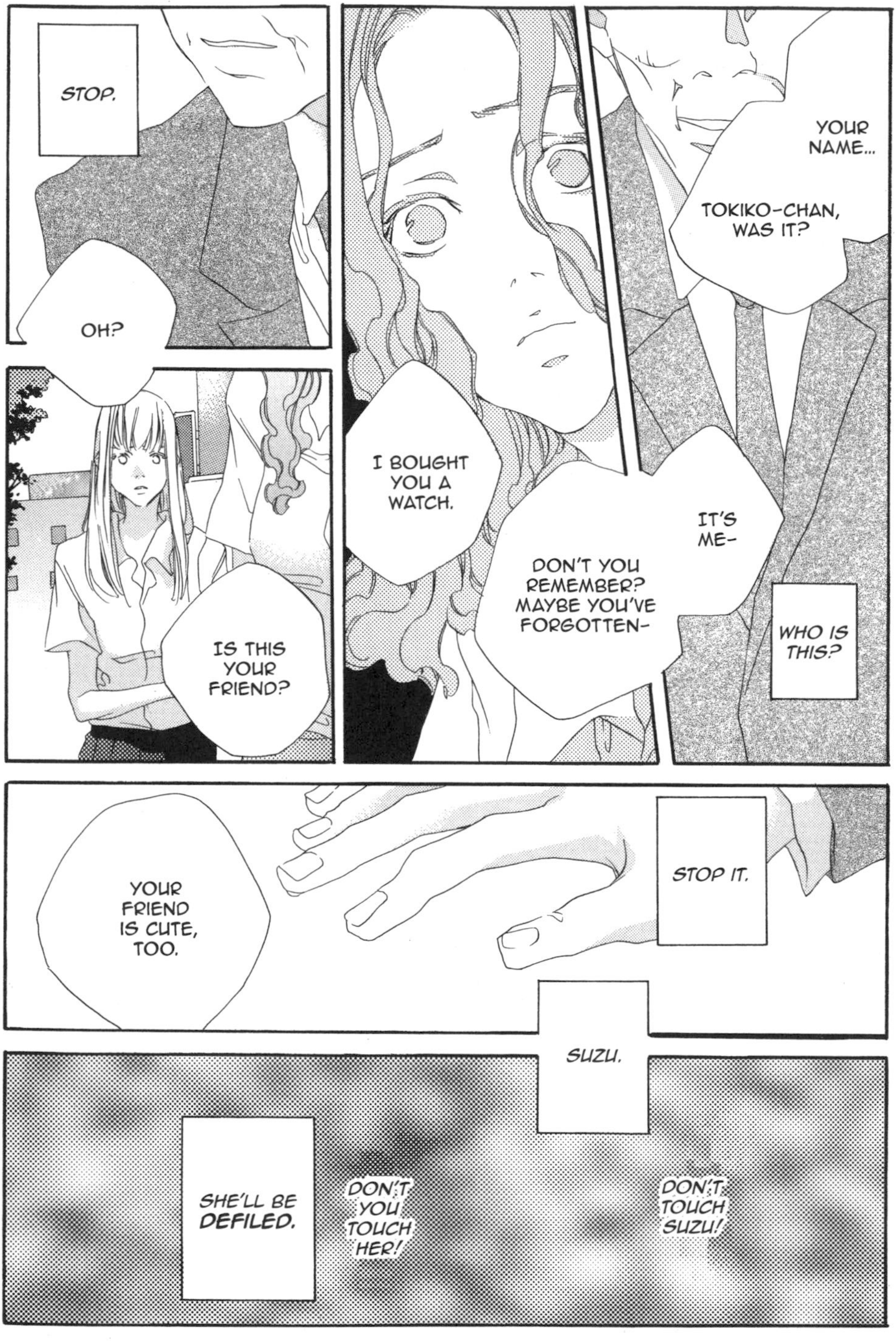
YOUR NAME...
TOKIKO-CHAN, WAS IT?
WHO IS THIS?
IT'S ME-
DON'T YOU REMEMBER? MAYBE YOU'VE FORGOTTEN-
I BOUGHT YOU A WATCH.
STOP.
OH?
IS THIS YOUR FRIEND?
STOP IT.
YOUR FRIEND IS CUTE, TOO.
SUZU.
DON'T TOUCH SUZU!
DON'T YOU TOUCH HER!
SHE'LL BE DEFILED.

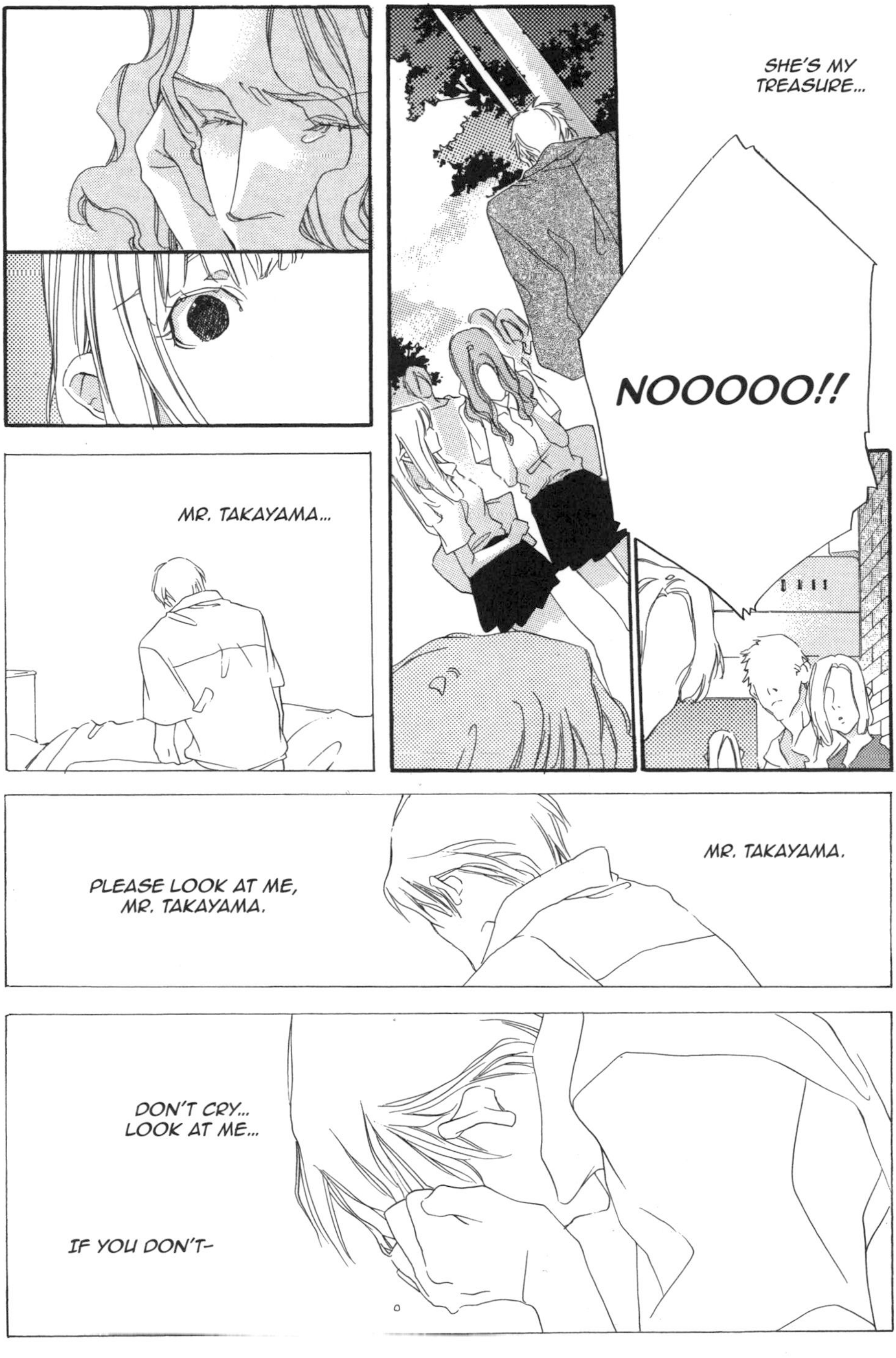
SHE'S MY TREASURE...
NOOOOO!!
MR. TAKAYAMA...
MR. TAKAYAMA.
PLEASE LOOK AT ME, MR. TAKAYAMA.
DON'T CRY... LOOK AT ME...
IF YOU DON'T-

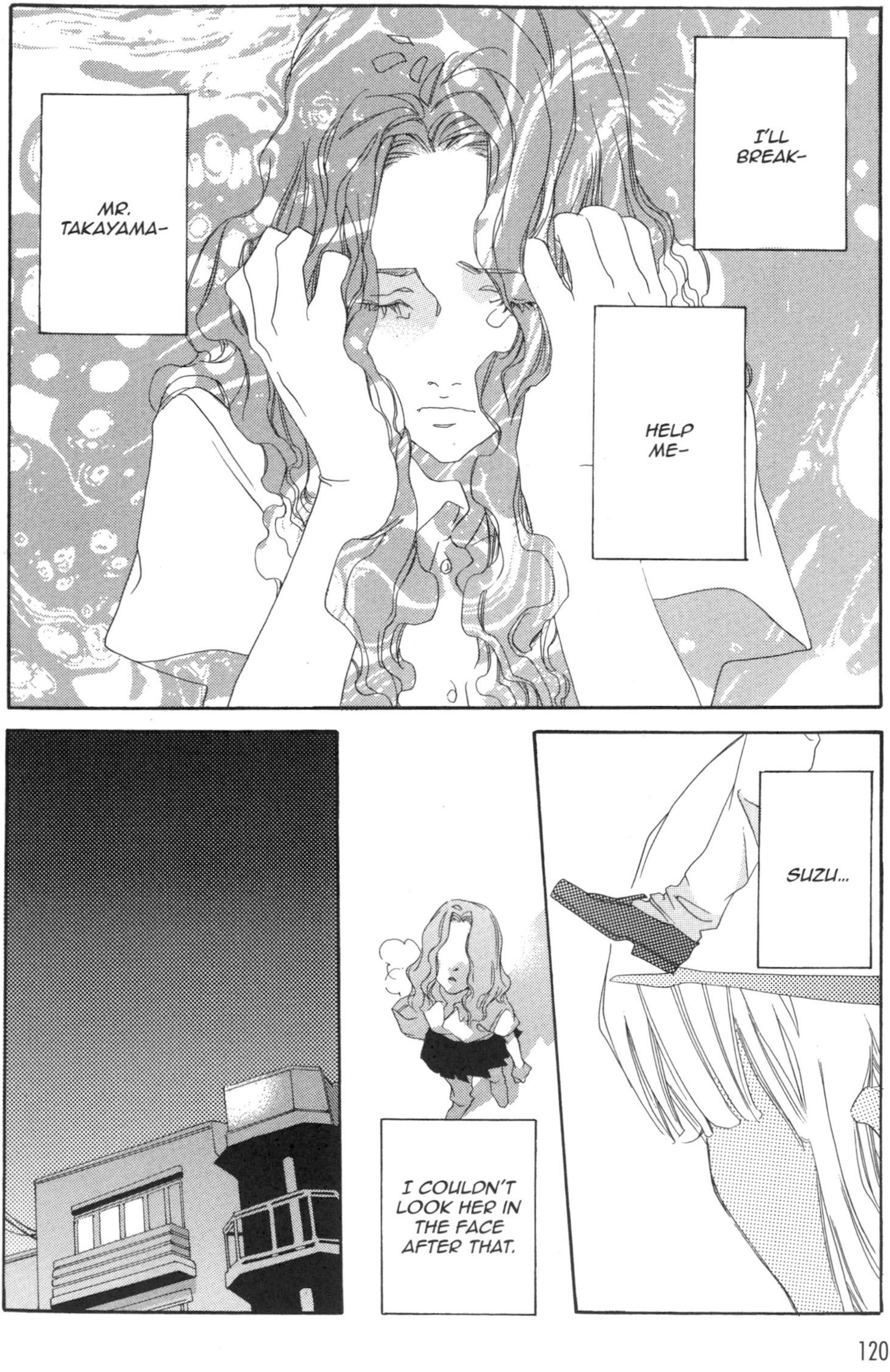
I'LL BREAK-
HELP ME-
MR. TAKAYAMA-
SUZU...
I COULDN'T LOOK HER IN THE FACE AFTER THAT.

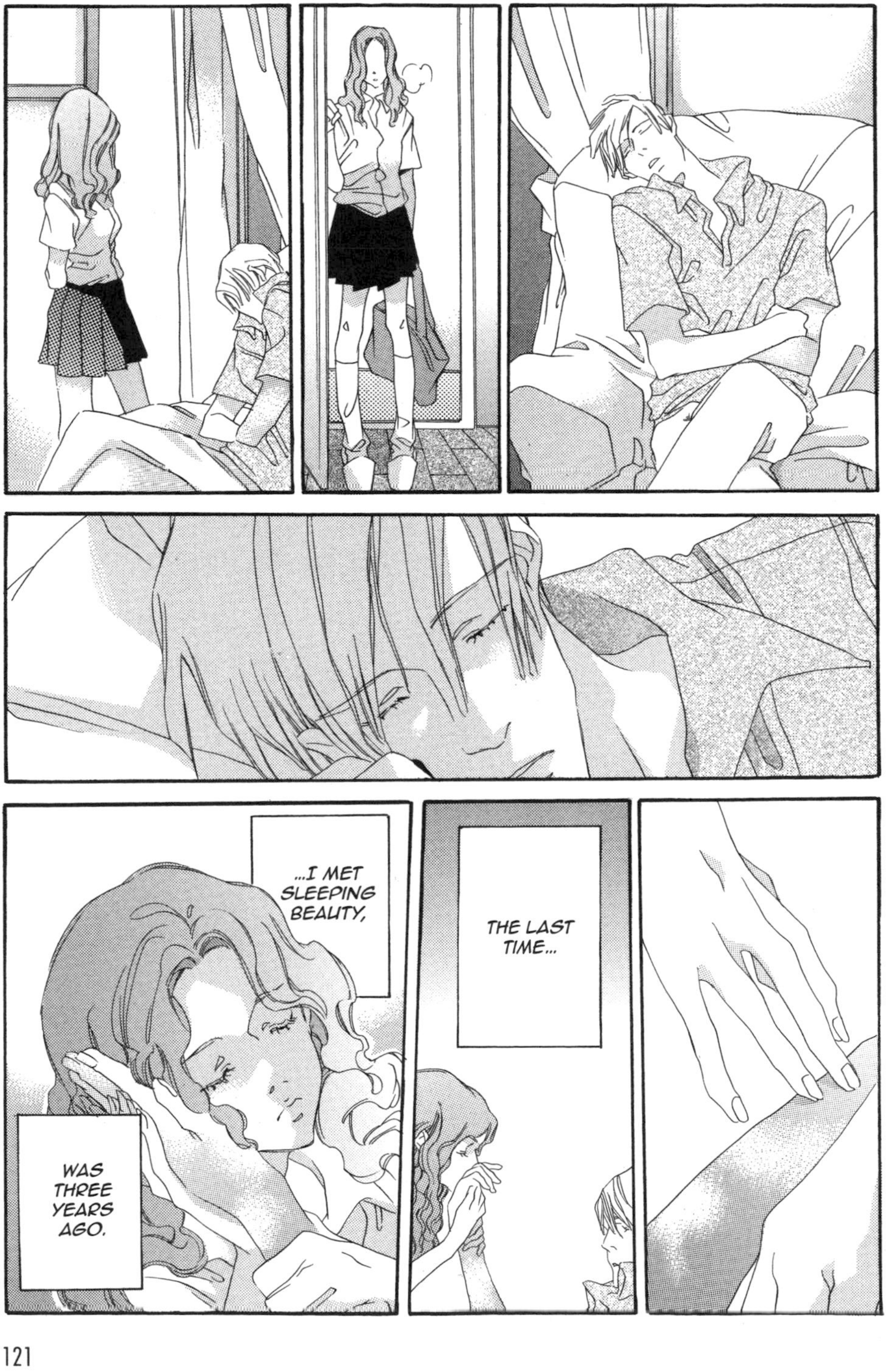
THE LAST TIME...
...I MET SLEEPING BEAUTY,
WAS THREE YEARS AGO.

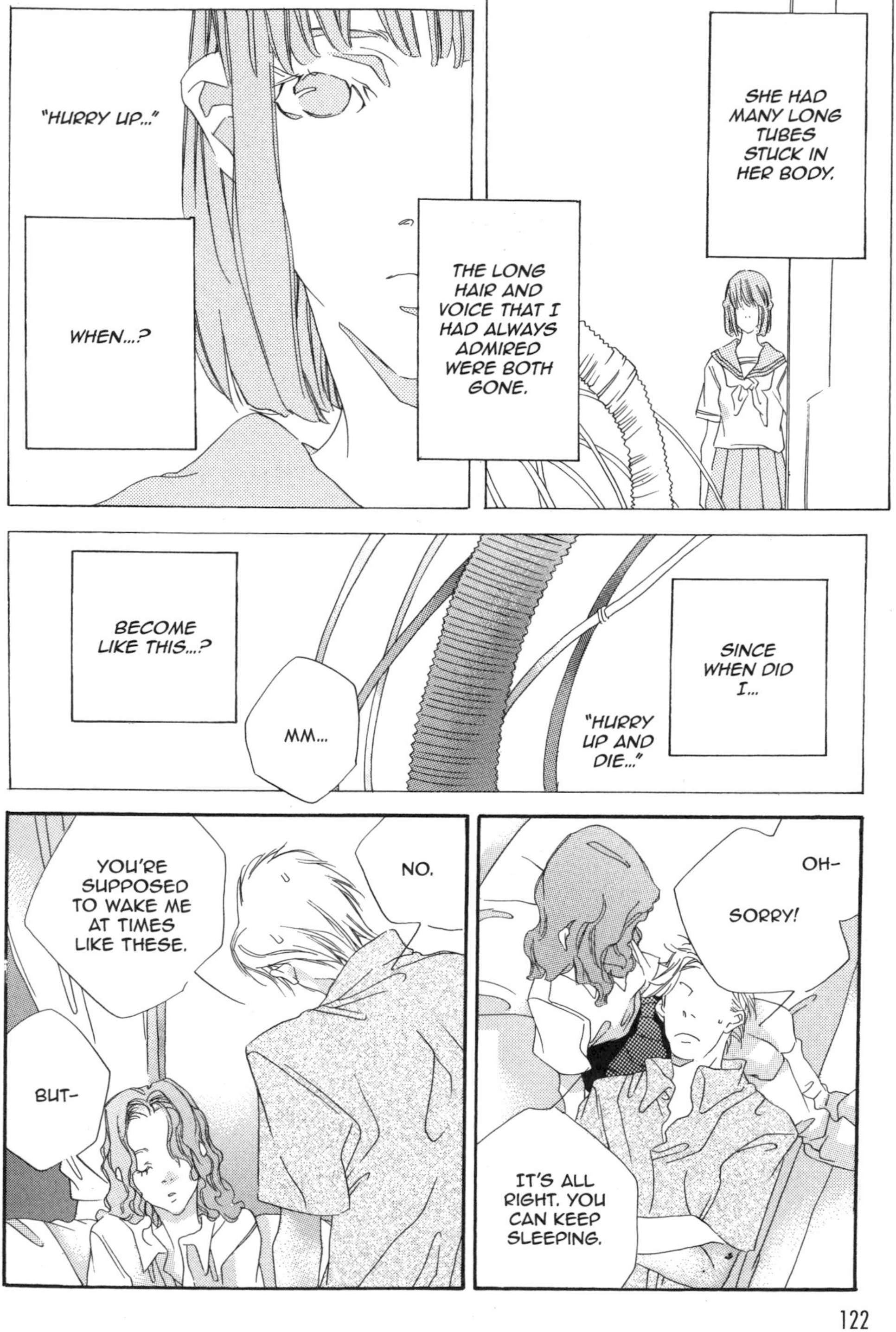
SHE HAD MANY LONG TUBES STUCK IN HER BODY.
THE LONG HAIR AND VOICE THAT I HAD ALWAYS ADMIRED WERE BOTH GONE.
"HURRY UP..."
WHEN...?
SINCE WHEN DID I...
"HURRY UP AND DIE..."
MM...
BECOME LIKE THIS...?
OH-
SORRY!
IT'S ALL RIGHT. YOU CAN KEEP SLEEPING.
NO.
YOU'RE SUPPOSED TO WAKE ME AT TIMES LIKE THESE.
BUT-

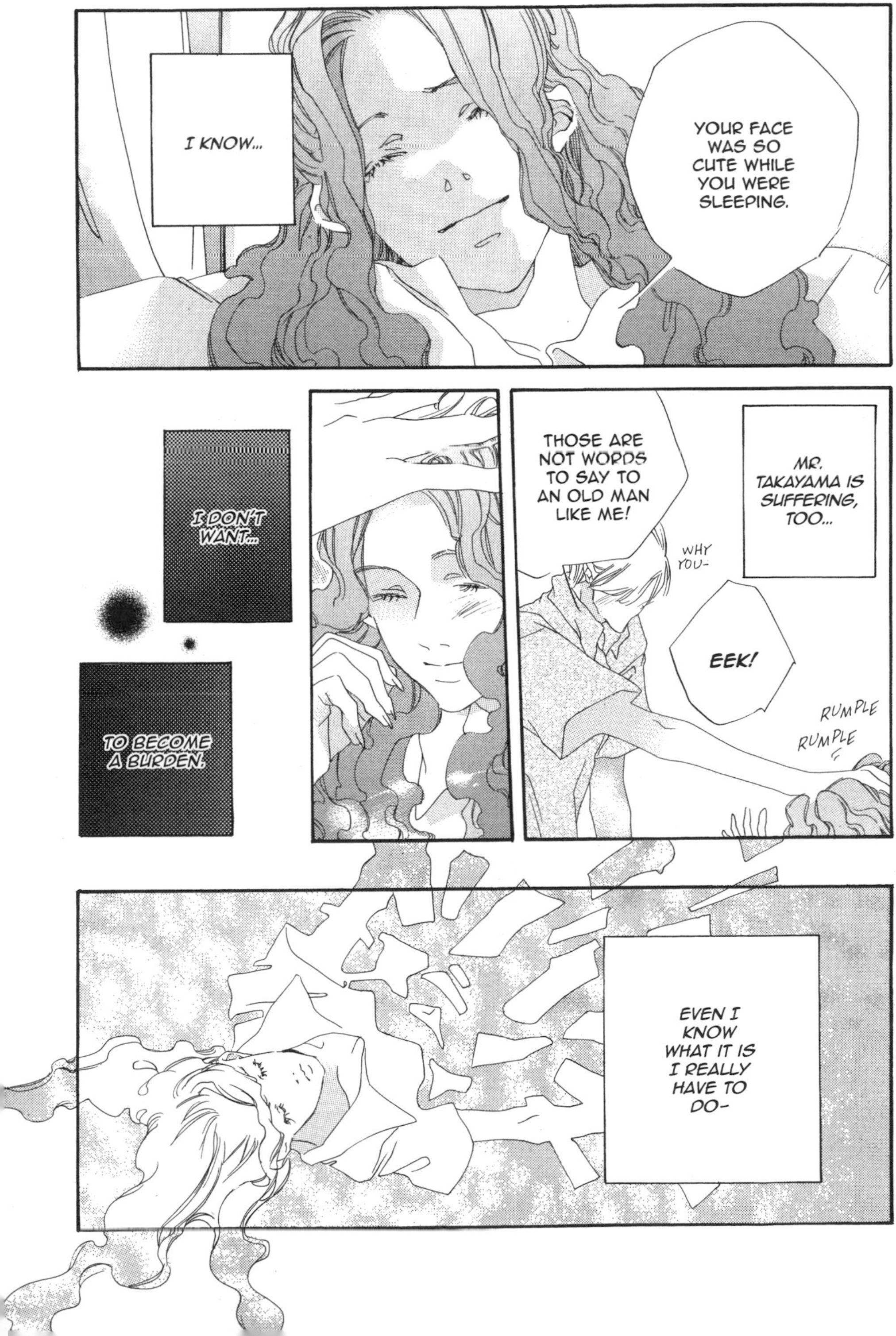
YOUR FACE WAS SO CUTE WHILE YOU WERE SLEEPING.
I KNOW...
MR. TAKAYAMA IS SUFFERING, TOO...
THOSE ARE NOT WORDS TO SAY TO AN OLD MAN LIKE ME!
WHY YOU-
EEK!
RUMPLE RUMPLE
I DON'T WANT...
TO BECOME A BURDEN.
EVEN I KNOW WHAT IT IS I REALLY HAVE TO DO-

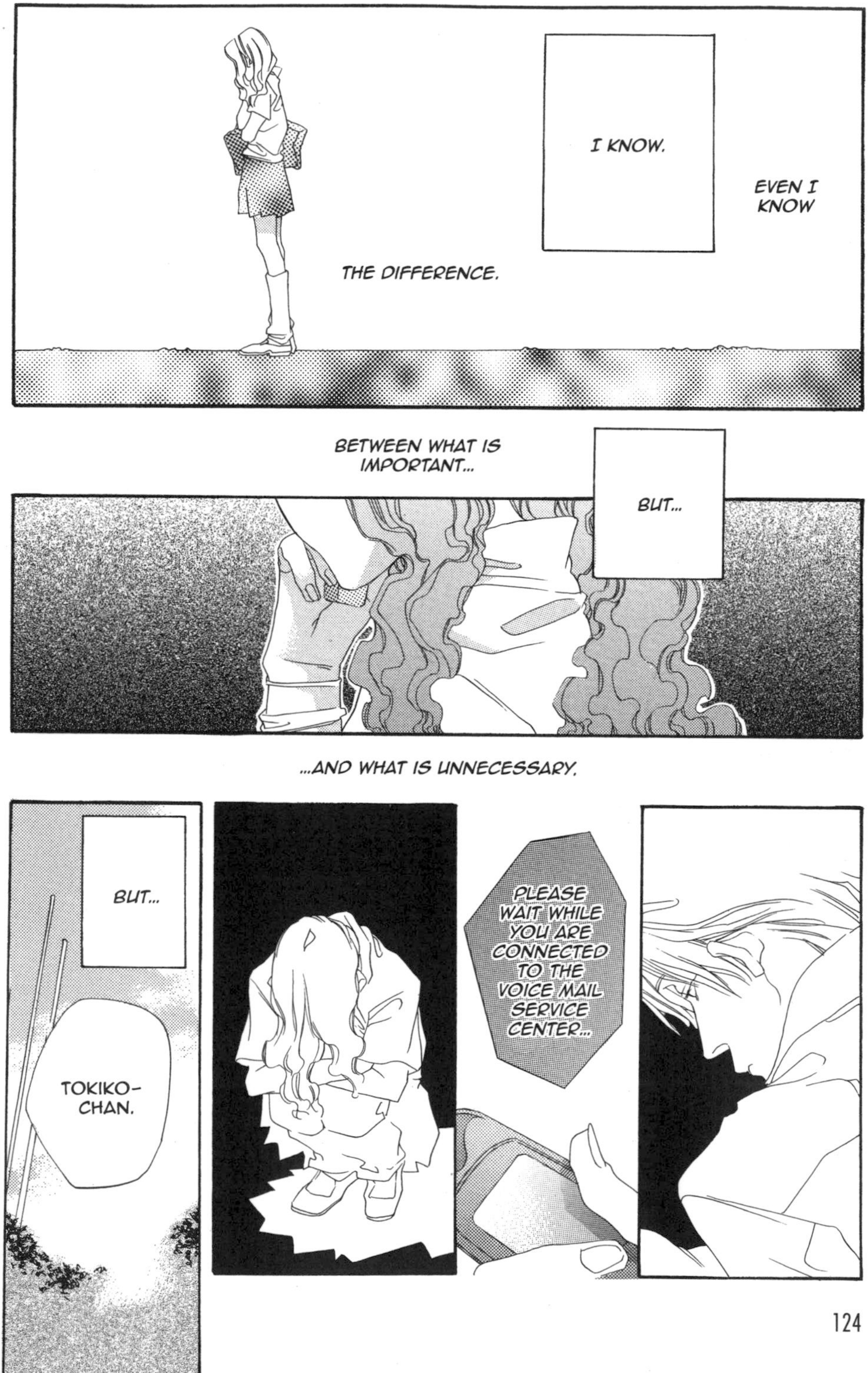
I KNOW.
EVEN I KNOW
THE DIFFERENCE.
BETWEEN WHAT IS IMPORTANT...
...AND WHAT IS UNNECESSARY.
BUT...
PLEASE WAIT WHILE YOU ARE CONNECTED TO THE VOICE MAIL SERVICE CENTER...
BUT...
TOKIKO-CHAN.

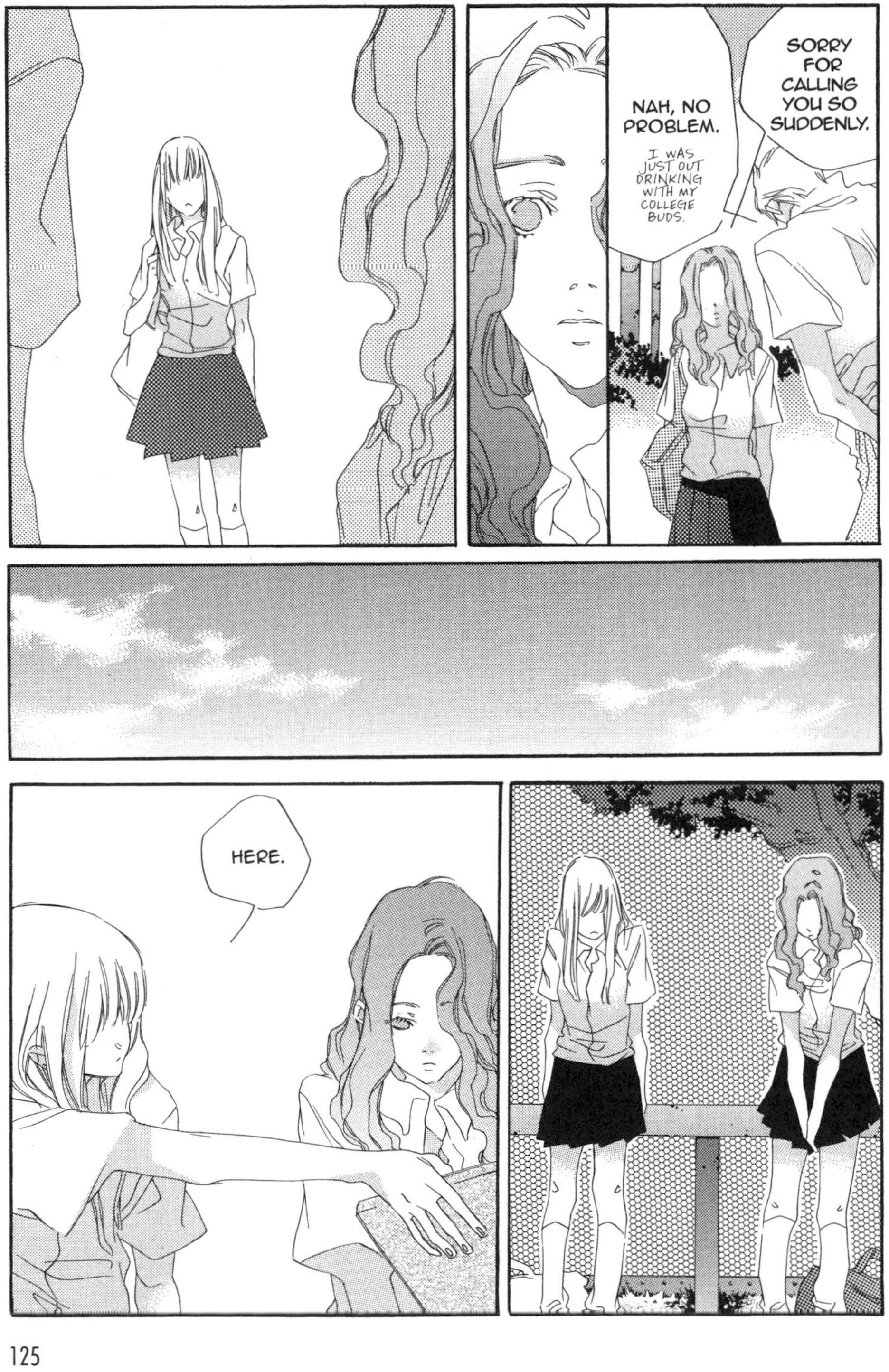
SORRY FOR CALLING YOU SO SUDDENLY.
NAH, NO PROBLEM.
I WAS JUST OUT DRINKING WITH MY COLLEGE BUDS.
HERE.

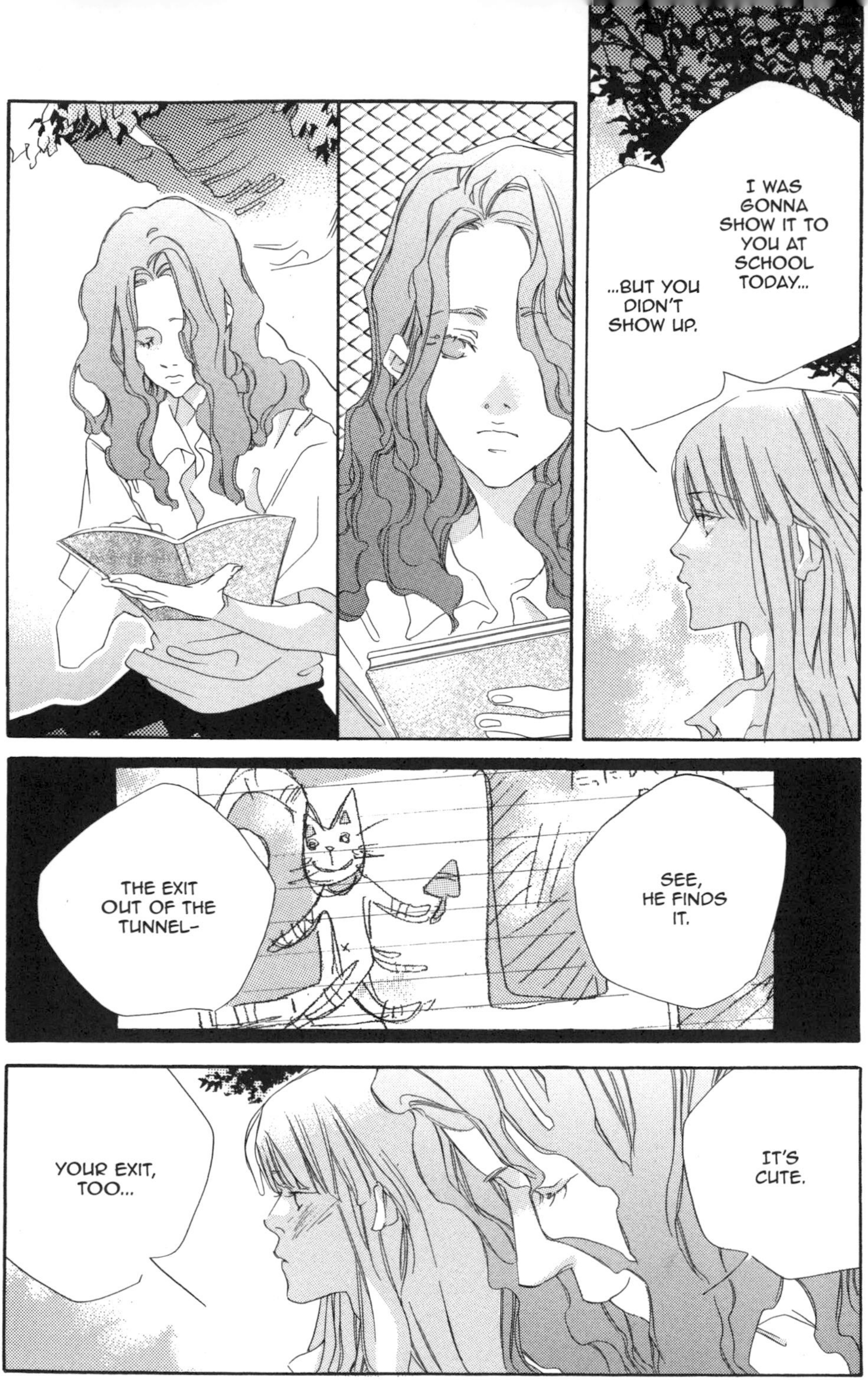
I WAS GONNA SHOW IT TO YOU AT SCHOOL TODAY...
...BUT YOU DIDN'T SHOW UP.
SEE, HE FINDS IT.
THE EXIT OUT OF THE TUNNEL-
IT'S CUTE.
YOUR EXIT, TOO...

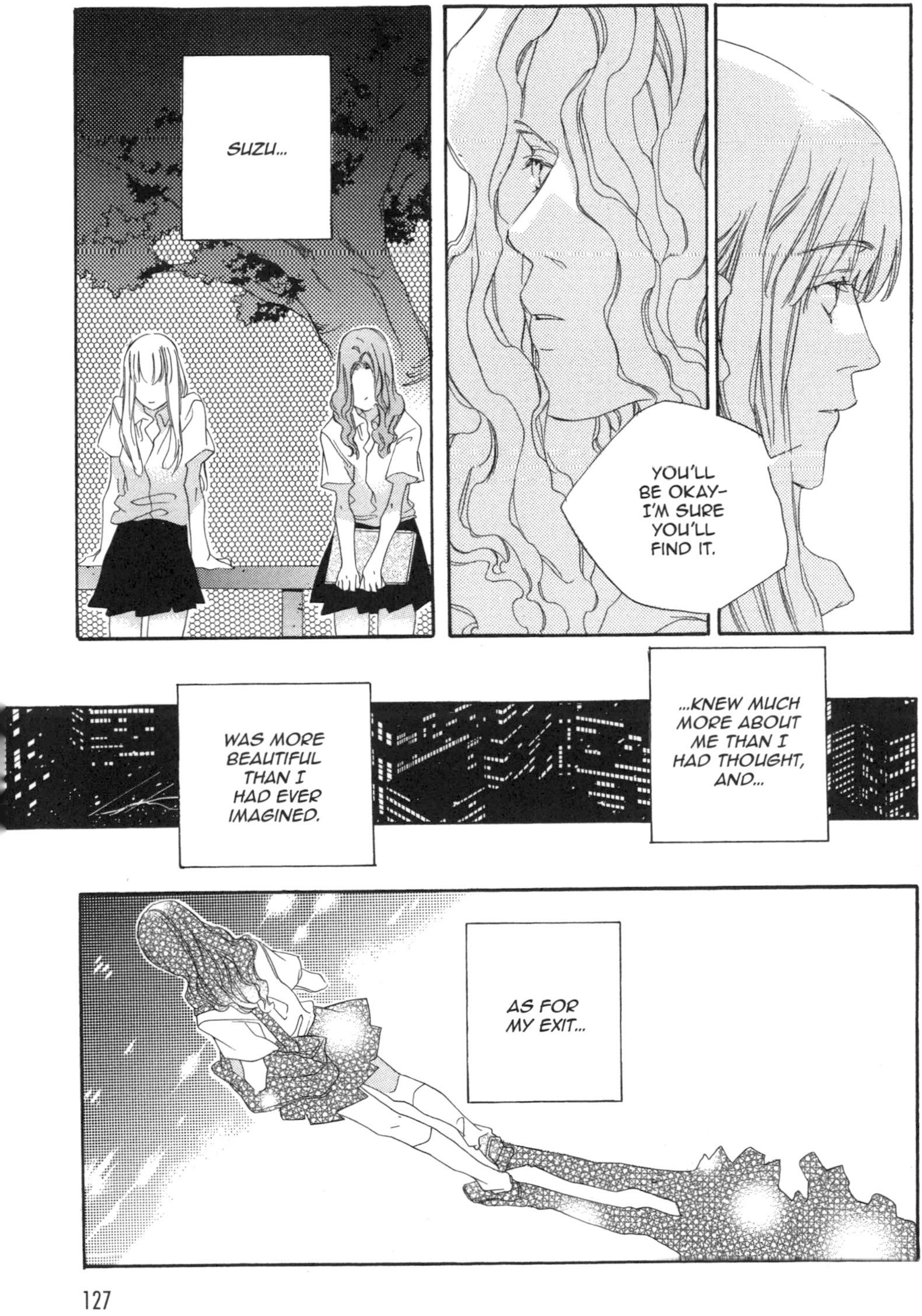
YOU'LL BE OKAY- I'M SURE YOU'LL FIND IT.
SUZU...
...KNEW MUCH MORE ABOUT ME THAN I HAD THOUGHT, AND...
WAS MORE BEAUTIFUL THAN I HAD EVER IMAGINED.
AS FOR MY EXIT...

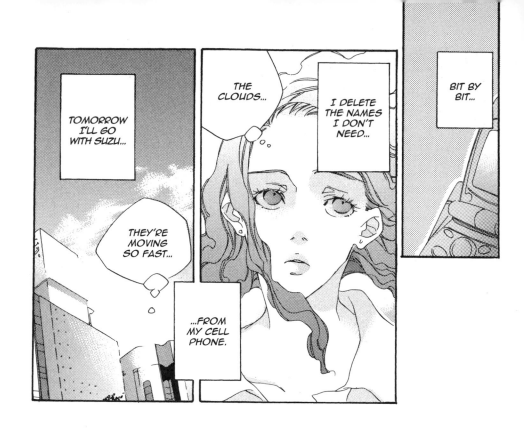

BIT BY BIT...
I DELETE THE NAMES I DON'T NEED...
THE CLOUDS...
...FROM MY CELL PHONE.
TOMORROW I'LL GO WITH SUZU...
THEY'RE MOVING SO FAST...

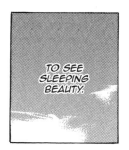

TO SEE SLEEPING BEAUTY.

BLUE CAT TUNNEL / END

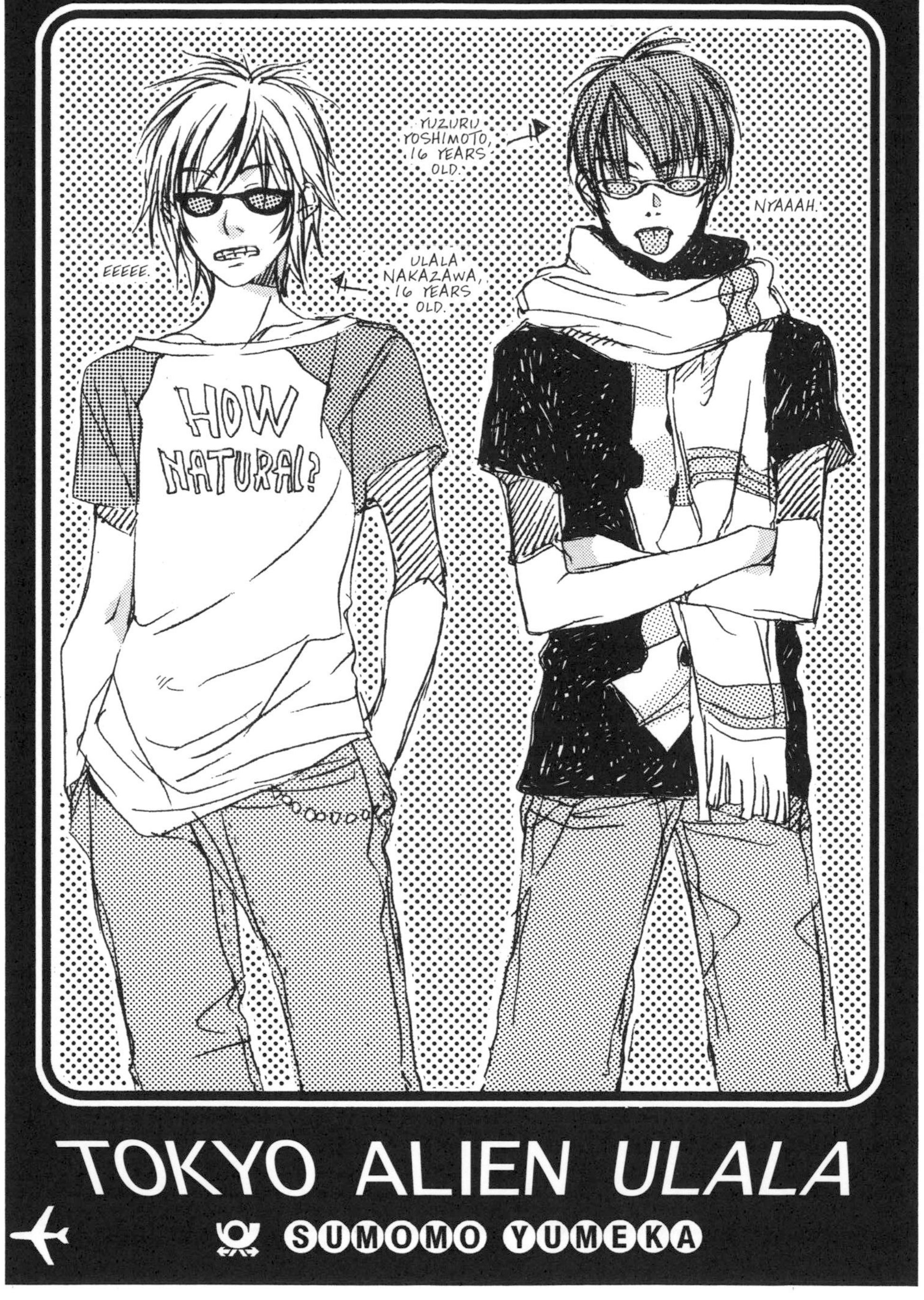
NYAAAH.
YUZURU YOSHIMOTO, 16 YEARS OLD.
ULALA NAKAZAWA, 16 YEARS OLD.
EEEEE.
HOW NATURAL?

TOKYO ALIEN *ULALA*

SUMOMO YUMEKA

ULALA NAKAZAWA (16), CURRENTLY RESIDING IN TOKYO, HAS A DREAM THAT IS BOTH IDIOTIC AND GRAND.

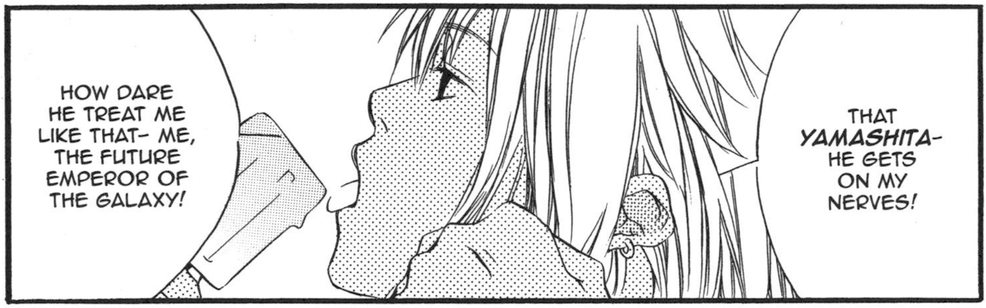
THAT YAMASHITA- HE GETS ON MY NERVES!
HOW DARE HE TREAT ME LIKE THAT- ME, THE FUTURE EMPEROR OF THE GALAXY!

THOUGH TIMID, A SELF-PROCLAIMED RULER.

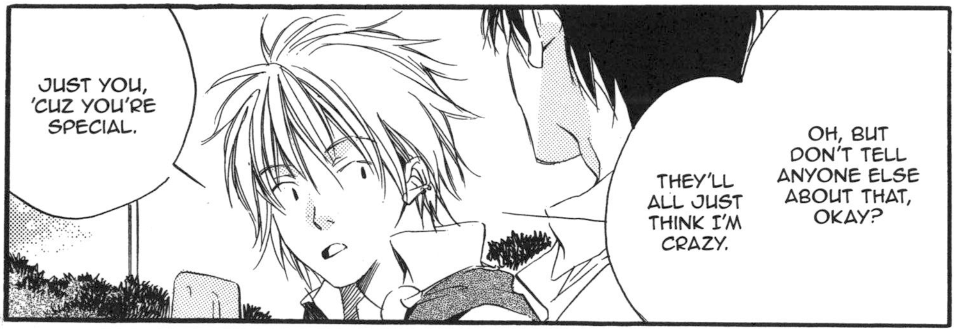
OH, BUT DON'T TELL ANYONE ELSE ABOUT THAT, OKAY?
THEY'LL ALL JUST THINK I'M CRAZY.
JUST YOU, 'CUZ YOU'RE SPECIAL.

HIS PHRASE OF HABIT: "I LOVE YOU, YUZURU."

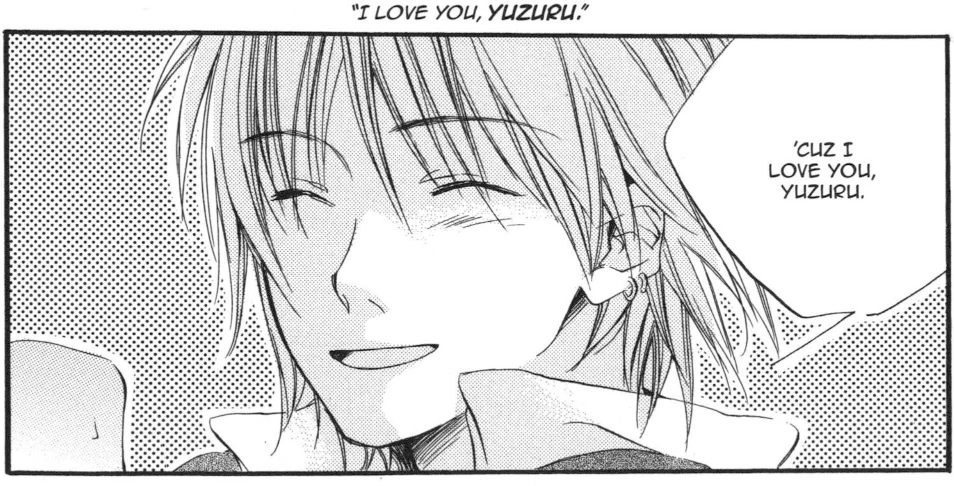
'CUZ I LOVE YOU, YUZURU.

ALIENESE.

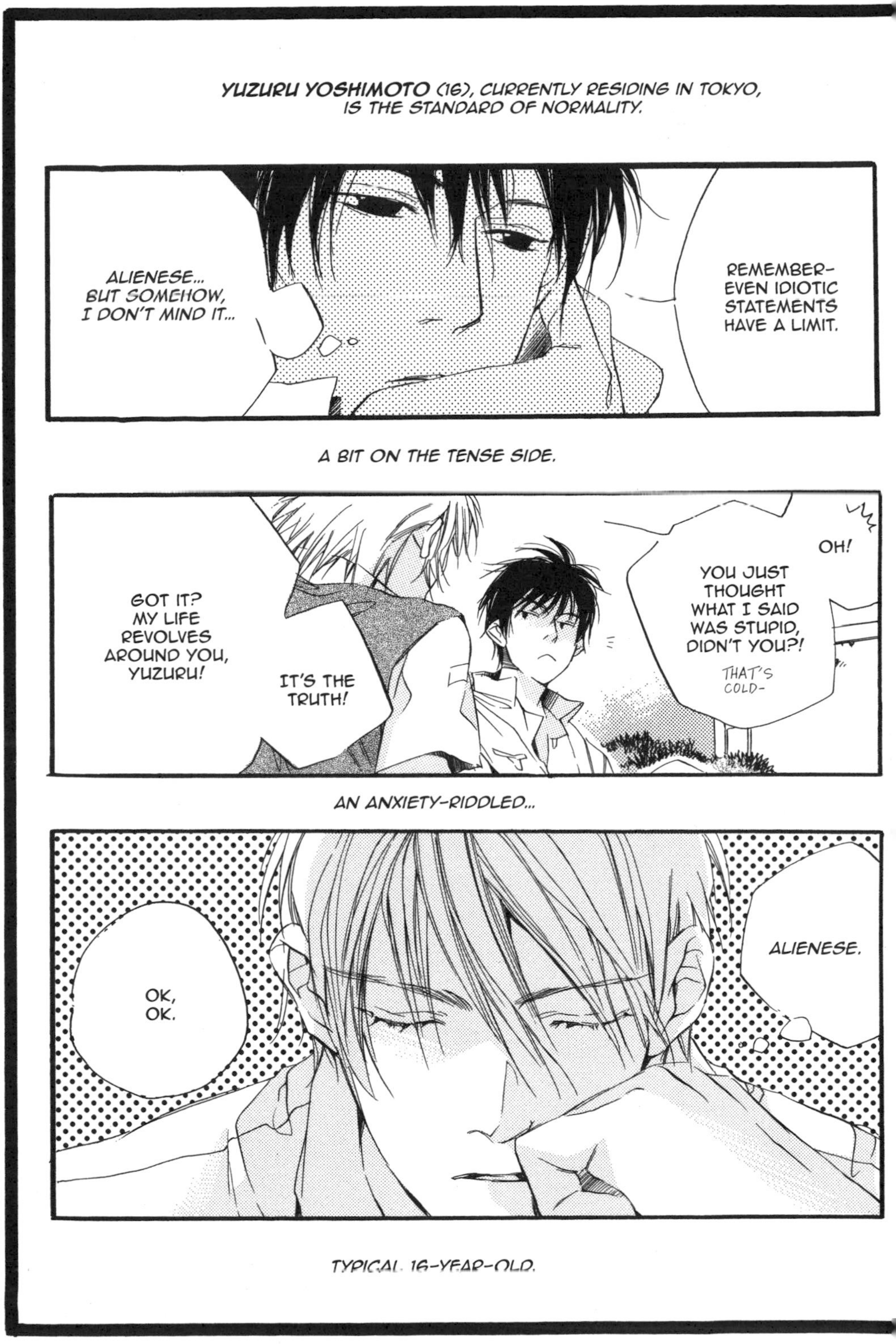
YUZURU YOSHIMOTO (16), CURRENTLY RESIDING IN TOKYO, IS THE STANDARD OF NORMALITY.
REMEMBER- EVEN IDIOTIC STATEMENTS HAVE A LIMIT.
ALIENESE... BUT SOMEHOW, I DON'T MIND IT...
A BIT ON THE TENSE SIDE.
OH!
YOU JUST THOUGHT WHAT I SAID WAS STUPID, DIDN'T YOU?!
THAT'S COLD-
GOT IT? MY LIFE REVOLVES AROUND YOU, YUZURU!
IT'S THE TRUTH!
AN ANXIETY-RIDDLED...
ALIENESE.
OK, OK.
TYPICAL 16-YEAR-OLD.

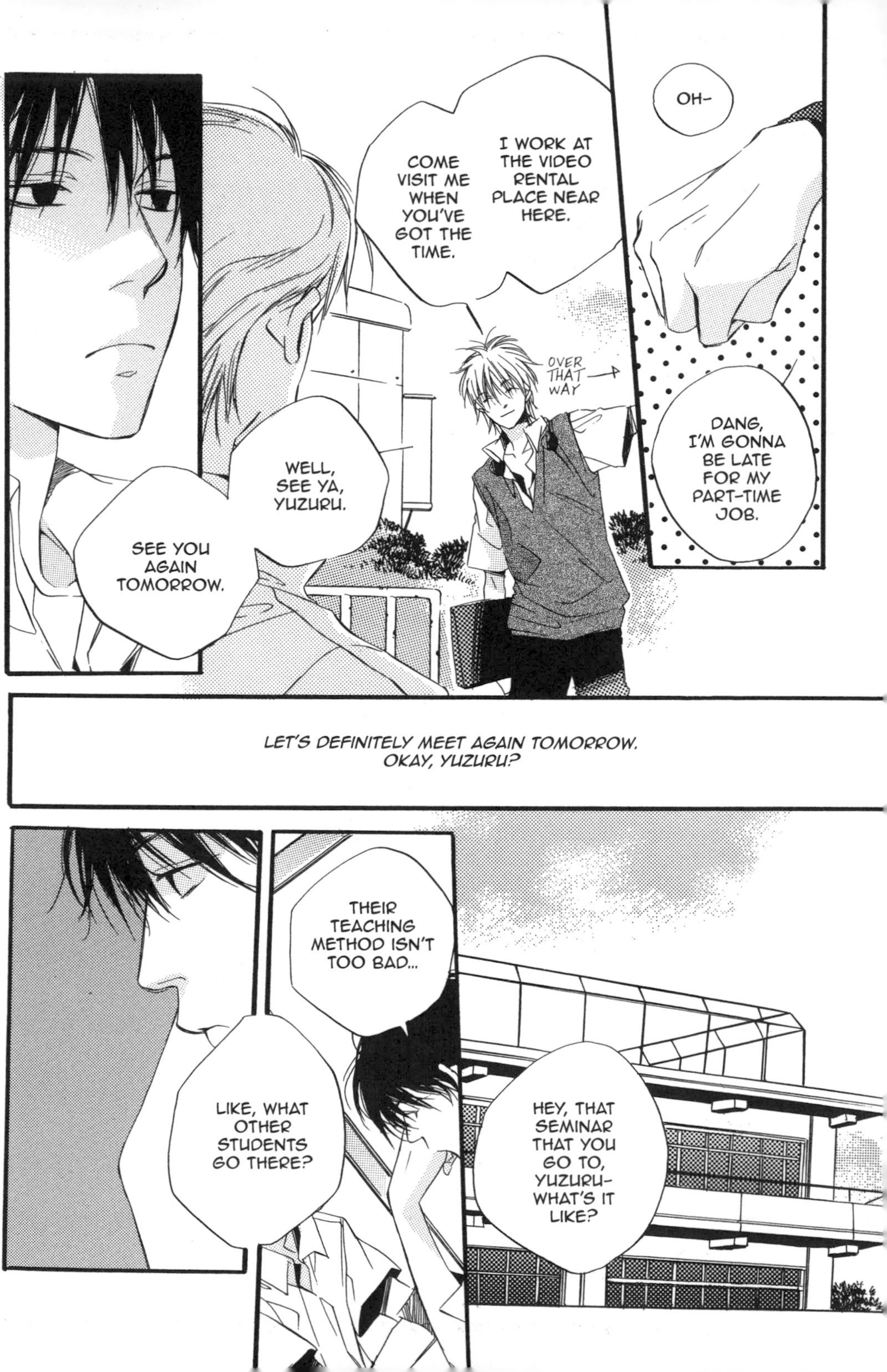
OH-
DANG, I'M GONNA BE LATE FOR MY PART-TIME JOB.
I WORK AT THE VIDEO RENTAL PLACE NEAR HERE.
COME VISIT ME WHEN YOU'VE GOT THE TIME.
OVER THAT WAY
WELL, SEE YA, YUZURU.
SEE YOU AGAIN TOMORROW.
LET'S DEFINITELY MEET AGAIN TOMORROW. OKAY, YUZURU?
HEY, THAT SEMINAR THAT YOU GO TO, YUZURU- WHAT'S IT LIKE?
LIKE, WHAT OTHER STUDENTS GO THERE?
THEIR TEACHING METHOD ISN'T TOO BAD...

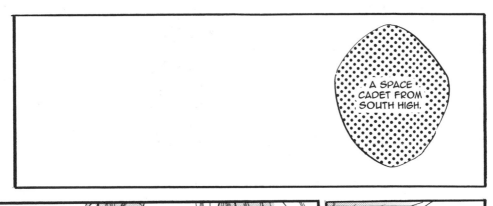

A SPACE CADET FROM SOUTH HIGH.

AND THEN, AND THEN—

HE SAYS, "WHICH ONE OF THE DORA-CHAN SERIES MAKES YOU CRY THE MOST?"

THIS OLD SKINHEAD DUDE!

IT TOTALLY ROCKED.

WHAT'S WRONG, YUZURU?

SPACING OUT LIKE THAT.

CONK

OH...

DID I BORE YOU?

WITH THAT STORY—

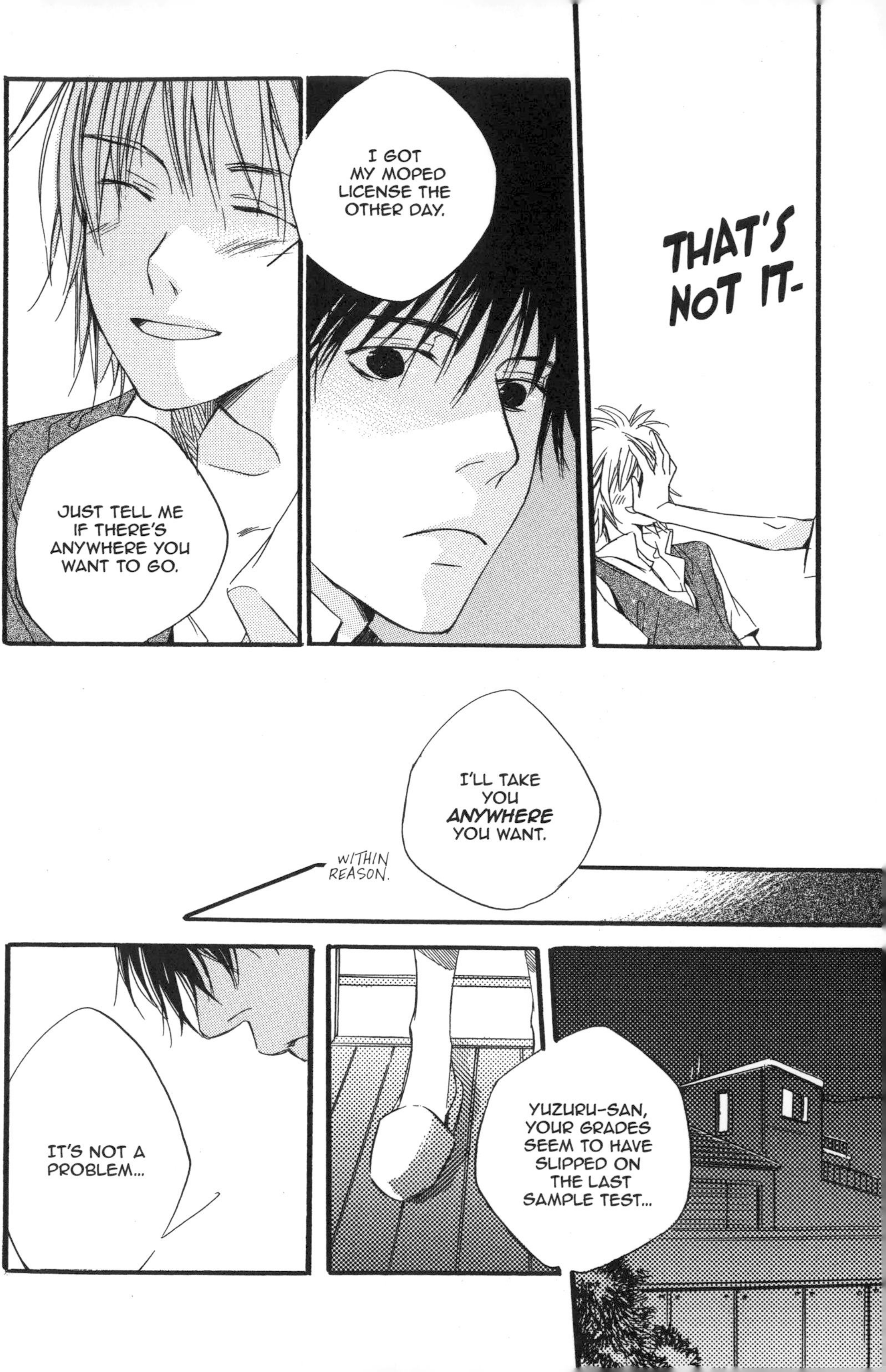
THAT'S NOT IT-
I GOT MY MOPED LICENSE THE OTHER DAY.
JUST TELL ME IF THERE'S ANYWHERE YOU WANT TO GO.
I'LL TAKE YOU ANYWHERE YOU WANT.
WITHIN REASON.
YUZURU-SAN, YOUR GRADES SEEM TO HAVE SLIPPED ON THE LAST SAMPLE TEST...
IT'S NOT A PROBLEM...

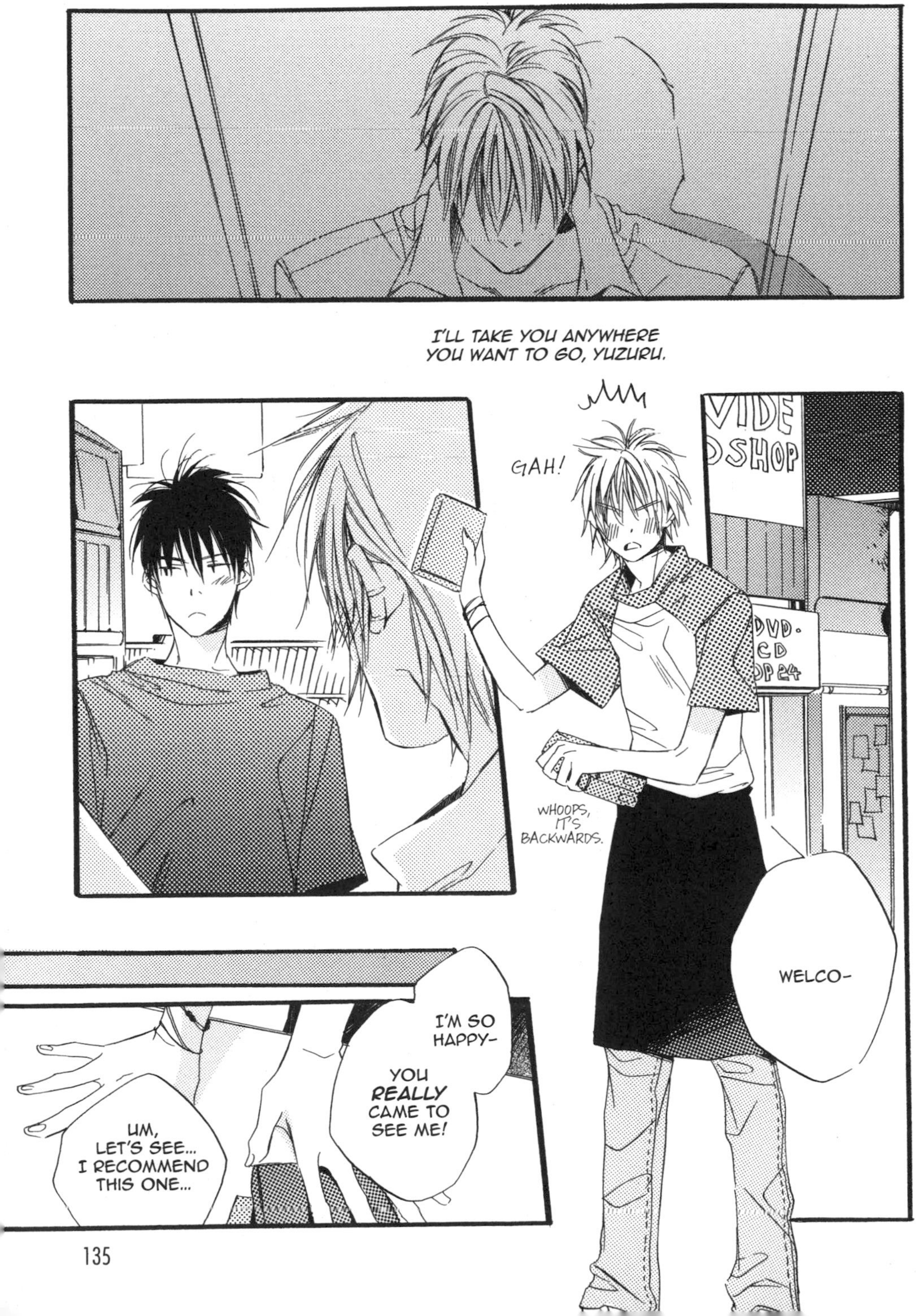
I'LL TAKE YOU ANYWHERE YOU WANT TO GO, YUZURU.
GAH!
WHOOPS, IT'S BACKWARDS.
WELCO-
I'M SO HAPPY-
YOU **REALLY** CAME TO SEE ME!
UM, LET'S SEE... I RECOMMEND THIS ONE...

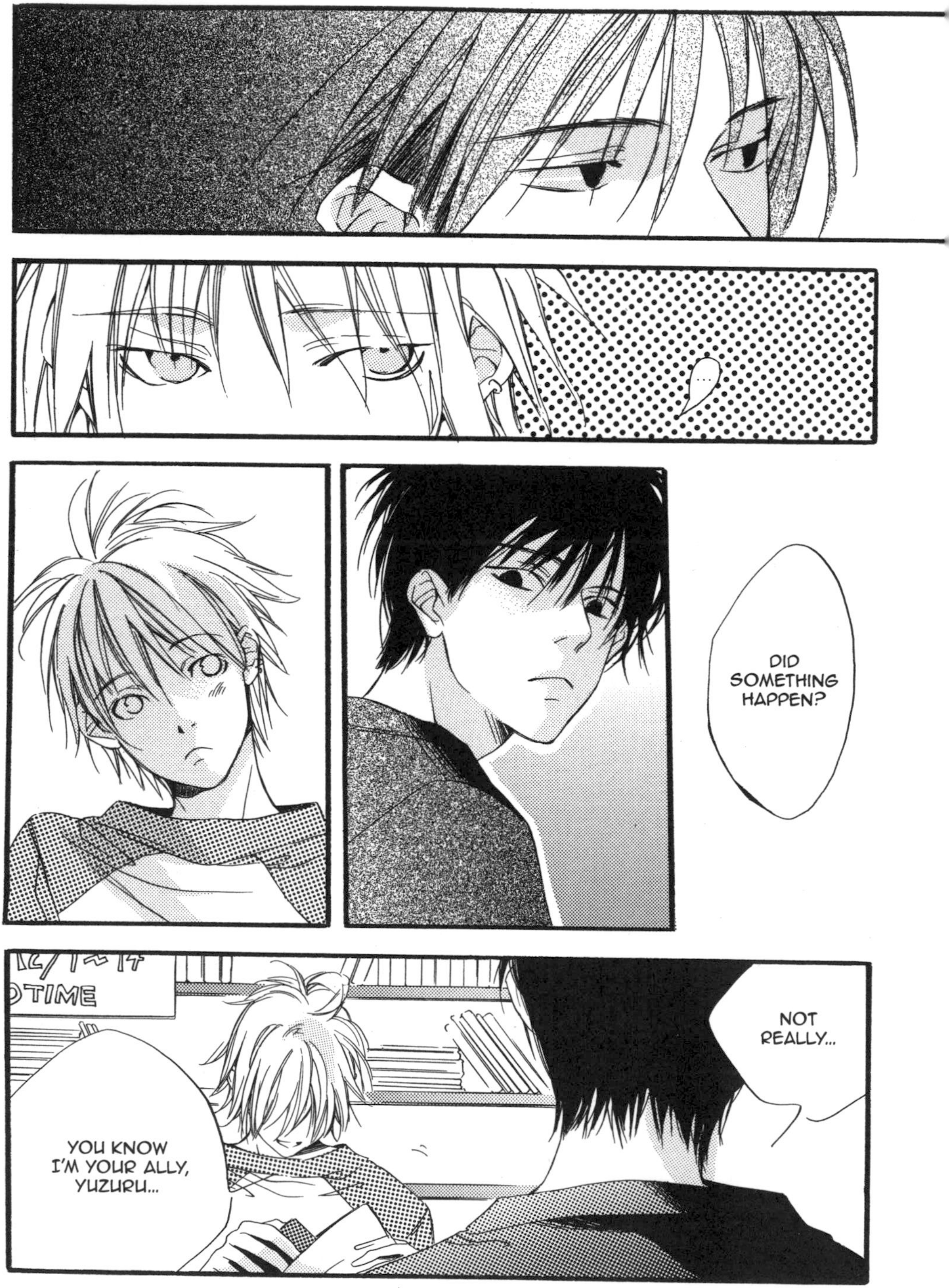
...
DID SOMETHING HAPPEN?
NOT REALLY...
YOU KNOW I'M YOUR ALLY, YUZURU...

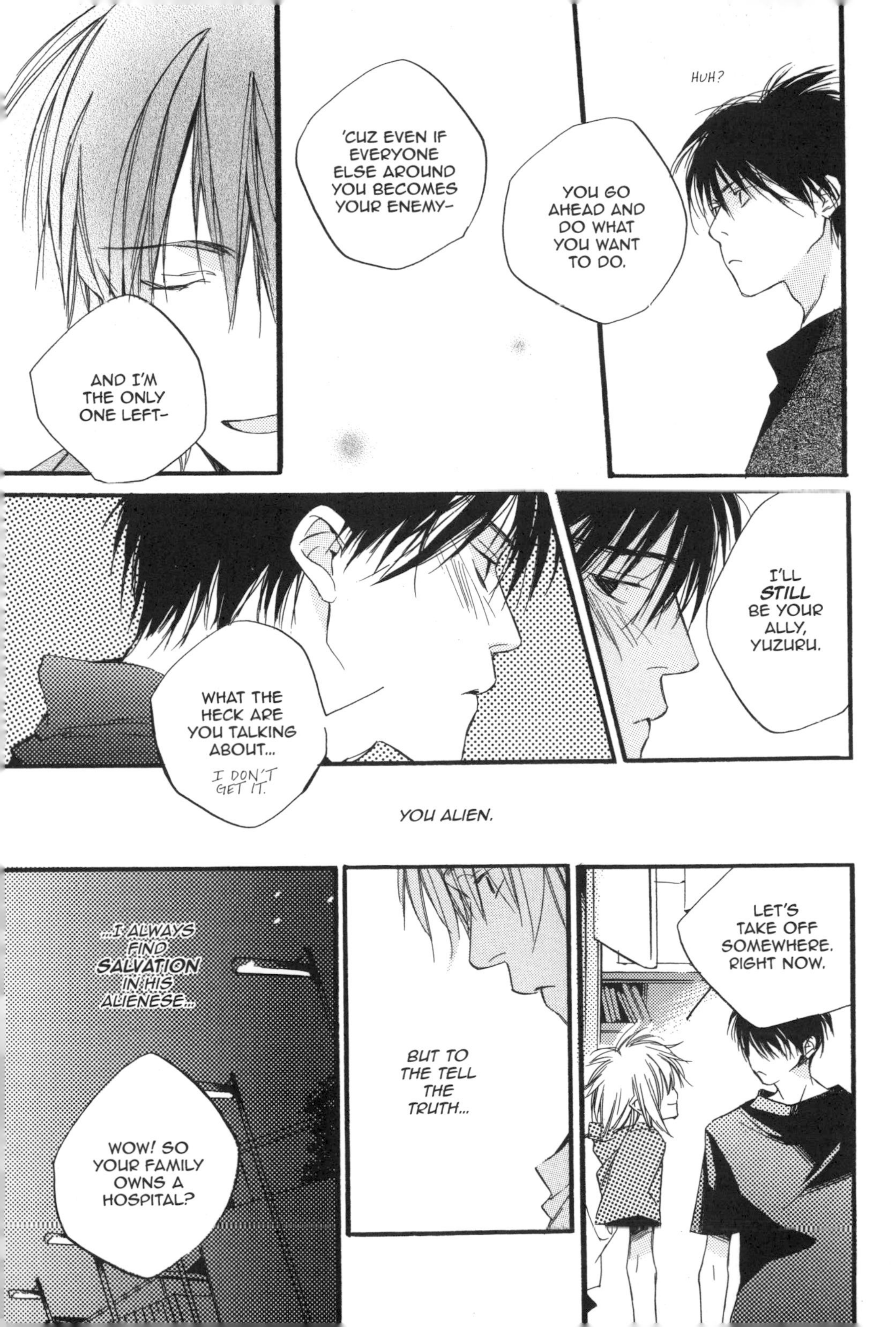

HUH?
YOU GO AHEAD AND DO WHAT YOU WANT TO DO.
'CUZ EVEN IF EVERYONE ELSE AROUND YOU BECOMES YOUR ENEMY-
AND I'M THE ONLY ONE LEFT-
I'LL STILL BE YOUR ALLY, YUZURU.
WHAT THE HECK ARE YOU TALKING ABOUT...
I DON'T GET IT.
YOU ALIEN.
LET'S TAKE OFF SOMEWHERE. RIGHT NOW.
BUT TO THE TELL THE TRUTH...
...I ALWAYS FIND SALVATION IN HIS ALIENESE...
WOW! SO YOUR FAMILY OWNS A HOSPITAL?

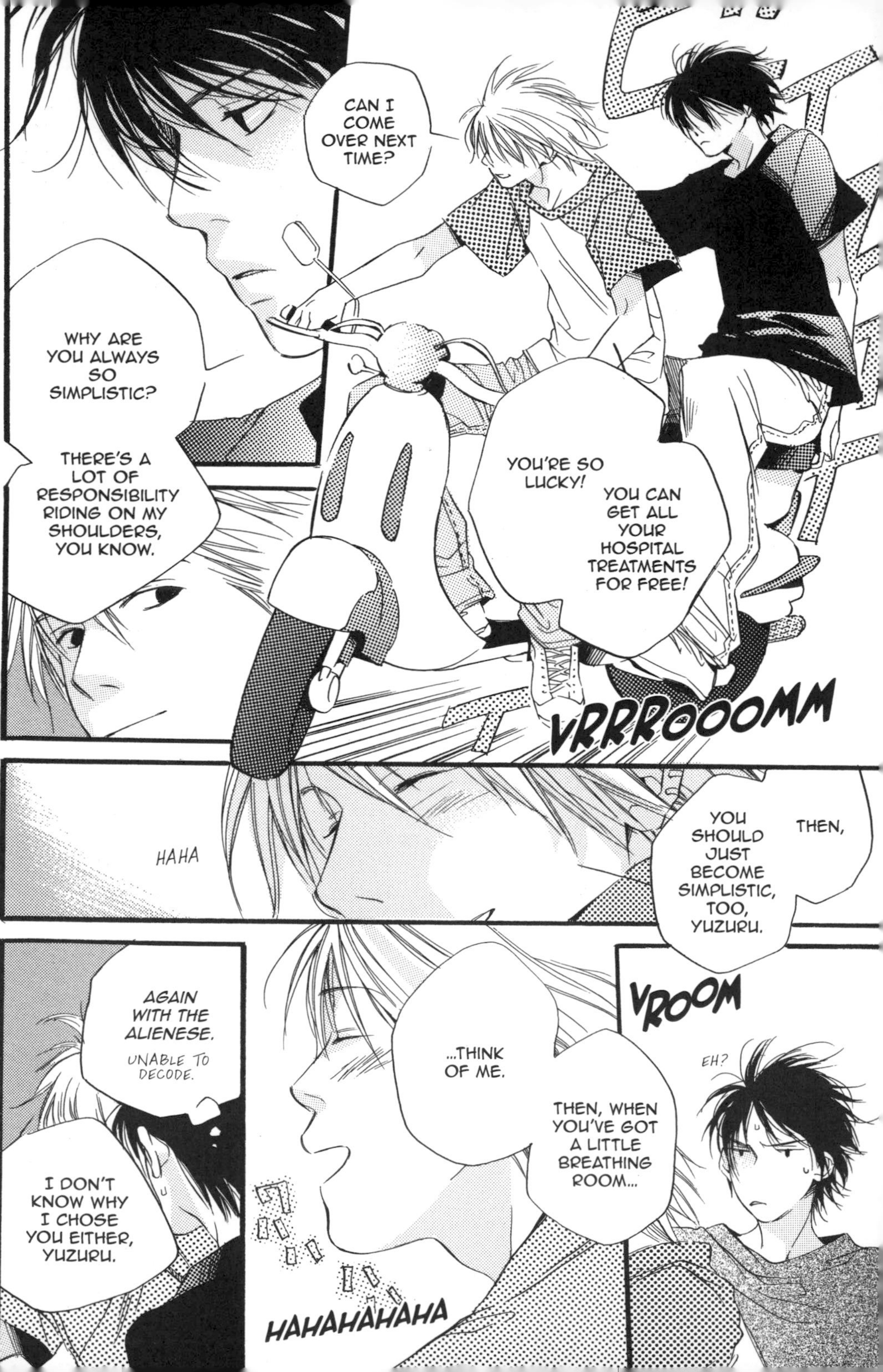
CAN I COME OVER NEXT TIME?
YOU'RE SO LUCKY!
YOU CAN GET ALL YOUR HOSPITAL TREATMENTS FOR FREE!
VRRROOOMM
WHY ARE YOU ALWAYS SO SIMPLISTIC?
THERE'S A LOT OF RESPONSIBILITY RIDING ON MY SHOULDERS, YOU KNOW.
THEN,
YOU SHOULD JUST BECOME SIMPLISTIC, TOO, YUZURU.
HAHA
VROOM
EH?
THEN, WHEN YOU'VE GOT A LITTLE BREATHING ROOM...
...THINK OF ME.
HAHAHAHAHA
AGAIN WITH THE ALIENESE.
UNABLE TO DECODE.
I DON'T KNOW WHY I CHOSE YOU EITHER, YUZURU.

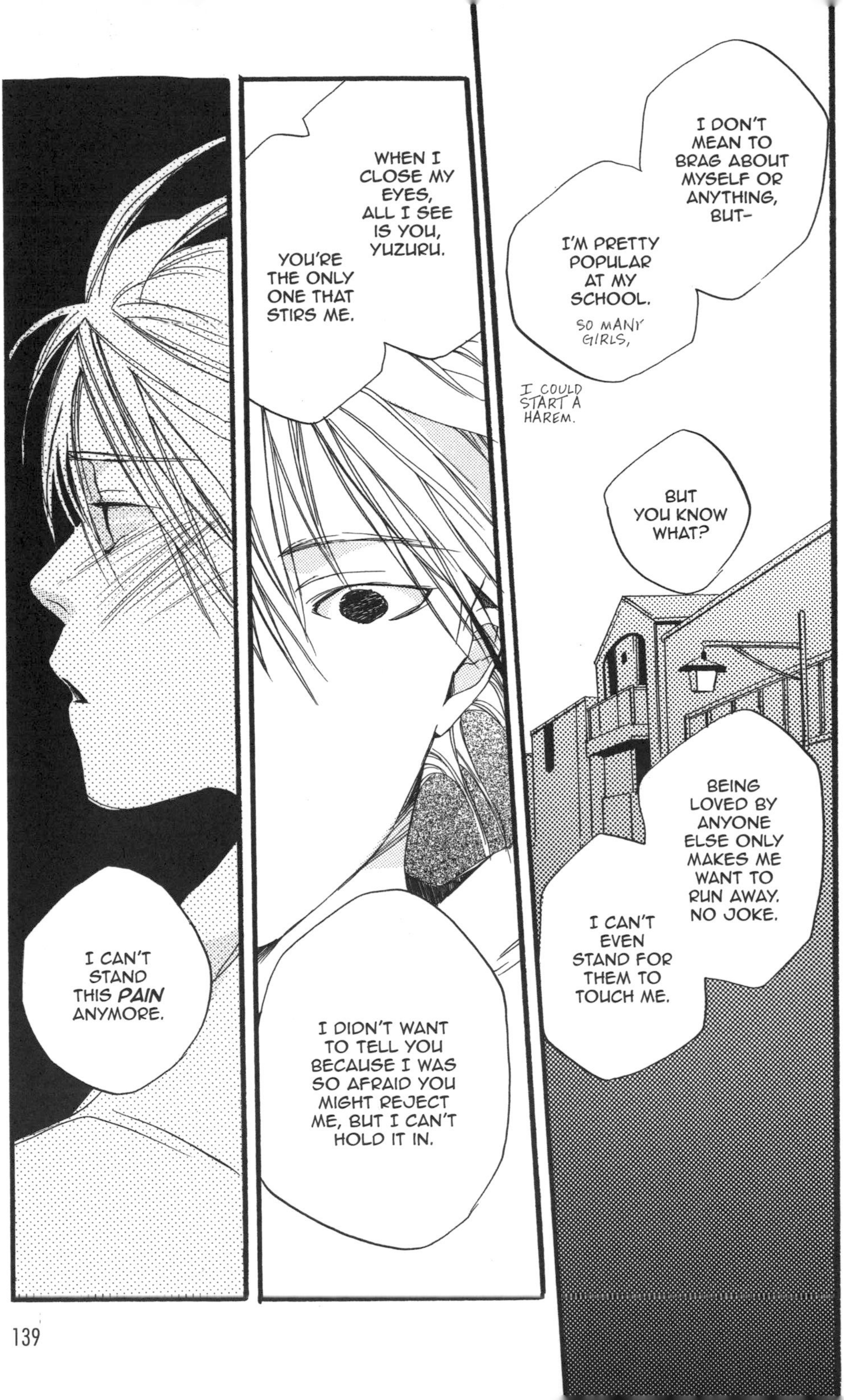
I DON'T MEAN TO BRAG ABOUT MYSELF OR ANYTHING, BUT-
I'M PRETTY POPULAR AT MY SCHOOL.
SO MANY GIRLS,
I COULD START A HAREM.
BUT YOU KNOW WHAT?
BEING LOVED BY ANYONE ELSE ONLY MAKES ME WANT TO RUN AWAY. NO JOKE.
I CAN'T EVEN STAND FOR THEM TO TOUCH ME.
WHEN I CLOSE MY EYES, ALL I SEE IS YOU, YUZURU.
YOU'RE THE ONLY ONE THAT STIRS ME.
I DIDN'T WANT TO TELL YOU BECAUSE I WAS SO AFRAID YOU MIGHT REJECT ME, BUT I CAN'T HOLD IT IN.
I CAN'T STAND THIS *PAIN* ANYMORE.

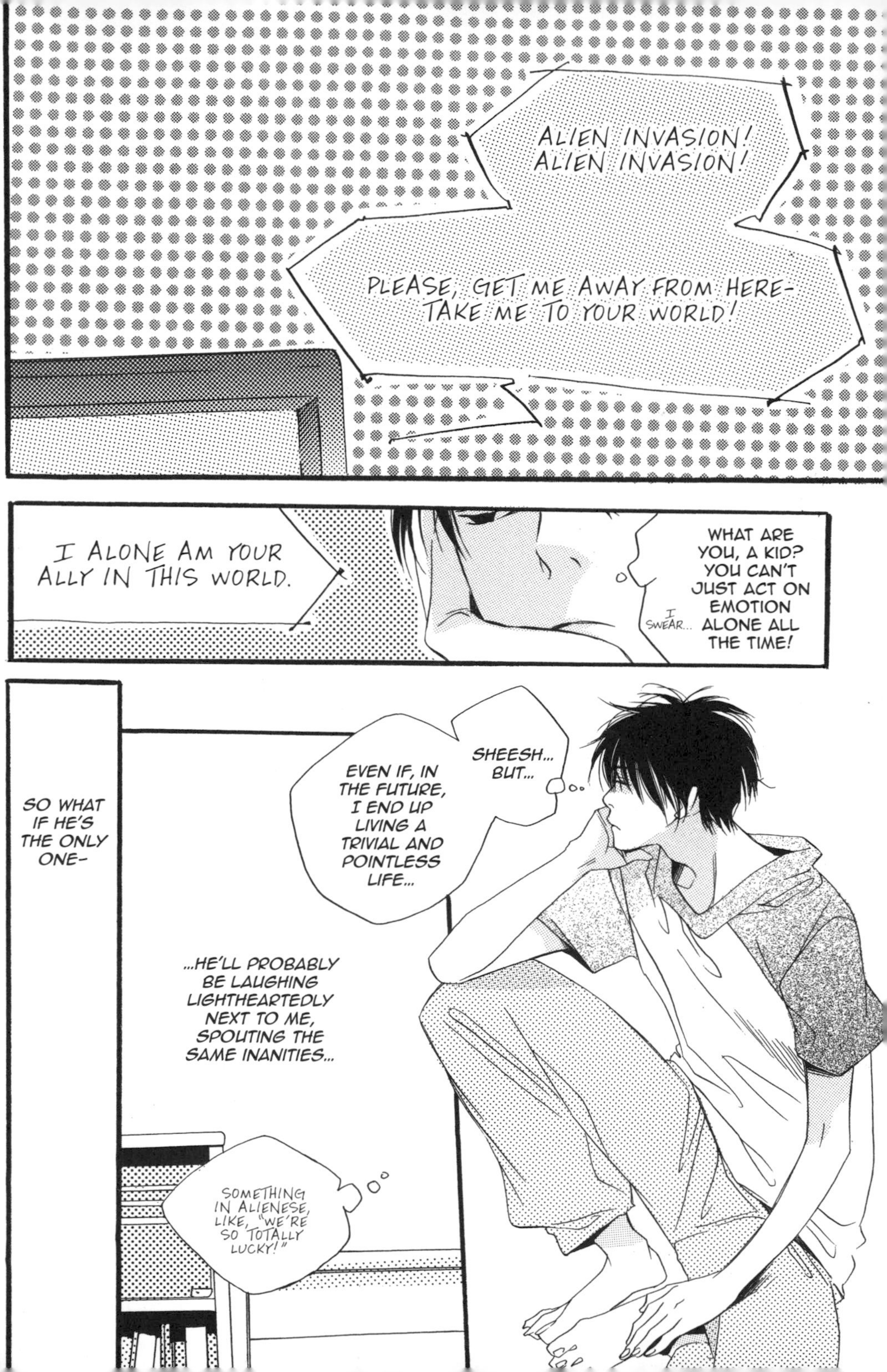
ALIEN INVASION! ALIEN INVASION!
PLEASE, GET ME AWAY FROM HERE-TAKE ME TO YOUR WORLD!
WHAT ARE YOU, A KID? YOU CAN'T JUST ACT ON EMOTION ALONE ALL THE TIME!
I SWEAR...
I ALONE AM YOUR ALLY IN THIS WORLD.
SHEESH... BUT...
EVEN IF, IN THE FUTURE, I END UP LIVING A TRIVIAL AND POINTLESS LIFE...
SO WHAT IF HE'S THE ONLY ONE-
...HE'LL PROBABLY BE LAUGHING LIGHTHEARTEDLY NEXT TO ME, SPOUTING THE SAME INANITIES...
SOMETHING IN ALIENESE, LIKE, "WE'RE SO TOTALLY LUCKY!"

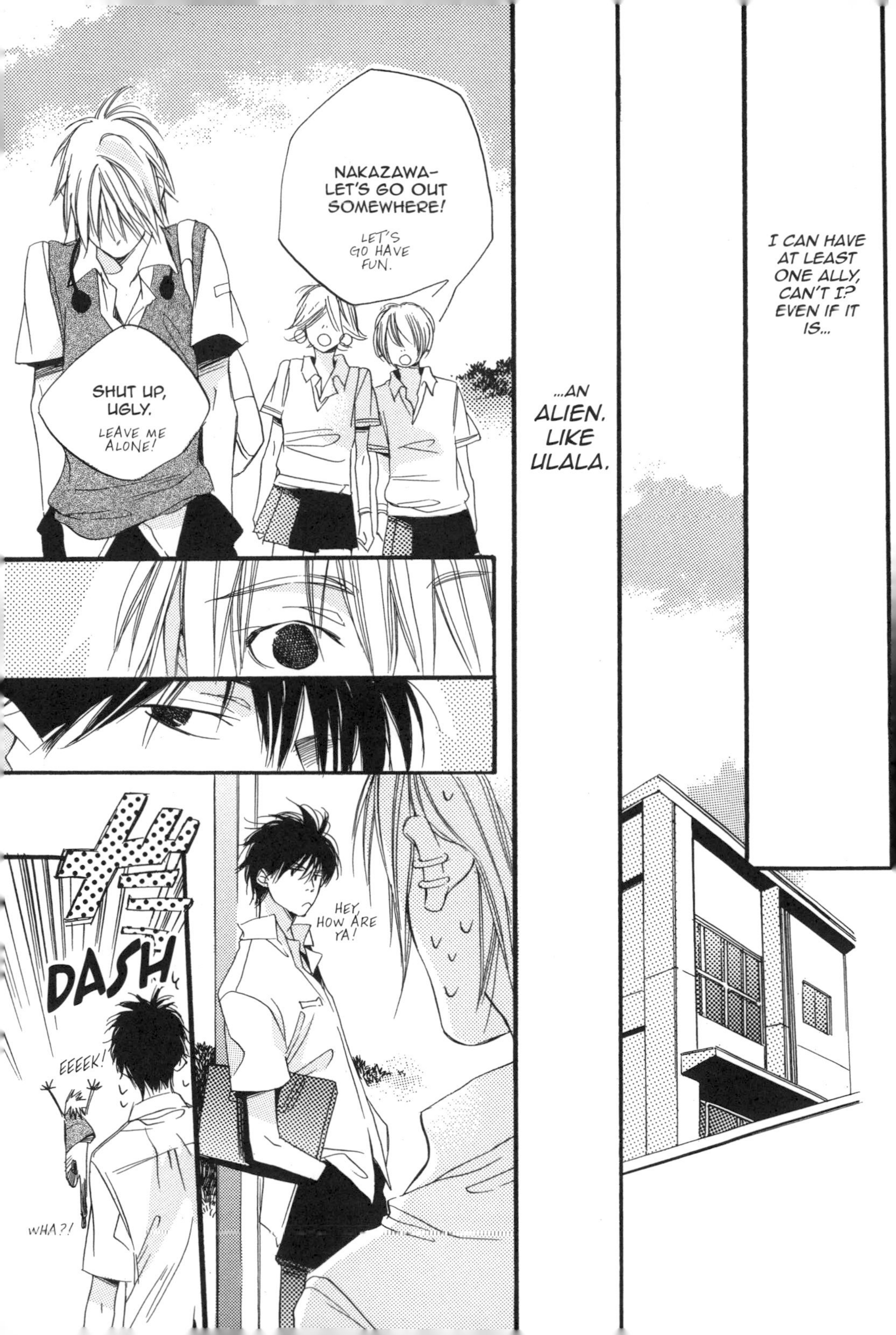
I CAN HAVE AT LEAST ONE ALLY, CAN'T I? EVEN IF IT IS...
...AN ALIEN. LIKE ULALA.
NAKAZAWA-LET'S GO OUT SOMEWHERE!
LET'S GO HAVE FUN.
SHUT UP, UGLY.
LEAVE ME ALONE!
HEY, HOW ARE YA!
DASH
EEEEK!
WHA?!

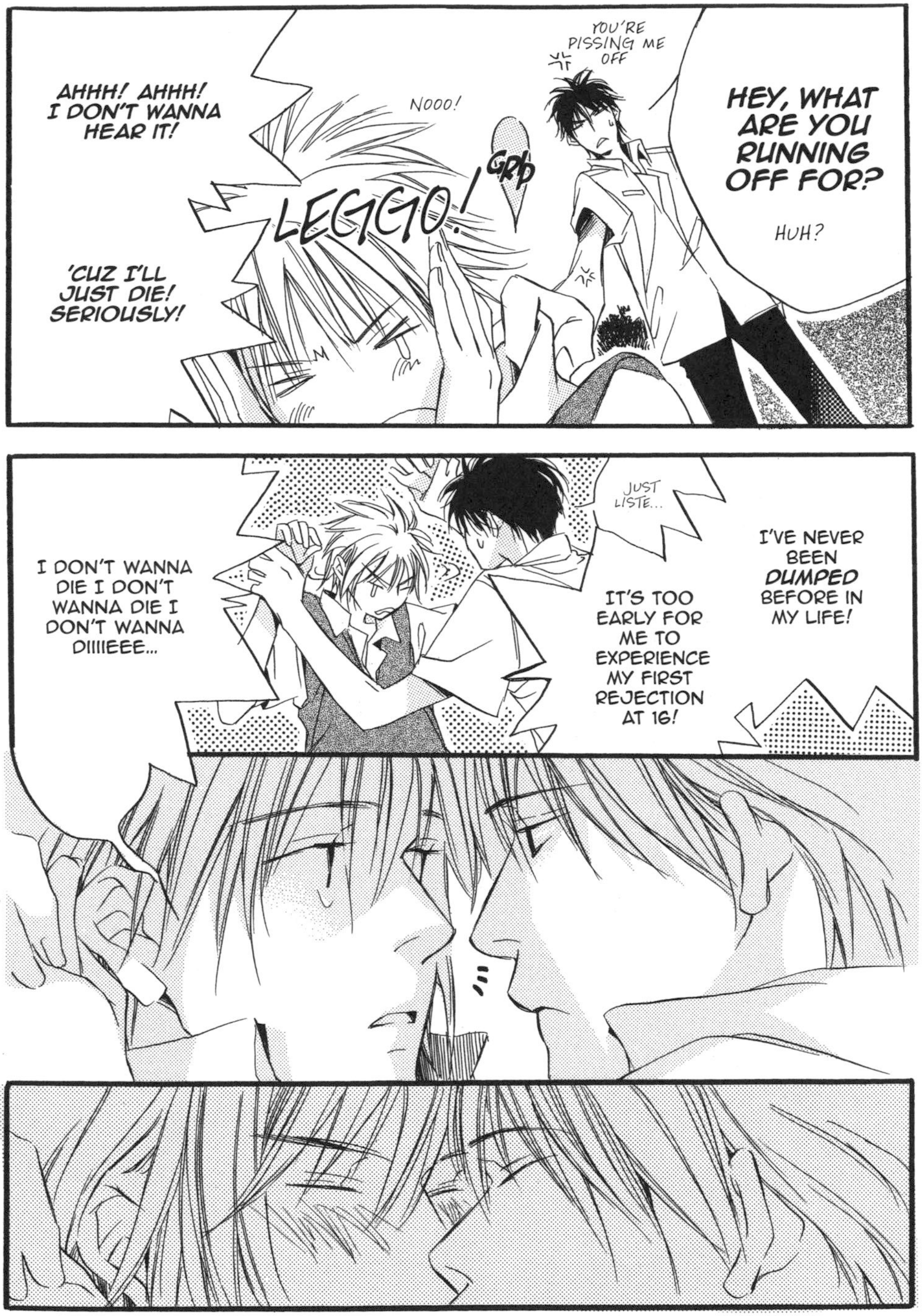
HEY, WHAT ARE YOU RUNNING OFF FOR?
HUH?
YOU'RE PISSING ME OFF
NOOO!
GRP
LEGGO!
AHHH! AHHH! I DON'T WANNA HEAR IT!
'CUZ I'LL JUST DIE! SERIOUSLY!
JUST LISTE...
I'VE NEVER BEEN DUMPED BEFORE IN MY LIFE!
IT'S TOO EARLY FOR ME TO EXPERIENCE MY FIRST REJECTION AT 16!
I DON'T WANNA DIE I DON'T WANNA DIE I DON'T WANNA DIIIIEEE...

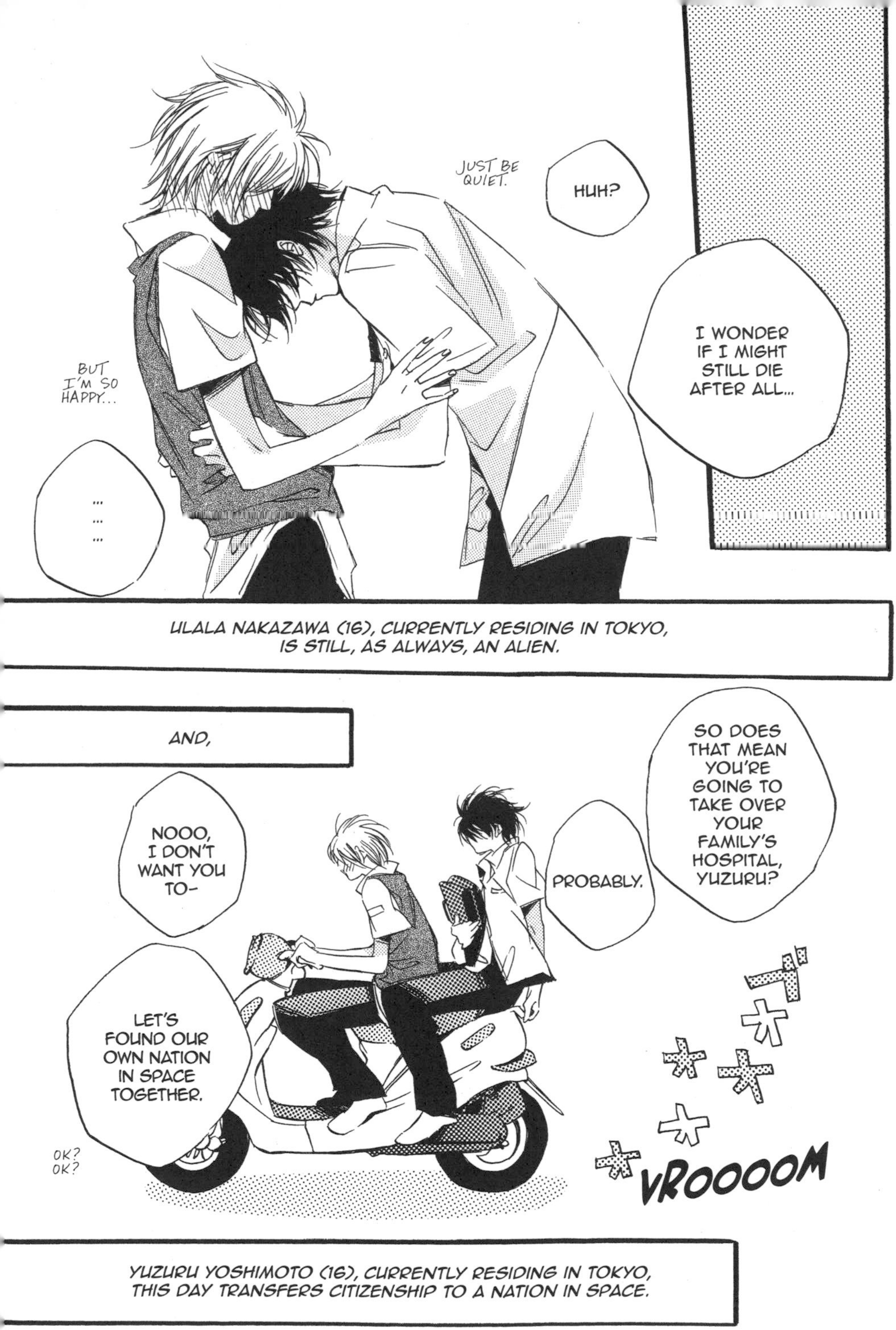
I WONDER IF I MIGHT STILL DIE AFTER ALL...
HUH?
JUST BE QUIET.
BUT I'M SO HAPPY...
... ...
ULALA NAKAZAWA (16), CURRENTLY RESIDING IN TOKYO, IS STILL, AS ALWAYS, AN ALIEN.
AND,
SO DOES THAT MEAN YOU'RE GOING TO TAKE OVER YOUR FAMILY'S HOSPITAL, YUZURU?
PROBABLY.
NOOO, I DON'T WANT YOU TO-
LET'S FOUND OUR OWN NATION IN SPACE TOGETHER.
OK? OK?
VROOOOM
YUZURU YOSHIMOTO (16), CURRENTLY RESIDING IN TOKYO, THIS DAY TRANSFERS CITIZENSHIP TO A NATION IN SPACE.

TOKYO ALIEN ULALA / END

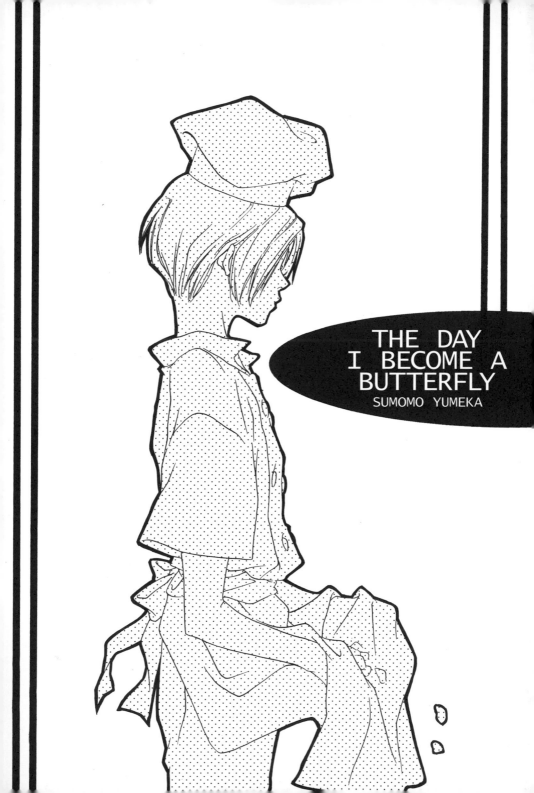

THE DAY I BECOME A BUTTERFLY

SUMOMO YUMEKA

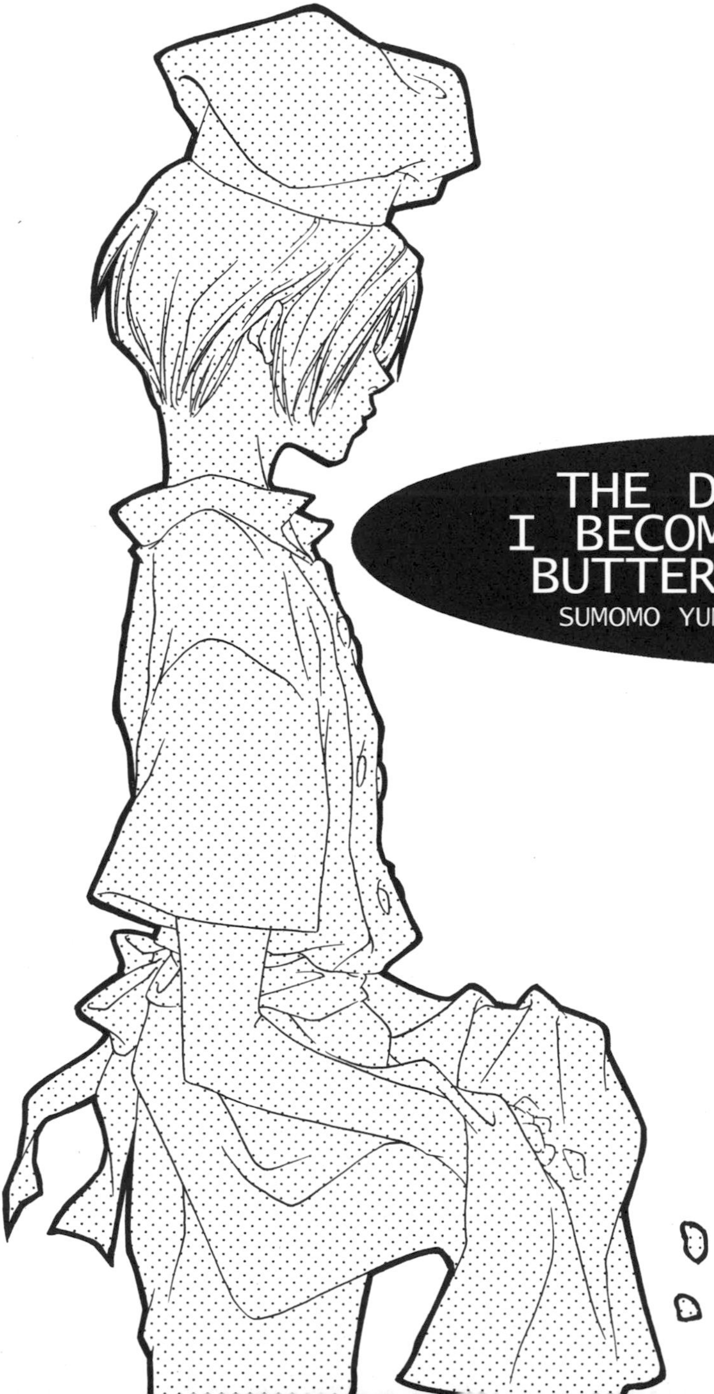

PLANET yours

SUMOMO YUMEKA

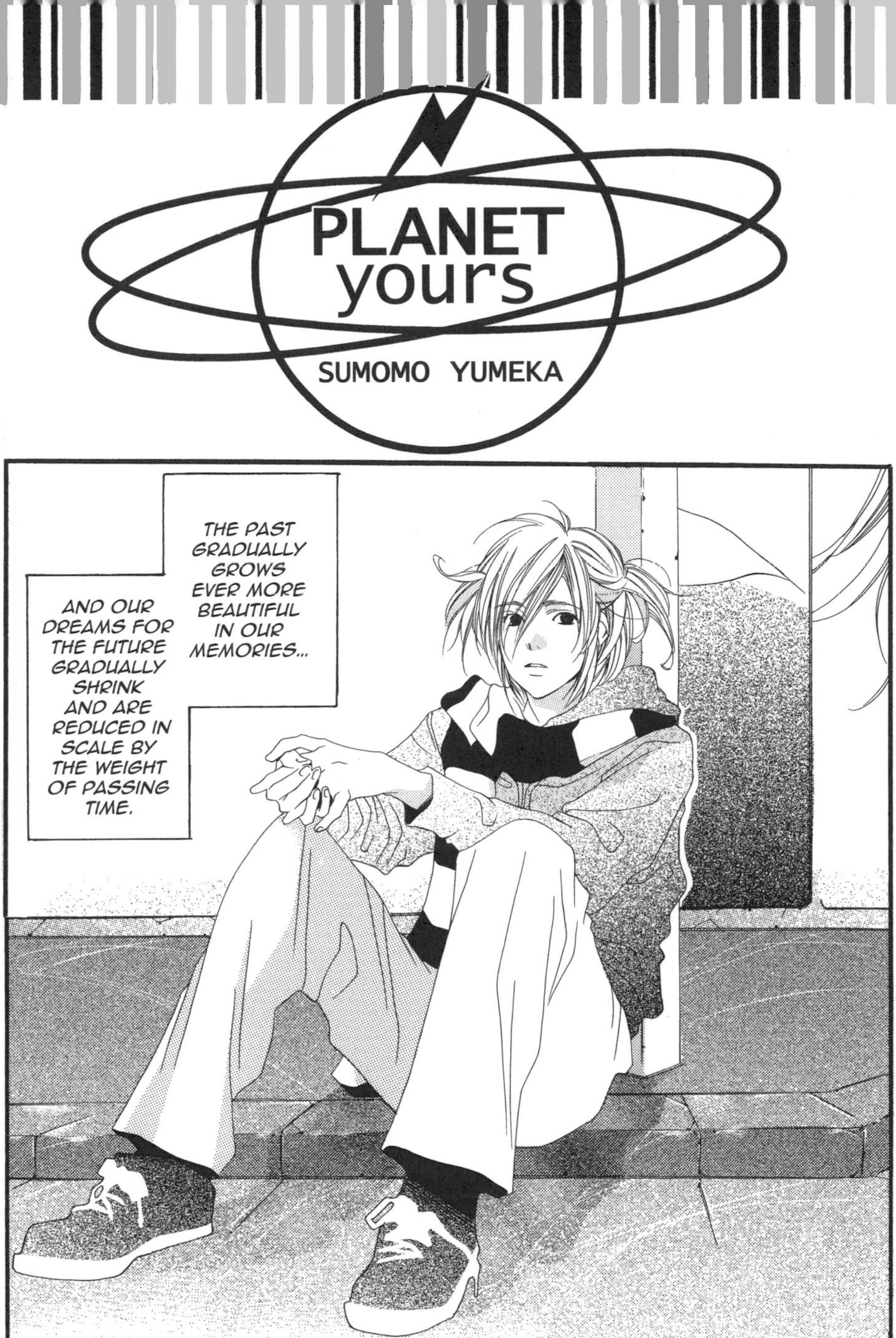
THE PAST GRADUALLY GROWS EVER MORE BEAUTIFUL IN OUR MEMORIES...
AND OUR DREAMS FOR THE FUTURE GRADUALLY SHRINK AND ARE REDUCED IN SCALE BY THE WEIGHT OF PASSING TIME.

AKIRA'S STORY

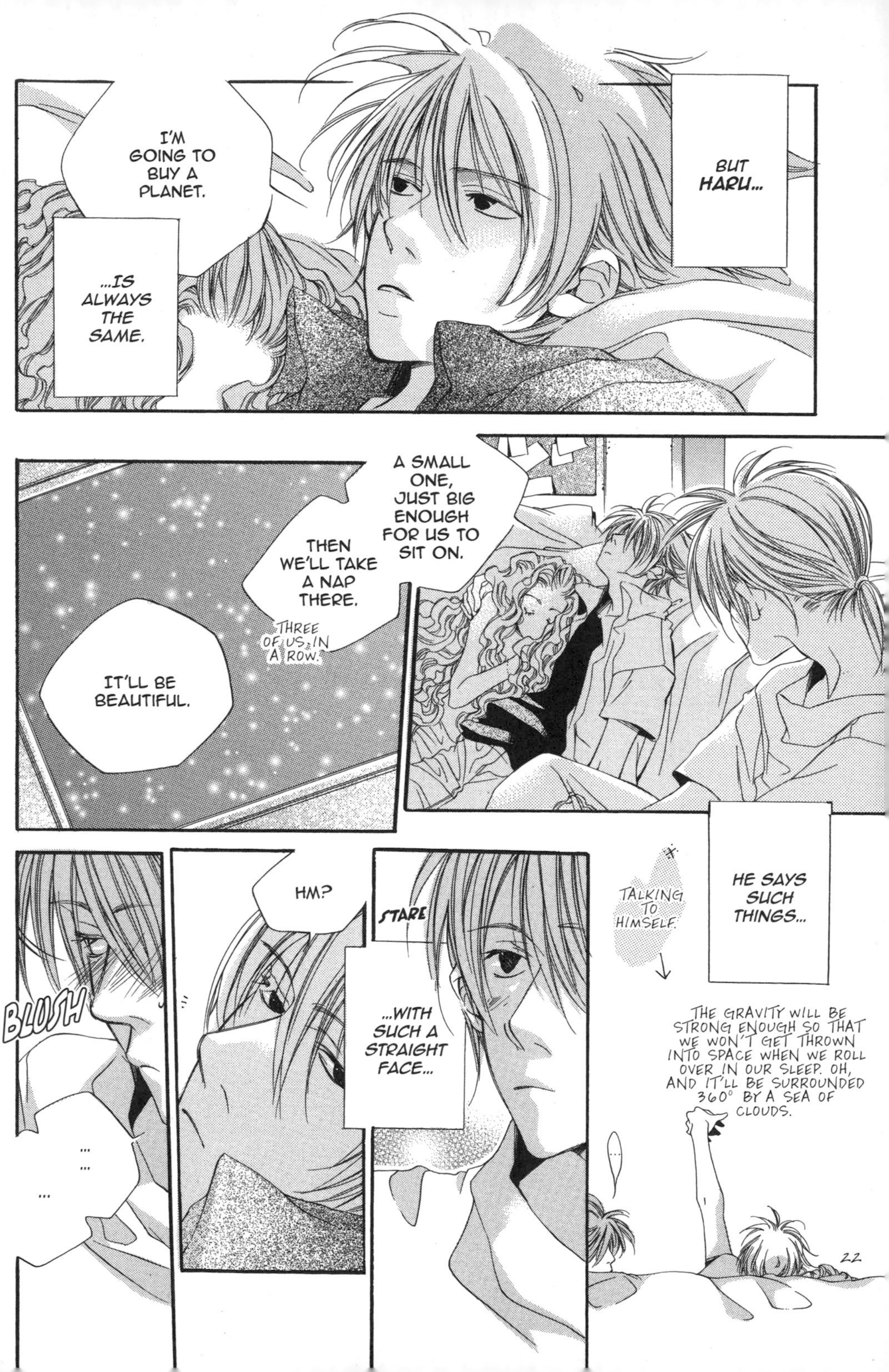

BUT HARU...
I'M GOING TO BUY A PLANET.
...IS ALWAYS THE SAME.
A SMALL ONE, JUST BIG ENOUGH FOR US TO SIT ON.
THEN WE'LL TAKE A NAP THERE.
THREE OF US IN A ROW.
IT'LL BE BEAUTIFUL.
HE SAYS SUCH THINGS...
TALKING TO HIMSELF.
THE GRAVITY WILL BE STRONG ENOUGH SO THAT WE WON'T GET THROWN INTO SPACE WHEN WE ROLL OVER IN OUR SLEEP. OH, AND IT'LL BE SURROUNDED 360° BY A SEA OF CLOUDS.
...
STARE
...WITH SUCH A STRAIGHT FACE...
HM?
BLUSH
...
...
...

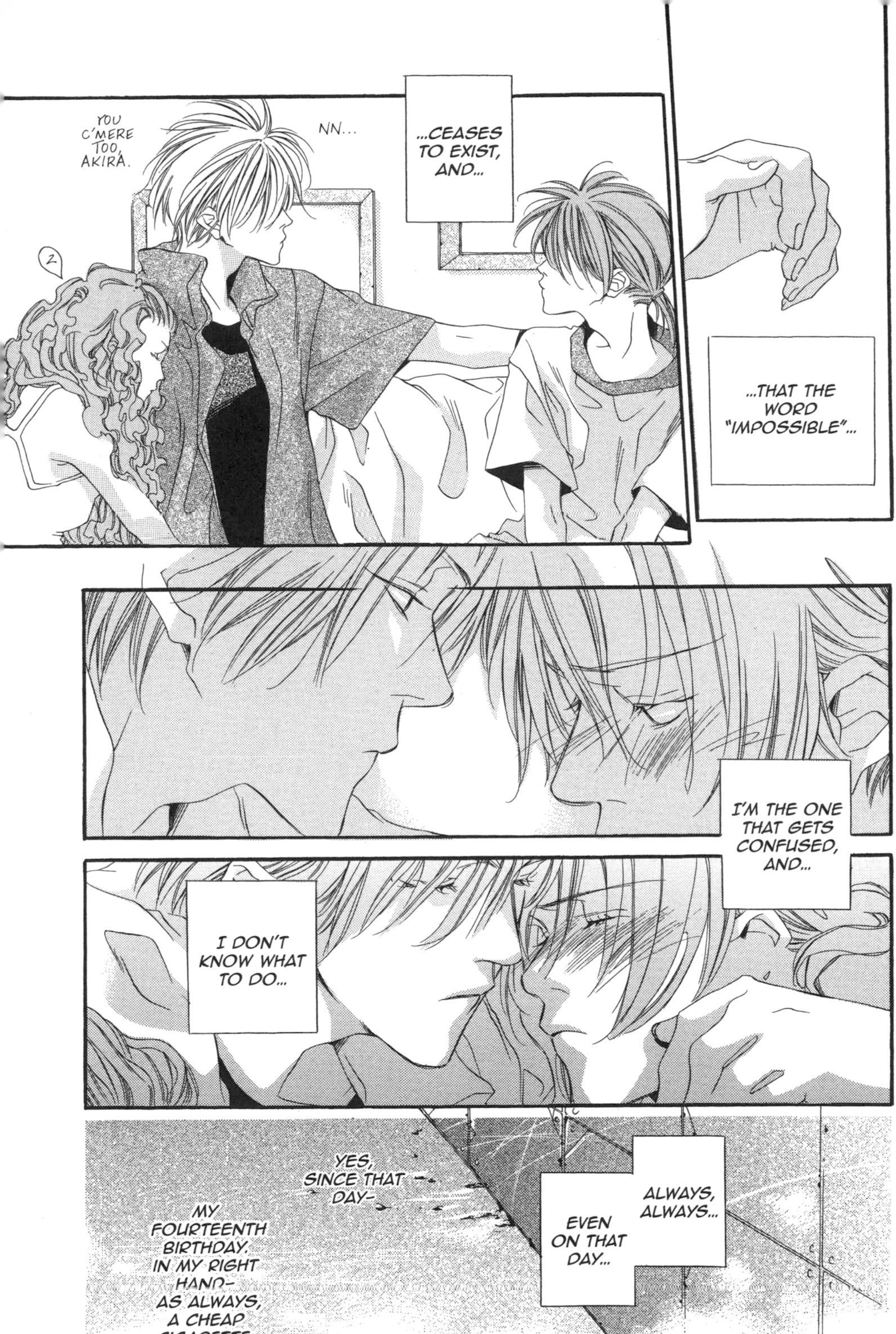
...THAT THE WORD "IMPOSSIBLE"...
...CEASES TO EXIST, AND...
NN...
YOU C'MERE TOO, AKIRA.
I'M THE ONE THAT GETS CONFUSED, AND...
I DON'T KNOW WHAT TO DO...
ALWAYS, ALWAYS...
EVEN ON THAT DAY...
YES, SINCE THAT DAY-
MY FOURTEENTH BIRTHDAY. IN MY RIGHT HAND- AS ALWAYS, A CHEAP CIGARETTE.

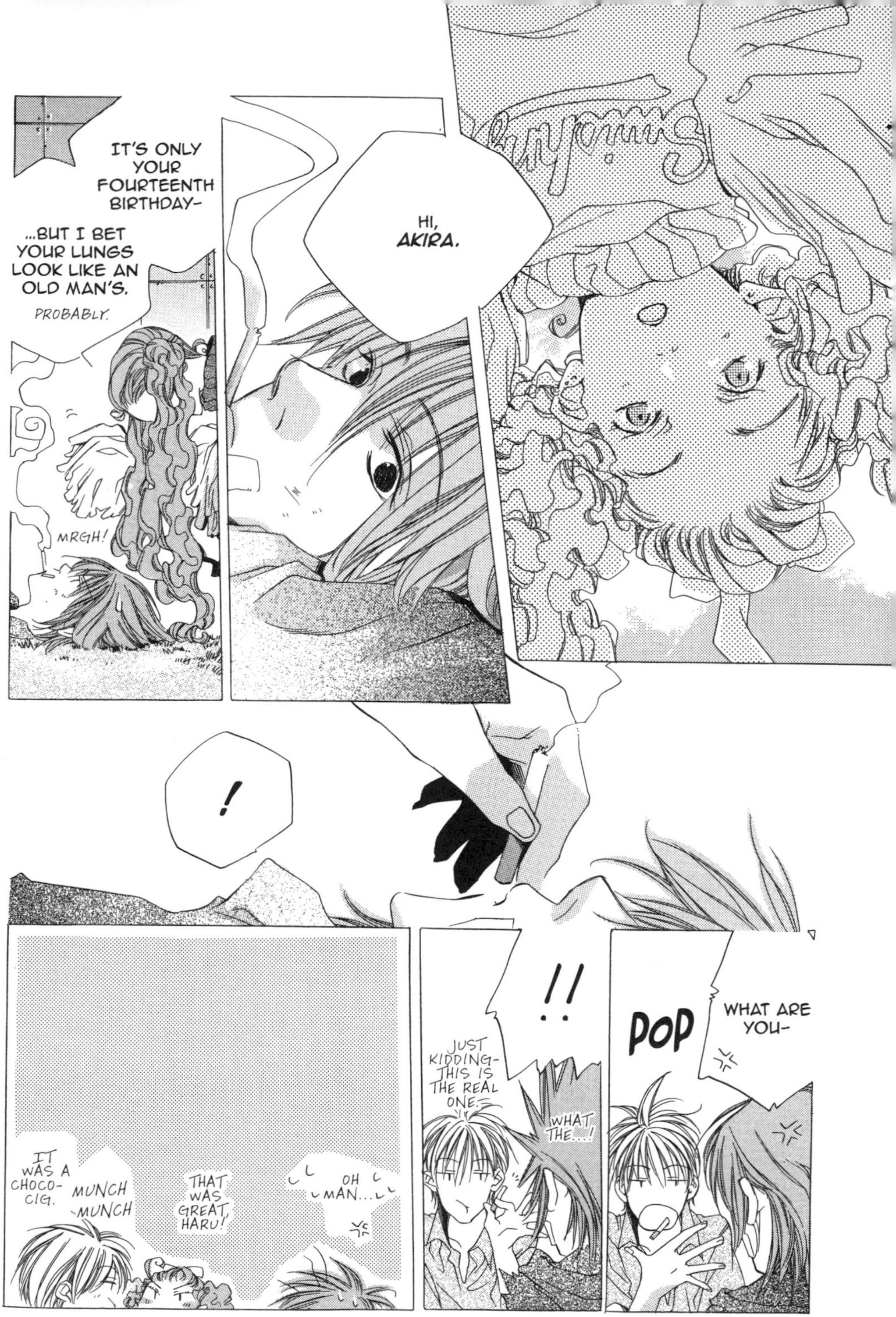
HI, AKIRA.
IT'S ONLY YOUR FOURTEENTH BIRTHDAY-
...BUT I BET YOUR LUNGS LOOK LIKE AN OLD MAN'S.
PROBABLY.
MRGH!
!
WHAT ARE YOU-
POP
!!
JUST KIDDING- THIS IS THE REAL ONE.
WHAT THE...!
OH MAN...
THAT WAS GREAT, HARU!
MUNCH MUNCH
IT WAS A CHOCO-CIG.

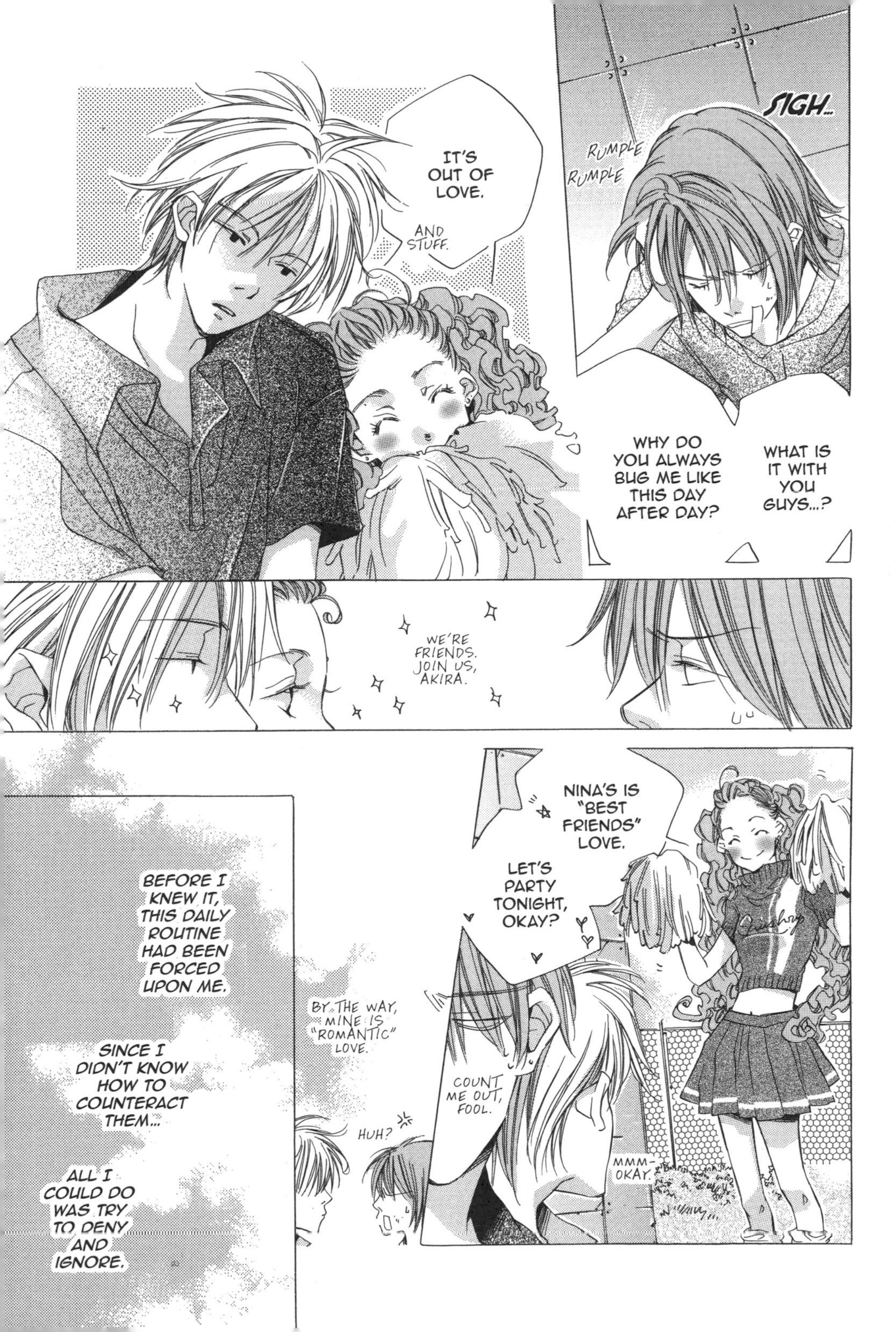
SIGH...
RUMPLE
RUMPLE
WHAT IS IT WITH YOU GUYS...?
WHY DO YOU ALWAYS BUG ME LIKE THIS DAY AFTER DAY?
IT'S OUT OF LOVE.
AND STUFF.
WE'RE FRIENDS. JOIN US, AKIRA.
NINA'S IS "BEST FRIENDS" LOVE.
LET'S PARTY TONIGHT, OKAY?
BY THE WAY, MINE IS "ROMANTIC" LOVE.
COUNT ME OUT, FOOL.
MMM-OKAY.
HUH?
BEFORE I KNEW IT, THIS DAILY ROUTINE HAD BEEN FORCED UPON ME.
SINCE I DIDN'T KNOW HOW TO COUNTERACT THEM...
ALL I COULD DO WAS TRY TO DENY AND IGNORE.

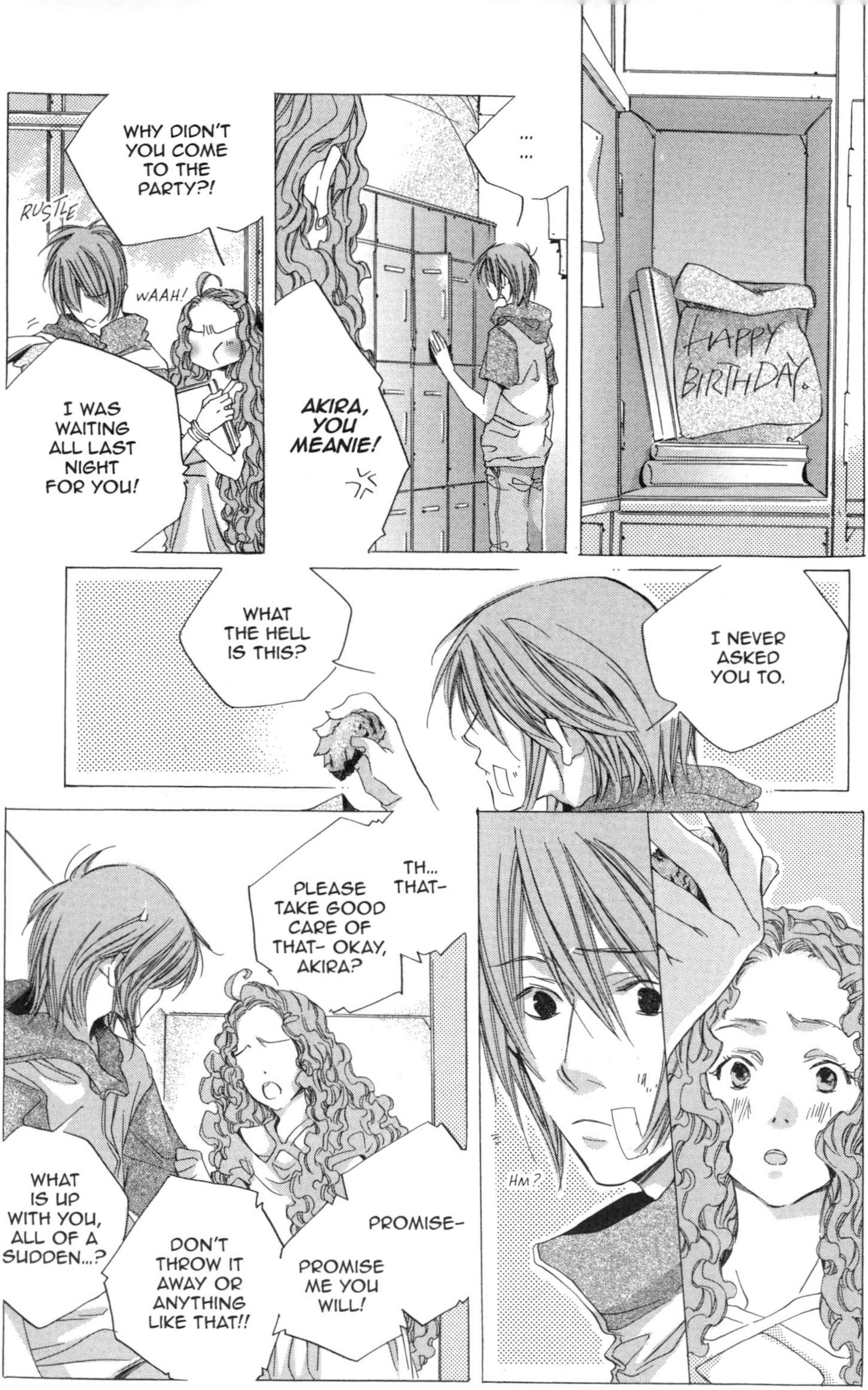
HAPPY BIRTHDAY.
...
...
AKIRA, YOU MEANIE!
WHY DIDN'T YOU COME TO THE PARTY?!
RUSTLE
WAAH!
I WAS WAITING ALL LAST NIGHT FOR YOU!
WHAT THE HELL IS THIS?
I NEVER ASKED YOU TO.
HM?
TH... THAT-
PLEASE TAKE GOOD CARE OF THAT- OKAY, AKIRA?
PROMISE-
PROMISE ME YOU WILL!
DON'T THROW IT AWAY OR ANYTHING LIKE THAT!!
WHAT IS UP WITH YOU, ALL OF A SUDDEN...?

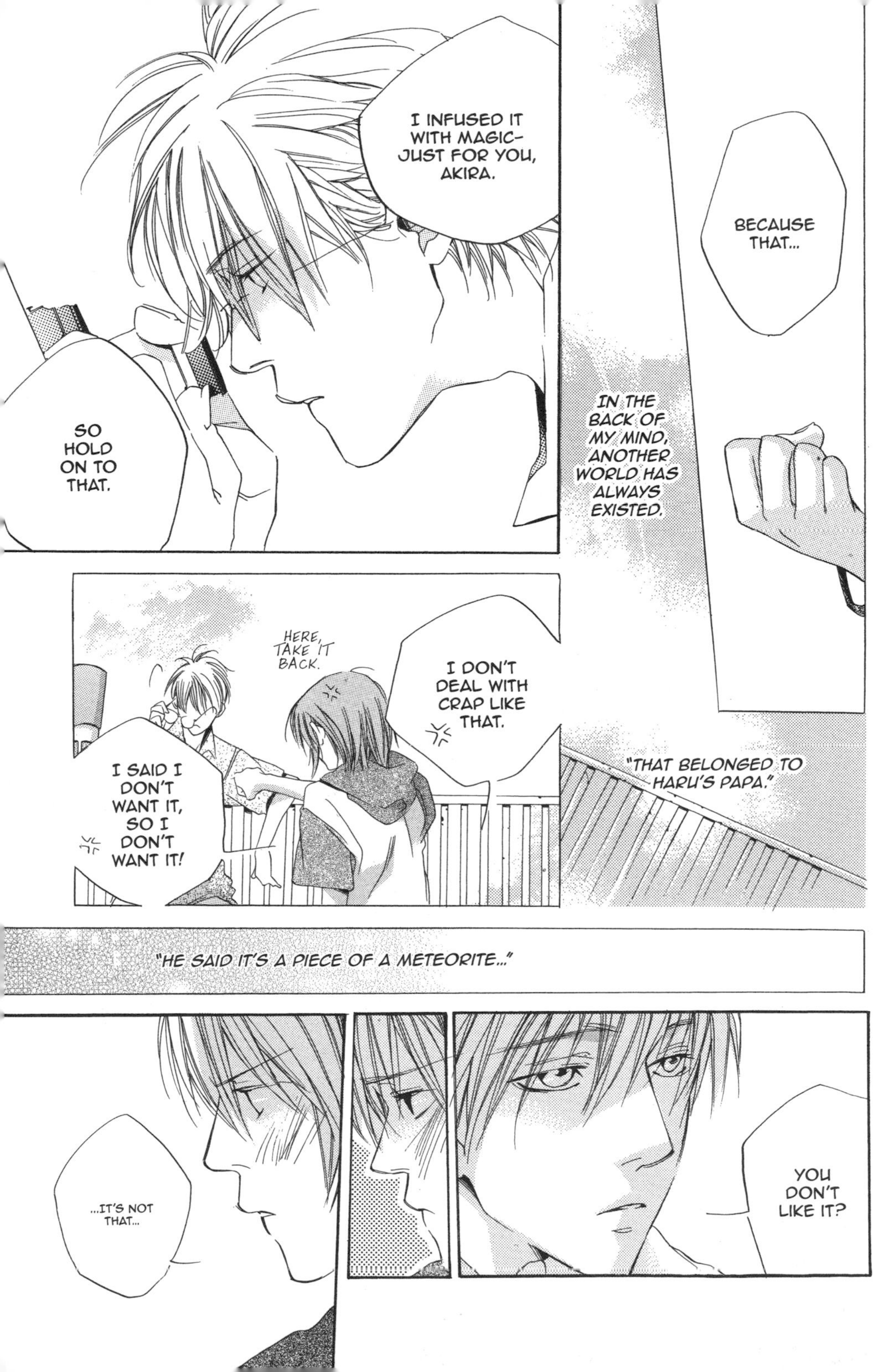

BECAUSE THAT...
IN THE BACK OF MY MIND, ANOTHER WORLD HAS ALWAYS EXISTED.
I INFUSED IT WITH MAGIC- JUST FOR YOU, AKIRA.
SO HOLD ON TO THAT.
"THAT BELONGED TO HARU'S PAPA."
I DON'T DEAL WITH CRAP LIKE THAT.
HERE, TAKE IT BACK.
I SAID I DON'T WANT IT, SO I DON'T WANT IT!
"HE SAID IT'S A PIECE OF A METEORITE..."
YOU DON'T LIKE IT?
...IT'S NOT THAT...

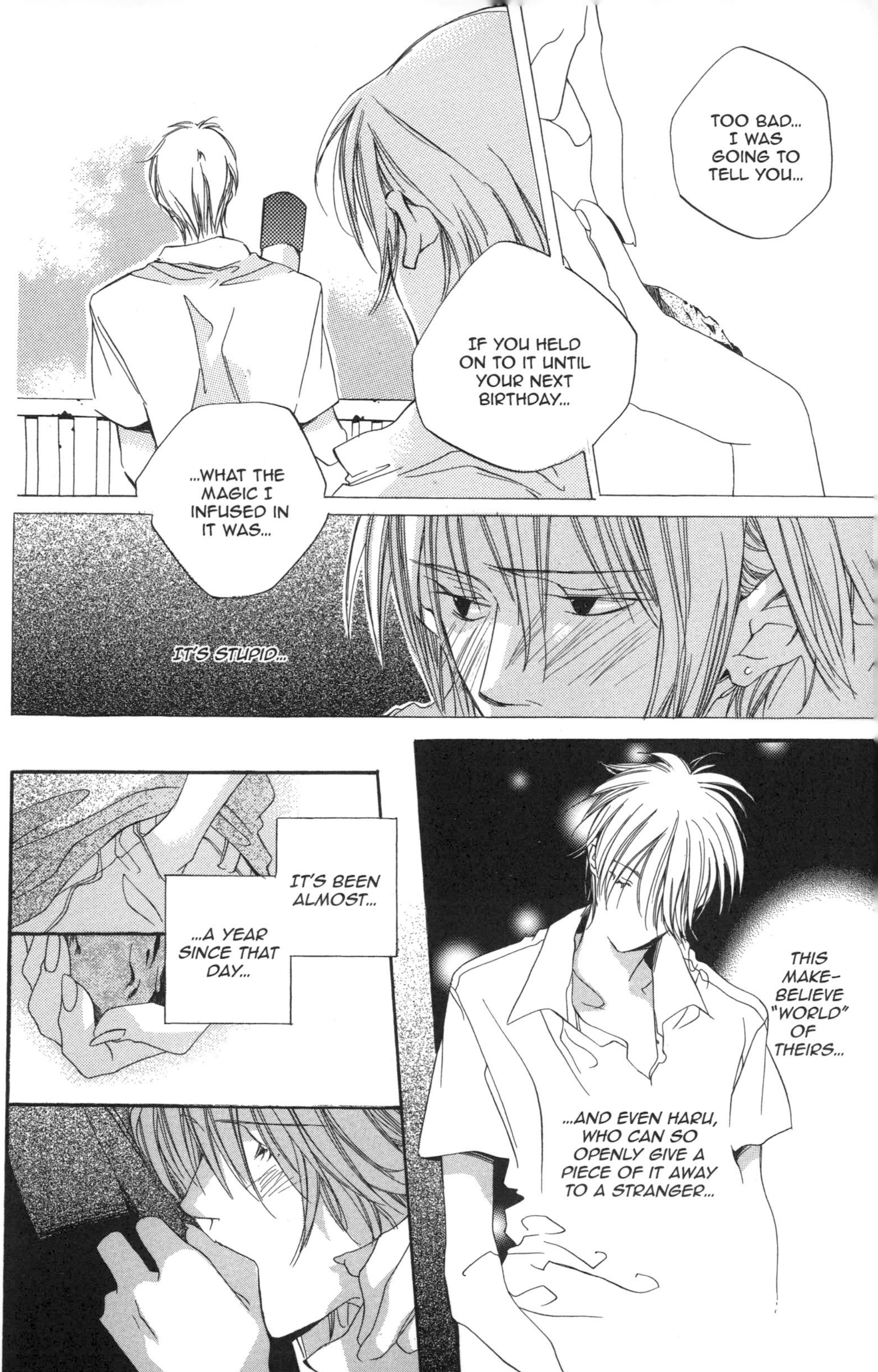
TOO BAD... I WAS GOING TO TELL YOU...
IF YOU HELD ON TO IT UNTIL YOUR NEXT BIRTHDAY...
...WHAT THE MAGIC I INFUSED IN IT WAS...
IT'S STUPID...
THIS MAKE-BELIEVE "WORLD" OF THEIRS...
...AND EVEN HARU, WHO CAN SO OPENLY GIVE A PIECE OF IT AWAY TO A STRANGER...
IT'S BEEN ALMOST...
...A YEAR SINCE THAT DAY...

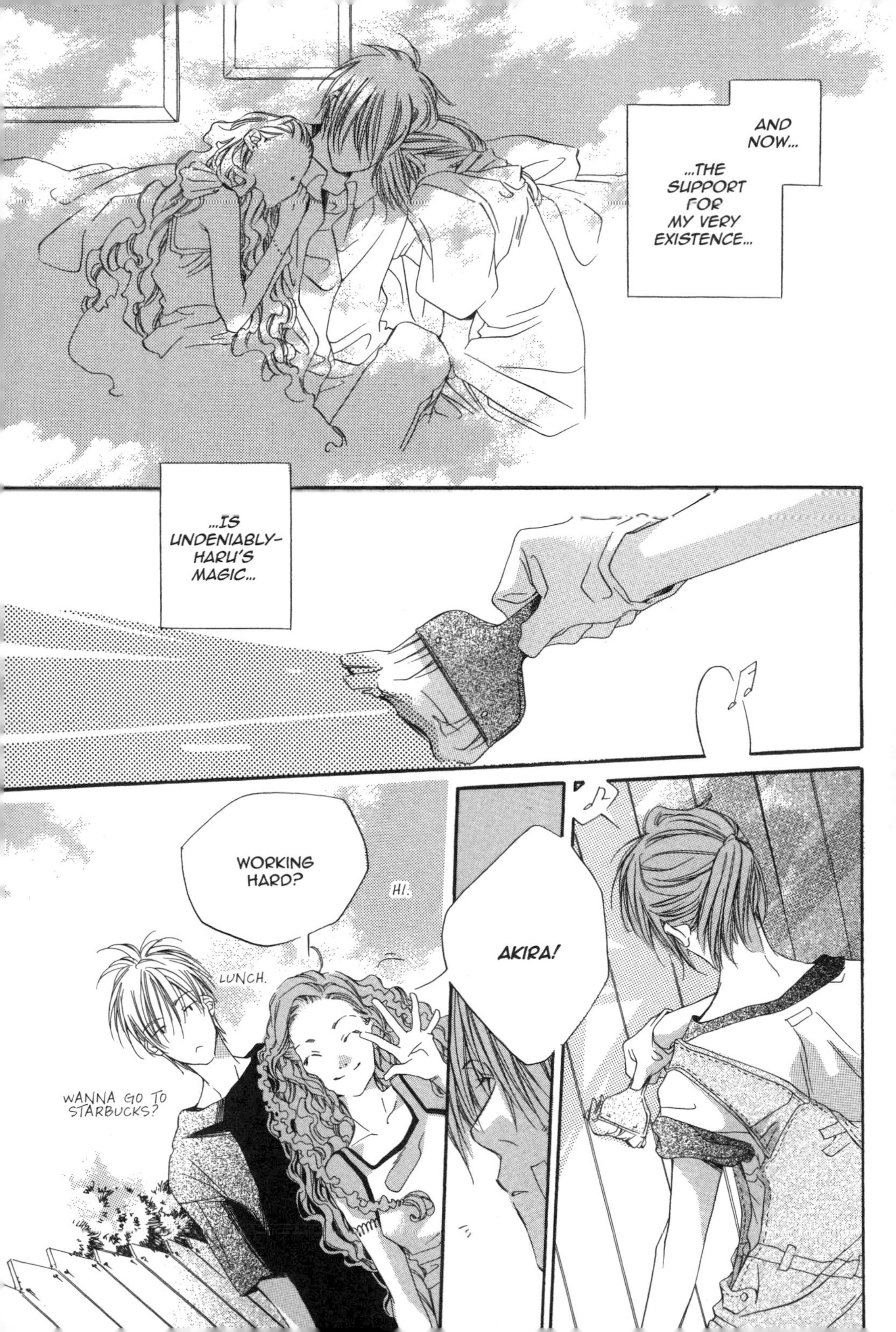
AND NOW...
...THE SUPPORT FOR MY VERY EXISTENCE...
...IS UNDENIABLY- HARU'S MAGIC...
AKIRA!
WORKING HARD?
HI.
LUNCH.
WANNA GO TO STARBUCKS?

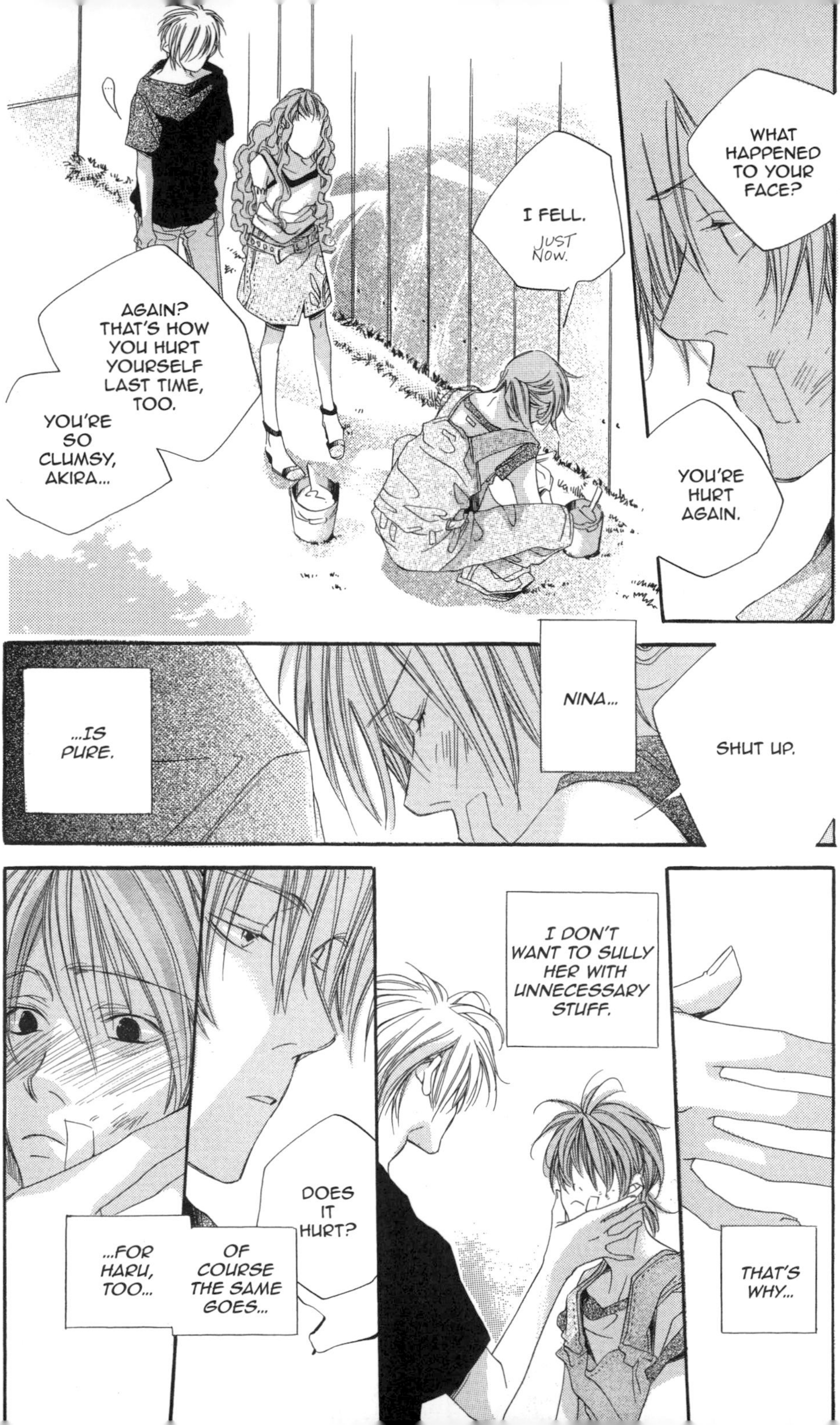
WHAT HAPPENED TO YOUR FACE?
YOU'RE HURT AGAIN.
I FELL.
JUST NOW.
…
AGAIN? THAT'S HOW YOU HURT YOURSELF LAST TIME, TOO.
YOU'RE SO CLUMSY, AKIRA...
SHUT UP.
NINA...
...IS PURE.
THAT'S WHY...
I DON'T WANT TO SULLY HER WITH UNNECESSARY STUFF.
DOES IT HURT?
OF COURSE THE SAME GOES...
...FOR HARU, TOO...

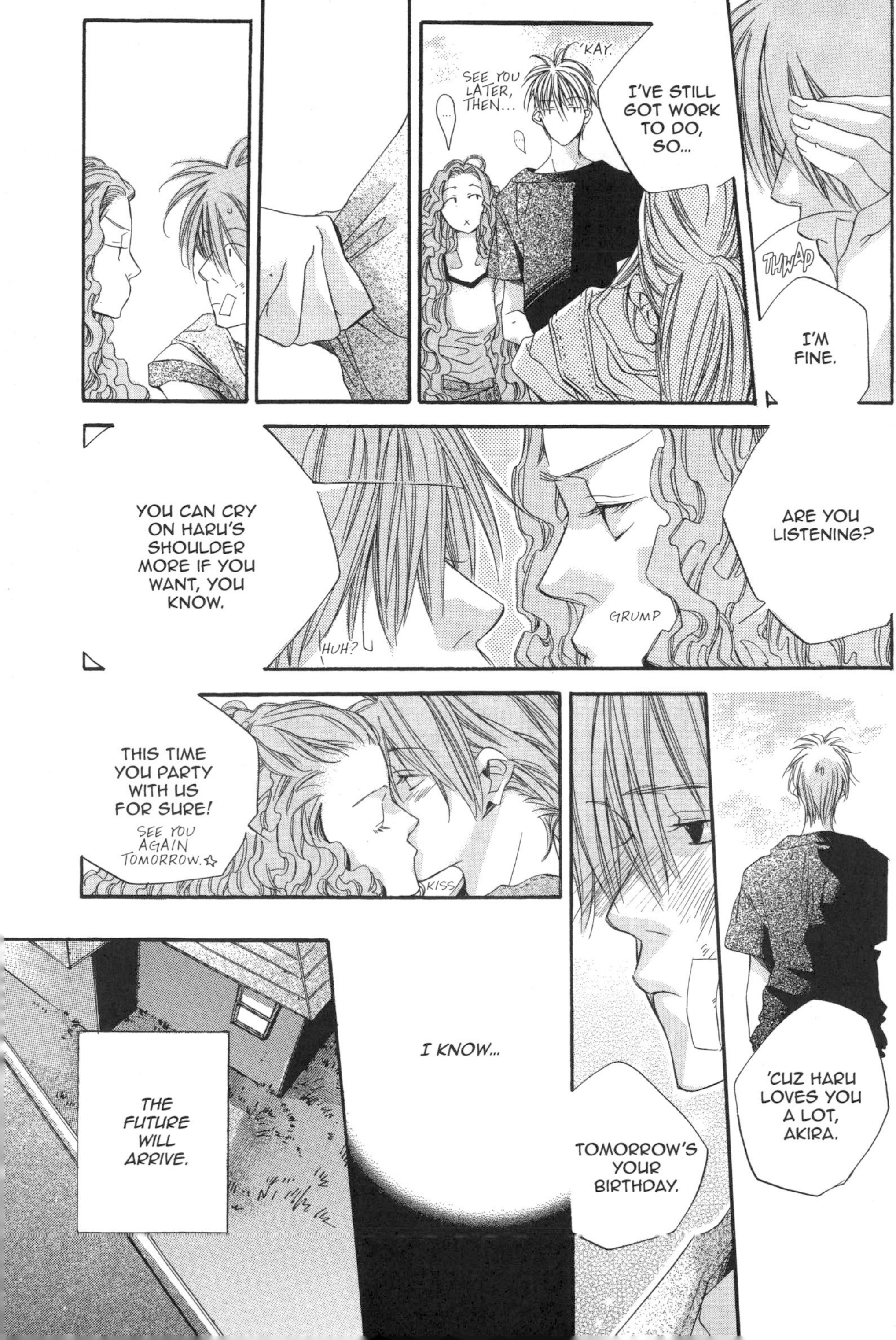
THWAP
I'M FINE.
'KAY.
I'VE STILL GOT WORK TO DO, SO...
SEE YOU LATER, THEN...
...
...
ARE YOU LISTENING?
GRUMP
HUH?
YOU CAN CRY ON HARU'S SHOULDER MORE IF YOU WANT, YOU KNOW.
'CUZ HARU LOVES YOU A LOT, AKIRA.
TOMORROW'S YOUR BIRTHDAY.
THIS TIME YOU PARTY WITH US FOR SURE!
SEE YOU AGAIN TOMORROW.☆
KISS
I KNOW...
THE FUTURE WILL ARRIVE.

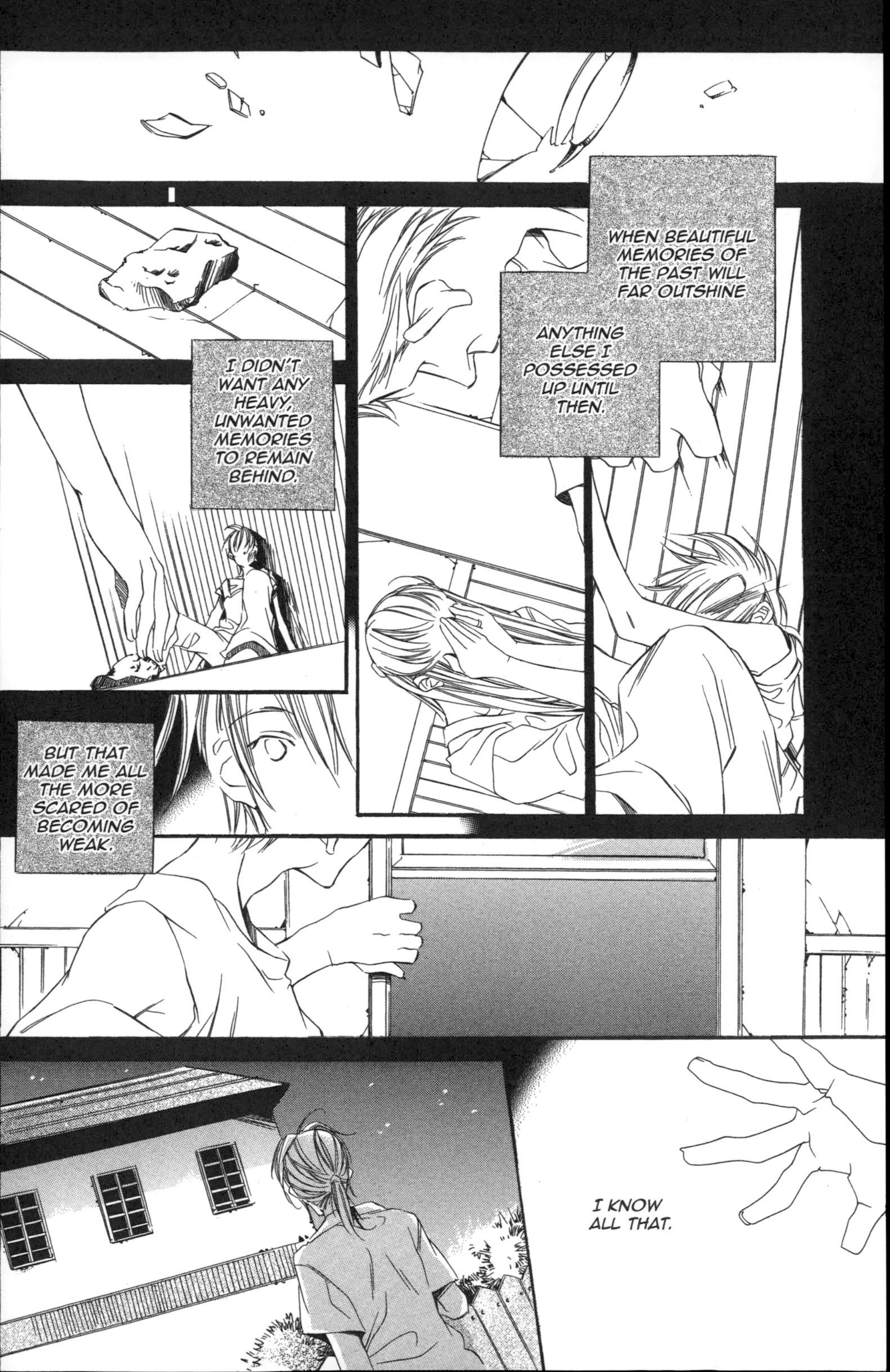
WHEN BEAUTIFUL MEMORIES OF THE PAST WILL FAR OUTSHINE
ANYTHING ELSE I POSSESSED UP UNTIL THEN.
I DIDN'T WANT ANY HEAVY, UNWANTED MEMORIES TO REMAIN BEHIND.
BUT THAT MADE ME ALL THE MORE SCARED OF BECOMING WEAK.
I KNOW ALL THAT.

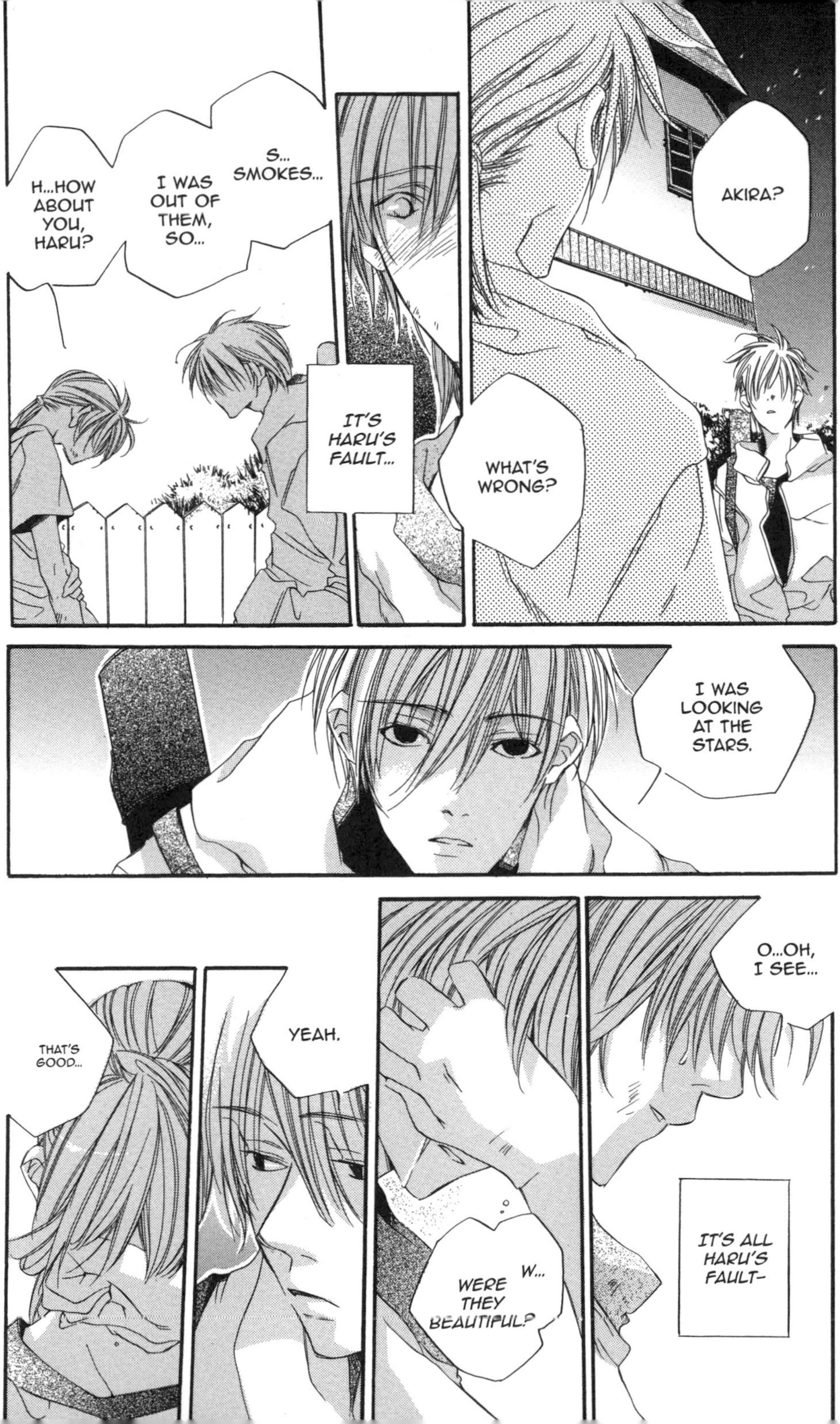
AKIRA?
WHAT'S WRONG?
IT'S HARU'S FAULT...
S... SMOKES...
I WAS OUT OF THEM, SO...
H...HOW ABOUT YOU, HARU?
I WAS LOOKING AT THE STARS.
O...OH, I SEE...
IT'S ALL HARU'S FAULT-
W... WERE THEY BEAUTIFUL?
YEAH.
THAT'S GOOD...

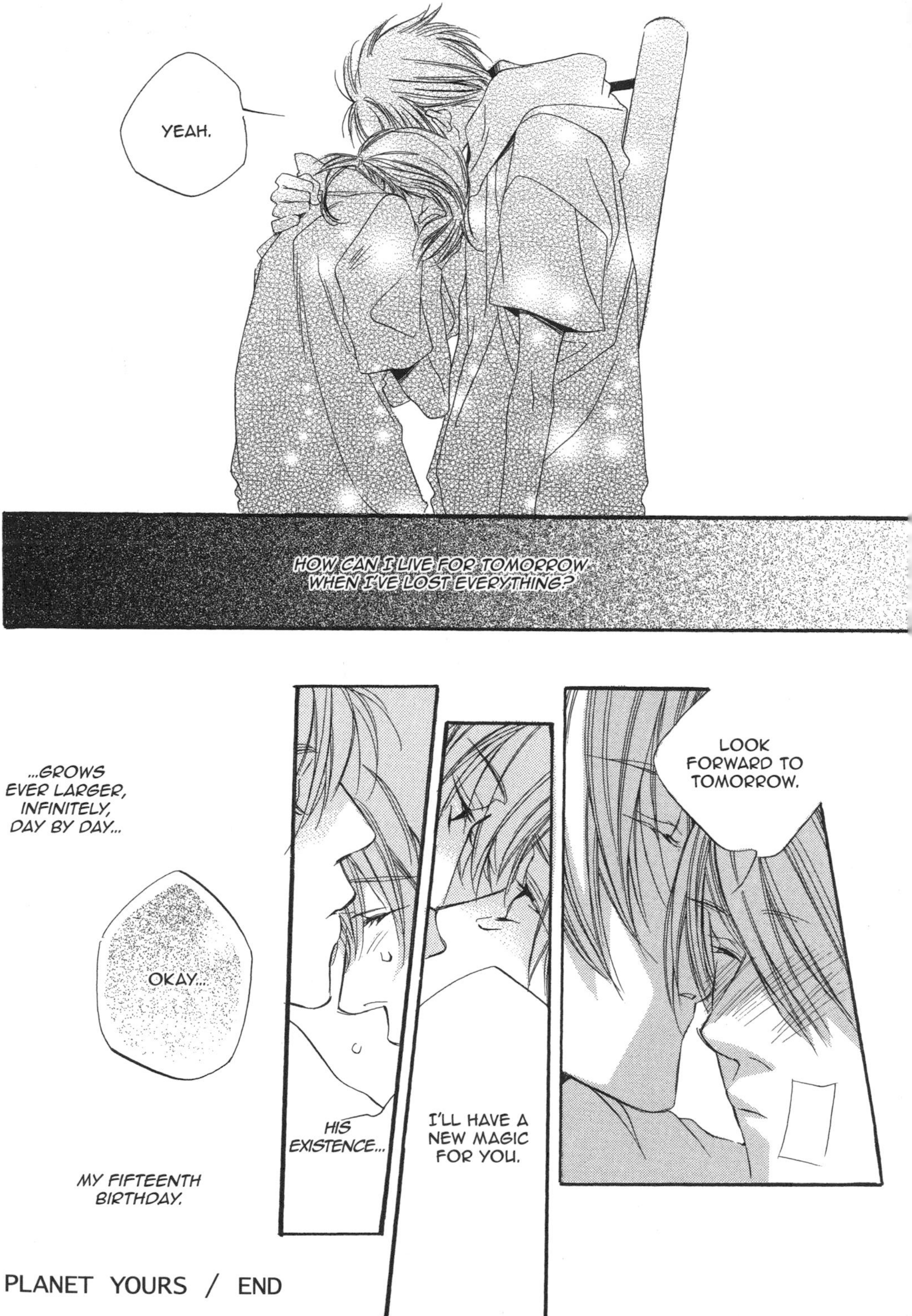

YEAH.
HOW CAN I LIVE FOR TOMORROW WHEN I'VE LOST EVERYTHING?
LOOK FORWARD TO TOMORROW.
I'LL HAVE A NEW MAGIC FOR YOU.
HIS EXISTENCE...
...GROWS EVER LARGER, INFINITELY, DAY BY DAY...
OKAY...
MY FIFTEENTH BIRTHDAY.

PLANET YOURS / END

THE DAY I BECOME A BUTTERFLY

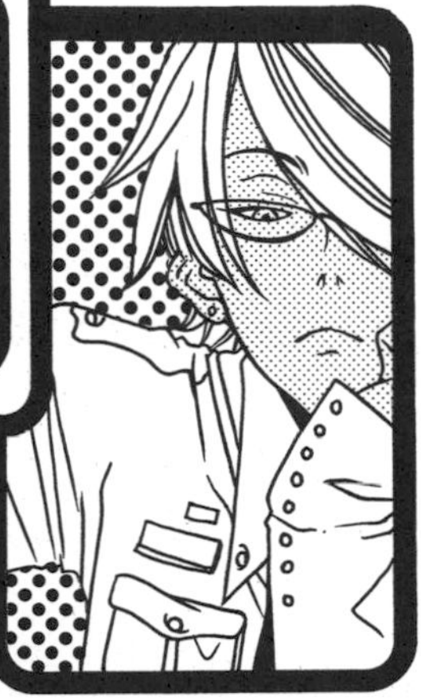

ENDING

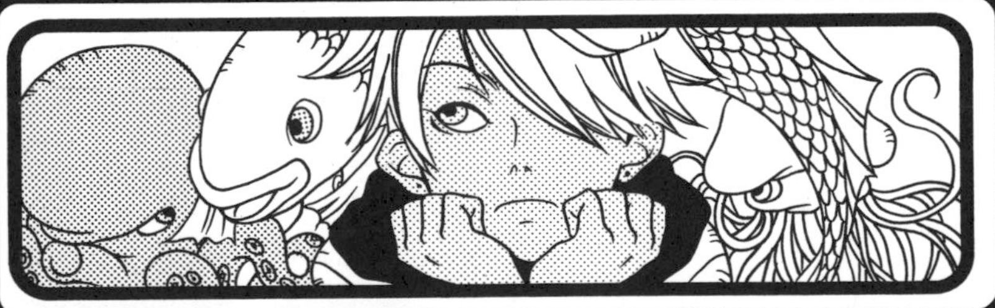

ALL PRODUCED BY SUMOMO YUMEKA

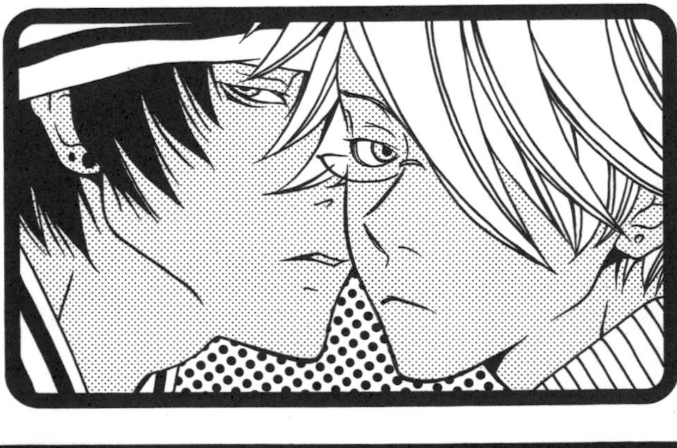

I AM BOTH EXTREMELY ASHAMED AND GRATEFUL THAT MY WORK, SUCH AS IT IS, AWKWARD AND INADEQUATE AS ALWAYS, HAS BEEN COLLECTED TOGETHER IN SUCH A FASHION AS THIS.

"THE DAY I BECOME A BUTTERFLY" IS A WORK I DISLIKE PERSONALLY BECAUSE THERE ARE VARIOUS THINGS I REGRET ABOUT IT. I ADMIT I DON'T EVEN FULLY UNDERSTAND THE PIECE MYSELF.

TO MY EDITOR, UTSUNOMIYA-SAN, THANK YOU VERY, VERY MUCH. I WISH YOU A LOVELY LIFE TOGETHER WITH YOUR PRINCE.

"THE LONELY WAR" AND "BLUE CAT TUNNEL" WERE STORIES THAT I WANTED TO HAVE MORE OF AN UPLIFTING "VIBRANT YOUTH" QUALITY, BUT IT TURNED OUT TO BE ON THE DEPRESSING SIDE.

ENDING

"TOKYO ALIEN ULALA" IS NONSENSE, AS USUAL. "PLANET YOURS" IS... WELL, MY BRAIN CELLS MUST HAVE BEEN DEAD DURING THAT ONE BECAUSE I DON'T REMEMBER IT AT ALL... SORRY.

IN THE END, I REGRET THAT ALL MY WORK IS SO INEXPLICABLE. I AM DEEPLY GRATEFUL TO YOU ALL FOR YOUR SUPPORT. THANK YOU VERY MUCH.

2003.JUNE.

SUMOMO YUMEKA

I SOMETIMES UPDATE A FOOLISH JOURNAL HERE:

HTTP://WWW5E.BIGLOBE.NE.JP/~SASSHI-/

SAME CELL ORGANISM

by Sumomo Yumeka

Different... yet alike...

How can two people be so completely different from one another, yet be so in tune with love?

junemanga.com

ISBN: 1-56970-926-2 $12.95

Same-Cell Organism/Dousaibou Seibutsu © Sumomo Yumeka 2001.
Originally published in Japan in 2001 by Taiyo Tosho Co., Ltd.

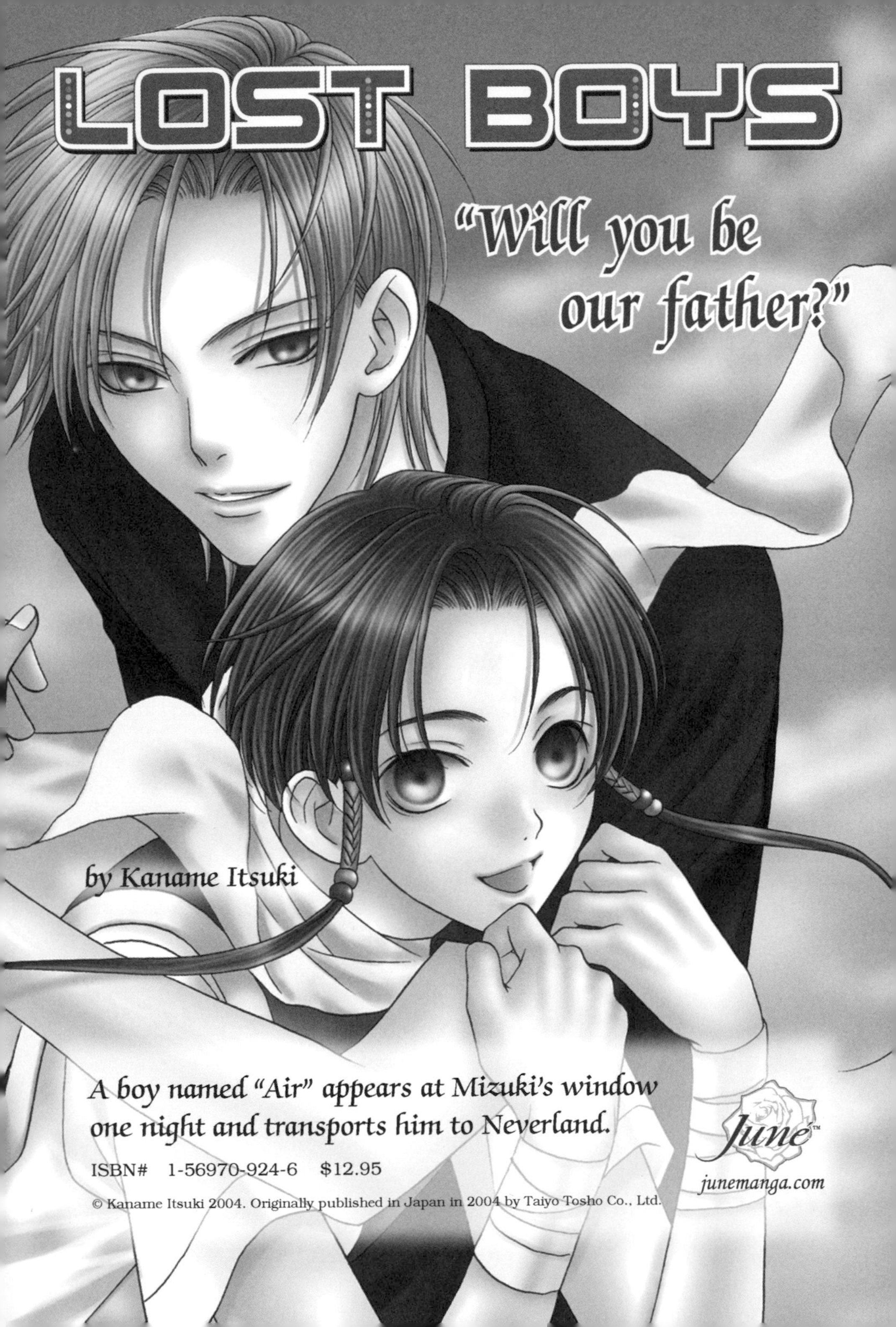
LOST BOYS
"Will you be our father?"
by Kaname Itsuki
A boy named "Air" appears at Mizuki's window one night and transports him to Neverland.
ISBN# 1-56970-924-6 $12.95
June™
junemanga.com
© Kaname Itsuki 2004. Originally published in Japan in 2004 by Taiyo Tosho Co., Ltd.

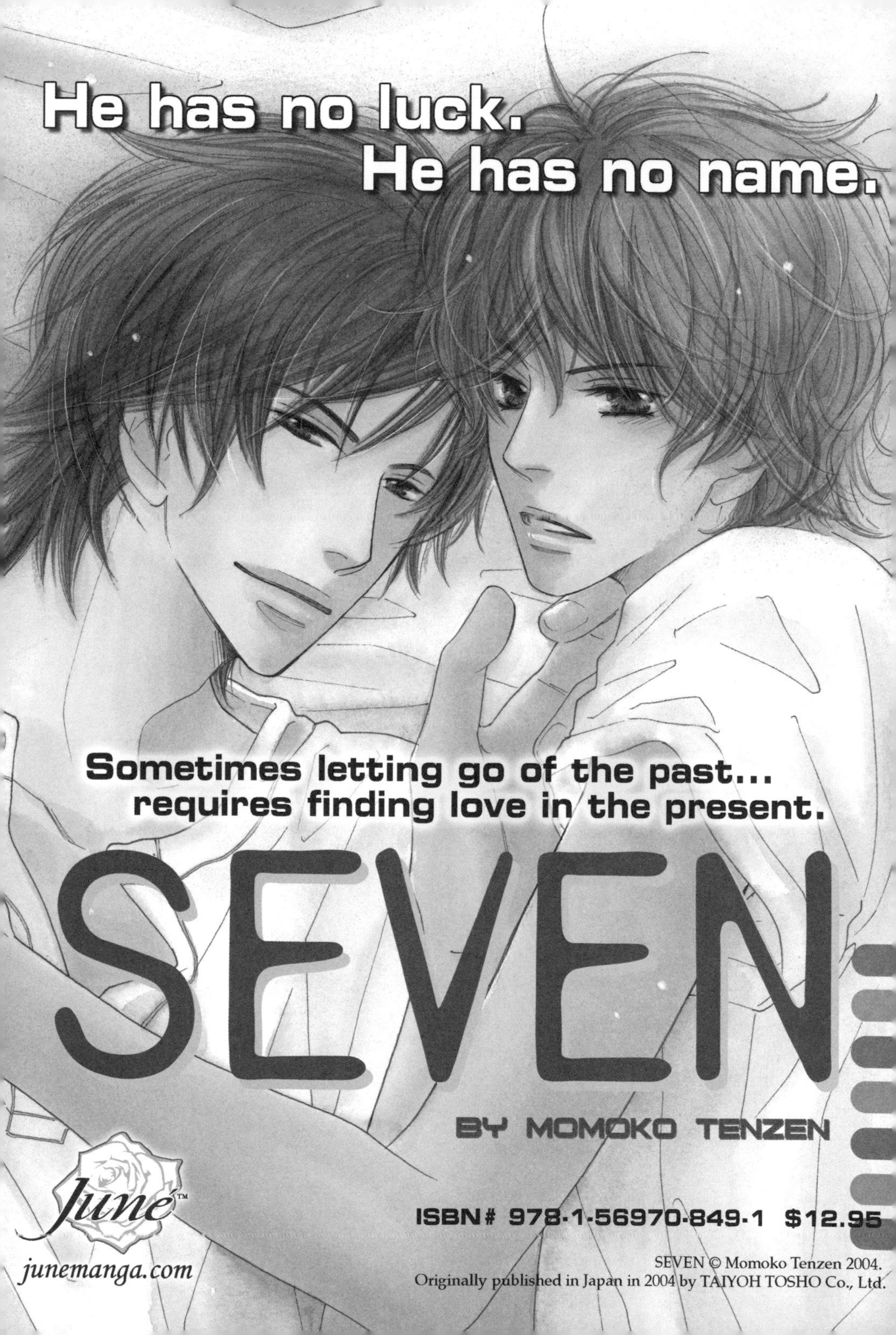
He has no luck.
He has no name.
Sometimes letting go of the past...
requires finding love in the present.
SEVEN
BY MOMOKO TENZEN
June™
junemanga.com
ISBN# 978-1-56970-849-1 $12.95
SEVEN © Momoko Tenzen 2004.
Originally published in Japan in 2004 by TAIYOH TOSHO Co., Ltd.

YOU & HARUJION

by Keiko Kinoshita

All is lost . . .

Haru has just lost his father,
Yakuza-esque creditors are
coming to collect on his
father's debts, and the
bank has foreclosed
the mortgage on
the house…

When things go from bad to worse,
in steps Yuuji Senoh…

ISBN# 1-56970-925-4 $12.95

June™

junemanga.com

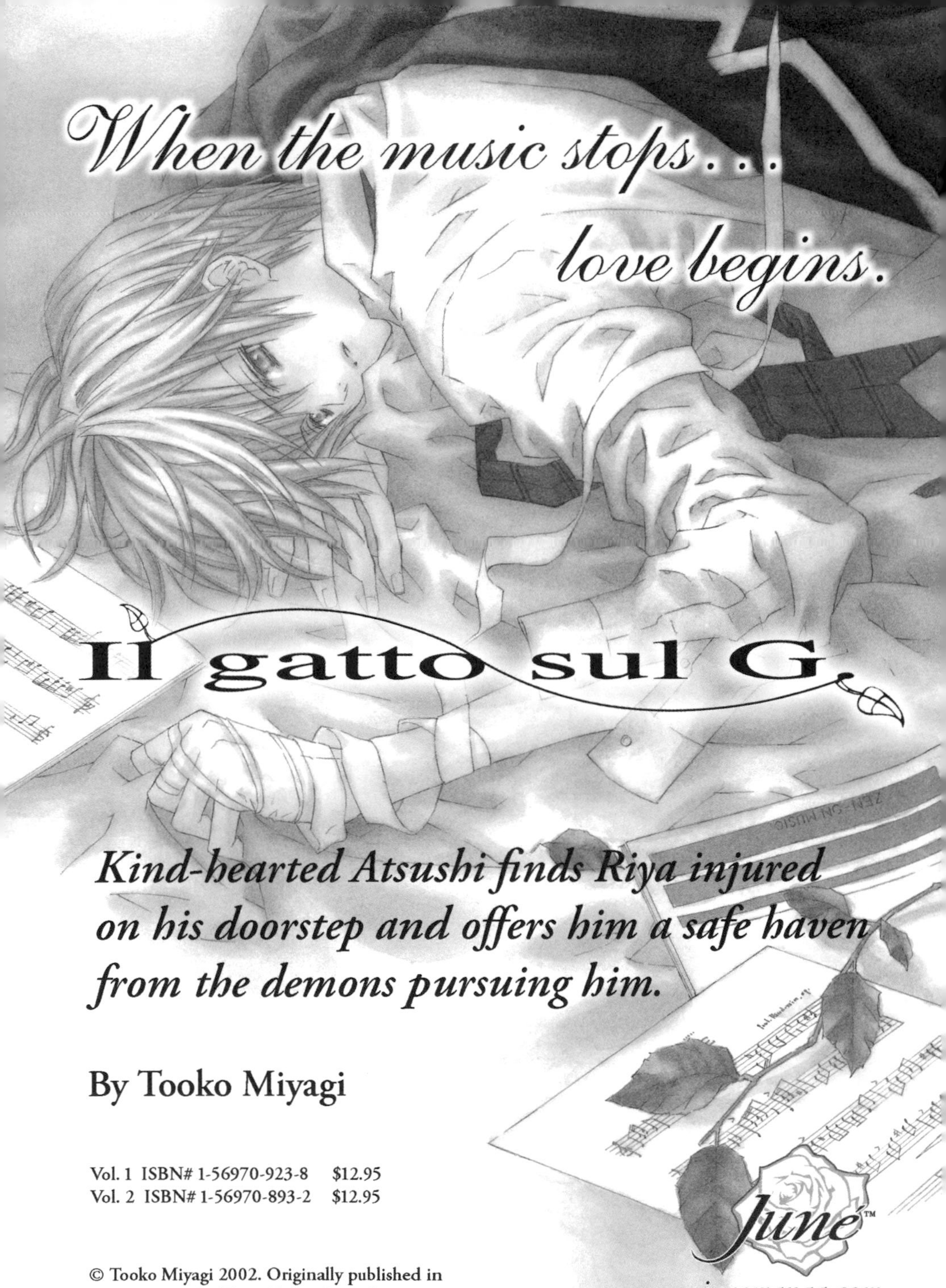
When the music stops . . .
. . . love begins.
Il gatto sul G
Kind-hearted Atsushi finds Riya injured on his doorstep and offers him a safe haven from the demons pursuing him.
By Tooko Miyagi
Vol. 1 ISBN# 1-56970-923-8 $12.95
Vol. 2 ISBN# 1-56970-893-2 $12.95
© Tooko Miyagi 2002. Originally published in Japan in 2002 by Taiyo Tosho Co.,Ltd.
June™
junemanga.com

The Moon and Sandals Vol. 1

月とサンダル

See me After Class!

THE MOON & SANDALS 1 © 1996 Fumi Yoshinaga. All rights reserved. First published in Japan in 1996 by HOBUNSHA CO., LTD., Tokyo

ISBN# 978-1-56970-802-9 SRP $12.95

june
by DMP

As a newly appointed high school teacher, Ida has yet to gain confidence in his abilities. His insecurity grows worse when he feels someone staring intensely at him during class. The piercing eyes belong to a tall, intimidating student—Koichi Kobayashi. What exactly should Ida do about it? Is it discontent that fuels Kobayashi's sultry gaze… or could it be something else?

Written and Illustrated by:
Fumi Yoshinaga

junemanga.com

STOP

This is the back of the book!
Start from the other side.

NATIVE MANGA readers read manga from *right to left*.

1
1
2
2
3
3
4
4
5
5
6
6
7
8

*If you run into our **Native Manga** logo on any of our books... you'll know that this manga is published in it's true original native Japanese right to left reading format, as it was intended. Turn to the other side of the book and start reading from right to left, top to bottom.*

Follow the diagram to see how its done.
Surf's Up!

NATIVE MANGA
READ RIGHT TO LEFT